John K. Goodrich is Assistant Professor of Bible at Moody Bible Institute, Chicago. He has published articles in *New Testament Studies*, the *Journal for the Study of the New Testament* and the *Journal of Biblical Literature*.

PAUL AS AN ADMINISTRATOR OF GOD IN 1 CORINTHIANS

This book looks in detail at Paul's description of apostles in 1 Corinthians 4 and 9 as divinely appointed administrators (*oikonomoi*) and considers what this tells us about the nature of his own apostolic authority. John K. Goodrich investigates the origin of this metaphor in light of ancient regal, municipal, and private administration, initially examining the numerous domains in which *oikonomoi* were appointed in the Graeco-Roman world, before situating the image in the private commercial context of Roman Corinth. Examining the social and structural connotations attached to private commercial administration, Goodrich contemplates what Paul's metaphor indicates about apostleship in general terms, as well as how he uses the image to defend his apostolic rights. He also analyses the purpose and limits of Paul's authority – how it is constructed, asserted, and contested – by examining when and how Paul uses and refuses to exercise the rights inherent in his position.

JOHN K. GOODRICH is Assistant Professor of Bible at Moody Bible Institute, Chicago. He has published articles in *New Testament Studies*, the *Journal for the Study of the New Testament* and the *Journal of Biblical Literature*.

SOCIETY FOR NEW TESTAMENT STUDIES

MONOGRAPH SERIES

General Editor: John M. Court

152

PAUL AS AN ADMINISTRATOR OF
GOD IN 1 CORINTHIANS

SOCIETY FOR NEW TESTAMENT STUDIES

MONOGRAPH SERIES

Recent titles in the series:

Paul as an Administrator of God in 1 Corinthians

JOHN K. GOODRICH

CAMBRIDGE
UNIVERSITY PRESS

CAMBRIDGE UNIVERSITY PRESS
Cambridge, New York, Melbourne, Madrid, Cape Town,
Singapore, São Paulo, Delhi, Mexico City

Cambridge University Press
The Edinburgh Building, Cambridge CB2 8RU, UK

Published in the United States of America by Cambridge University Press, New York

www.cambridge.org
Information on this title: www.cambridge.org/9781107018624

First published 2012

Printed in the United Kingdom at the University Press, Cambridge

A catalogue record for this publication is available from the British Library

Library of Congress Cataloguing in Publication data
Goodrich, John, 1981–
    Paul as an administrator of God in 1 Corinthians / John Goodrich.
      p. cm. – (Society for New Testament Studies monograph series ; 152)
    Revision of the author's thesis (doctoral)–University of Durham, 2010.
    Includes bibliographical references (p.) and indexes.
    ISBN 978-1-107-01862-4 (hardback)
    1. Bible. N.T. Corinthians, 1st–Criticism, interpretation, etc.
    2. Paul, the Apostle, Saint.   3. Authority–Biblical teaching.
    4. Apostles–Biblical teaching. I. Title.
    BS2675.52.G665   2012
    227'.206–dc23
    2012007317

ISBN 978-1-107-01862-4 Hardback

CONTENTS

ACKNOWLEDGMENTS

This book is a revised version of a doctoral thesis submitted to the University of Durham in March 2010. The project benefited from a number of people who in various ways provided much-needed support, and I am indebted to each of them for their time, wisdom, and prayers. In the first place, I wish to thank Dr John Court for accepting this volume into the SNTSMS, as well as Laura Morris, Anna Lowe, and everyone else at Cambridge University Press for their editorial assistance and expertise.

Many thanks are particularly due to Professor John Barclay for his gracious and attentive supervision over the duration of my research. Since even before my arrival in Durham he readily made himself available to me, and did so especially during the finishing stages of the project, even while he was on sabbatical in Dunedin. For this I am exceedingly grateful, as well as for his constant encouragement and for the many penetrating insights he has shared with me about Pauline theology and the ancient world.

I am additionally grateful to my examiners, Professor Francis Watson and Dr Simon Gathercole, for their kind and constructive feedback, as well as to Drs Stephen Barton and William Telford for reading and commenting on portions of my work at various stages. The thesis benefited further from insights gained through conversations with members of Durham's Department of Classics and Ancient History, most notably Professors J. David Thomas and Peter Rhodes, and Dr Paola Ceccarelli. I owe the inception of the project to Tyndale House, Cambridge, where my initial interest in Graeco-Roman antiquity was sparked through the library's 2006 summer tutorial led by Revd Dr Bruce Winter.

I wish to thank Compass Bible Church and Christchurch Durham for providing much-needed Christian fellowship for several formative years. I will also forever be indebted to the excellent studymates I had at 37 North Bailey, especially Kristian Bendoraitis, Ben Blackwell, David Briones, and Nijay Gupta. All were a constant source of reflection, encouragement, and good humour in the day-to-day grind of postgraduate research.

Thanks are additionally due to my wonderful colleagues at Moody Bible Institute for welcoming and supporting me as one of their own. It was this very faculty who first introduced me to the academic study of the Bible, and it is an honour to have the opportunity now to teach alongside them. I am particularly grateful to my department chair and good friend Gerald Peterman for his kind and capable leadership. His wise counsel, both personal and professional, has made the past two of years at MBI a joy.

Words cannot express the depth of my appreciation for my family, John and Julie Goodrich, Jeremy and Whitney Goodrich, Mark, Nancy, and Dotty Rush, Michael and Liz Rush, and Ryan and Melissa Cox. Their love and generosity made our adventure abroad a reality. Above all, I am immeasurably grateful to my beautiful wife, Christin. My work over the years has demanded much from her, yet in her devotion and self-sacrifice she has modelled no less than the very grace of God. She is the best friend I could ask for, and as I look forward to our many more years together doing ministry and raising Justin, it is my pleasure to dedicate this book to her. *Soli Deo gloria.*

ABBREVIATIONS

References to ancient literature generally follow the conventions established by Patrick H. Alexander, *et al.* (eds.), *The SBL Handbook of Style* (Peabody, MA: Hendrickson, 1999), and the translations used are those from the Loeb Classical Library unless otherwise indicated. Abbreviations for inscriptions generally follow the recommendations of B. H. McLean, *An Introduction to Greek Epigraphy of the Hellenistic and Roman Periods from Alexander the Great down to the Reign of Constantine (323 BC–AD 337)* (Ann Arbor: University of Michigan Press, 2002). For papyri, see John F. Oates, *et al.* (eds.), *Checklist of Editions of Greek, Latin, Demotic, and Coptic Papyri, Ostraca, and Tablets* (5th edn; Bulletin of the American Society of Papyrologists Supplements 9; Oakville: American Society of Papyrologists, 2001).

AB	Anchor Bible
AGJU	Arbeiten zur Geschichte des antiken Judentums und des Urchristentums
AGSU	Arbeiten zur Geschichte des Spätjudentums und Urchristentums
AJA	*American Journal of Archaeology*
ANRW	*Aufstieg und Niedergang der römischen Welt: Geschichte und Kultur Roms im Spiegel der neueren Forschung*
ANTC	Abingdon New Testament Commentaries
ARIDSup	Analecta Romana Instituti Danici Supplement
AusBR	*Australian Biblical Review*
Austin	M. M. Austin, *The Hellenistic World from Alexander to the Roman Conquest: A Selection of Ancient Sources in Translation* (2nd edn; Cambridge University Press, 2006)
AYB	Anchor Yale Bible

Bagnall/Derow	Roger S. Bagnall and Peter Derow, *The Hellenistic Period: Historical Sources in Translation* (Oxford: Blackwell, 2003)
BASP	*Bulletin of the American Society of Papyrologists*
BBR	*Bulletin for Biblical Research*
BDAG	W. Baur, W. Danker, W. F. Arndt, and F. W. Gingrich, eds., *Greek–English Lexicon of the New Testament and Other Early Christian Literature* (3rd edn; University of Chicago Press, 2001)
BDF	F. Blass and A. Debrunner, *A Greek Grammar of the New Testament and other Early Christian Literature* (trans. and rev. R. W. Funk; University of Chicago Press, 1961)
BECNT	Baker Exegetical Commentary on the New Testament
Behr	P. Aelius Aristides, *The Complete Works* (trans. Charles A. Behr; 2 vols.; Leiden: Brill, 1981)
BETL	Bibliotheca Ephemeridum Theologicarum Lovaniensium
BICS	Bulletin of the Institute of Classical Studies
BNTC	Black's New Testament Commentaries
BTB	*Biblical Theology Bulletin*
BZNW	Beihefte zur Zeitschrift für die neutestamentliche Wissenschaft
CBET	Contributions to Biblical Exegesis and Theology
CBQ	*Catholic Biblical Quarterly*
CJ	*Classical Journal*
CQ	*Classical Quarterly*
Crawford	Michael H. Crawford, *Roman Statutes* (2 vols.; BICS 64; London: Institute of Classical Studies; University of London, 1996)
Crawley	Thucydides, *The History of the Peloponnesian War* (trans. Richard Crawley; London: J. M. Dent, 1910).
CRF	Otto Ribbeck, *Comicorum Romanorum Fragmenta* (3rd edn; Leipzig: Teubner, 1897)
ECC	Early Christianity in Context
EKK	Evangelisch-katholischer Kommentar zum Neuen Testament
GRBS	*Greek, Roman, and Byzantine Studies*
GRS	Thomas Wiedemann, *Greek and Roman Slavery* (London: Routledge, 1981)
HNT	Handbuch zum Neuen Testament

HTR	*Harvard Theological Review*
HTS	Harvard Theological Studies
HUT	Hermeneutische Untersuchungen zur Theologie
ICC	International Critical Commentary
JBL	*Journal of Biblical Literature*
JETS	*Journal of the Evangelical Theological Society*
JGRChJ	*Journal of Greco-Roman Christianity and Judaism*
JHS	*Journal of Hellenic Studies*
JÖAI	*Jahreshefte des Österreichischen archäologischen Instituts*
JRA	*Journal of Roman Archaeology*
JRASup	Journal of Roman Archaeology Supplementary Series
JRS	*Journal of Roman Studies*
JSNT	*Journal for the Study of the New Testament*
JSNTSup	Journal for the Study of the New Testament Supplement Series
JTS	*Journal of Theological Studies*
KEK	Kritisch-exegetischer Kommentar über das Neue Testament (Meyer-Kommentar)
LCL	Loeb Classical Library
LNTS	Library of New Testament Studies
LSJ	H. G. Liddell, R. Scott, H. S. Jones, *A Greek–English Lexicon* (9th edn with revised supplement; Oxford University Press, 1996)
MM	J. H. Moulton and G. Milligan, *The Vocabulary of the Greek Testament* (Peabody, MA: Hendrickson, 1997)
NICNT	New International Commentary on the New Testament
NIGTC	New International Greek Testament Commentary
NovT	*Novum Testamentum*
NovTSup	Supplements to Novum Testamentum
NSBT	New Studies in Biblical Theology
NTS	*New Testament Studies*
OCD	S. Hornblower and A. Spawforth, eds., *Oxford Classical Dictionary* (3rd rev. edn; Oxford University Press, 2003)
ÖTK	Ökumenischer Taschenbuch-Kommentar
PNTC	Pillar New Testament Commentary
PRSt	*Perspectives in Religious Studies*
ResQ	*Restoration Quarterly*
SBL	Studies in Biblical Literature
SBLDS	Society of Biblical Literature Dissertation Series
SJT	*Scottish Journal of Theology*
SNTSMS	Society for New Testament Studies Monograph Series

SNTW	Studies of the New Testament and Its World
TDNT	G. Kittel and G. Friedrich, eds., *Theological Dictionary of the New Testament* (trans. G. W. Bromiley; 10 vols.; Grand Rapids: Eerdmans, 1964–76)
THKNT	Theologischer Handkommentar zum Neuen Testament
TNTC	Tyndale New Testament Commentaries
TynBul	*Tyndale Bulletin*
Watson	*The Digest of Justinian* (trans. Alan Watson; 2 vols.; rev. edn; Philadelphia: University of Pennsylvania Press, 1998)
WBC	Word Bibilical Commentary
WUNT	Wissenschaftliche Untersuchungen zum Neuen Testament
ZNW	*Zeitschrift für die neutestamentliche Wissenschaft und die Kunde der älteren Kirche*
ZPE	*Zeitschrift für Papyrologie und Epigraphik*
ZTK	*Zeitschrift für Theologie und Kirche*
Zulueta	*The Institutes of Gaius* (trans. Francis de Zulueta; 2 vols.; Oxford: Clarendon Press, 1946)

1

APOSTOLIC AUTHORITY IN 1 CORINTHIANS

> If to others I am not an apostle, at least I am to you.
>
> 1 Cor 9.2

Paul's first epistle to the Corinthians[1] provides a unique and fascinating insight into the social realities and ethical pitfalls that enveloped one of the apostle's earliest and most cherished faith communities. Throughout its sixteen chapters, Paul's letter repeatedly attests to the conflicts that erupted within the church at Corinth and the volatility of the community's boundaries with the unbelieving world. The church's discord – apparent in political factions (1.10–4.21), civil litigation (6.1–8), libertarianism (6.12; 8.1–11.1), gender disputes (11.3–16; 14.33–6), segregated dining (11.17–34), and charismatic bias (12.4–31) – is indicative of the competitive and dissenting spirit that permeated the city's congregations. Furthermore, the high degree of *fragmentation* that plagued the community seems to have been fuelled intensely by its widespread *integration* with non-Christian society; indeed, there was almost no sense of separation between the church and the unbelieving world from which it was called.[2] An assembly obviously fraught with internal conflict, preoccupied with non-Christian ethics, and consumed with popular forms of education and leadership, the church in Corinth struggled perhaps

---

[1] The canonical 1 Corinthians was not Paul's initial correspondence with the Corinthian church (cf. 1 Cor 5.9–11), but this form of reference will be utilised throughout for the sake of convenience.

[2] As Barclay (1992: 57–8) has astutely observed, 'One of the most significant, but least noticed, features of Corinthian church life is the absence of conflict in the relationship between Christians and "outsiders". In contrast to the Thessalonian church, the believers in Corinth appear neither to feel hostility towards, nor to experience hostility from, non-Christians... Clearly, whatever individual exceptions there may be, Paul does not regard social alienation as the characteristic state of the Corinthian church.' Cf. de Vos (1999); Robertson (2001: 53–113). For the influence of non-Christian ethics on the Corinthian believers, see Clarke (1993); Winter (2000: x). For Paul's portrayal of the Corinthian church as an ideologically distinct community, see Horsley (2005); Adams (2000: 147–9).

more than any other of the apostle's early faith communities to grasp and embody the new 'symbolic order' of Pauline Christianity.[3]

While the nature of the Corinthians' shortcomings distinguished them from Paul's other churches, it is the manner in which Paul utilised the gospel to remedy these complications that distinguishes 1 Corinthians from the rest of the Pauline corpus. First Corinthians reveals in a way unlike any other Pauline epistle the apostle's theology *in practice*, that is, the applicability of the gospel to real people and ordinary problems.[4] According to Gordon Fee, it is this ability of Paul to bring the good news to bear in the marketplace, to facilitate the message as it works its way out in the exigencies of everyday life, that demonstrates the 'truth[fulness] of his gospel', and finds unique expression in 1 Corinthians.[5]

Paul's apostolic authority

Among the many ways that Paul applies his theology to the lives of the believers in Corinth, few are as prevalent and important in 1 Corinthians as the elucidation of apostolic power and authority.[6] As James Dunn maintains, 'The opportunity to compare Paul's theology and his practice, or, better, his theology in practice, is nowhere so promising as in the case of apostolic authority', and '[o]n the day-to-day reality of Paul's apostolic authority, the most instructive text is undoubtedly 1 Corinthians'.[7] The basis of Dunn's two assertions seems clear: the conceptualisation of apostles and apostleship was a matter of great concern between the Corinthian believers themselves, as well as between the church and its founder, and so much so that it was the first topic Paul sought to resolve in the letter (1.10–4.21), one he would soon revisit (9.1–27), and one that would eventually occupy further reflection in later correspondence (2 Corinthians). Clarifying who, or what, Paul and the other apostles were and how they were to be perceived was therefore a matter of real

---

[3] Horrell (1996: 53–9); cf. Tucker (2010).

[4] Barrett (1968: 26); Conzelmann (1975: 9); R. F. Collins (1999: 29); Furnish (1999: 122–3).

[5] Fee (1987: 16).

[6] Scott (2001: 3) defines *social power* as 'the socially significant affecting of one agent by another in the face of possible resistance'. In this investigation various forms of power will be identified. One such form is *authority*, which we understand to be an expression of what Scott refers to as *persuasive influence*, which involves 'processes of legitimation and signification that can be organised into complex structures of command and expertise' (17). It is by virtue of his position in the ecclesiastical structure that Paul issues the commands and possesses the apostolic rights which will occupy our attention in this study.

[7] Dunn (1998: 571–2).

urgency in Paul's rhetorical strategy as he undertook to direct the church toward ecclesial unity and Christian maturity. At the same time, because the letter is not as polemical as Galatians or 2 Corinthians, it provides an exceptional window into the power dynamics of an apostle playing a relatively unscripted role.

Inasmuch as apostolic authority remains a pertinent topic of study in Pauline theology in general and in 1 Corinthians in particular, the enquiry remains complicated in modern NT research by the multiplicity of scholarly approaches being employed. Not only do these different points of entry leave many interpreters with competing perspectives about the nature of Paul's authority and apostolic practice, but, as the following survey seeks to demonstrate, they too often fail to consider important hermeneutical factors relevant to interpreting Paul's discourses, including their socio-historical and rhetorical contexts.

Authority constructed

Numerous studies in 1 Corinthians have sought to illuminate the nature of apostleship and the authority Paul possessed by examining the theological implications of the many illustrative ways the apostle *constructs*, or *describes*, the apostolate. Countless studies, for instance, have investigated Paul's use of the title ἀπόστολος (1 Cor 1.1, 17; 4.9; 9.1–2, 5; 12.28–9; 15.7, 9), aiming to expose the nature of apostleship by deciphering the origin of the title. While a few interpreters have suggested that the Pauline concept originated in Christianity or Gnosticism,[8] a growing consensus of scholars – following the initial proposal of J. B. Lightfoot and its later development by Karl Rengstorf – suggest that Paul's particular brand of apostleship had its origin in Judaism and was in some way related to the office of the שליח ('delegate').[9] Going in a similar direction, Karl Sandnes has examined Paul's identification with the Hebrew prophets (2.6–16; 9.15–18), suggesting that Paul understood and portrayed his apostolic role as an extension of the OT prophetic tradition.[10] John N. Collins, on the other hand, has focused on Paul's use of the term διάκονος (3.5), arguing quite controversially that Paul's metaphor depicts the apostle as an embassy from God to the church, rather than as a servile position as the term is conventionally understood

---

[8] For the apostolate as a Christian invention, see, e.g., Munck (1950); Ehrhardt (1953: 15–20). For its origin in Gnosticism, see Schmithals (1969: 98–110).

[9] Lightfoot (1865: 92–101); Rengstorf (1964: 407–45). More recently, Agnew (1986); Frey (2004: 180).

[10] Sandnes (1991: 77–130).

to mean.[11] Stephan Joubert and Trevor Burke have independently targeted Paul's father metaphor (4.14–21), while Beverly Gaventa has concentrated on Paul's maternal language (3.1–2).[12] Finally, Zeba Crook, utilising the relational framework of patronage, portrays Paul as a client and beneficiary who out of loyalty labours to 'convert' other clients to his patron God (9.1, 16–17; 15.8–10).[13]

While normally being socio-historically and exegetically focused, most studies investigating Paul's metaphorical representations of apostleship, however, neither seek nor are able to address what are arguably the most fundamental theological matters concerning apostolic authority: its basis, scope, purpose, and limits. However, this lacuna has in large part been filled by John Schütz, who was one of the first to address Paul's authority utilising modern theory. Combining detailed exegesis with sociology, Schütz demonstrated that Paul's conceptualisation of *apostolic* authority significantly varied from Max Weber's model of *charismatic* authority, since the apostle's authority did not rest on the legitimation of others.[14] Instead, after examining a number of Pauline texts (including 1 Corinthians 1–4 and 15), Schütz reasoned that Paul's authority transcended the legitimating power of the community and rested on two 'figures of interpretation': (i) the *gospel*, itself 'a power or force in human affairs, the field or sphere in which those called by it now stand and through which they move to a future already adumbrated and in some sense present in the gospel'; and (ii) the *apostle* himself, whose power derives not from an institution – 'Paul does not regard apostolic authorization as a sometime thing, as a limited endowment of representative authority' – rather, as the apostle embodies the gospel in his life and ministry, his authority becomes 'inseparable from the whole of the person authorized'.[15] 'Hence, both the gospel and the apostle are manifestations of a single power and *are* "authority" in that sense.'[16] Deeply learned and nearly comprehensive in scope, Schütz's work remains a leading theological analysis of Paul's authority-concept.

Even Schütz's investigation, however, was not able to address every significant facet of Pauline apostolic power and authority, as he himself ignored how Paul's authority was actually exercised. That is to say, while Schütz's treatment provides an intriguing study on Paul's ideology of authority, it remains one-dimensional insofar as it fails to analyse how Paul asserted his authority over his Christian communities.

Authority asserted

While the studies mentioned above have examined how Paul *constructed* apostolic authority, a number of other studies have sought to expose and evaluate how Paul *asserted* authority. Looking beyond Paul's apostolic representations, these investigations often utilise modern theory to detect, compare, and assess the use of power and authority in Paul's letters. Bengt Holmberg, whose analysis of the 'structures of authority' in the early church is now quite famous for helping to usher in an age of sociological exploration of the NT, is another who has left a massive imprint on the landscape of Pauline authority studies. Whereas Schütz examined Paul's authority as an ideological abstraction, Holmberg pursued the matter as a sociological reality, utilising 'concrete social facts' to establish what 'actually happened between Paul and his churches'.[17] Relying therefore on both Acts and the Pauline letters to supply his historical data, Holmberg compared Paul's power to the Weberian authority models and concluded that the primitive church operated under the influence of a complex structure of ecclesial power based mainly on charismatic authority, and contained mixed degrees of institutionalisation. Moreover, while Holmberg contended that Paul's Gentile mission was largely dependent on, though not subordinate to, the Jerusalem church,[18] he argued that Paul possessed a large measure of regional authority, having been superordinate to his missionary co-workers and having had the necessary leverage over the local churches he founded to admonish them and to expect from them financial support in return for preaching.[19] In fact, according to Holmberg, it was Paul's *over*-involvement in those churches that disrupted their development of local political structures (cf. 1 Corinthians 12 and 14).[20]

Although Holmberg's analysis yielded rich results, his methodology has been criticised by scholars reluctant to impose anachronistic and unsubstantiated models onto ancient texts.[21] There is, to be sure, much to be gained by using modern theory in the study of biblical literature. Theories, frameworks, and models can at the very least function as useful

---

[17] Holmberg (1980: 203), who charges Schütz and his methodological predecessors with committing 'the fallacy of idealism'.

[18] Holmberg (1980: 55–6).   [19] Holmberg (1980: 70–93).

[20] Holmberg (1980: 116).   [21] Judge (1980: 210); Clarke (1993: 3–6).

heuristic tools 'for the purpose of developing new approaches to and opening up new questions about early Christianity'.[22] Still, the criticisms directed against Holmberg's analysis have served to remind interpreters of the need to verify interpretive claims and methodologies with sufficient historical data. As Holmberg himself remarks,

> [A] detailed knowledge of the historical setting of the early Christians is indispensable for any historical reconstruction of their real life. Historiography cannot operate without historical data that can serve as evidence, nor can it neglect any available historical data, just because they cannot be easily fitted into one's own outlook or 'model'. Socio-historical fieldwork is what hypotheses, models, and theories work on and are constructed from. This means also that models or theories cannot substitute for evidence, by filling in gaps in the data, as it were.[23]

Future efforts to elucidate and appraise Paul's apostolic authority must therefore situate Paul's letters in their historical context and validate the use of modern theory and expectations with sufficient textual evidence.

This warning is particularly germane to critics who are expressly suspicious of the apostle's exercise of authority and have sought to expose its suppressive nature without reconstructing the context in which it was employed. Graham Shaw, for instance, while conceding that Paul's letters advocate liberation and reconciliation, aggressively argues that those tenets are wholly incompatible with the oppressive ethos of Paul's political practice.[24] Paul's assertion of authority is, according to Shaw, 'complex but unrelenting', as he manipulated churches to rely on him, all the while concealing his dependence on them and alienating those believers who failed to ally.[25] Furthermore, Paul's abusive exercise of power is to be credited to the apostle's mistaken sense of authorisation: 'the brittle, arbitrary and divisive nature of Paul's leadership', Shaw remarks, 'is intimately connected with self-delusion about the resurrection, and a mistaken value attributed to charismatic phenomena'.[26] Targeting several Pauline letters, in addition to Mark's Gospel, Shaw has particularly harsh words for Paul's rhetoric in 1 Corinthians:

---

[22] Horrell (2000: 93). Cf. Esler (2000); Horrell (2009).
[23] Holmberg (2004: 269–70). Cf. Holmberg (1990).
[24] Shaw (1983: 181–4). Despite his criticisms of Paul's assertion of authority, Shaw attempts to exonerate Paul's intentions by conceding that the apostle was 'learning to exercise freedom and love' (184).
[25] Shaw (1983: 181).   [26] Shaw (1983: 182).

This letter, which contains the most famous of all Paul's writings, the lyrical passage on love in ch. 13, is in other respects an exercise of magisterial authority. Its keynote is struck in the second verse – the Lordship of Christ. In the name of that Lord Paul demands unity and obedience. He is to be seen subduing critics, subjecting the faithful to his unsolicited censure, and giving firm rulings to their most intimate queries. It is a style that the officials of the Vatican can rightly claim as their own. It is perhaps a sign of Paul's confidence in the exercise of his authority that only a few verses of the letter are devoted to prayer. He briefly thanks God for the spiritual achievement of the Corinthians ... and declares his confidence that God will maintain their loyalty – sentiments which both confirm the Corinthians in their position of obedience and rule out of court the possibility of their defection. Here he needs neither to flatter nor cajole, and so he proceeds to command.[27]

Although Shaw's concerns are refreshingly candid, his rhetoric is habitually overstated and his analysis fails to place any of Paul's discourses in their historical context. As Dunn remarks with reference to Shaw's criticisms on 1 Corinthians, 'A fairer reading ... would be much more sensitive to the rhetorical character of the letter and to the social factors at play in Corinth, particularly when we cannot hear the other sides of the debates and do not know how much the issues were caught up in the social tensions of Corinth, not least between patrons and their clients.'[28]

Elizabeth Castelli's treatment of Paul's call to imitation (μίμησις), while offering another stimulating appraisal of the apostle's 'strategy of power', ultimately suffers from a similar kind of contextual neglect.[29] Critical of past interpreters who 'either have ignored the implicit articulation of power present in the advocacy of mimetic relations or have rendered the power relationship unproblematic and self-evident',[30] Castelli has sought, on the basis of the theory of Michel Foucault, to expose the power buried in Paul's rhetoric by showing how the perpetuation of sameness was used to repress deviance and proliferate a single Christian ideology – Paul's own – with the ultimate consequence of monopolising truth and determining who would and would not be saved. Castelli's thesis has particular relevance for 1 Corinthians, where Paul's call to become his imitators surfaces twice in significant sections of the letter.

---

[27] Shaw (1983: 62).   [28] Dunn (1998: 575–6).
[29] Castelli (1991: 15).   [30] Castelli (1991: 33).

'Imitation of Paul in both contexts (4:16 and 11:1)', Castelli states, 'has to do fundamentally with the social arrangement of the Corinthian community (unity and identity) and always refers back to the singular authoritative model of Paul.'[31] But Castelli's insistence on Paul's manipulation of the Corinthians fails to account for how his call to imitation originally functioned in the letter, that is, as a pattern of suffering and of *sacrificing* one's authority, rather than *exploiting* it (cf. 4.9–13; 9.19). Castelli attempts to circumvent the matter of authorial intention by dismissing its accessibility to modern exegetes.[32] However, as Margaret Mitchell has noted, such neglect is at odds with Castelli's own rhetoric as well as the postmodern theory on which her thesis rests.[33] Moreover, once the socio-rhetorical context of 1 Corinthians is given fuller attention, it is plain that the Corinthians, not Paul, were those fixated on power.[34]

Sandra Polaski, who is also informed by Foucauldian methods of detecting power, analyses Paul's autobiographical discourses in order to move behind what Paul *states* about his power to identify what Paul *implies* about it. Even though she has no wish to apply a 'hostile reading' to the text, nor 'to vilify Paul's power claims from the outset', nor 'to dismiss them as deceitfully self-serving', Polaski openly employs a hermeneutic of suspicion whereby she attempts to detect in Paul 'evidence of power relations which the surface meaning of the text may mask'.[35] This leads her to investigate Philemon, Galatians, and Paul's references to the divine grace given to him (e.g. 1 Cor 3.10) in order to demonstrate how the apostle possessed a sense of revelatory authority which he used to persuade his audiences to obey. While he always afforded his audiences the opportunity to refuse, to do so would have been an affront to him and, just as Castelli observed, would have resulted in placement outside the ideological community.[36]

Whereas Shaw, Castelli, and Polaski have raised serious questions about the motives and effects of Paul's apostolic authority, other

---

[31] Castelli (1991: 114–15). See also Wanamaker (2003), who is indebted to Castelli's approach and further emphasises Paul's use of ideology to assert power.

[32] It is significant that Scott (2001: 2) notes how a 'power relation cannot ... be identified unless there is some reference to the intentions and interests of the actors involved and, especially, to those of the principal'.

[33] M. M. Mitchell (1992).

[34] Cf. Clarke (1998: 342–7); Copan (2007: 181–218).

[35] Polaski (1999: 21).

[36] Polaski (1999: 71): 'Paul moves from relationship-language that is already accepted by his readers ... to another set of terms, commercial, familial, and even corporeal in nature, which, taken together, describe a universe in which Paul is very close to God in authority.'

interpreters have suggested that the power relations operating between Paul and his communities were far more complex than some modern critics realise. Ernest Best, for instance, while recognising that Paul possessed authority derived from the gospel, argued that Paul only made claim to his apostleship and apostolic authority when addressing his relationship with other church leaders.[37] In so doing, Best attempted to mitigate the charge of Paul's abuse of specifically *apostolic* authority, insisting that Paul exercised authority over his churches only on the basis of his status as their *founder* ('father').[38] But Best's distinction between Paul's roles as apostle and church founder seems artificial; despite Best's attempts to do so, there does not appear to be any reason to separate Paul's apostolic and missional roles. Moreover, determining which role Paul occupies when he exercises authority over his converts seems to require evidence beyond what his letters provide.

Kathy Ehrensperger, followed by Adrian Long and Rick Talbott, has also given Paul's exercise of authority a sympathetic reading, attempting to explain how Paul used his authority constructively, that is, not to suppress his churches, but to empower them toward Christian maturity. While she grants that Paul and others in the early Christian movement exercised power *over* their communities and operated within an asymmetrical hierarchy, Ehrensperger places Paul's rhetoric into conversation with contemporary feminist theories of power in order to explain that Paul's authority, far from being domineering, had a transformative objective which sought to enable early believers to reach a status of maturity on a par with their leaders.[39] As Ehrensperger herself remarks, 'Paul emphasizes again and again that the aim of his teaching is to *empower* those within his communities to *support each other*. He acts as a parent-teacher using power-over them to empower them and thus render himself, and the power-over exercised in this role, obsolete.'[40]

---

[37] Best (1986: 8–12, 22).

[38] Best (1986: 22): 'There is no doubt Paul claimed to be an apostle, and that of the type of Peter. There is no doubt that he exercised authority. There must be doubt that these two ideas are necessarily related.'

[39] Ehrensperger (2007: 179).

[40] Ehrensperger (2007: 136, original emphasis). See also Adrian Long (2009: 56–147): '[W]hen contextualized within both the Corinthians' situation and especially within his self-presentation in the Corinthian correspondence, it would seem safer to find in Paul's claim to be the community's father a statement of power which is gospel-defined; which aims not at self-aggrandizement but at the edification of the community through service and love' (130). Moreover, Talbott (2010: 93–161) shows that Paul holds in tension the notions of 'kyriarchy' (structural power and superiority) and 'kyridoularchy' (exercising power on behalf of social subordinates so as to empower them), implementing a kyridoularchal vision in his churches while addressing with kyriarchical rhetoric those who failed

Ehrensperger's approach involves analysing and re-evaluating many of the same metaphors and motifs examined by her predecessors, such as Paul's grace language, apostleship terminology, parental metaphors, and imitation motif. But although her exegesis is socio-historically grounded and her thesis about the empowering role of the apostolate deserves serious consideration, the assumption that the apostles sought eventually to eliminate the ecclesial hierarchy seems unwarranted. At what point was apostolic authority rendered obsolete, and was this goal actually achievable, or merely hypothetical? Ehrensperger simply goes beyond the evidence when she utilises her framework to impose this ecclesiastical goal.

Authority contested

In addition to considering the social context of power, one of the most significant complications with analysing Paul's power and authority in Corinth is that there existed within and without the community various contestants for power and various understandings of it. Reconstructing the competing power relations operative in the church is therefore an essential hermeneutical step in the interpretive process. Although there is certainly no consensus in modern scholarship about the precise social circumstances facing the community at the time 1 Corinthians was written, what is known (or hitherto found to be historically plausible) must be taken into serious consideration, especially when assessing Paul's power claims and assertions. As Dunn explains, 'Difficult though it is, the reconstruction of social context is necessary for any full understanding of the letter': 'as different reconstructions are proffered, or as different facets of the complex historical context of 1 Corinthians are illuminated, so different emphases and facets of the letter itself will be thrown into prominence (and others into shadow)'.[41]

Dunn's warning is particularly applicable in our case. Most would agree, for instance, that one of the major ethical failings of the Corinthian community was its preoccupation with personal power, exercised through honour, boasting, and patronage, and perhaps most apparent in the church's political, legal, and dietary disputes.[42] As L. L. Welborn

---

to align with his vision. But empowering others did not render one's power obsolete. As Talbott explains, 'Kyridoularchy did not necessarily require one to forfeit his or her status or economic means simply to identify with lower-status members. The object was not repudiating one's power but ascribing honor to others' (100).

[41] Dunn (2004: 296, 309).

[42] See, e.g., Chow (1992: 113–66); Clarke (1993: 59–107).

has rightly and memorably remarked, 'It is a power struggle, not a theological controversy, which motivates the writing of 1 Corinthians 1–4.'[43] Intensifying these local feuds still further were the disproportionate power and patronage ascribed to individual leaders, including not only apostolic figures such as Paul, Apollos, and Cephas, but perhaps also local dissenters, such as the Corinthian prophetesses and popular orators.[44] Finally, it is important also to recall the role occupied by God/ Christ in Paul's apostolic undertaking, particularly as the one who exercised power over him and would judge his ministry at its completion.[45] These kinds of power relations must be factored into any discussion of Paul's portrayal and assertion of apostolic authority, as they are foundational to the reconstruction of the occasion of the letter and indispensible for identifying its rhetorical, perhaps even apologetic, objectives.

Summary

As this survey has shown, Pauline interpreters have employed a variety of methods and approaches in seeking to elucidate Paul's apostolic authority. But many who have investigated the concept have restricted their analyses either to the construction *or* assertion of his authority. For Paul, however, theology is inseparable from practice, so it is important that both aspects be examined together when possible. It has also been shown that many studies neglect certain hermeneutical factors that must be accounted for when addressing apostolic power and authority. Scholars utilising modern theories of analysis are especially prone to identify power claims without adequately demonstrating that such forms and expressions of power are substantiated by historical data. Beyond this, many of these studies ignore that there were in Corinth various contestants for power whose own power assertions disrupted the community and set the tone for Paul's subsequent response. Because Paul's power relations are so complex, it is important that his exercise of authority not be treated, as Andrew Clarke warns, 'in simplified terms, essentially dealing exclusively with Paul's mechanisms of asserting power'.[46] Rather, Clarke recommends, 'Paul's power rhetoric and his power dealings need to be explored within their wider context, including the ways in which Paul defined the limits of his power, the ways in which he

---

[43] Welborn (1987b: 89).   [44] Cf. Wire (1990); Winter (2002).

[45] As Schütz (1975: 285) remarks: 'The final judgment is the final and unmistakable manifestation of power.'

[46] Clarke (2008: 106; cf. 108–9).

undermined the power that was inherent in his own position, [and] how he responded to the power plays of others.'[47] What is therefore needed is an investigation that considers both Paul's construction *and* assertion of authority, one that is sensitive to the letter's socio-historical and rhetorical contexts.

Paul as an administrator of God: a neglected metaphor

One image that too often goes overlooked, yet can be utilised to address the concerns raised by Clarke, is Paul's portrayal of apostles as administrators (οἰκονόμοι) of God.[48] Paul's metaphor appears in two important passages in 1 Corinthians (4.1–5; 9.16–23), and in both pericopae Paul indicates that his apostleship was being scrutinised by his own converts. Paul therefore employs the metaphor in both texts to correct fundamental misunderstandings about his apostolic role, rights, and responsibilities. In fact, the strategic placement of this metaphor indicates that Paul believed it cogently communicated some of his chief apostolic attributes; indeed, the directive in 1 Cor 4.1 (οὕτως ἡμᾶς λογιζέσθω ἄνθρωπος) suggests that Paul considered this metaphor to be a more reliable illustration of the apostolate for his current readership than the other images he employed in 1 Corinthians 3–4. Furthermore, Paul's reinstatement of the same metaphor in 9.17 demonstrates his continued confidence in the image's ability to convey his role to this particular church. Beyond this, Paul's metaphor affords the reader a promising way to analyse Paul's construction *and* assertion of authority in 1 Corinthians, for both 1 Cor 4.1–5 and 9.16–23 offer representations of apostleship and the authority inherent in that position, as well as show how the apostle exercised (or even refused to exercise) his authority in an effort to resolve specific problems in the church. Paul's use of this metaphor therefore provides a multi-faceted portrait of apostleship and emphasises aspects of his authority that many previous scholarly investigations have overlooked.

---

[47] Clarke (2008: 106).

[48] The terms οἰκονόμος and οἰκονομία are used metaphorically for apostleship in four passages in the Pauline epistles. Although Paul uses οἰκονόμος in Rom 16.23 for the civic magistracy held by Erastus and in Gal 4.2 as a metaphor for the pre-Christian function of the Mosaic Law, the only undisputed Pauline letter where the metaphor is used to represent apostleship is 1 Corinthians, where it appears in 4.1–2 (οἰκονόμος (2x)) and 9.17 (οἰκονομία). In the disputed letters, the abstract noun οἰκονομία appears metaphorically for Paul's apostolic commission in Eph 3.2 and Col 1.25. Οἰκονόμος is also used in Titus 1.7 as a metaphor for an ἐπίσκοπος and οἰκονομία refers in Eph 1.10, 3.9, and 1 Tim 1.4 to the divine plan/administration of God. The metaphor is implied in the Pauline *Haustafeln* (Eph 6.9; Col 4.1); cf. Harrill (2006: 85–117).

Unfortunately, there remains much debate in NT scholarship about Paul's *oikonomos* metaphor. The confusion is, on the surface, due to the fact that there have been an insufficient number of studies completed on the metaphor by biblical scholars. There exists, for instance, no book-length treatment to date exclusively devoted to explaining this image, whether in 1 Corinthians or anywhere else in Paul's letters. But this oversight by biblical scholars is perhaps only indicative of the general unfamiliarity with the concept among ancient historians; indeed, there remains a conspicuous lacuna even in ancient historical scholarship due to the lack of a definitive treatment of the term οἰκονόμος by classicists. Although some studies have been conducted on the use of οἰκονόμος, οἰκονομία, and related terminology, they are few, quite dated, generally inaccessible as unpublished doctoral theses, and have limited aims so that they do not bring much light to bear directly on Paul's metaphor.[49] In fact, as will be demonstrated in this study, appropriately interpreting Paul's *oikonomos* metaphor requires familiarity with socio-legal and economic aspects of the ancient world that are not immediately obvious in 1 Corinthians and that many NT exegetes have failed to consider heretofore.

There also remains confusion among scholars about the derivation of Paul's metaphor. Even though Paul's description of apostles as *oikonomoi* has long been recognised as a metaphor with a *source domain* originating somewhere in the administrative landscape of the ancient world,[50] the precise social context and connotations of the analogy remain disputed. Many interpreters are even reluctant to identify a specific area of derivation, since *oikonomoi* were ubiquitous in Graeco-Roman antiquity.[51] But failing to identify the metaphor's source domain accurately will bring, and indeed has already brought, added confusion to the exegetical task. Not only do these varying opinions about the metaphor attribute competing legal statuses to Paul's apostolic profile (which affects, for instance, the social perception of apostleship, as well as how one interprets the volitional aspect of his preaching in 1 Corinthians 9), but the failure to

---

[49] Landvogt (1908); Reumann (1957). Cf. Lehmeier (2006).

[50] Kövecses (2002: 4): 'The conceptual domain from which we draw metaphorical expressions to understand another conceptual domain is called source domain, while the conceptual domain that is understood this way is the target domain... The target domain is the domain that we try to understand through the use of the source domain.'

[51] Tooley (1966: 75–6) considered 1 Cor 4.1–2 to be 'the most pregnant use of the metaphor in the NT', yet failed even to propose a possible source domain, despite distinguishing between several social contexts in which *oikonomoi* were appointed. See also the indecision of Michel (1967: 150); Conzelmann (1975: 83); Horsley (1998a: 67, 129–30); Collins (1999: 168–9); Fitzmyer (2008: 212).

distinguish between source *domains* can easily lead to the indiscriminate use of source *materials*. It is therefore critical that Paul's metaphor be situated in the right administrative context in order to ensure that it is interpreted appropriately.

Survey of interpretations

The first sustained scholarly treatment of Paul's *oikonomos* metaphor attempted to locate the origin of the image in the religious matrix of the Graeco-Roman world. In the middle of the last century, John Reumann, following the *religionsgeschichtliche Schule*, pursued the expression οἰκονόμους μυστηρίων θεοῦ (1 Cor 4.1) by examining a number of Greek inscriptions depicting variously ranked *oikonomoi* in a range of religious capacities. Reumann then proposed that Paul probably adopted the title 'stewards of the mysteries of God' from this Graeco-Roman religious context, especially the mystery cults. Reumann remarked,

> [R]ather than any ... theological explanation, it is the background in Greco-Roman life and use of the term with already existing religious connotations which provide the immediate and most obvious insight into Paul's designation of himself and others as 'stewards of God' and his mysteries; as in other instances, he is borrowing terminology current in the religious world of his day.[52]

Despite Reumann's impressive sample of texts featuring *oikonomoi* performing religious rites and responsibilities, the mystery cult hypothesis influenced very few interpreters. Not only does the reading fail to account for the monetary use of the metaphor apparent in 1 Cor 9.17, where Paul's apostolic wage (μισθός) is the issue in dispute, but nearly a decade later Reumann himself abandoned his own proposal in favour of a more ambiguous reading.[53] Moreover, in this later work Reumann

---

[52] Reumann (1958: 349). Cf. Windisch (1934: 221). Much of Reumann's work in Paul was directed against Oscar Cullmann's decontextualised rendering of *oikonomia* as *Heilsgeschichte*. Cullmann's (1951: 33) understanding of the term was largely influenced by its later-Pauline occurrences (Eph 1.10; 3.2, 9; Col 1.25). Cullmann then imported this later cosmic sense into Paul's self-designation as an '*oikonomos* of God's mysteries' (1 Cor 4.1) so that Paul's metaphor indicated the apostle was not just entrusted 'an administration of the divine teaching about salvation but also of the active realization of the redemptive history' (223). In support of Cullmann's reading is the fact that a number of patristic authors subsequently utilised *oikonomia* to refer to God's cosmic plan of redemption; cf. Richter (2005). Nevertheless, Reumann (1967) convincingly showed that the earlier-Pauline uses of *oikonomia*-terminology do not refer to God's redemptive plan.

[53] Reumann (1967: 161). Still, Reumann (1992: 14) maintained that the mystery cult interpretation would have resonated with many in Paul's world. But as Schrage (1991: 321)

intimated that the phrase 'stewards of the mysteries of God' may in fact have been a Semitism borrowed from Second Temple Judaism, a theory that continues to carry some currency in modern scholarship.

The Semitic hypothesis has, for instance, been advocated by Benjamin Gladd in his recent monograph on Paul's use of μυστήριον in 1 Corinthians. Although he concedes that 'Paul may have invented this stewardship metaphor without any reference to the OT, Second Temple Judaism, or Mystery Religions', Gladd observes certain resonances between 1 Cor 4.1–5 and Theodotion's Greek text of Daniel, which eventually lead him to suppose that Paul's *oikonomos* metaphor was a familiar image in Jewish apocalyptic.[54] But Gladd's proposal fails to convince, since, as he himself admits, the Greek phrase is found nowhere in Jewish literature or anywhere else in Graeco-Roman antiquity.[55] Raymond Brown and Markus Bockmuehl, on the other hand, suggest that a Hebrew parallel may exist from Qumran, both briefly noting the similarities between Paul's designation of apostles as οἰκονόμοι μυστηρίων (1 Cor 4.1) and the intriguing phrase [א]נשי משמרת לרזיכה ('the men who guard your mysteries', 1Q36 16.2).[56] The resemblance is certainly striking, but we should not minimise the differences between the actions and responsibilities implied by the Greek noun οἰκονόμος and the Hebrew verb שמר, especially because the former was directed to Gentile urbanites, the latter to sectarian Jews. While there may be some implied functional overlap between the two terms, they are not strictly equivalent: οἰκονόμος implies the accumulation, administration, and dispensing of resources; שמר generally indicates protection and safekeeping. Furthermore, the fragmentary nature of 1Q36 leaves us with virtually nothing by which to identify who the guardians were and how they were supposed to protect their mysteries, rendering the text basically useless to interpreters of Paul's metaphor.[57] Beyond this, a Jewish apocalyptic context, just as the

remarks, 'Obwohl ihnen nach Paulus μυστήρια θεοῦ anvertraut sind, ist zu bezweifeln, daß der Sprachgebrauch der Mysterienkulte von Einfluß war. Die Apostel sind keine Mystagogen.'

[54] Gladd (2008: 172). Gladd, who regards Daniel as a 'steward of mysteries', argues that the shared use of εὑρίσκω and πιστός in 1 Cor 4.2 and Dan 6.4 (Theo) substantiates the claim that Paul was alluding to the Danielic episode. But in the latter text, εὑρίσκω has no syntactical relationship with πιστός; God is not even the subject of the verb, as he is implied to be in 1 Cor 4.2.

[55] Gladd (2008: 171); cf. Bockmuehl (1990: 166 n. 42). The infrequent and insignificant use of οἰκονομία-terminology in the LXX has been noted by Reumann (1967: 151).

[56] Brown (1968: 45); Bockmuehl (1990: 166).

[57] Such is perhaps the reason why neither Brown nor Bockmuehl suggest how 1Q36 might illuminate the Pauline phrase, and why Gladd (2008: 270), who is aware of the text, draws no comparison between it and 1 Cor 4.1. Even Harvey (1980: 331), who refers to the

mystery religions hypothesis, fails to offer an explanation for Paul's clear monetary use of the metaphor in 1 Cor 9.17.

Another recent treatment has sought to show that Paul's metaphor was derived from the regal administrative contexts of the Hellenistic and Roman periods. Relying exclusively on papyrological evidence, Peter Arzt-Grabner and Ruth Kritzer argue that Paul's image has close structural correspondences with officials appointed within the public domain (*öffentlichen Bereichs*), especially certain high-ranking financial officers who served in imperial hierarchies.[58] Moreover, because official, Ptolemaic documentation uses the verb εὑρίσκω for the calling to account of a regal *oikonomos* (P.Rev. 49), it is suggested that Paul was probably even well acquainted with the terminological conventions of those political systems, since he employs the verb in a similar manner in 1 Cor 4.2.[59] This, however, seems to minimise the significant differences that existed between the Hellenistic regal *oikonomoi* and their Roman counterparts, since the Roman *oikonomoi* who served in the administration of Caesar were in fact imperial slaves who managed his household and economic interests. By ignoring their individual job descriptions and distinct social and legal statuses, these interpreters confuse the two categories, portraying both kinds of official as if they occupied a single office. A similar confusion is also apparent in the way Kritzer relates the relevant Pauline discourses. Although she indicates that Paul's metaphor in 1 Cor 4.1–2 implied free status, in her comments on 9.16–17 she suggests that Paul's preaching was involuntary and unpaid. She then likens his office to a public liturgy. But since liturgies were normally municipal offices, the comparison seems only to obscure the image further by introducing another political category.[60] It is not finally clear, then, whether Paul's metaphorical language was drawn from a regal, civic, or private context, or even whether 1 Cor 4.1–2 and 9.16–17 cohere in any sense.

It has also become common to propose that Paul adopted his *oikonomos* metaphor from the Hellenistic moral philosophers. Abraham Malherbe, followed by John Byron and Lincoln Galloway, suggests that Paul's use of the analogy in 1 Cor 9.17 should be read in light of the

---

Qumran expression as an 'almost exact equivalent' to the Pauline metaphor, cannot exclude the possibility that Paul's image was derived from another context.

[58] Arzt-Grabner, Papathomas, Kritzer, and Winter (2006: 163).

[59] Arzt-Grabner, Papathomas, Kritzer, and Winter (2006: 164): 'Paulus verwendet hier einen Vergleich aus dem Amtsbereich (ἐν τοῖς οἰκονόμοις), und wie die Belege zeigen, ist er mit der Terminologie einer "amtlichen Feststellung" gut vertraut, und zwar bis ins Detail.' But the use of εὑρίσκω was also used for the calling to account of other kinds of *oikonomoi* (cf. Luke 12.43).

[60] Arzt-Grabner, Papathomas, Kritzer, and Winter (2006: 354).

figurative use of the same image in Epictetus (*Diatr.* 3.22.3).[61] Epictetus' *oikonomos* metaphor has as its target domain the 'true Cynic', and likens the person who assumes the Cynic lifestyle without first being assigned to it by God to the person who appoints himself as the *oikonomos* of a well-ordered house and begins insolently giving orders: he will of course be disciplined by his κύριος. Although there are fascinating similarities between Epictetus' construal of the true Cynic and Paul's portrayal of Christian apostleship (cf. *Diatr.* 3.22.23; 1 Cor 1.17), those who rely exclusively on Epictetus' metaphor to make sense of Paul's analogy face one major problem: Epictetus' portrayal of the true Cynic as an *oikonomos* is itself a metaphor. Epictetus, just as Paul, drew from a particular source domain – namely, estate management – and then applied very specific attributes of the manager to the Cynic, several of which are different from those which Paul himself underscores. Conspicuously absent from Epictetus' metaphor, for example, is the subject of money. Yet remuneration is plainly a central concern in Paul's metaphor in 1 Cor 9.17. Therefore, unless it can be demonstrated that Paul and Epictetus used their metaphors identically – and they clearly did not – then it is imperative that the interpreter trace Paul's *oikonomos* metaphor back to its original, *literal* source domain before applying attributes to the apostle.

The most common approach to Paul's *oikonomos* metaphor, then, has been to interpret it against the backdrop of literal managerial slavery. Dale Martin's treatment of the metaphor has been particularly influential in this respect. Martin, who limits his focus to 1 Corinthians 9, argues that the expression οἰκονομίαν πεπίστευμαι (9.17) implied that Paul identified himself as Christ's enslaved, representative leader.[62] Although most biblical scholars once regarded ancient slavery only as a brutal and oppressive institution, Martin sought to demonstrate that slavery functioned for some in the Roman world as an opportunity for social advancement. Legally, slaves had no family, possessed no money, and were to be restricted to a low social stratum. Martin, however, through an extensive use of literary and non-literary evidence, argued that some slaves circumvented these restrictions, acquiring spouses, children, allowances (*peculia*), and even relatively prominent social standing, experiencing significant social mobility through association with high-power owners. Martin therefore

---

[61] Malherbe (1994: 249–51); Byron (2003: 249–53); Galloway (2004: 184–6). See also Ierodiakonou (2007: 65), who credits the terminological similarities between Epictetus and Paul to their shared use of 'the common conversational language of the day, which reflects a common way of thinking about things in this period'.

[62] D. B. Martin (1990); cf. Lehmeier (2006: 219–65); R. H. Williams (2006: 76–83); Zeller (2010: 173).

contended that Paul's metaphorical depiction of himself as the οἰκονόμος of the divine κύριος would have elicited a positive impression from persons of a low social condition. While free persons within the church would have responded negatively to Paul's menial self-representation, slaves and others from humble origins would have regarded the metaphor as a designation of honour, power, and authority.[63]

But even as some interpreters agree that the phrase οἰκονομίαν πεπίστευμαι (9.17) indicates a claim to slavery and leadership, others contend that the title is legally ambiguous and cannot support the social implications advanced by Martin. Murray Harris, for example, states that Paul's designation in 1 Cor 9.17

> scarcely validates the inference that Paul views himself as a high-status managerial slave (*oikonomos*) in Christ's household, especially since Paul has already used that actual term *oikonomos* twice in the same letter in reference to stewards who are commissioned to expound 'the mysteries of God' (1 Cor. 4:1–2), 'managers' authorized to divulge God's hidden truths (= the gospel), a role that in fact makes Paul 'the scum of the earth' (1 Cor. 4:13).[64]

Harris also challenges the assumption that either Paul or the Corinthians would have associated managerial slavery with the positive social implications advanced by Martin. According to Harris, managerial slaves 'formed such a small minority that we may question whether that particular connotation of slavery would have ousted the dominant notion of slavery as humble subjection to a master in the minds of Paul's converts'.[65] Moreover, 'Any suggestion of Paul's personal concern about "status" ... seems foreign to an evangelist-pastor who earlier in 1 Corinthians has depicted himself and the other apostles as doomed gladiators entering

---

[63] D. B. Martin (1990: 84):
It is important to see ... that up through [1 Cor] 9:18, according to one form of discourse, at least, Paul has made no move toward humility or self-lowering, even though he has defined himself as a slave of Christ. He has, however, redefined the categories for leadership and authority. Instead of thinking about leaders in the normal ways – as patrons, wealthy, kings, those who are free and do as they will – Paul moves the debate into the common discourses of early Christianity, which talks of its leaders as slaves of Christ. Again, this is not to make Christian leaders less powerful or authoritative but to insist that the discussion be carried on in the context of Christian discourse rather than in that of the upper class or of moral philosophers. Far from giving up his authority, Paul seeks in 9:1–18 to establish it beyond question.

[64] M. J. Harris (1999: 129).   [65] M. J. Harris (1999: 129–30).

the arena of human scorn at the end of the procession (1 Cor. 4:9–10), and who aligned himself with menial slavery by pursuing the servile, manual trade of tent-making (Acts 18:3).'[66]

John Byron has also challenged Martin's treatment of the *oikonomos* metaphor. Byron conducted his study first by critically assessing Martin's historical analysis of *oikonomoi*, especially in the inscriptions, and eventually assembled a case for the legal ambiguity of the title.[67] Unlike Martin, Byron took into consideration Paul's metaphor in 1 Cor 4.1–2, where Paul also portrays the apostle as a ὑπηρέτης ('servant'). While Byron supposed that the title οἰκονόμος is legally ambiguous, he argued that ὑπηρέτης plainly indicates free status. This, along with an unconventional reading of 1 Cor 9.16–18, led Byron to conclude that Paul's *oikonomos* metaphor implies that the apostle was a free-will servant.

But Byron's analysis is not without its own complications. In his reassessment of the legal status of *oikonomoi*, Byron failed to distinguish between the very different kinds of administrator in antiquity that bore this title, comparing municipal *oikonomoi* of the likes of Erastus from Rom 16.23 with private *oikonomoi* of the likes of the Unjust Steward from Luke 16.1–8.[68] Such is a case of verbal *parallelomania* ('excerpt versus context'),[69] for Byron conflates the evidence, assuming that different kinds of *oikonomoi* in antiquity can at once serve as appropriate comparisons for Paul's use of the term in 1 Corinthians. Nevertheless, Byron (perhaps inadvertently) has brought into question Martin's assumption that managerial slavery serves as the most plausible source domain of Paul's metaphor.[70] It is therefore imperative that we revisit the ancient evidence in order to identify from which source domain Paul was borrowing and what apostolic attributes the metaphor implies.

Research aims, methods, and procedure

Given the confusion that continues to shroud the interpretation of Paul's *oikonomos* metaphor, it is appropriate that we examine it afresh in this

[66] M. J. Harris (1999: 130).   [67] Byron (2003: 241–53).
[68] Byron (2003: 243–4).
[69] Sandmel (1962: 7):

> It would seem to me to follow that, in dealing with similarities we can sometimes discover exact parallels, some with and some devoid of significance; seeming parallels which are so only imperfectly; and statements which can be called parallels *only by taking them out of context*. I must go on to allege that I encounter from time to time scholarly writings which go astray in this last regard. It is the question of *excerpt versus context* (emphasis added).

[70] Byron, for instance, has significantly influenced Galloway (2004: 184 n. 148).

study in order to clarify those socio-historical, exegetical, and theological matters in dispute. It is important at the outset therefore to raise
the following research aims and questions: in antiquity, what were the
main administrative contexts in which *oikonomoi* were appointed? What
were the major social, legal, and structural differences between those
administrators? To what kind of *oikonomos* was Paul comparing himself? What attributes was Paul applying to himself through the metaphor?
Addressing these socio-historical and exegetical issues will comprise the
bulk of the following study, since the answers to these questions will
determine how the relevant Pauline texts are interpreted and how one
understands Paul's theology of apostleship and apostolic authority.

In order to meet these aims, it is important that we pay close attention to certain methodological considerations. One of the main methodological contributions of this study will be the differentiation it makes
between words and concepts in a way that certain previous studies have
neglected. The first way this differentiation will be observed is by distinguishing between the various persons (concepts) designated as *oikonomoi*. By paying careful attention to these diverse source domains, this
study seeks to use the relevant source materials responsibly, so as to
avoid any parallelomanic pitfalls.

The second way that the word-concept distinction will be observed is
by investigating each of those diverse roles (concepts), not only through
the designation *oikonomos*, but, when possible, also through a variety of
Greek synonyms and Latin correlatives. Along these lines, L. Michael
White and John Fitzgerald have emphasised the importance, when drawing parallels, of examining 'semantic fields' rather than 'individual key
words', warning that 'the data used in making comparisons must not be
restricted to instances of verbal identity or similarity', since '[s]ome of
the most striking parallels between Christian and non-Christian texts are
primarily conceptual and involve little or no verbal agreement between
the two'. 'In future studies', they therefore advise,

> it will be crucial to investigate such terms, not simply in iso-
> lation from one another but as part of the conceptual 'linkage
> group' to which they belong and with increased attention to the
> social worlds in which they are used. Similarly, attention will
> need to be given to combinations of Greek words as well as
> to equivalent terms and similar expressions in Latin and other
> languages.[71]

---

[71] L. M. White and Fitzgerald (2003: 31).

Awareness of both of these kinds of word-concept distinction will be of central importance in this investigation, since each has been overlooked in previous studies.[72]

The second main methodological contribution of this study involves the utilisation of ancient sources. There has been a growing concern among NT scholars in recent years regarding the kinds of extra-biblical material that should be employed to establish the interpretive context of early Christianity. Those working especially in the Pauline epistles have been challenged to be discriminant about their use of ancient sources due to the limited light certain kinds of evidence can bring to bear on the socio-cultural environment of Paul's churches, not least the Corinthian community. According to Justin Meggitt, for instance, there exists 'a fundamental problem that hampers all interpretations of the Corinthian epistles to a significant extent: *the problem of dependence on elite sources* (written and nonwritten)'.[73] Meggitt remarks,

> Although most scholars use a variety of sources in their analysis of the letters, and believe that their employment of them is increasingly sensitive and sophisticated, failure to recognise the *atypical* and *unrepresentative* nature of much of the material that is employed to reconstruct the context within which the letters are interpreted renders much of what is written about them of little value.[74]

Therefore, NT scholars, Meggitt maintains, must reconsider their 'evidential presuppositions' and 'undergo a significant change in perspective'.[75] Meggitt takes his recommendation further still: 'If New Testament scholars wish to make sense of the preoccupations and expectations of both Paul and the Corinthian community, we must seek out … those sources, both literary and nonliterary, that give voice to the world of the nonelite, that articulate what could be termed the *popular culture* of the

---

[72] If, for example, Byron had focused on the same concept, or role, that Martin had expressly targeted, that is, *private* estate managers, Byron would have eliminated from his investigation those free *oikonomoi* who served in *municipal* roles and then probably reached different conclusions. Alternatively, had Byron opened up his study to Greek and Latin correlatives for private estate managers (e.g. ἐπίτροπος, πραγματευτής, *vilicus, actor, dispensator*), he would have also realised that the slave status of private *oikonomoi* during the Roman period was far more uniform than he supposed, since the legal status of estate managers is generally clearer in the evidence bearing those other terms.

[73] Meggitt (2004: 242, original emphasis).

[74] Meggitt (2004: 242, original emphasis).

[75] Meggitt (2004: 242).

first century.'[76] Unfortunately, what precisely Meggitt means by 'popular culture', what concepts require such a scrutinising approach to the source materials, and which sources are then able to bring this world to light are less than clear. Nevertheless, his warning remains applicable for many working in Pauline studies generally and 1 Corinthians in particular. One cannot simply assume that most or even many of the numerous extant literary works from antiquity characterise the thoughts, attitudes, practices, and beliefs of the early believers just because they are contemporary, correspond geographically, and relate thematically with Paul's letters. As Meggitt states, 'If we wish to find more representative sources with which to construct our understanding of the context within which the Corinthian correspondence was written and read, and to interpret such sources appropriately, it is necessary to look beyond New Testament scholarship' and 'to benefit from those who have made the study of "popular culture" their central preoccupation'.[77]

Accordingly, much of the evidence to be assembled in this study will rely on the work of ancient social, economic, and legal historians, that is, the specialists in the periods, regions, and subjects central to this investigation. Moreover, the reconstructions will necessarily rely on an eclectic collection of evidence, including ancient literature, inscriptions, and papyri. Admittedly, when describing ancient forms of servile administration, every type of evidence has limitations. As J. Albert Harrill laments, 'In the end, we find that none of our sources fulfills our expectations; together, they allow a reconstruction of slavery that few historians specializing in modern periods would find satisfactory.'[78] But Harrill concedes that a diligent pursuit of reliable sources can result in a faithful reconstruction of ancient slavery. This requires that the highly informative *theoretical* sources (e.g. agricultural handbooks, novels, dreambooks, biblical literature, legal texts) be supplemented with *actual* portrayals of real-life slaves (e.g. inscriptions, papyri).[79] Harrill, in fact, provides as an example how the profile of Petronius' fictional and seemingly exaggerated former steward Trimalchio (*Satyr.* 26–78), an archetypal *nouveau riche*, is in certain ways validated by Seneca's real-life counterpart, Calvisius Sabinus (*Ep.* 27).[80] 'With care', Harrill thus concludes, 'imaginative literature can yield important historical insights.'[81]

---

[76] Meggitt (2004: 241–2, original emphasis).
[77] Meggitt (2004: 243).
[78] Harrill (1995: 29); cf. W. Fitzgerald (2000: 8).
[79] Harrill (1995: 28–9).
[80] For additional examples of wealthy former slaves, see Mouritsen (2011: 228–47).
[81] Harrill (1995: 29); cf. McCarthy (2000: 8).

Harrill's opinion is shared by Fergus Millar, whose analysis of Apuleius' second-century CE novel the *Metamorphoses* reveals the historical and contextual insights that can be obtained from certain kinds of ancient fiction. '[T]he invented world of fiction', Millar affirms, 'may yet represent – perhaps cannot help representing – important features of the real world.'[82] Similar kinds of general historical insight can also be gathered from certain gospel parables. 'At its simplest', explained C. H. Dodd, 'the parable is a metaphor or simile *drawn from nature or common life.*'[83] More suitable definitions of the parable genre have been offered in recent years,[84] but Dodd nonetheless discerns how several of Jesus' parables reflect conceivable scenarios and thus provide reasonably reliable data with which to produce sketches of actual people and the ancient world. Even Fabian Udoh, who believes the NT slave parables are 'literary constructs that transmit the *slaveholders*' fantasies, fears, ideals, values, and agenda' and therefore 'do not completely "reflect" the practice of slavery in the Roman Empire', ultimately maintains that the parabolic slave, 'if he is to be comprehensible', must have 'an underlying social reality'.[85] Thus, in this investigation a host of sources will be utilised to reconstruct the relevant forms of ancient administration, not least ancient fiction and biblical parables. These theoretical and occasionally elitist sources will be especially useful in this investigation, since even Paul's metaphor considers, to a certain extent, the expectations of his administrative superior (ζητεῖται ἐν τοῖς οἰκονόμοις, 1 Cor 4.2). By relying on the testimonies of various kinds of text, a range of voices will be heard, and the portraits which are assembled will be, it is hoped, all the more reliable.

Cognisant of these aims and methodological concerns, this study will proceed in two parts. First, in Chapters 2–4 the main three administrative contexts in which the title *oikonomos* was used (regal, municipal, private) will be examined separately in order to illumine the varying social, structural, legal, and remunerative characteristics associated with each domain. Analysis of these contexts will enable us to develop a general profile of the *oikonomoi* who served in them so that in Chapter 5 those profiles can be compared to Paul's own apostolic portrait constructed in 1 Cor 4.1–5 and 9.16–23. By comparing those profiles with the characteristics of Paul's image, a plausible source domain for the metaphor will become apparent. Secondly, after having identified the metaphor's source domain, in Chapters 6–7 those two passages where Paul applies

---

[82] Millar (1981: 75).   [83] C. H. Dodd (1935: 16, emphasis added).
[84] See, e.g., Snodgrass (2008: 7–9).   [85] Udoh (2009: 328).

the metaphor (4.1–5; 9.16–23) will be analysed in order to determine how an informed understanding of the metaphor influences and instructs the interpretation of those important Pauline texts. Finally, in Chapter 8 (the conclusion), and on the basis of our understanding of how Paul utilised the *oikonomos* metaphor in 1 Corinthians, the implications of this self-portrayal will be discussed and their significance for Paul's apostolic authority accounted for.

PART I

Oikonomoi as administrators in Graeco-Roman antiquity

A good modern treatment of the office of the oeconomus is still a desideratum.[1]

Almost eighty years have passed since eminent ancient historian Michael Rostovtzeff lamented the above scholarly lacuna, yet still it remains. This is not to suggest that in modern scholarship no studies have appeared which treat *oikonomoi* in any detail; in the past half-century several works have been published which examine the individuals bearing the title in specifically defined geopolitical contexts. Virtually nothing, however, has been written which attempts a comprehensive analysis of *oikonomoi* from the Hellenistic to the early Roman period, and much confusion regarding the nature of these officials remains as a result. Indeed, many important questions have been inadequately treated, while others have never been advanced in scholarly dialogue: what are the main contexts in which *oikonomoi* were employed? What are the constituent parts of the office in each context? What responsibilities were entrusted to them? Where were *oikonomoi* located in their respective administrative hierarchies? Were *oikonomoi* recognised as persons of authority, menial servitude, or somewhere in between? What other characteristics were normally attributed to them and what methods of accountability, or disciplinary measures, including rewards and punishment, would they have faced from their superiors? Such questions require answers if biblical scholars, as well as ancient historians, desire a satisfactory understanding of the use of this title.

The conspicuous absence of a full-scale analysis of *oikonomoi* comes as little surprise once one is introduced to the difficulty of such a task. The abundance of the documentary evidence together with the elasticity of the term and the evolution of its use from Classical Greece to the Hellenistic era through the

---

[1] Rostovtzeff (1933: 67 n. 1); cf. Rostovtzeff (1922: 148). This remark applied originally to Ptolemaic regal *oikonomoi*, but is equally relevant to other domains.

Roman Empire and into the Byzantine period demonstrates that *oikonomoi* performed a variety of regal, civic, commercial, and even ecclesial services in a number of social contexts while belonging to several social strata. The term, then, must be treated carefully by paying close attention to its uses in particular regions and time periods, so as not to confuse its meaning and connotations in one historical context with that in another. In the following three chapters we shall survey the administrators who bore the title *oikonomos* in regal, civic, and private contexts – those in which *oikonomoi* have been most often attested during the periods just before and immediately following the birth of the church – in order to construct a general profile of those officials and their respective offices. Of central importance in our reconstruction of those positions are their structural hierarchy, administrative responsibilities, sociolegal status, and methods of accountability. By analysing their attributes it will become clear that, although these administrators share some significant similarities, their differences require that they be conceptually distinguished.

2

OIKONOMOI AS REGAL ADMINISTRATORS

The *oikonomoi* shall take care that the orders by the king ... are kept without alteration.

IG XII *Suppl.* 644

Within just a few years following the death of Alexander the Great in 323 BCE, his vast empire was partitioned into territories, which were then disproportionately issued to his military generals. Alexander's successors (διάδοχοι), which included the likes of Ptolemy, Seleucis, Antigonus, Lysimachus, and others, established independent kingdoms in the regions they formerly governed while under Alexander's regime. Although individually these civilisations paled in comparison with the size of Alexander's empire, each procured large territories and great wealth while developing the administrative infrastructure necessary to operate independently of one another. While they were often preoccupied with lengthy military campaigns, in just a short span of time each of the kingdoms from the Hellenistic era (*c.* 323–30 BCE) implemented its own political, military, and economic structure, 'a structure that was to survive almost unchanged until they were incorporated in the Roman Empire and even later'.[1]

Some of the earliest non-literary evidence for *oikonomoi* in the Mediterranean basin attests to their functioning as financial administrators in these very kingdoms. Among the Hellenistic monarchies, the Ptolemies, Seleucids, Attalids, and Macedonians deposited the most illuminating evidence for the regal *oikonomos*. Between the literary, epigraphic, and papyrological data from this period, the papyri provide the fullest portrait of *oikonomoi*, although they derive strictly from Egypt and so are limited in relevance almost exclusively to Ptolemaic administration. The inscriptions, on the other hand, reveal less detail than do the papyri about the nature of the office, but on the whole they provide more reliable testimony than do literary works and represent the office in

---

[1] Rostovtzeff (1941: 189).

a wider geographical spread than do the papyri, attesting to the title's use in the administrations of each of the main Hellenistic political powers.[2] All of these documents, whose dates range from the mid fourth century BCE to the end of the Hellenistic era, exhibit many of the same traits of *oikonomoi*, including (i) their elevated social and administrative rank as regional managers within their respective hierarchies, (ii) their many delegated responsibilities concerning the financial matters of a particular territory, and (iii) the promise of professional advancement or penalty depending on the outcome of their tenure.

The Hellenistic administrations, although patterned after the scheme instituted by Alexander, also resembled the political and economic models inherited from the governments that preceded the Greeks. Most historians therefore agree, 'The regions brought under the control of the Hellenistic kingdoms showed little economic unity or uniformity.'[3] Thus, even though the *oikonomoi* who served in each of these kingdoms share many of the same attributes, in our survey we shall examine the kingdoms individually due to the structural dissimilarities that existed between them.

Ptolemaic Kingdom

The Ptolemaic Kingdom provides historians with a wealth of data for reconstructing the role of the *oikonomos* as a regal administrator. Much of the evidence for the office has been preserved in papyri from Egypt. But mainland Egypt was not the only region controlled by the Ptolemies. For almost the entire period of Ptolemaic rule (*c.* 305–30 BCE), the Ptolemies also inhabited and efficiently governed the more distant 'possessions' of Cyprus, Cyrene, Cyrenaica, Syria, Phoenicia, and Palestine. Furthermore, for some years of this period Lycia, Caria, parts of Ionia, the Black Sea region, certain Aegean islands, and even the Peloponnese formed the distant sub-sections of the kingdom.[4] Due, then, to the abundance of the epigraphic and papyrological evidence left by the Ptolemies, as well as their possible influence on the administrations of other Hellenistic states, we begin our examination with the Ptolemaic Kingdom.

Hierarchy

Among the most notable traits of the Ptolemaic regal *oikonomos* was his middle managerial rank in the kingdom's administrative

---

[2] F. W. Walbank (1984b: 11).
[3] Davies (2003: 504).   [4] Cf. Bagnall (1976).

hierarchy. Although he was given charge of a large administrative division, the *oikonomos* was a delegate and, in that respect, subordinate to a chain of organisational superiors. Precisely where in the administrative hierarchy of the Ptolemaic Kingdom his post was located is of some debate and especially dependent on the period in view.[5] For the sake of the present study, we shall adopt the structure of the third-century BCE kingdom, from where most of the relevant primary evidence derives.[6]

The Ptolemaic state, from the vantage point of the king, was a household (οἶκος). Its administration began with the king as head of the household (κύριος), and all civil, financial, military, and legal matters ultimately reported to him.[7] But with the arrival of new economic institutions imported from the Greek world (e.g. banking, tax farming, auctions of property), the Ptolemaic economy became in need of an infrastructure that would support itself.[8] The king therefore delegated many of his responsibilities to royal officials, most notably the διοικητής, in order to manage the kingdom efficiently. As the chief financial officer, the διοικητής oversaw all of the kingdom's financial matters, including its revenue and expenditures; he in turn appointed *oikonomoi* to manage the kingdom's regional divisions, the nomes (νομοί).[9]

Within the nome, a complex network of additional delegates existed. The nome administration was divided into three branches. First, the bureau of the nomarch, with the aid of his locally commissioned subordinates (the toparchs and komarchs), supervised the nome's agricultural production. Secondly, the bureau of the *oikonomos*, together with his checking clerks (ἀντιγράφεις), was given charge of the nome's finances. Finally, the bureau of the royal scribe (βασιλικὸς γραμματεύς) maintained the necessary official records, with the help of his subordinates, the district and village scribes (τοπογραμματεῖς, κωμογραμματεῖς). The

---

[5] For a comparison of the third-century BCE chain of command with that from the second and first centuries BCE, see Reumann (1957: 253–4).

[6] On the *terminus post quem* for the disappearance of the Ptolemaic *oikonomos* in the early first century BCE, see Kruse (2002: 890); Falivene (2009: 527).

[7] For the Ptolemaic administrative divisions, see Falivene (1991).

[8] Manning (2003: 137).

[9] Some debate remains on whether or not the centrally located διοικητής supervised a group of subordinate regional διοικηταί. Thomas (1978) argues that those papyri indicating that διοικηταί held regional offices either utilised the title as shorthand for ὑποδιοικηταί (P.Cair.Zen. 59236) or belonged to a phase in the second century BCE when power may have been temporarily decentralised. Thomas supposes that 'such a decentralisation, if it ever took place, quickly proved unworkable (though this does not prove that it was not tried) and the government rapidly reverted to the old situation' (191). On the other hand, P.Ord.Ptol. 21–2 (Bagnall/Derow §64), dated to 260 BCE, suggests that Syria had its own διοικητής, who was supervised by the διοικητής in Alexandria.

head of each of these bureaus, including the *oikonomos* in the financial branch, reported to the διοικητής in Alexandria.[10]

An important document that highlights the hierarchical structure of the financial branch of the kingdom is P.Tebt. 703, a late third-century BCE memorandum generally agreed to have been an appointment charter from a διοικητής to an οἰκονόμος.[11] Dubbed 'the jewel of Greek administrative papyri',[12] P.Tebt. 703 shows the superordinate rank of the author as he repeatedly instructs the addressee with verbs in the imperative mood. But this hierarchy is especially apparent at the end of the document when the author orders the recipient 'to keep the instructions in hand, and to report on everything as has been ordered [περὶ ἑκάστων ἐπιστέλλε(ιν) καθὰ συντέτακται]'.[13] More than any other feature in the document, the need to give an account to the commissioning party attests to the subordinate rank of the *oikonomos*.

The subordinate role of *oikonomoi* is further underscored on occasions when civilians file complaints against them and request their superiors to overturn their decisions. Such was the case when in 254/253 BCE a certain peasant (Neoptolemos) wrote to the διοικητής (Diotimos) to appeal a ruling concerning taxation on his vineyards in the Aphroditopolite Nome. The original ruling was made jointly by the nome *oikonomos* (Theokies) and βασιλικὸς γραμματεύς (Petosiris) and cost Neoptolemos' father (Stratippos) an unusually large sum (P.Cair.Zen. 59236). Neoptolemos therefore wrote to the διοικητής requesting that the local and regional officials, including the *oikonomos*, reimburse Stratippos for the expenses he incurred. A similar request was also made in 248 BCE by Theopropos, a Kalyndian landholder, whose tenant farmer had supplied wine for a city festival without receiving payment from the city administration in exchange for those goods. Theopropos therefore wrote to the διοικητής (Apollonios) requesting that he contact the *oikonomos* overseeing Kalynda and instruct the official to reimburse Theopropos for the 250 drachmas plus interest he was owed for the wine (P.Cair.Zen. 59341a). In these instances, appeals by certain individuals over the heads of *oikonomoi* demonstrate that the decisions of such regional officials ultimately rested on the approval of higher authorities – in these cases the διοικητής – and any executive decisions made by διοικηταί were binding on *oikonomoi*.

---

[10] Bagnall (1976: 3–4); cf. Manning (2003: 137).

[11] Although the document does not specify the rank of the two officials, Rostovtzeff argues that 'the subjects of the memorandum coincide with matters dealt with by the oeconomus in the third century B.C.' (Rostovtzeff 1933: 67 n. 1). Cf. Samuel (1971).

[12] Turner (1984: 147).   [13] Trans. Bagnall/Derow §103.

Oikonomoi were not only subordinate to the διοικητής. The king himself was also regarded as their superior, for he possessed the authority to appoint *oikonomoi* to office. One inscription from Labraunda in Caria dating to 267 BCE records that a certain Apollonius, son of Diodotos, was appointed *oikonomos* by the king (κατασταθεὶς οἰκο[νό]μος ὑπὸ βασιλέως Πτολε[μαίου], *ILabraundaMcCabe* 2/*ILabraunda* 43). A second inscription from Limyra in Lycia dating to 288/287 BCE follows a similar formula. Honouring two Caunian *oikonomoi* (Amyntas Eythonos and Sosigenes of Zopyros), the text indicates that King Ptolemy had appointed the two officials as *oikonomoi* of the land (κατασταθέντες ὑπὸ βασιλ[έως] [Π]τολεμαίου οἰκονόμοι τῆς χώρας, *SEG* 27.929).[14] Admittedly, officials who did not report directly to the king were normally assigned to their positions by his representatives – in the case of the financial bureau, by the διοικητής. It is therefore uncertain in these two instances whether the king assigned the *oikonomoi* directly or was merely credited with their commission. Even so, it is clear from these documents that *oikonomoi* were subordinate officials in the Ptolemaic Kingdom and that they recognised the διοικητής and the king as their administrative superiors.

Despite their position beneath the kingdom's highest-ranking officials, *oikonomoi* occupied an impressive regional supervisory position. 'The Ptolemaic state functioned', remarks Joseph Manning, 'by stressing the vertical ties to the ruler through a bureaucratic hierarchy that connected the villages to the nome capitals, and these in turn to the capital at Alexandria.'[15] The representative role that *oikonomoi* occupied in the nome, then, afforded them great structural authority in their respective regions. Within these territories *oikonomoi* supervised numerous officials who managed the nome subdivisions (toparchies), which were further divided into villages. Moreover, the *oikonomoi* employed a series of subordinate collectors (λογευταί), auditors (λογισταί, ἐκλογισταί), and checking clerks (ἀντιγράφεις) who functioned as their personal agents.

This structural authority of *oikonomoi* is apparent in the papyri which describe their many responsibilities. The Revenue Laws (259 BCE), for instance, detail the regulations governing tax farming, vineyard supervision, wine production, and oil distribution, while frequently mentioning the responsibilities of *oikonomoi* in these commercial and economic divisions. Column 20 of the papyrus explains with particular clarity the

---

[14] For discussion of the text, especially the difficulty of determining the jurisdiction implied by τῆς χώρας, see Wörrle (1977).

[15] Manning (2003: 131).

authority derived representatively from the king and entrusted to the *oikonomoi*. The column reads, 'Any tax farmers who fail to balance their accounts with the *oikonomos*, when he desires them to do so and summons them, shall pay 30 minas to the Crown and the *oikonomos* shall at the same time compel them' (P.Rev. 20).[16] Two parts of the passage are of interest here. First, the relationship between tax farmers and the *oikonomos* was clearly asymmetrical. Tax farmers were required to report to the *oikonomos* and balance accounts with him when he desired (β[ο]υ[λο]μέν[ου] τοῦ οἰκονόμου), clearly demonstrating the structural authority of the *oikonomos* over his delegates. His administrative authority is also underscored when the law states that the *oikonomos* is able to compel (συναναγκάζω) the delinquent tax farmer to balance accounts. Such compulsion suggests that the *oikonomos* possessed the structural leverage and legal authority to force his subordinates into action when encountering delay or resistance. But the source of his authority is also worthy of clarification. The regal *oikonomos* derived his authority from his association with the king. As stated later in the column, the *oikonomos*, the ἀντιγράφεις, and their agents (οἱ π[αρ' αὐτῶν]) were 'officials of the Crown' (lit. those administering royal things: οἱ τὰ βασι[λ]ικὰ πραγματευόμενοι) appointed to carry out the king's plan to completion.[17] Indeed, it was the king's vision, after descending down through the chain of command, which was enacted in the nomes. Consequently, in tax collection, just as much as in his other supervisory duties, the *oikonomos* represented Ptolemy in the nome as one authorised to command on his behalf.

P.Tebt. 703 also portrays *oikonomoi* as possessing authority in their day-to-day responsibilities. Early in the document, the διοικητής instructed the *oikonomos* to encourage and inspire the local farmers (παρακαλεῖν καὶ εὐθαρσεστέρους παρασκευάζειν, lines 42–3). The *oikonomos* was not only required to carry out these instructions verbally (τοῦτο μὴ μόνον λόγωι γίνεσθαι, lines 43–4) and interpersonally, but also by intervening on behalf of the farmers when they were unfairly harassed by local officials. As the charter states, '[I]f any of them complain of the *komogrammateus* or the *komarchs* about any matter touching agricultural work, you should make inquiry [ἐπισκοπεῖν] and put a stop to such doings' (lines 44–9).[18] Numerous papyri show that it was commonplace for farmers

[16] Trans. Bagnall/Derow §114.
[17] For more on the agent of the *oikonomos* (ὁ παρὰ τοῦ οἰκονόμου), see Clarysse (1976).
[18] Trans. Bagnall/Derow §103.

to write to their regional *oikonomos* to appeal for assistance with these kinds of disturbance. According to Alan Samuel, 'Such appeals are by no means exceptional, and they show that the resolution of disputes in agricultural matters was a normal administrative task for the oikonomos in the third century B.C.'[19] By instructing the *oikonomos* to intervene in village affairs on behalf of farmers, this document underscores the administrative authority that the *oikonomos* exercised over village officials, particularly the village scribe and komarch. As Samuel affirms, 'A number of third century appeals [from villagers] to the oikonomos illustrate that his administrative authority was recognized.'[20]

Responsibilities

Charged with the management of the nome's revenue and expenditures, the responsibilities of the *oikonomos* were mostly financial in nature. But the *oikonomos* was not a mere accountant or dispenser of public funds; those jobs were done by the royal scribe and checking clerk. Instead, the *oikonomos* developed and implemented the plan for the nome's economy. He was responsible for the nome's agricultural production, for ensuring that seed was issued to farmers, and even for encouraging them when the harvest was poor. He was responsible for oil production and linen manufacturing. He also oversaw the entire commercial sector, including the scheduling of deliveries from farms to the market and for regulating its prices. But perhaps the chief financial responsibility of the *oikonomos* in Ptolemaic administration was organising tax collection. Tax farming in antiquity was a complex system of state revenue acquisition, involving

---

[19] Samuel (1971: 452).

[20] Samuel (1971: 452). For another look at the power dynamics involved in the central and peripheral administrative sectors of the kingdom, see the above-mentioned P.Cair. Zen. 59341a. This letter reveals the great authority of the *oikonomos* in two ways. First, the jurisdiction of the *oikonomos* in Caria appears to have overlapped considerably with that of the στρατηγός. Not only is he paired with the στρατηγός as his associate during a financial dispute, but, as a later portion of this letter reveals, his responsibilities extended well beyond matters of finance and into military administration (P.Cair.Zen. 59341b–c). As Bagnall (1976: 245) observes, 'The *oikonomos* was evidently the colleague of the *strategos*, not his subordinate... And the *oikonomos* was at least the equal if not somewhat higher in rank than the commandant' (cf. 99–101). Secondly, the *oikonomos* possessed the authority to arbitrate between individuals (Theopropos) and an entire city (Kalynda) in matters of finance. Although he refused to involve himself directly in the repayment of the debt, he and the στρατηγός were nevertheless perceived by Theopropos, the two treasurers, and the city officials (πρυτάνεις, γραμματεύς) as having the authority to resolve the dispute. As Samuel (1966: 446) remarks, 'A review of the evidence shows that the oikonomos had no real judicial role, but as any administrator could and would do, he decided matters which affected the satisfactory accomplishment of his tasks.'

the auctioning of collection responsibilities to tax farmers, who, after each monthly collection, would balance accounts with the *oikonomos* and checking clerk to make certain that the proper sum was accumulated. The *oikonomos* then balanced his accounts with the διοικητής to ensure the same.[21] The responsibilities of the *oikonomos* in tax farming are nowhere better preserved than in the Revenue Laws. The document is much too long and detailed to cite or explain at length. It is sufficient to say here that the kingdom's economy was buttressed by tax revenue, and the involvement of the *oikonomos* in the collection of taxes ensured the financial viability of the kingdom.

Many of the remaining duties of the *oikonomos* have been preserved in P.Tebt. 703.[22] According to the papyrus, the *oikonomos* was responsible for maintaining the depth, strength, and cleanliness of the canals that ran through and hydrated the fields (lines 29–40). He was required to inspect the landscape carefully to ensure that the fields were sown well (lines 49–54), with the correct kinds of crop, according to the sowing schedule (lines 57–8). At the harvest, he was to make certain that the grain was transported punctually to Alexandria (lines 70–87). He was to maintain a list of the uses of cattle in agriculture (lines 63–70; 163–74) and to take care that the calves were fed adequately (lines 183–91), especially the offspring of royal cattle (lines 67–8). All of the specifics concerning the operation of weaving houses (lines 87–117) and oil factories (lines 134–63) fell within the jurisdiction of the *oikonomos*. He was responsible for auditing the revenue accounts, village by village if possible, otherwise by toparchy (lines 117–34). Moreover, he regulated the prices of items sold in the market (lines 174–82), ensured that trees were planted on schedule (lines 191–211), and organised the maintenance for the royal houses and gardens (lines 211–14). He oversaw the custody of deserting soldiers and sailors prior to their journey to the capital (lines 215–22). Finally, he was responsible for providing the nome with a sense of public as well as financial security, realising that the two concerns influenced one another (lines 222–34).

Beyond itemising the main responsibilities of the *oikonomos*, P.Tebt. 703 also discusses the official's idealised character traits and work ethic. These attributes were considered absolutely necessary (δεῖν, line 261) for performing the job well. According to the author, the *oikonomos* was to be characterised by honesty (καθαρῶς, lines 262–3), goodness (βέλτιστος, line 263), justice (δίκαιος, line 266), and blamelessness (ἀνέγκλητος,

---

[21] Turner (1984: 152).
[22] Many of the concerns in P.Tebt. 703 are also addressed in P.Rev.

line 276). Moreover, the papyrus includes numerous admonitions about the manner in which the official should complete his tasks. For instance, he was expected to inspect the various agricultural, industrial, and commercial sectors of the nome carefully (ἐπιμελῶς, *passim*) and zealously (προθύμως, line 120). The ideal character profile of the *oikonomos*, then, was a central concern in P.Tebt. 703, just as it was in many documents outlining the duties of state officials in Egypt.

In P.Tebt. 27, for instance, the late second-century διοικητής Eirenaios reprimanded Hermias, the superintendent of revenues, for appointing a poorly qualified *oikonomos*, along with certain other officials. Eirenaios accused Hermias of appointing men who were 'without exception evil and worthless persons [πᾶσι δὲ κακοῖς καὶ οὐδενὸς ἀξίοις]', instructing him rather to nominate 'persons of repute' (ἀξιόλογοι).[23] Dorothy Crawford, in fact, drew heavily from P.Tebt. 27 and 703 when she compiled a list of traits commonly associated with royal officials over the three centuries of Ptolemaic rule. Her profile of the archetypal 'good official' resembles the *oikonomoi* portrayed in both Tebtunis papyri:

> The duty of the official was universal care, ἡ τῶν ὅλων φροντίς, he should be πασίφιλος [friendly to all], and exhibit qualities of care, ἐπιμέλεια, goodwill, εὔνοια, foresight, πρόνοια, keenness and alacrity, σπουδή, προθυμία, or ἐκτενία, and acumen in decision, ἀκρίβεια. He must always show attention, ἐπιστορφή or προσοχή, vigilance, τήρησις or ἀγρυπνία, and care, ἀντίληψις, for those with whom he had contact; the aim of his actions should be justice for all men, ὅπως τὰ δίκαια γίνηται τοῖς ἀνθρώποις.[24]

Although these documents only prescribe the make-up of the *oikonomos* from the vantage point of the top of the hierarchy, they nevertheless supply an idealised description of the official, indeed, one of the perspectives we are seeking here.

Accountability

Despite the clearly defined responsibilities entrusted to the *oikonomos*, he may have struggled to meet the demands of his superiors while also maintaining a healthy relationship with the inhabitants of the nome. As Crawford explains,

---

[23] Trans. Bagnall/Derow §110.   [24] Crawford (1978: 195–6).

Officials were those used by the king to look after his interests, whilst protecting those of the peasants; it was necessary that they collected as much profit in the form of rents and taxes as was compatible with the continuing co-operation of the peasants. If they were over-zealous on the king's behalf the peasants would refuse to co-operate; if they were over-kind to the peasants the king would be displeased.[25]

Therefore, in order to maintain the dependability of *oikonomoi*, the chief Ptolemaic administrators offered incentives to their subordinates for their achievements, while also penalising them for poor performance. In either case, accountability was implemented by the διοικητής and king to motivate their regional supervisors to serve as instructed.

In the conclusion of P.Tebt. 703, for instance, the author of the papyrus remarks, 'If you act thus, you will fulfil your official duty and your own safety will be assured [ὑμῖν ἡ πᾶς ἀσφάλεια ὑπάρξει]' (lines 255–8).[26] The statement implies that the office carried with it the potential for removal, or demotion, for a poor performance. Other documents also indicate that *oikonomoi* could be fined for negligence, such as making late payments to the διοικητής (cf. P.Rev. 19, 51–2). While nothing is known about the monetary compensation of *oikonomoi*,[27] the author of P.Tebt. 703 also promises professional advancement for the *oikonomos* who manages well. The papyrus declares, '[I]f you are without reproach in this, you will be held deserving of higher functions [γένησθε μειζόνων ἀξιωθήσεσθαι]' (lines 276–8).[28] These kinds of positive and negative incentives were to keep the *oikonomos* aligned with the interests of his superiors.[29] Thus, even though it may be, as E. G. Turner maintains, that in Ptolemaic administration 'no regular system of promotion, no *cursus honorum* or specially quick promotion to reward initiative has been traced',[30] Crawford is probably correct to suspect the existence of an informal system of promotion, whereby professional advancement could

[25] Crawford (1978: 195).   [26] Trans. Bagnall/Derow §103.

[27] It could be that *oikonomoi* received a portion of the taxes raised in their respective nome or certain non-monetary privileges. According to the Zenon archive, for instance, διοικηταί were provided δωρεαί, temporary grants of land given by the king in substitution for a salary; cf. Rostovtzeff (1922: 42–55). It could be that *oikonomoi* were afforded similar gifts.

[28] Trans. Bagnall/Derow §103.

[29] It is perhaps for this reason that 'good officials' (i.e. those found acceptable to both the king and his subjects) were rather scarce in the Ptolemaic administration. As the abundance of written complaints and royal decrees suggest, 'many officials were both wicked and corrupt' (Crawford 1978: 199).

[30] Turner (1984: 147).

be attained through 'acceptable performance and not antagonizing one's superior'.[31]

Seleucid Kingdom

The administration of the Seleucid Kingdom (*c*. 305–63 BCE) differed from the Ptolemaic system primarily by its Achaemenid origin. Whereas historians generally agree that the Ptolemies inherited and immediately adapted the Pharaonic form of financial administration, creating the modified Macedonian system outlined above, the Seleucids similarly laid a Macedonian-style economy atop the existing Achaemenid administration, which they inherited from the Persians.[32] Thus, even though the basic structure of the Seleucids and their utilisation of *oikonomoi* deserve independent comment, there are few major differences between the administrative structures implemented by the Seleucids and Ptolemies.

One of the sources which best illuminates the framework of the Seleucid financial administration is Pseudo-Aristotle's *Oeconomica*.[33] In the second book of the treatise (*Oec*. 1345b), the author outlines the administrative structure used by the Seleucids, distinguishing between its four administrative spheres (οἰκονομίαι): the regal (βασιλική), satrapal/provincial (σατραπική), municipal (πολιτική), and private (ἰδιωτική).[34] The governing of satrapies and cities are our primary concern here. The satrapies, which at the kingdom's height spanned from Anatolia to central Asia, further divided into hyparchies and required a vast network of subordinate officials through whom the king could regulate the economy, collect taxes, and sell and lease privately and publicly owned land.[35]

Hierarchy

The greatest difference between Seleucid and Ptolemaic administration lies in the offices at the top of the chain of command. Similar to the Ptolemaic structure, the Seleucid διοικηταί were directly subordinate to the king as his chief financial officers. But rather than appointing a single διοικητής to represent the king, as was practised by the Ptolemies, the

---

[31] Crawford (1978: 199).
[32] Rostovtzeff (1941: 440); Sherwin-White and Kuhrt (1993: 42); Aperghis (2004: 264–9).
[33] Aperghis (2004: 7).
[34] The LCL reads: 'the administration of a king; of the governors under him; of a free state; and of a private citizen'.
[35] Sherwin-White and Kuhrt (1993: 45–6).

Seleucid king appointed numerous διοικηταί both centrally and region-ally, placing the majority of them in the satrapies and various other sub-divisions (e.g. Coele-Syria). There they supervised finances, serving alongside the governor (στρατηγός), who oversaw civil matters.[36] Some of the titles given to administrative officials beneath the διοικηταί also diverge from those of the Ptolemaic Kingdom. The ἐκλογισταί were the officials responsible for establishing the level of taxation and for super-vising the λογευταί, who carried out the collection. Οἱ ἐπὶ τῶν ἱερῶν managed the temples and their revenue. The *oikonomoi*, on the other hand, supervised the royal land and revenue, while controlling expen-ditures in their financial districts within the satrapy (οἰκονομίαι; *SEG* 39.1289/*OGI* 179).[37] They also co-operated with the hyparchs, who oversaw all civil and military matters within the districts.[38]

Much of what is known about the role and responsibilities of Seleucid regal *oikonomoi* derives from the so-called Ptolemaios Dossier (*c.* 190 BCE), a compilation of inscriptions from Scythopolis (*SEG* 29.1613). In Text 4, the στρατηγός and high priest (Ptolemaios) petitioned the king (Antiochos III) to allow certain regional misdemeanours to be handled by local leaders, while those matters of some severity were to be dealt with by leaders of the satrapy. Antiochus then forwarded the request to two διοικηταί (Kleon and Heliodoros), before it was formalised on a stele. The document reads as follows:

> To King Antiochus III, memorandum from Ptolemy the *strate-gos* and high priest; concerning any disputes that may arise: I request that written instructions be sent so that disputes aris-ing in my villages [ἐν ταῖς κώμαις] and involving peasants with each other should be settled by my agents [ἐπὶ τῶν παρ' ἐμοῦ], but those arising with peasants from the other villages should be investigated [ἐπισκοπῶσιν] by the *oikonomos* and the offi-cial in charge of the district [(ὁ τοῦ τόπ)ου πρ(ο)εστηκώς], and if they concern murder or appear to be of greater significance they should be referred to the *strategos* in Syria and Phoenicia; the garrison commanders and those in charge of the districts [τοὺς δὲ φρουράρχους (καὶ τοὺς ἐ)πὶ τῶν τόπων τεταγμένους]

---

[36] Scholars have been unable to agree on the title given to the Seleucid Kingdom's most senior financial officer, if even there was one.

[37] For discussion of the οἰκονομίαι and *SEG* 39.1289, see Gauthier (1989: 129–34) and Ma (1999: 136). Aperghis (2004: 276–7) proposes that ὁ ἐπὶ τῶν προσόδων was equiva-lent to and came to replace the *oikonomos* in the later stages of the kingdom.

[38] Aperghis (2004: 295).

should not ignore in any way those who call for their interven-
tion. The same letter to Heliodorus.[39]

Even though some of the specifics about the administrative and jurid-
ical divisions in the satrapy remain unclear, this inscription reveals significant details about the role and responsibilities of *oikonomoi* in those
regions.[40] The stele clearly distinguishes between villages (κῶμαι) and
collections of villages, or districts (τόποι). Districts were governed by
an *oikonomos* and toparch (ὁ τοῦ τόπου προεστηκώς). These two officials were most likely those identified as Ptolemaios' agents (τῶν παρ'
ἐμοῦ). But while both were in some sense subordinate to the στρατηγός
(the general appointed over the satrapy and all of its respective districts
and villages), the διοικητής (the financial counterpart to the στρατηγός)
was the immediate supervisor of the *oikonomoi*. The Seleucid regal
oikonomos, while remaining at least two or three positions removed from
the top of the administrative hierarchy, therefore still occupied a high-
ranking office as the chief financial administrator at the district level.

Responsibilities

In addition to possessing great administrative authority in their respective
regions, the Seleucid *oikonomoi* shared the same area of administrative
responsibility as the Ptolemaic *oikonomoi*. As the chief financial official
in the district, the *oikonomos* supervised the region's royal land and revenue. Their oversight of Seleucid territory is apparent, for instance, in the
Laodike Dossier, a mid-third-century inscription from Didyma in Ionia,
which reports a real-estate transaction that took place between the king's
officials and Laodike, the king's ex-wife.[41] In this scenario, the hyparch
allocated the king's real estate (village, mansion, property, and peasants)
to Laodike by way of Arrhidaios, her estate manager (τῶι οἰκονομοῦντι
τὰ Λαοδίκης). The regal *oikonomos* Nikomachos was then responsible
for authorising the transaction on behalf of the king (κατὰ τὸ παρὰ
Νικομάχου τοῦ οἰκονόμου πρόσταγμα).[42]

---

[39] Trans. adapted from Austin §193.
[40] For discussion, see Aperghis (2004: 269–73).
[41] *SEG* 16.710/19.676/*OGI* 225/*IDidymaMcCabe* 128. For text, translation, and discussion, see Landvogt (1908: 29); Welles (1934: 102–4 (§20)); Aperghis (2004: 315–18 (§3));
cf. Bagnall/Derow §25; Austin §173.
[42] It is also significant that the author draws a distinction between ὁ οἰκονόμος and
ὁ οἰκονόμων τὰ Λαοδίκης. Here ὁ οἰκονόμος is a regal official under whose jurisdiction the
real-estate transaction took place. The other manager, Arrhidaios, was the private administrator who supervised Laodike's personal affairs. During this period, private *oikonomoi* of
elite persons could possess some wealth (cf. *ILaodikeiaLykos* 1/*SEG* 47.1739; Austin §168;

The Seleucid *oikonomoi* also possessed a certain measure of judicial authority, as the earlier Scythopolis text indicates. Although oversight of the royal land and revenue in the districts was their primary concern, the responsibilities of the *oikonomos* extended beyond financial matters and, together with the toparch, included jurisdiction over any number of civil disputes between the peasants and even over minor criminal offences. The pair of officials probably maintained their own areas of competency when possible, but because many civil matters also concerned private and public finances, occasionally it was fitting that the two settled certain disputes together.

Attalid Kingdom

The Attalid (or Pergamene) Kingdom was the undersized state that remained following the death of Lysimachus in 281 BCE. With Pergamon as its capital, the dynasty controlled a small sector of the northwest corner of Asia Minor until the land was bequeathed to the Romans in 133 BCE. In comparison with the Ptolemaic and Seleucid Kingdoms, evidence for the inner workings of Attalid administration is rather meagre. Without question, Pergamon was the administrative centre throughout the dynasty, and the remainder of the kingdom continually struggled to develop around it. But the city was governed quite differently from the other Hellenistic capitals in the early years following its inception.[43] The king's control over Pergamon was quite limited before the Treaty of Apameia in 188 BCE. Technically, he stood apart from the city council (βουλή) and its management of civic finances, although the council στρατηγοί and ταμίαι were appointed by him and provided him opportunities to direct civic policy.[44] Following the treaty, however, the king developed a hierarchy featuring more empowered civic officials (i.e. στρατηγοί, ὁ ἐπὶ τῆς πόλεως, ὁ ἐπὶ τῶν ἱερῶν προσόδων; cf. *OGI* 483), which increased his control over Pergamon considerably. This hierarchical evolution probably occurred in the outer Attalid territories as well, although those smaller regions required far less developed administrative structures than did those of their Near Eastern neighbours. Whereas the

---

for discussion, see Wörrle (1975)). Nevertheless, their administrative domain was quite different from that of their regal counterparts, as they operated on a far more modest socioeconomic plane. As Ma (1999: 149) observes, 'It comes as no surprise that Antiochos II and his subordinates should have distinguished between a Seleukid officer, ὁ οἰκονόμος, and the private manager of Laodike I, ὁ οἰκονομῶν τά Λαοδίκης... [Even the] peasants could differentiate between institutions of the central state ... and their landlord's managers.'

[43] Allen (1983: 159).   [44] Allen (1983: 167–8).

Ptolemies divided their land into nomes and the Seleucids into satrapies, the Attalids partitioned their main territories into τόποι.⁴⁵ Each of these regions was governed politically by a στρατηγός and financially by an οἰκονόμος, both of whom were personally appointed by the king.

The use of οἰκονόμος in the financial administration of the Attalid Kingdom was not confirmed textually until the 1996 discovery of a mid-second-century inscription at a shrine in Pleura, near Sardis.⁴⁶ The document contains a list of initiates (μύσται) and reports the decision to erect the stele in the shrine at the request of the priest. The text reads:

> When Euthydemus was chief-priest and Kadoas, son of Pleri, was priest. Memorandum to the chief-priest Euthydemus from Kadoas, priest of Apollo in Pleura, who has held the priesthood for a long time. Earlier, when Antiochus was king, I asked the chief-priest Nikanor to give permission that I set up a stele in the sanctuary, on which I record his name, my own and those of the *mystai*, and now I ask you, if it seems right to you, to give order [συντάξαι] to write to Asclepiades, the *oikonomos*, to assign me a place [ἵνα παραδείξῃ μοι τόπον] where I may set up the stele on which I record your name, my own, and those of the *mystai*.⁴⁷

The inscription does not reveal much about the profiles of the *oikonomos* or the other mentioned officials, and disagreement therefore remains about their rank, duties, and jurisdiction.⁴⁸ What is clear is that the *oikonomos* (Asclepiades) was a financial official responsible for allocating space for sanctuary inscriptions. The chief priest (Euthydemos) was responsible for authorising the decision and for instructing (συντάσσω) the *oikonomos* to allocate (παραδέχομαι) space for the stele. This, however, does not necessarily indicate that the chief priest was superordinate to the *oikonomos*. Euthydemos apparently forwarded the request to a certain Diophantos, who then forwarded the letter to one Attinas. The two latter-named officials are of unknown rank, but probably served in the royal administration and were 'in charge of a large territory or of a

⁴⁵ Malay (1996: 84). Due to the variety of communities which were included in the τόποι, E. V. Hansen (1947: 172) suggests that the 'places' were not strict administrative subdivisions, but ill-defined demarcations of land.

⁴⁶ Even so, historians have for some time been importing Seleucid models into their reconstructions of Attalid administration and thus assumed all along that the Attalids utilised *oikonomoi* in provincial management; cf. E. V. Hansen (1947: 169–70).

⁴⁷ For text, translation, and discussion, see Malay and Nalbantoğlu (1996).

⁴⁸ Cf. Ma (1999: 146–7); Dignas (2002: 50–6); Aperghis (2004: 277–8).

wide range of matters' in the region of the shrine.[49] Attinas apparently informed the *oikonomos* Asclepiades about Euthydemos' authorisation. Thus, the *oikonomos* was probably subordinate to Attinas and perhaps also to Diophantos.[50]

Since Attalid *oikonomoi* were apparently responsible for the erection of stelae at local shrines, they probably occupied a less significant administrative position than did the Ptolemaic and Seleucid *oikonomoi*. Clearly, they were involved in the payment of various civic and sacred expenses.[51] But even so, the competencies of Attalid *oikonomoi* were similar to their Seleucid counterparts', being responsible for at least some of the region's finances.[52] Thus, they were officials with some administrative authority.

Macedonian Kingdom

The financial administration of the Macedonian (or Antigonid) Kingdom remains in relative obscurity in comparison with its Asian and Near Eastern counterparts. At various times during their rule (*c.* 294–168 BCE), the Antigonids controlled all of Macedonia, parts of Achaea and southern Thrace, certain Aegean Islands, and Caria. Much evidence is lacking, however, about how these regions were governed, due in part to the focus of the Antigonid kings on warfare rather than administrative development.[53] Local economic structures are attested, but the relationship between the cities and districts, and between districts and king, remains unclear, creating difficulty for those who wish to reconstruct the administrative framework of the Macedonian Kingdom. This is especially disappointing because the balance of power between the king and his people made Macedonia the most distinct of the major Hellenistic powers.[54] Although certain kings instituted structures which resemble

[49] Dignas (2002: 54 n. 84).

[50] Aperghis (2004: 278). *Contra* Malay and Nalbantoğlu (1996: 78), who suggest that Diophantos and Attinas were 'royal functioners serving under the chief-priest or the *oikonomos*'.

[51] Dignas (2002: 55) probably overstates her case when she suggests that the *oikonomos* was 'involved in matters that did not concern land at all, not even sacred territory. The post must have had a very down to earth profile, if Asclepiades was really going to assign a place for a single stele in a small sanctuary.'

[52] Ma (1999: 136). In fact, Malay and Nalbantoğlu (1996: 78) suggest that the *oikonomos* was 'a royal official responsible for the royal land (βασιλικὴ γῆ) as well as for the sanctuaries', and was 'adopted by the Attalids from the Seleucid administration'.

[53] It is of further significance that Macedonia has so far been inadequately excavated.

[54] Hatzopoulos (1996a: 420) remarks that 'the whole structure of the Macedonian state is less elaborate, less hierarchical, and bears less the imprint of an all-pervasive and

those of neighbouring kingdoms,[55] those systems changed regularly, so simply importing a bureaucratic model from a contemporary state to provide a skeleton on which to build will not do. Neither will it suffice to rely too much on evidence dating from before the Antigonid dynasty. While it has been suggested that the kingdom's structure changed little following the death of Alexander,[56] recent studies have noted significant changes in city and state organisation, not only immediately following the division of the Alexandrian Empire, but even between the reigns of various Antigonid kings.[57] For our purposes, then, we shall focus all of our attention on reconstructing part of only one administrative policy, that of Philip V.

Of all those of the Macedonian kings, the reign of Philip V has preserved the most illuminating data with which to work in the Hellenistic period, and it is from his rule that we possess the only extant documents attesting to the appointment of *oikonomoi* in Macedonian regal administration. During the forty-three years of his reign (222–179 BCE), Philip spent no more than eight at peace.[58] For this reason it is not at all surprising that the two inscriptions mentioning regal *oikonomoi* in Macedonia were discovered in army garrisons (*IG* XII *Suppl.* 644; *SEG* 51.640bis).[59] In these two nearly identical texts, *oikonomoi* emerge as financial administrators, just as they were in the more abundantly documented kingdoms. But some of their responsibilities included tasks somewhat unfamiliar to those expounded in the Ptolemaic, Seleucid, and Attalid texts examined above. The late third-century BCE inscription found in Chalcis (*IG* XII *Suppl.* 644), for instance, portrays *oikonomoi* as responsible for the inspection and replacement of basic supplies in Philip's military fortresses (φρούρια).[60] The inscription was originally a διάγραμμα and, though much too lengthy to quote at length, provides significant data with which to reconstruct the office.[61]

strictly structured bureaucracy than that of the Ptolemies... Macedonia emerges as more "democratic", if not egalitarian, and relying more on local initiative and autonomy than on a centralised civil service'; *contra* Errington (1990: 218–29). For a balanced view, see F. W. Walbank (1984a: 225–9).

[55] Billows (1990: 268) suggests that something akin to the Achaemenid administration was instituted during the reign of Antigonos Monophthalmos (306–301 BCE).

[56] Rostovtzeff (1941: 250).   [57] F. W. Walbank (1984a: 225–7).

[58] F. W. Walbank (1940: 259).

[59] *IG* XII *Suppl.* 644, found in Chalcis, was preserved in its entirety. For discussion, see Welles (1938: 252–4); Hatzopoulos (1996b: 36–8). *SEG* 51.640bis, found in Kynos, contains lines 36–53 of the previous text.

[60] The φρούριον in Chalcis was among the 'fetters of Greece', the three most strategically located Macedonian fortresses located in Demetrias, Corinth, and Chalcis.

[61] I am grateful to Professor John Barclay and Dr Paola Ceccarelli for their assistance with working with this text.

Hierarchy

The *oikonomoi* in *IG* XII *Suppl.* 644 were clearly regal administrators and subordinate to the king, since the orders they received were issued directly by him (τὰ διαταχθέντα ὑπὸ τοῦ βασιλέως, line 1). Because the document also contains instructions to the garrison commanders (φρούραρχοι) and agents of the *oikonomos* (χειρισταί τῶν οἰκονόμων), we can reconstruct a basic chain of command: the king served as head of the monarchy and delegated oversight to his military and financial subordinates, the φρούραρχοι and *oikonomoi*; the *oikonomoi* then further delegated tasks to their agents (χειρισταί). While the φρούραρχοι were required to grant permission to the *oikonomoi* before opening the fortress's storage bins, and to notify the king of any mismanagement on the part of the *oikonomoi* and their agents, the *oikonomoi* were probably not subordinate to the φρούραρχοι. Rather, they were officers of equal rank in complementary departments.[62] This is most apparent when the text indicates that the king himself, rather than the φρούραρχοι, gave the directives and would condemn them (καταγινώσκω, lines 33, 36) for any case of negligence. Thus, the *oikonomoi* were subordinate officials who, according to this inscription, served directly beneath the king.

The document also shows that the *oikonomoi* possessed some measure of authority. Although the text does not state explicitly which official is in view for most of the instructions, the supervisory nature of the duties together with the opening address suggest that all the instructions were intended for the *oikonomoi* unless otherwise indicated. But the presence of the χειρισταί (lines 9, 27) indicates that *oikonomoi* did not personally handle all the storage matters in each fortress. Final responsibility for the replenishment of the fortresses's supplies belonged to the *oikonomoi*, but since the χειρισταί maintained possession of the keys to the storage bins (τὰς μὲν κλεῖδας τῶν ἀποθηκῶν, line 8), the actual task of replenishing supplies was probably carried out by those agents. Thus, *oikonomoi*, even though subordinate to the king, possessed supervisory authority in the fortresses, and probably over the provinces of the kingdom.

Responsibilities

The responsibilities of the *oikonomoi*, as they pertain to the fortress, are made quite clear in the inscription. Once they took inventory of the

---

[62] F. W. Walbank (1940: 294).

stored goods (lines 3–6), they were responsible for bringing in the new grain (lines 15–16) and for arranging the old grain to be sown in the local fields (lines 17–18). Furthermore, they were responsible for replacing the wine and wood every five years (lines 18–19) and for inspecting and repairing the granaries (lines 21, 25–6, 30). The purpose of the surplus is not entirely clear. C. Bradford Welles suggests that the ordinance was given 'to maintain in a state of constant readiness the "first class" military supplies, grain, wine, and wood' in case of an enemy siege.[63] On the other hand, the supplies may have been intended for emergency civilian use, since the peasants would have probably found protection in the fortress during an attack.

Although the inscription only lists responsibilities associated with the maintenance of army surplus, it is reasonable to surmise that the Macedonian *oikonomoi* were entrusted with responsibilities beyond those listed on this stele, and perhaps outside military matters. Clearly, the φρούραρχος was appointed to a particular fortress (ὁ φρούραρχος ὁ τεταγμένος ἐν ὧι ἂν τόπωι, lines 40–1), but this may not have been the case for the *oikonomos*. When the text states that an *oikonomos* might be 'transferred over to another place [μετάγηται ἐφ' ἕτερον τόπον]' (lines 49–50), the location in view may not have been a fortress, but an administrative region, similar to the τόποι managed by the Seleucid and Attalid *oikonomoi*. Moreover, it is plausible, as Welles suggests, that the *oikonomoi* performed duties in addition to those mentioned in the document.[64] When the text refers to 'the rest of the concerns of the office [τῶν λοιπῶν τῶν ἐκ τῆς οἰκονομίας]' (lines 52–3), it indicates that *oikonomoi* performed tasks not mentioned in this διάγραμμα, tasks which may have required supervision beyond the fortress. Indeed, the appointment of χειρισταί probably suggests that the responsibilities of *oikonomoi* were so numerous and geographically extensive that personal agents were required to fulfil them. In fact, the regularly scheduled instructions mentioned in the text required attention only once every ten days at most during the winter (lines 23–4), undoubtedly the most demanding season of the year. Therefore, it is likely that the *oikonomoi* had more tasks entrusted to them than those listed in the inscription. If so, they would have been regarded as persons of great authority in the regal administration of the Macedonian Kingdom.

---

[63] Welles (1938: 253). It is curious that nothing is stated about weaponry.
[64] Welles (1938: 253).

Accountability

The διάγραμμα also makes clear that the office of the *oikonomos* required thoughtfulness (φροντιζέτωσαν, lines 19–20), punctuality (εὐθέως, lines 16–17; παραχρῆμα, line 26), and, above all, carefulness and precision (ἐπιμελείσθωσαν ὅπως τὰ διαταχθέντα … διατηρῆται ἄφθαρτα, lines 1–2). According to the inscription, negligence was unacceptable to the king, and in any such cases the offenders would suffer whatever sentence the king issued (ἐλεγχθέντες παθέτωσαν ὅτι ἂν αὐτῶν ὁ βασιλεὺς καταγνῶι, lines 32–3), which might have consisted of termination from office (ἀφιῆται ἀπὸ τῆς χρείας, lines 50–1), or perhaps worse. In any case, the *oikonomoi* were warned by way of this inscription to follow the king's orders closely.

Summary

In the preceding investigation we carefully examined the use of the title οἰκονόμος in the regal administrations of the Hellenistic kingdoms.[65] It is notable that during this period the title was used in each of the four main Hellenistic political powers: the Ptolemaic, Seleucid, Attalid (Pergamene), and Macedonian (Antigonid) Kingdoms. Due to the minor structural differences that existed between the monarchies, we examined them individually, so as not to confuse the use of the title in one administrative system with that in another. Despite this discriminating approach to the source materials, several consistent features surfaced in our analysis.

Oikonomoi were always shown to be subordinate financial officials at least one step removed from the top of the administrative hierarchy, and in most cases they were at least two steps away. At the same time, *oikonomoi* were without exception regional managers entrusted with the oversight of large territories. As a result, they normally had several delegates at their immediate disposal and supervised numerous other local officials. With such a high administrative rank, *oikonomoi* would have possessed significant social status and structural authority. But the administrative competencies of *oikonomoi* were usually limited to financial matters, so that their responsibilities typically involved various kinds

---

[65] In the Roman period, the *oikonomoi* of Caesar, though clearly belonging to the emperor and forming a category of administration somewhat distinct from the private, public, and regal domains, more closely resembled private than regal administrators, as they belonged to the *familia Caesaris*; cf. Swiderek (1970); Weaver (1972). We shall therefore integrate our discussion of the *oikonomoi* of Caesar into Chapter 4.

of revenue acquisition as well as the provision of and payment for needs and supplies in the regional economic sector. They served in certain judicial capacities on occasion, but usually this was necessary when the offences involved were financial in nature. In any case, *oikonomoi* were held accountable for their oversight by administrative superiors. Several documents indicate that professional advancement was a real possibility for those who carried out the king's wishes. Alternatively, termination and eventual sentencing by the king or an immediate supervisor awaited those who were found guilty of mismanagement.

3

OIKONOMOI AS CIVIC ADMINISTRATORS

The *oikonomoi* shall pay for the writing of all these things from
the revenue which they have for the administration of the city.
IMagnMai 98/IMagMcCabe 2

The epigraphic remains from both the Hellenistic and Roman periods
also attest to the appointment of *oikonomoi* as administrators of Greek
and Roman cities. Just as with the evidence for regal *oikonomoi*, texts
featuring *oikonomoi* who served in civic contexts have been found
throughout the Mediterranean basin and range in date from just before
the death of Alexander the Great to the mid third century CE. But before
an analysis of these municipal officials can be undertaken, several methodological difficulties must be addressed.

First, despite the widespread geographical attestation of the title, the
inscriptions mentioning municipal *oikonomoi* are not evenly distributed.
Many of these inscriptions surface in clusters and in specific geographical regions, most notably western Asia Minor, the Aegean Islands, the
coastal cities of the Black Sea, and southern Greece, creating a lack of
uniformity across the Mediterranean. It is possible that this clustering is
due to modern archaeology's patchy excavating of Greek societies, but it
should be noted that there are even very few attestations of *oikonomoi* in
some cities that have been heavily excavated.[1]

In spite of the scattered attestation of *oikonomoi*, it is significant for
our purposes that the best-attested regions are those located at the edges
of the Hellenistic kingdoms where an abundance of self-governing cities developed.[2] It is not surprising, then, that cities in these peripheral

---

[1] Take for example Athens, from which there have been tens of thousands of inscriptions
published and just one known instance of *<o>ikonomos* (*IG* II/2 11492/*CIG* 963/*CIL* III
555), which, incidently, attests to a private slave administrator, not a civic official.

[2] Although much of western Asia Minor and the Black Sea region fell within the board-
ers of the monarchies, quite often the cities located within those distant territories were
given the opportunity to govern themselves, so long as tributes were regularly paid to the

regions were managed differently from those governed more closely by the Hellenistic kings and employed titles not normally utilised in cities falling within the direct jurisdiction of the monarchies. In fact, many of the titles used for magistrates in these 'independent' cities were the same as those used for regional administrators in the Hellenistic kingdoms. After all, in the peripheral, independent cities there would have been little concern for titular overlap with regal administrators.

It is also significant that there are genetic links between many of the cities that appointed *oikonomoi*. It has been well documented, for instance, that the Greek civilisations of western Asia Minor were colonised by cities in southern Greece. Moreover, the Greek civilisations found in the Black Sea region were largely colonised by the cities of western Asia Minor, particularly Miletus.[3] Because these regions have hereditary ties, it is not surprising that the titles used for their city officials quite frequently overlapped.

A second difficulty with examining the profile of municipal *oikonomoi* is that the inscriptions which mention them rarely reveal anything of real significance. As David Magie laments, 'Unfortunately, the extant documents – principally decrees passed by the Assemblies – yield little information concerning the details of government and the actual administration of public affairs in the Asianic city-states during the Hellenistic period.'[4] We are not implying that nothing can be ascertained about their civic responsibilities and administrative power. Inscriptions featuring *oikonomoi* indicate much about their involvement in civic purchases and certain public events. Beyond this, however, not much is known directly from those texts. If it can be assumed that every *oikonomos* serving in a municipal context was entrusted with exactly the same responsibilities, then more can be deduced. But as previously stated, most cities where the title was used were autonomous, constructed their own constitutions, and so were governed differently. It is not entirely clear, therefore, why certain cities appointed entire boards of *oikonomoi*, why some elected only one, and why some appear to have had none. To complicate things further, the titles given to the individuals who fulfilled the duties normally performed by *oikonomoi* were not always the same. It is quite unclear why some cities used the title οἰκονόμος, others ταμίας, and still others ὁ ἐπὶ τῆς διοικήσεως. Were these titles synonymous? If so, why

kings. For the 'independence' of Greek cities, see, e.g., M. H. Hansen (1995); Ma (1999: 150–74).

[3] Tsetskhladze (2004: 124): 'Virtually all the colonies in the Black Sea region were founded by Miletus.'

[4] Magie (1950: 59).

do they occasionally appear in the same city, and even side by side (cf. *SEG* 39.1243; 52.659; *IMylasa* 301; *ISmyrna* 771; 772)?[5] And why do certain titles surface in some periods, disappear for well over a century, only to reappear again in the same city in a later era?[6] Such questions create difficulties in the reconstruction of city administrations and have to be taken into consideration when investigating the responsibilities and power of civic *oikonomoi*.

We must, nevertheless, attempt to synthesise what the evidence does suggest. In an effort to do so, we shall divide the data into three historical and municipal contexts. We shall first analyse the responsibilities and administrative power possessed by those *oikonomoi* serving in Greek cities during the Hellenistic period. We shall then proceed to those characteristics of *oikonomoi* in Greek cities from the Roman period. Finally, we shall examine the same traits of *oikonomoi* serving in Roman colonies and *municipia*. While minor differences existed in each of these civic contexts, several consistent features of *oikonomoi* will become apparent over the course of our analysis. In each of these municipality-types, *oikonomoi* normally functioned as financial magistrates and possessed considerable socio-economic status within their respective communities (it is noteworthy, however, that a number of municipal *oikonomoi* serving in Greek cities during the Roman period appear to have been public slaves; e.g. *SEG* 24.496; 38.710; 47.1662).[7] But despite their prominence, these officials never possessed any significant political and decision-making authority. Furthermore, the measures taken to ensure their dependability differed between historical and municipal contexts. In fact, it is quite significant that *oikonomoi* serving in these civic roles were neither offered any tangible incentives

---

[5] It could be that, within a city, local tribes referred to a single municipal office by different titles (cf. *IMylasa* 201; 301). In Priene, on the other hand, οἰκονόμος, νεωποίης, and ὁ ἐπὶ τῆς διοικήσεως were all used for financial magistrates. But νεωποίαι clearly managed sacred funds, suggesting that *oikonomoi* served in the central treasury. The jurisdiction of οἱ ἐπὶ τῆς διοικήσεως is trickier, since they made the same payments as *oikonomoi*. Asboeck (1913: 112) concluded that ὁ οἰκονόμος and ὁ ἐπὶ τῆς διοικήσεως referred to the same public office: 'Die Befugnisse beider sind, soweit wir sie kennen, identisch.' This may have been the case, but not necessarily so, since ὁ ἐπὶ τῆς διοικήσεως only surfaces four times in Priene, the last attestation being in the second century BCE, while οἰκονόμος appears more than ten times through the first century BCE. Migeotte (2006a: 388) therefore suggests that a reform took place during the second century BCE that eliminated ὁ ἐπὶ τῆς διοικήσεως and retained only the *oikonomos*, entrusting all public funds to him.

[6] See, e.g., the titular variety of the Athenian treasury (cf. Henry 1982; Henry 1984; Oliver 2007: 223–7).

[7] Still, many other municipal *oikonomoi* in Greek cities during the Roman period were citizens and magistrates (e.g. *CIG* 2811; *SEG* 26.1044; *TAM* 5.743; *ISmyrna* 761; 771; 772; *IStratonikeia* 1). Cf. A. Weiss (2004: 50–9).

for managing well nor held accountable directly to a superior official. Instead, municipal *oikonomoi* were answerable either to the entire community or to a representative body.

Hellenistic Greek cities

We begin our survey of Graeco-Roman municipal administration with the Greek πόλις of the Hellenistic period. In contrast to our studies on regal and private administrators, we shall initially analyse the responsibilities of municipal *oikonomoi*, since deciphering their political rank requires first that we adequately grasp what duties they performed. We shall then examine the administrative hierarchy and means of political accountability operative in these cities.

Responsibilities

The *oikonomoi* who served in Greek cities during the Hellenistic period were treasurers, elected magistrates, and citizens. This much is clear from the interchangeable use of οἰκονόμος with ταμίας (treasury magistrate) in civic publications.[8] According to the epigraphic record, the most commonly repeated statement mentioning municipal *oikonomoi* reads as follows: 'And let the *oikonomos* pay the expense for the stele [τὸ δὲ ἀνάλωμα τὸ εἰς τὴν στήλην δοῦναι τὸν οἰκονόμον]' (*OGI* 50). While regularly varying in word-order and word-choice, this formula is mentioned in at least twenty-five inscriptions dated between the fourth and first centuries BCE, as well as in an additional eight inscriptions whose dates are unknown, but whose provenances suggest that they too belonged to the Hellenistic period.[9] Significantly, the formula resembles that which was used to authorise the purchases made by ταμίαι and other financial magistrates in many other Greek cities during this timeframe.[10]

Oikonomoi were also responsible for the payment and provision of numerous gifts and crowns for ambassadors, athletes, and benefactors. A third-century BCE inscription from Ephesus has been restored to report how an *oikonomos* was charged with the responsibility of awarding a

---

[8] While A. Weiss (2004: 56) deduces that in some cases οἰκονόμοι and ταμίαι held entirely different offices, he concedes that 'der οἰκονόμος τῆς πόλεως in einigen Städten den ταμίας ersetzte'. Cf. Reumann (1957: 234–5). Landvogt (1908: 19–21) also observed the considerable overlap between the responsibilities of οἰκονόμοι and ταμίαι, although he ultimately rejected a formal equivalence.

[9] For the municipal *oikonomoi* payment formulas, see Goodrich (2010a: 102–6).

[10] Cf. Henry (1989: 259–60).

certain man a gift in return for his benefactions: 'And the *oikonomos* should send to him the gift of hospitality [ξένια] so that all might know that the people highly honour the favours being offered for the benefits of the city' (*IEphMcCabe* 88/*IBM* 469). Although the recipient is not specified in what remains of the inscription, it is clear from another Ephesian publication dating to the same period that such ξενίαι were offered to wealthy visitors whose favours the city sought to secure (*IEphMcCabe* 60/*OGI* 10/*IBM* 453). Such gifts were probably sanctioned by law, as indicated in a third-century BCE inscription from Colophon: 'And the *oikonomos*, Koronos, should give the gift of hospitality [ξένια] to the ambassador [τῶι πρεσβευτῆι], which is in accordance with the law [τὰ ἐκ τοῦ νόμου]' (*SEG* 49.1502). *Oikonomoi* were also responsible for purchasing and distributing crowns to accomplished athletes and politicians. In one inscription (*IEphesos* 1448), an Ephesian *oikonomos* was commissioned to pay for the crowns presented to Antigonus and Demetrius, whereas in another the *oikonomos* in Ephesus was instructed to distribute cash to the victor of a contest so the athlete could purchase the crown himself (*IEphesos* 1415/*IEphMcCabe* 69/*IBM* 415).[11] Finally, a second-century BCE inscription from Colophon shows that an *oikonomos* was responsible annually for financing a celebration in honour of a prominent deceased citizen.[12] Here it is significant to observe that, while other city officials were integrally involved in the planning of this municipal event, which included cultic as well as athletic oversight, the only responsibility of the *oikonomos* in this instance and in many others was the dispensing of the necessary funds.

Oikonomoi did on occasion perform duties beyond making public payments. Two lengthy texts reveal their participation in religious festivals and processions. A second-century BCE inscription from Magnesia on the Maeander mentions a board of *oikonomoi* to which was delegated certain cultic duties on behalf of the city (*IMagnMai* 98/*IMagMcCabe* 2).[13] It was resolved that, in the last month of the year, they should buy a bull. Then, at the beginning of the new year, when seed was to be sown, they should offer the bull as a sacrifice at a public festival for the purpose of soliciting city-wide protection

[11] According to the text, Athenodoros was to be awarded the prize in cash from the Ephesian *oikonomos*. Presumably, the victor would then use the money to purchase his own crown. The interesting feature of this award is that it was delivered by Ephesus, even though the athletic contest was held in Nemea. It was probably the case that the policy in Ephesus, and perhaps in other cities as well, was to award gifts to any champion who named the city as his residence; cf. Slater and Summa (2006: 298).

[12] Macridy (1905: 163); cf. Dmitriev (2005: 36).

[13] For translation, see Price (1999: 174 (§3)).

(φυλακή) from Zeus. Their participation in the sacrifice, as well as their ongoing prayer for the city's peace and prosperity, highlights their representative role, not only in financial matters, but also in the religious activities of the community.[14] But this and other inscriptions show that, even when *oikonomoi* performed cultic duties, they were not in such contexts only, or even primarily, acting as 'religious' officials, since the religious responsibilities of *oikonomoi* were always accompanied by administrative tasks.[15] In this inscription, for instance, it is significant that the *oikonomoi* were responsible for offering and dividing sacrifices (seemingly religious tasks) *as well as* for purchasing the animals, drawing up a contract, then having the decree engraved on a stele, placed in the sanctuary, and paid for by the central treasury (seemingly administrative tasks).[16]

Additional inscriptions also present *oikonomoi* who were entrusted with both religious and administrative duties. For example, in one late fourth-century BCE inscription from Ephesus (*IEphesos* 1448/*IBM* 448/*IEphMcCabe* 108), the pairing of an *oikonomos* together with a priestess as officiants of a sacrifice demonstrates once more that religious responsibilities were occasionally delegated to municipal *oikonomoi*.[17] But, as noted before, the participation of city administrators in public rituals was quite normal in Graeco-Roman antiquity, since magistrates

---

[14] As Reumann (1958: 342) observes, the duties of the *oikonomos* 'go beyond check-signing, for he takes part in the sacrificial rites, if not as a cult official, at least as an intermediary of the municipal government'.

[15] Of course the sharp distinction between sacred and secular did not exist in the Graeco-Roman world, so one should not categorise *oikonomoi* or any city official as serving in a purely secular context. As Rhodes (2009: 1) remarks, 'In Athens, and in the Greek world generally, the notion of a separation between church and state was unthinkable.' MacMullen (1981: 43) further explains, '[I]t must be remembered how far from purely secular were most elected officials in cities of Greek or Roman derivation. This year to the gods, the next to the city – such was the pattern of service rendered by the local aristocracy.' Nevertheless, some delineation between public and sacred was recognised in Graeco-Roman cities. Dignas (2002: 272) maintains that 'a clear destinction between sacred and public finances, as well as between sacred and public land, existed in the communities of both Hellenistic and Roman Asia Minor'.

[16] Dmitriev (2005: 29–30) notes that Greek city officials occasionally supervised affairs in different administrative contexts because

> city offices in Hellenistic Asia were not grouped into any a priori defined fields of city administration. One city official could have different kinds of responsibilities and was classified in more than one category, while officials with different ranges of responsibility could participate in the same kind of activity. The Greeks conceptualized city administration not as a sum of administrative fields but as individual offices which they grouped as the situation required.

[17] [θύειν δὲ καὶ][εὐ]αγγέλια τῆι Ἀρτέμιδι τοὺς ἐσσῆνας καὶ [τὴν ἱέρειαν][καὶ τ]ὸν οἰκονόμον.

served as community representatives not only in political matters, but also in religious observance. The *oikonomos* in this text should therefore not be confused with a purely cultic official, especially because the payment instructions in the latter part of the inscription indicate that the *oikonomos* also oversaw the city's finances.[18] As Reumann remarks, '*[A]ll* state officials in antiquity had religious duties to perform, and the fact that an ἄρχων took part in a sacrifice did not make him a cult official. Likewise with the political *oikonomos*.'[19]

In summary, while a handful of inscriptions mention the cultic duties occasionally delegated to municipal *oikonomoi*, it is apparent in each case that religious oversight only accompanied the administrative responsibilities normally entrusted to them.[20] Cumulatively, then, the texts mentioning municipal *oikonomoi* reveal that, during the Hellenistic period, they were always treasurers and often the chief financial magistrates of the Greek cities where they were appointed, having been commissioned to disburse public funds for various civic expenses. As Peter Landvogt explained, 'Die Hauptkompetenzen des οἰκονόμος in diesen Freistaaten bestehen in der Sorge für Aufschrift und Aufstellung von Psephismen und Statuen, in Bestreitung der Kosten für jene Besorgungen sowie für Kränze und Gastgeschenke… Kurz, das Charakteristische für die ganze Amtstätigkeit des οἰκονόμος … in dieser Periode ist, daß er lediglich als Kassen- oder Finanzbeamter fungiert.'[21]

Hierarchy

As treasury magistrates, municipal *oikonomoi* were, in one sense, considered civic leaders. But their elevated social status and political rank did not translate into great administrative authority like the *oikonomoi* who served in the hierarchies of the Hellenistic kingdoms. Hellenistic cities simply – and quite intentionally – lacked the deep political structure that characterised the monarchies. Instead, political power was designed to be shared by the members of the community. Certain kinds of socio-economic power could be obtained and exploited effectively in these municipalities. But *oikonomoi* and other local politicians possessed very limited structural leverage with which they might control the community.

---

[18] τοῦ δὲ ἀναλώματος τοῦ εἰς τὴν θυ[σίαν ἐπιμελεῖσθαι] τ[ὸν ο]ἰκονόμον … τοῦ δὲ στεφάνου ἐπιμε[λεῖσθαι τὸν οἰκονόμον].

[19] Reumann (1958: 344, original emphasis).

[20] Reumann (1958: 344): 'At best we can say that these governmental *oikonomoi* at times had cultic duties along with financial ones.'

[21] Landvogt (1908: 17).

The typical independent Greek city of the Hellenistic period was democratic by constitution and instituted three main political bodies to ensure that it was ruled by the people (δῆμος).[22] The first institution, the assembly (ἐκκλησία), consisted of all the male citizens of the city of at least 21 years of age. Just as in Athens,[23] most city assemblies convened for standard meetings about thirty times a year and for the chief meeting (ἐκκλησία κηρία) ten additional times a year.[24] At assembly meetings, which were always summoned by the president (e.g. πρύτανις, ἡγεμών), the citizens made collective decisions, normally by vote, concerning matters proposed by the council. Such matters included the passing of decrees and legal revisions, although the latter were also required to be confirmed by legislative jurors (νομοθέται).[25]

The second institution, the council (βουλή), consisted of annually elected magistrates (ἄρχοντες), such as *oikonomoi*, who carried out the executive duties of the city.[26] Normally, magistrates in the πόλις were required to be male citizens, at least 30 years of age (although exceptions have been noted),[27] free of any criminal charges, and not seeking re-election to an office held the previous year (cf. Aristotle, *Ath. pol.* 55.3). In keeping with the democratic principle, they were to have gained their position either by vote or by lot.[28] While certain cities required a single official for a given magistracy, other cities further reduced the control of elected officials by electing entire boards to a particular office, such as the city treasury.[29] But, whereas the right to pass public decisions was reserved for the assembly, magistrates were entrusted with the responsibility of preparing decisions for the assembly and implementing those policies passed collectively by the people. A resolution normally originated with the magistrates, and, after a formal motion had been passed by the council, it became a preliminary resolution (προβούλευμα). It was then presented before the assembly for vote, where, if passed, the resolution became a decree.[30] Thus, both the

[22] A. H. M. Jones (1940: 157).

[23] Finley (1983: 70–1) considers it methodologically acceptable to draw general conclusions by comparing Athens with other large city-states.

[24] M. H. Hansen (1999: 133).   [25] M. H. Hansen (1999: 167–9).

[26] Dmitriev (2005: 56); A. H. M. Jones (1940: 165).

[27] Dmitriev (2005: 46–56) discusses instances when women and children (and even kings and deities) were elected to public office.

[28] Magistrates were normally elected in order to protect the sovereignty of the people. A. H. M. Jones (1940: 162) explains, 'It was an essential principle of Greek democracy to curb as far as possible the power of the executive, the magistrates, and to ensure that the magistracies were equally accessible to all citizens.'

[29] A. H. M. Jones (1940: 163); Migeotte (2006a: 393–4).

[30] Rhodes (1972: 104).

people – via the assembly – and the council were integral to the decision-making process, as announced in the enactment formulas of many
civic publications: ἔδοξεν τῆι βουλῆι καὶ τῶι δήμωι.[31] These statements
are suggestive of the great administrative authority and responsibility
entrusted to both the assembly and the council. The two bodies functioned complementarily, so that the council was always charged with
the important task of proposing and carrying out the decisions made
by the assembly.[32] Nevertheless, the entire procedure underscores the
sovereignty of the people and the supportive roles of the council and its
magistrates.

The third institution of the Greek city was the people's court
(δικαστήριον), which further highlights the restricted power of magistrates. If the council was the executive branch of the δῆμος, then the court
functioned as its judicial embodiment and was the political establishment with which the final word and source of power rested.[33] Although
every city had a single δικαστήριον, several courts might convene every
day in a given city, each comprising upward of several hundred male
jurors (δικασταί) who were at least 30 years of age and selected daily by
lot from a large panel of eligible citizens. These courts tried both public
and private cases, but those which most often came before the people's
court were political hearings.

The distribution of power between each of these three civic bodies has
significant implications for how we regard the authority entrusted to the
oikonomoi appointed in Hellenistic cities. Since Greek cities sought to
restrict the authority of their politicians by placing the bulk of the decision-
making power in the hands of the citizens, the structural authority of the
typical elected official was quite limited. Beyond this, treasurers such as
oikonomoi do not appear to have possessed much, if any, structural authority, since their role was largely to dispense public funds at the instruction

---

[31] Rhodes and Lewis (1997: 4).

[32] A. H. M. Jones (1940: 164):

> All Greek cities, however democratic, recognized that the primary assembly
> was a dangerously irresponsible body, and therefore, while leaving to it the
> ultimate decision on every point of importance, took care that no ill-considered
> proposal could be suddenly sprung upon it and passed in a snap division. One
> precaution, which seems to have been universal, was that no measure might be
> brought before the assembly which had not been considered and approved by
> the council.

[33] The precise relationship between the δῆμος and δικαστήριον is disputed.
M. H. Hansen (1974: 18) argues that '[t]he authority of the courts is greater than that of
the Assembly, and it is the jurors who are the protectors of democracy'. Cf. M. H. Hansen
(1975); M. H. Hansen (1990). Rhodes, on the other hand, maintains that both the assembly and people's court were embodiments of the δῆμος; cf. Rhodes (1979, 1980).

of the council. Still further, this responsibility was occasionally distributed among a treasury board, affording the individual *oikonomos* a rather inconsequential role in the establishment of public policy.

Accountability

According to the Athenian court system, political hearings generally took four forms.[34] Before any elected person could take office, he had to undergo (i) a scrutiny of his legal qualifications (δοκιμασία).[35] While in office, he could be removed during any ἐκκλησία κηρία (ii) by vote (ἀποχειροτονία), due simply to the dissatisfaction of the people,[36] or (iii) by impeachment (εἰσαγγελία) for criminal behaviour.[37] Lastly, at the end of his term, he had to undergo (iv) a final review of his conduct and a financial audit (εὔθυναι). Only when this final scrutiny was completed could the magistrate honourably return to civilian life. These kinds of political election and trial were essential for the survival of democracy in Hellenistic cities. According to Peter Rhodes and David Lewis, 'If a Greek state was to be considered in any sense democratic, it was essential that, even if the offices were not open to all citizens, the citizens should have the right to appoint the office-holders and call them to account.'[38]

The role of the assembly and court therefore created a balance of power in the Hellenistic cities, so that civic magistrates, such as *oikonomoi*, could occupy elected office and possess administrative responsibility without being afforded great structural power like the *oikonomoi* of the Hellenistic monarchies. Certain offices utilised titular prefixes which imply subordination (ὑπο-), but as Sviatoslav Dmitriev explains, 'The development of subordinate relations took place only inside

---

[34] Although the majority of evidence for the accountability of Greek city officials is from fourth-century BCE Athens, political trials in other Hellenistic cities resemble the Athenian system; cf. Rhodes and Lewis (1997: 528–9); Fröhlich (2004: 361–2).

[35] The δοκιμασία was not an examination of the candidate's competence, but his 'formal qualifications, conduct and political convictions' (Hansen 1999a: 218). Cf. Roberts (1982: 14); Adeleye (1983).

[36] Hansen (1999: 221).

[37] Εἰσαγγελία εἰς τὸν δῆμον could be charged against any citizen for a political crime and normally resulted in the death penalty, exile, or such a heavy fine that the convict became a state debtor and ἄτιμος for life; cf. Roberts (1982: 28). Εἰσαγγελία εἰς τὴν βουλήν could only be brought against magistrates for the lesser charge of maladministration and resulted in a large fine; cf. M. H. Hansen (1999: 212–18).

[38] Rhodes and Lewis (1997: 528). The prosecution of junior magistrates is best represented by the trial of the acclaimed Athenian general Timotheus, whose sentence fell upon his ταμίας, Antimachus (Demosthenes, *Tim.* 49). Cf. Roberts (1982: 27, 42–3, 201 n. 54).

administrative colleges and social organizations and therefore did not create any hierarchical structure in Asian city administration.'[39] Again, because during this period magistrates – who do not appear normally to have been paid[40] – were often wealthy enough to finance their own administrations or promise some benefaction upon election, public officials were normally socially prominent persons in their respective communities.[41] But even though the population was apparently content with the political initiative of the elite, the δῆμος maintained the bulk of political power, as they possessed the final vote on all matters which entered the assembly and, perhaps more importantly, the opportunity to prosecute political crimes in the people's court. Thus, civic *oikonomoi* would not have possessed any decision-making power or structural authority stemming from a superior bureaucratic rank. Rather, as Mogens Hansen explains regarding the central treasury, '[T]he job of the Council and the Board of Receivers in relation to the public finances was purely administrative: they had only very limited power to take decisions about the use of the moneys they administered.'[42] David Magie concurs: 'As a rule ... treasurers had no authority of their own, their duties being

[39] Dmitriev (2005: 61).

[40] M. H. Hansen (1979) argues that the salary (μισθός) paid to Athenian magistrates was abolished in 411 BCE and never reintroduced. However, de Ste Croix (1975) presents evidence for members of the assembly in Iasus, as well as judges, assembly members, and councillors in Rhodes, receiving salaries. Regardless, the practice of paying magistrates was not widespread; cf. Dmitriev (2005: 34–5).

[41] By the Hellenistic period the typical Greek city was in enough financial disarray that the population was generally willing to succumb to the ambitious political careers of the economic elite so long as the city was compensated in return. Public benefactions and liturgies – often taking the form of generous donations to city building projects and funding of magistracies – eventually provided wealthy citizens avenues to secure long-term control of public offices; cf. Dmitriev (2005: 38–45). As A. H. M. Jones (1940: 168) explains,

> Democracy was ... in the Hellenistic age tempered by a convention that the rich should have a virtual monopoly of office, provided that they paid for it liberally. And on the whole the compromise seems to have worked very well. The sanguinary class war which was the curse of Greek politics in the fifth century died down, and the upper classes fulfilled their part of the bargain in no grudging spirit. A very strong sense of civic obligation grew up among them, and they served their cities loyally both with their persons and their purses, as countless inscriptions testify.

Greek cities during the Hellenistic period were therefore ideologically democratic, but functionally aristocratic.

[42] M. H. Hansen (1999: 263). The inscriptions mentioning the payments made by *oikonomoi* never specify which account was to be deducted when paying for stelae, gifts of hospitality, or crowns. It is reasonable to assume, though, that they were paid for by the council, who set aside an account to cover such expenses. For city budgets, see Dmitriev (2005: 36); Schuler (2005); Migeotte (2006b); Rhodes (2007).

to receive the income of the city and to make payments ordered by the Council or by a decree of the Assembly.'[43]

Roman Greek cities

With the spread of Rome came the inevitable deterioration of democracy and the introduction of top-heavy power structures in the cities of the eastern Mediterranean. Although not all democratic principles and practices were discarded outright during the Roman period, most Greek city governments came to function as aristocracies, rather than as the democracies so prevalent in the Classical and Hellenistic periods. Of course democracy's decline was neither instantaneous nor universal. The changes introduced in the Roman period were already present in infancy as early as the beginning of the Hellenistic era.[44] Moreover, not all cities adopted Rome's policies, so there remained features of the democratic model in a number of Asian cities that continued to function just as they had centuries earlier. But while the labels 'oligarchy' and 'aristocracy' never appear in city constitutions, in both form and function most Greek cities under Rome came to resemble miniature versions of the Roman Republic.

According to G. E. M. de Ste Croix, three factors led to the gradual 'destruction of Greek democracy'. The first cause was the growth of magisterial and conciliar control of the assembly.[45] In many Greek cities during this period, the people maintained some involvement in the creation of public policy. Indeed, the councils of certain cities continued to require the approval of the assembly in the policy-making process. But the assembly's power to reject proposals was largely theoretical and rarely utilised. The epigraphic evidence from the Roman Empire demonstrates that the ἐκκλησία convened mainly for the purpose of ratifying honorary decrees and the proposals that the magistrates chose to present to the people. The assembly, then, had become little more than a confirmatory body and its power largely nominal.[46]

A second factor that led to the demise of democracy and the rise of oligarchy in the Greek city was the attachment of liturgies to civic magistracies.[47] Like the magistracies of the Hellenistic period, city officials under Rome were elected annually by the assembly of adult male

---

[43] Magie (1950: 61).
[44] Abbott and Johnson (1926: 69): 'When Rome entered Greece, the era of the independent city-state had already passed.'
[45] de Ste Croix (1981: 300); cf. Abbott and Johnson (1926: 75).
[46] Magie (1950: 641).   [47] de Ste Croix (1981: 300).

citizens. During the Roman period, however, the annual lists of magisterial candidates were produced by the council, and the assembly's only
responsibility in elections was the selection of the candidates from the
pre-approved list of nominees.[48] During this period magistracies also
came attached with property qualifications, often because magistrates
were expected to finance their own administrations.[49] A third-century CE
inscription from Thessalonica demonstrates this reciprocal exchange as
it recognises the generosity of a certain Zosimos, the city's *oikonomos*
and benefactor (τὸν εὐεργέτην, *IG* X/2.1 150). But the property quali-
fication was not an entirely new observance during the Roman period.
As A. H. M. Jones remarks, it simply 'gave legal sanction to what was
already the general practice, making illegal for the future what had in the
past been theoretically possible – that the people might elect to office
radically minded politicians of humble station'.[50] The use of elections
was a small concession to democracy, but in some cities even voting
rights were restricted to a few, which is implied by the differentiation
between 'ecclesiasts' and 'citizens' in certain inscriptions.[51]

   With council nominations out of the poor's reach, magisterial posts
became almost hereditary and perpetually controlled by the elite. This
is even demonstrated in several *oikonomoi* inscriptions from the Roman
period. One *oikonomos* from Cos, for instance, is said to have served his
post for well over two decades: 'Philetos, *oikonomos* of the city of Cos,
managing [οἰκονομήσαντος] blamelessly for 23 years' (*IKosPH* 310).[52]
A funerary column of a well-respected citizen from Crete, moreover,
mentions the man's three sons, all of whom apparently served as *oikonomos* in their lifetime: '[Kletonymos] certainly did not extinguish his life
in old age glowing like some star, through the imprudence of his *dai-
mon*, while protecting his country with his counsels. Rather the *oikonomoi*, pillars of his reputation [δοξῆς κίονες], prevailed in good foresight.
For he left three sons of his own.'[53] These examples demonstrate that

---

[48] Magie (1950: 640–1).
[49] Dmitriev (2005: 140–57); Zuiderhoek (2009).
[50] A. H. M. Jones (1940: 171).
[51] Magie (1950: 640); cf. Abbott and Johnson (1926: 75–6).
[52] The date of this inscription remains uncertain, but is estimated to be before the first
century BCE. Dmitriev (2005: 223) considers the *oikonomos* to have been a magistrate. But
Fraser (1972: 115) suggests that the individual was a public slave, arguing that 'the words
τῆς πόλεως seem normally to be used of state-employment of a humble sort ... and would
not be appropriate to a regularly elected official or magistrate'. Cf. Sherwin-White (1978:
222). But Fraser's generalisation cannot be applied to numerous οἰκονόμοι who were both
magistrates and bore the qualifier τῆς πόλεως (e.g. *IPriene* 83; 99; 109; 117; *TAM* 5.743;
IAphrodMcCabe 275).
[53] For text, translation, and discussion, see Baldwin Bowsky (1989). The date of this
inscription is probably the late second century BCE.

magistracies, including the office of the *oikonomos*, were important roles in city administration and were controlled by certain socio-economic groups, even individual families. Thus, by the Roman period the elite clearly had a tight monopoly on political office.

The third factor contributing to democracy's demise while under Rome was the elimination of the popular law courts.[54] In the democratic city the δικαστήριον held the magistrates accountable for political crimes, ensuring that the council operated in the best interests of the people. But in the Roman period, the juries were largely non-functioning bodies, so that the council was left without accountability or any built-in restrictions.[55] Some ancients still regarded the popular courts as operative during this period (e.g. Plutarch, *Mor.* 805a; Dio Chrysostom, *Or.* 49.15).[56] But the involvement of the courts in the prosecution of the ruling class is almost completely absent from the epigraphic record.[57] Without the people's court, the council became sovereign.[58] As Jones explains, 'When [the council] came to be no longer a mere committee of the assembly, renewed at frequent intervals and responsible to the popular courts for its acts, but a permanent and therefore irresponsible body, it inevitably became the governing body of the city.'[59]

Rome's aristocratic and timocratic policies dominated the majority of the cities of the eastern Mediterranean. Even though each of these features was already present during the Hellenistic period, the power exercised over *oikonomoi* in the Greek cities under the Roman Empire changed markedly in this period. No longer were they mere administrative functionaries serving as representatives of the δῆμος. During the Roman period, the *oikonomoi* serving as treasury magistrates – though largely remaining unpaid[60] – belonged to the socio-economic elite, were patrons of the city, and remained unaccountable to the general population. Still, the magistracy was not considered a position of great structural

[54] de Ste Croix (1981: 301).

[55] Some supervision was applied by the provincial governor and his imperial agents; cf. Abbott and Johnson (1926: 78); Bowman (1996: 366). But not much is known about the involvement of these imperial officials in the accountability of local magistrates; cf. Jacques (1984: 379–425).

[56] Dmitriev (2005: 157): 'The evidence for the *dokimasia* of city officials in preprovincial Asia and in various Roman provinces suggests that at least some city officials in the province of Asia also had to pass a *dokimasia* before being admitted to office.' Cf. C. P. Jones (1978: 98); Makarov (2007).

[57] Reynolds (1988: 31) maintains that 'in most cities the more important cases went to a Roman court'.

[58] Although Rome tried not to interfere in the legislation of cities in the east, the absence of official accountability in these cities might stem from the policy of magisterial immunity in the west; cf. Weinrib (1968: 36–7); Plescia (2001: 51–6).

[59] A. H. M. Jones (1940: 171).   [60] Dmitriev (2005: 141).

authority. Just as before, its administrative powers were restricted to making payments as decided by the council. While *oikonomoi* were able to utilise their wealth and social stature to obtain office, once elected their administrative power was quite limited.

Roman colonies and *municipia*

The appointment of *oikonomoi* in the colonies and *municipia* of the eastern Roman Empire requires that we also analyse the political structures of these cities, since they were governed quite differently from their Greek counterparts.[61] Unfortunately, the administrative rank and responsibilities of *oikonomoi* in these Roman cities remain disputed due to the uncertainty of the term's Latin equivalent(s).[62] Much debate has therefore ensued in an effort to identify, for instance, the rank and status of Erastus, the acquaintance of Paul and *oikonomos* of Corinth (Rom 16.23). NT specialists and ancient historians have proposed a number of possible Latin renderings for Erastus' title, including *arcarius/dispensator* (servile accountant), *quaestor* (treasury magistrate), and *aedilis* (public works magistrate). However, to date no consensus has emerged.[63]

The identification of at least one Latin equivalent for *oikonomos* in Roman *coloniae* and *municipia* has received some clarification in recent years by the discovery of an inscription from the Achaean colony of Patras. Paying tribute to the *oikonomos* Neikostratos, the inscription displays the man's *cursus honorum*, thus providing the opportunity to compare his current rank with that of his previously held municipal positions. The inscription was restored to read: 'Neikostratos, *oikonomos* of the colony [τὸν οἰκονόμον τῆς κολωνείας], twice the president of the games [δὶς ἀγωνοθέτην], having generously served as *agoranomos* [ἀγορανομήσαντα φιλοτείμως], having twice lavishly served as secretary [δὶς γραμματεύσαντα φιλοδόξως], having built the triclinium from its foundation, having laid the mosaic' (*SEG* 45.418).[64]

---

[61] During the republic and early empire, *coloniae* were newly established cities comprised largely of army veterans and freedmen settlers, while *municipia* were previously inhabited, conquered towns incorporated into the Roman state (Aulus Gellius, *Noct. att.* 16.13.8–9a); cf. Abbott and Johnson (1926: 3–9); Lintott (1993: 130).

[62] The confusion is due in part to the absence of a bilingual text from antiquity containing the Greek title and a Latin correlative.

[63] For *arcarius/dispensator*, see Cadbury (1931); Meggitt (1996); Friesen (2010). For *quaestor*, see Theissen (1974: 245); Goodrich (2010a); cf. A. Weiss (2010); Goodrich (2011). For *aedilis*, see *IKorinthKent* 232; Gill (1989); Clarke (1993: 46–56); Winter (1994: 179–97).

[64] Kokkotake (1992: 130). While the editors of *SEG* 45.418 have dated the inscription to the Roman period generally, through personal e-mail correspondence Joyce Reynolds has

Several details in this inscription are relevant for our enquiry. First, it is significant that Neikostratos, perhaps a freedman, was honoured here as the *oikonomos* of the colony after having held several prestigious posts earlier in his career. Of particular importance in Neikostratos' *cursus* is his tenure as ἀγωνοθέτης (cf. *Achaïe II* 136, 266).[65] The president of the games, as A. D. Rizakis indicates, was an office that only the wealthiest individuals of the city could afford to occupy: 'agonothètes et *munerarii* font partie de la tranche la plus riche de la société locale car ils sont appelés à faire des dépenses très élevées pour les jeux et les concours de la cité'.[66] The adverbs φιλοτείμως and φιλοδόξως also vividly describe the liberality of Neikostratos' previous administrations. They testify to the man's high social status while highlighting how he generously gave of his own wealth, probably in the form of benefactions – like the triclinium and mosaic (κατασκευάσαντα ἀπὸ θεμελίων τὸ τρέκλεινον ψηφοθετήσαντα) – in exchange for his offices and public admiration. As J. E. Lendon explains,

> In Greek, one of the usual terms for public benefaction was *phi-lo-timia*, an act of 'glory-love'. It was in honour terms that the rich man's motivation, involving so much trouble and expense, was chiefly understood: he devoted to the city his money and effort and got honour in return – cheering in the assembly and the voting of honorific decrees and monuments.[67]

In view of this description, it is clear that no mere slave (*arcarius/dispensator*) or aspiring citizen could have fitted Neikostratos' profile. Rather, as the text intimates, the office of *oikonomos* in an Achaean colony such as Patras was reserved for accomplished and highly visible aristocrats, and was indicative of social, economic, and political achievement.

Secondly, it should be observed how Neikostratos' *cursus* undermines the interpretation which equates the offices of οἰκονόμος and ἀγορανόμος in Achaean colonies. Bruce Winter, for example, seeking to identify Erastus the *oikonomos* from Rom 16.23 with Erastus the *aedilis* from *IKorinthKent* 232, has proposed that Corinth's unusual political structure permitted οἰκονόμος to be used interchangeably with ἀγορανόμος and ἀστυνόμος, two textually confirmed equivalents for *aedilis*.[68] However, Neikostratos' *cursus* in *SEG* 45.418 demonstrates that οἰκονόμος referred to a magistrate altogether separate from the ἀγορανόμος.

---

suggested to me that the lettering indicates a date perhaps no earlier than the late second century CE.

[65] Rizakis (1989: 184).   [66] Rizakis (1998: 30).   [67] Lendon (1997: 86).
[68] Winter (1994: 185–91); cf. Mason (1974: 175).

Still, the question remains. In Patras, to which magistracy did οἰκονόμος correspond? In Neikostratos' *cursus*, ἀγορανόμος (ἀγορανομέω) unquestionably corresponded to *aedilis*.[69] Moreover, since in Patras the Greek equivalents for *duovir* were στρατηγός (*Achaïe II* 110) and ἀρχὸς πενταέτηρος (*Achaïe II* 37),[70] the use of οἰκονόμος in Neikostratos' inscription indicates that he served as *quaestor*.[71] But where in the administrative hierarchy were *quaestores* located, and what kinds of administrative power and responsibility did they possess?

The reconstruction of the administrative structures of Roman colonies and *municipia* is made possible mainly through the remains of a number of Latin statutes. These texts were commissioned by the central Roman government in an effort to unify the civic administrations of their provincial settlements in the period when many of them were founded.[72] The *Lex Iulia Municipalis*, otherwise known as the *Tabula Heracleensis* (*ILS* 6085), for instance, is a collection of regulations instituted in 45/44 BCE to standardise local administration in the settlements both 'within the city of Rome or nearer the city of Rome than one mile' and 'in *municipia* or colonies or prefectures or *fora* or *conciliabula* of Roman citizens' (*passim*).[73] Equally significant are the remains of the four city charters discovered in Spain.[74] The *Lex Coloniae Genetivae Iuliae seu Ursonensis* (*ILS* 6087), for instance, comprises four bronze tablets from the colony of Urso dating to 45/44 BCE and contains many of the same stipulations concerning the responsibilities of the senate and the local magistrates included in the *Lex Iulia Municipalis*.

Both of these *leges* reveal much about how colonies were founded and governed in the late republic and early empire. Moreover, they have special relevance for this study because Corinth, as a Roman colony founded in early 44 BCE, was probably commissioned with a nearly identical charter.[75] Regrettably, neither the *Lex Iulia Municipalis* nor the *Lex Coloniae Genetivae Iuliae* mention the office of the *quaestor* or contain significant information concerning magisterial accountability. Much of this information, however, is supplemented by the well-preserved remains of three Spanish *municipium* charters dating to the Flavian period. The *Lex Salpensa* (*ILS* 6088), *Lex Malacitana* (*ILS* 6089), and

---

[69] Mason (1974: 19) equates ἀγορανομέω with *aedilis esse* in a municipal context.
[70] Rizakis (1998: 29).   [71] A. Weiss (2010: 578).
[72] Abbott and Johnson (1926: 57); Levick (1967: 80).
[73] Trans. Crawford 1.24.
[74] For the relevance of Spanish charters in the reconstruction of city constitutions across the empire, see, e.g., Curchin (1990: 12).
[75] Curchin (1990: 14).

Lex Irnitana are near-verbatim copies of what must have been a charter template and together provide close to a comprehensive account of city administration and magisterial responsibility in a typical Roman *municipium*. Using this assortment of laws and charters to inform our study, we can reconstruct the typical municipal government under the late republic and early empire in order to discover what administrative power was issued to and held over the municipal *quaestor*.

Hierarchy and responsibility

Political power in the ancient Roman city was unevenly shared between three civic institutions: the assembly of citizens (*comitia*), local senate (*ordo decurionum*), and magistrates (*magistratia*). Unlike the Hellenistic Greek city, power did not rest with the people or even the assembly. Rather, as in the lesser-privileged Greek cities under Rome, the only notable responsibility of the assembly was to elect civic magistrates nominated by the senate. Administrative power in the Roman colony and *municipium*, then, was entrusted to a few, the aristocrats, who controlled the primary decision-making bodies, the senate and the magistracies.

The *ordo* consisted of the local senators (*decuriones*), whose number differed between cities – being as low as 30, as high as 600, but often being around 100 – and was specified in the city's constitution (e.g. *Lex Irnitana* 31).[76] Candidates for admission to the *ordo* were elected annually and were required to meet basic legal, financial, and age qualifications before being elected by the existing decurions. Those qualifications ensured that the empowered elite maintained political authority and that any undesirable members were excluded.[77]

The magistrates were nominated annually from among the existing senators by the *ordo* and elected by the assembly. Candidates could not have held office within the five years leading up to their candidacy (*Lex Malacitana* 54/*ILS* 6089) and were expected to fund large portions of their own administrations, including certain expensive public services which were stipulated in the city constitution. The officials to be elected each year included two *duoviri*, two *aediles*, and in some cities two *quaestores*. Aspiring aristocrats often, but not always, progressed up the magisterial ranks according to the *cursus honorum*, taking office sequentially from *quaestor* to *aedilis* to *duovir*.[78]

---

[76] Curchin (1990: 22).   [77] Curchin (1990: 27).
[78] Curchin (1990: 29) doubts that there existed any fixed sequence.

The *duoviri* (*duumviri*) were the chief local dignitaries and presided over the senate. They also served as the judicial magistrates of the city. They might personally hear a number of smaller civil and criminal cases, although these cases could also be decided by juries made up of senators. The more costly and important cases were sent before the provincial governor, who became increasingly involved in local affairs through the centuries. Regarding the relationship of the *duoviri* to the lower magistracies, they possessed greater power than the *aediles* and *quaestores* and could apply *intercessio* against the acts of those lesser officials, provided this took place within three days of a complaint being received (*Lex Salpensa* 27/*ILS* 6088; *Lex Malacitana* 58/*ILS* 6089). The lesser officials, however, were not directly accountable to the *duoviri*. They were subject to the discretion of the *duoviri* in some administrative decision-making and could be prosecuted by them following their term, but the *duoviri* did not possess any direct political authority over the junior magistrates.

The *aediles* functioned as deputies to the *duoviri*. They might at times function in a judicial capacity, but were primarily entrusted with the management of public works and city maintenance, which involved overseeing the restoration of public roads and buildings as well as supervising the marketplace. Moreover, they were expected to sponsor annual athletic contests and religious festivals. Although little is said in the extant charters about the oversight of city finances by the *aediles*, there is little room to doubt that they handled public funds, especially in towns which had no *quaestor*.

The *quaestores* are completely absent in the earliest Spanish colony charters and may not have existed in all cities.[79] Therefore, not as much is known about their responsibilities and governing authority as that of the *duoviri* and *aediles*. What is known about the municipal *quaestores* in the provinces comes largely from the *Lex Irnitana*. Once in office, *quaestores* were responsible solely for the administration of public finances. As Chapter 20 of the charter indicates, 'The quaestors ... are to have the right and power [*ius potestasque*] of collecting, spending, keeping, administering and looking after the common funds ... at the discretion of the duumviri [*pecuniam commune ... exigendi erogandi custodiendi atministrandi dispensandi arbitratu{m}*

---

[79] Curchin (1990: 29–30): 'Clearly the quaestorship did not exist in all towns, and the quaestors' financial duties must have been undertaken by the other magistrates.' Cf. Bispham (2008: 332). Still, it is perhaps significant that certain Caesarian colonies elected *quaestores* (e.g. Tarraco), even though the office is not mentioned in the *Lex Ursonensis*; cf. Goodrich (2011).

IIuirorum].'[80] Even so, the quaestorship comprised considerably less political and judicial power than the senior magistracies. Although they were given command of their share of public slaves (*servi communes*), nowhere do the charters suggest that *quaestores* possessed any decision-making authority regarding public expenditures. Budget revisions were made by the senate in consultation with the *duoviri*, and instructions regarding public payments apparently came through the *duoviri* and at their discretion (*arbitratum*).[81] *Quaestores*, on the other hand, were simply entrusted with the unenviable task of making and receiving payments on behalf of the central treasury.

Regardless of the tedious nature of their work, *quaestores* were always assumed to possess high socio-economic status. According to Chapter 54 in the *Lex Malacitana* (*ILS* 6089), for instance, *quaestores* were required to be Roman citizens and *decuriones*, who were generally among the 100 wealthiest members of the city, possessing at least 100,000 sesterces (cf. Pliny, *Ep.* 1.19).[82] Chapter 60 in the *Lex Irnitana* additionally mandated all candidates for the quaestorship to deposit sizable 'securities' (*praedes*) for the office prior to the casting of votes on election day. Together these stipulations indicate that *quaestores* were prominent individuals in Roman communities, even if they lacked great administrative power. After all, Roman magistracies were indicative of social, rather than political, hierarchy, often requiring more personal munificence than professional competence.[83]

Political power in the Roman city, then, truly rested with the senate. This centralisation of administrative authority is underscored in Chapter 129 of the *Lex Ursonensis* (*ILS* 6087):

> Whoever shall be IIviri [*duoviri*], aediles, or prefect of the colonia Genetiva Iulia, and whoever shall be decurions of the colonia Genetiva Iulia, they are all diligently to obey and observe the decrees of the decurions without wrong deceit, and they are to see that whatever it shall be appropriate for any of them to undertake or do according to a decree of the decurions, they undertake or do all those things, as they shall deem it proper, without wrongful deceit.[84]

[80] For text, translation, and discussion, see Gonzalez and Crawford (1986); cf. Lebek (1994: 264–9).

[81] Rizakis (1998: 29).

[82] In most Roman cities magistrates were also required to be freeborn (cf. *Lex Malacitana* 54/*ILS* 6089), although exceptions were made in certain colonies; cf. Spawforth (1996: 169).

[83] Lendon (1997: 21).   [84] Trans. Crawford 1.25.

That all of the magistrates would be subject to the decrees and decisions of the *ordo* suggests that the senate had the final say in all matters relating to public policy.

Thus, even though the magistrates were entrusted with oversight of particular fields of administration, they – especially *quaestores* – were largely functionaries appointed to carry out the decisions of the *ordo*. It was the senate that was the ultimate decision-making body: the senate decided what buildings were to be erected, what expenses were to be paid, how taxes were to be collected, and what laws were to be passed.[85] They even functioned as the jury for many of the larger cases too important for the *duoviri* to decide themselves. But perhaps most significantly, the senate was the political body which called the magistrates to account.

Accountability

What is known from the remains of charters and *leges* about the accountability of magistrates in Roman colonies and *municipia* of the early empire suggests that cities feared very little that magistrates might abuse their political power. It was the senate, after all, that possessed the bulk of the city's decision-making power while functioning without any form of accountability to the general population. Thus, impeachment or political prosecution of magistrates for administrative corruption or negligence was not as much of a concern as in the Greek cities.

According to the charters, the primary administrative concern of the senate was embezzlement of public funds by those magistrates who had access to them. Therefore, instructions were provided mandating the provision of *praedes* by magisterial candidates prior to election. Chapter 60 of the *Lex Irnitana* and *Lex Malacitana* summarises the procedure:

> Those who in that municipium seek the duumvirate or the quaestorship … each of them, on the day on which the election is held, before the votes are cast, is to provide at the discretion of the person who holds that election *praedes* to the common account of the municipes, that their common funds which he handles in the course of his office will be kept safe for them (*ILS* 6089).[86]

These *praedes*, which could be paid for by the candidates directly or by bondsmen if the expense was too great, functioned as collateral on

---

[85] Curchin (1990: 59).
[86] For text, translation, and discussion, see Gonzalez and Crawford (1986).

behalf of the candidates ensuring that those magistrates who handled the public funds would not steal from the city treasury or flee from their responsibilities.[87]

With these deposits in hand, the primary means used by the senate to secure its treasury was a financial audit at the close of each magisterial term. As several *leges* indicate, each official was required to produce evidence for the purchases they made with community monies at the completion of their administration (*Lex Irnitana* 67).[88] If the accounts were found to be unbalanced or if the magistrate failed to provide sufficient documentation, the senate was able to appoint prosecutors, summon the alleged criminal before the senatorial court, and sue him for the money owed (*Lex Irnitana* 68–9). Beyond this, if a candidate refused to fulfil the duties of the office, he himself was liable for his obligations, but so were his bondsmen and his nominators. One can therefore imagine the pressure applied to an elected magistrate by his supporters to complete his term. Moreover, if a magistrate refused to fulfil his duties, the governor was entitled to intervene and compel him to complete his responsibilities (*Dig.* 50.4.9). Precautions were also instituted in order to prevent the official from fleeing the city. If, for example, a magistrate attempted to flee, then the city would seize his property and surrender all his possessions to his successor. And if he was caught, according to the early fourth-century CE Theodosian Code (12.1.16), the fugitive was forced to serve two terms rather than just one.[89] Such measures ensured the responsible completion of one's administration and show *quaestores* to be mainly functionaries in civic government.

Summary

In the preceding survey we encountered *oikonomoi* in three kinds of Graeco-Roman city and observed that the title carried slightly different connotations in each municipal context. After examining the role of *oikonomoi* in the political hierarchies of the Hellenistic Greek city, the Roman Greek city, and the Roman colony and *municipium*, we noted that the office was normally considered a civic magistracy (except in the few instances in the Roman period when the title referred to a public slave), and the responsibilities which were entrusted to these officials primarily and consistently included the administration of public finances,

---

[88] See also the *Lex Ursonensis* 80 (*ILS* 6087); *Lex Tarentina* 7–25 (*ILS* 6086).
[89] Abbott and Johnson (1926: 86).

particularly the payment of community expenses. The persons who occupied these prominent offices were therefore always citizens. And as political magistracies became monopolised by the socio-economic elite, the *oikonomos* became closely associated with public benefaction.

The social standing of these magistrates, however, did not have a direct bearing on the authority entrusted to them. Despite their social and legal privilege, *oikonomoi* possessed very little structural power. They had delegates at their disposal, but normally the officials who occupied the position were still considered administrative functionaries, serving as the bursar for the ruling body. The personal incentives for occupying this public office were also quite limited. Although serving as an *oikonomos/quaestor* functioned as one of several possible means of advancing one's social status, such honours were not accompanied by any immediate tangible or monetary benefits. Rather, as a public office, the position was normally quite costly, often requiring promises of munificence in order to receive election. But as long as one's administrative duties were fulfilled to the community's satisfaction, the annual term ended peacefully with a simple audit.

4

OIKONOMOI AS PRIVATE ADMINISTRATORS

> And summoning ten of his slaves, he gave them ten minas, and
> said to them, 'Conduct business with this until I come.'
>
> Luke 19.13

The private administrative sphere is the context in which *oikonomoi*
are most commonly attested. Scores of ancient literature, inscriptions, and papyri from across the Mediterranean basin and throughout
Graeco-Roman antiquity refer to these *oikonomoi* who served as managers of privately owned businesses and estates. The most voluminous
evidence for the service of private administrators in this area is ancient
literature, especially the economic handbooks from the Hellenistic
philosophical tradition. Many recent studies on ancient slavery, however, have distanced themselves from those literary sources, largely
because they are theoretical and prescriptive, as well as because they
present estate administration from the vantage point of the proprietor.
While recognising this perspective, the present investigation makes no
attempt to distance itself from those literary texts, since this chapter
seeks to produce a portrait of private administrators as they were popularly conceived. We are therefore just as interested in an imaginative
portrait of private administration as an actual one, and just as much
in the householder's point of view as the manager's. For these reasons,
the use of caricatures and stereotypes – even occasional depictions of
the 'perfect administrator' (ἀποτετελεσμένος ἐπίτροπος, Xenophon,
Oec. 13.3; *perfectus villicus*, Columella, *Rust.* 11.1.12) – will be useful for illuminating Paul's metaphor, especially when literary portrayals can be substantiated by real-life testimonies from inscriptions and
papyri.

Since much illuminating data derives from texts that refer to private administrators as something other than οἰκονόμοι, in the following
study we shall also use as supporting evidence (i) Greek sources which

prefer the titles ἐπίτροπος, πραγματευτής, and δοῦλος,[1] as well as (ii) Roman sources which employ Latin equivalents, such as *vilicus, actor, dispensator, institor*, and *servus*.[2] By supplementing our study with evidence that uses these correlative terms, we will benefit from a more comprehensive analysis of the *concept* of the private administrator without the liabilities that accompany surveys unnecessarily restricted to a single word. Moreover, the use of such (near) synonyms is especially important in this study since, while detailed descriptions of *oikonomoi* appear in literary sources from the Classical and Hellenistic Greek periods, the Latin *vilicus* and other titles are used far more abundantly and in more illuminating ways in the sources from the early empire.

In this chapter, then, we shall provide an overview of the private administrative sphere in order to show that business administrators were popularly conceived of as subordinate and servile managers subject to the total (structural and legal) dominance of the master and proprietor. They were responsible for the prosperity of the enterprise entrusted to them, which afforded them considerable representative authority over

---

[1] The relationship between οἰκονόμος and other Greek and Latin administrative titles is disputed. Aubert (1994: 33–4) suggests that οἰκονόμος corresponded to *vilicus*, and ἐπίτροπος to *procurator*. The epigraphic record, however, demonstrates that οἰκονόμος could be translated: *vilicus* (*CIL* III 447/*ILS* 1862; *CIL* III 555/*ILS* 1867); *actor* (*CIL* IX 425/*ILS* 3197/*IG* XIV 688, with *IGRR* 1.464/*CIG* 5875); and *dispensator* (*CIL* III 333/*ILS* 1539/*IGRR* 3.25; *SB* 6.9248). Moreover, that ἐπίτροπος can be translated *vilicus* is apparent when Columella (*Rust.* 11.1.5) quotes Cicero's translation of Xenophon (*Oec.* 12.3–4). Other Greek terms were also used for private administrators (e.g. χειριστής, φροντιστής). It is probable, then, that the Greek terms for private managers were somewhat interchangeable and could indicate a range of administrative roles; cf. Rathbone (1991: 62); Carlsen (1995: 15–16; 2002: 117–18).

[2] The Latin titles normally referred to specific administrative positions, although they evolved over time. Harrill (2006: 103–4) explains that in the Latin tradition the *ordo mancipiorum* had a threefold chain of command: (i) *procurator* (steward-attorney, or full representative), followed by (ii) *vilicus* (bailiff) and (iii) *praefectus, monitor*, or *magister* (overseer, foreman). Other designations were also utilised (*actor, atriensis, dispensator, institor*), but their specific functions varied according to context. For some of the regional complexities involving the use of both Greek and Latin terms, see Crawford (1976: 51–2). Despite the minor differences that may have existed between these administrators, their close conceptual overlap permits us to draw insights from a range of titles. As Tietler (1993: 210) explains,

> Although the mutual relationships between these *vilici, actores, oikonomoi, pragmateutai et ceteri*, the hierarchy among some of them and the precise content of their tasks are not as sufficiently known as one might wish, one thing at least seems clear: in one way or another they could be put in charge of the management, the supervision or the administration of an estate. In that respect it seems justified to place them together under a common denominator, regardless of subtle distinctions.

the workforce and in trade negotiations with third contracting parties. Finally, their loyalty to the owner's interests – demonstrated through obedience resulting in the moderate success of the business – determined whether the administrator would reap reward or punishment.

Hierarchy

While the employment of delegate estate managers was considered beneficial from very early in Graeco-Roman society, the title οἰκονόμος originally applied to the heads of households who personally supervised their own estates (Xenophon, *Oec.* 1.1–4; Aristotle, *Pol.* 1252a). But as estates grew larger, military and political obligations weightier, and the migration of rural settlers to urban centres more popular, the burden of running estates and directing labourers became heavier as well.[3] Landowners who desired to cultivate their estates while participating in non-agrarian interests were therefore forced to make a functional compromise: they developed various systems of absentee landownership involving the appointment of estate administrators. Not every estate owner could afford to entrust their livelihood to another, but this was often the solution for the elite. As Aristotle explains, '[A]ll people rich enough to be able to avoid personal trouble have a steward [ἐπίτροπος] who takes this office, while they themselves engage in politics and philosophy' (*Pol.* 1255b35–7).[4] Although absentee landownership during the fourth century BCE was perhaps a rare privilege even among the rich, by the second century BCE it had become quite commonplace among the landed elite to entrust the responsibilities of business administration to various kinds of delegate.[5]

[3] Aubert (1994: 120). Erdkamp (2005: 12) estimates that in antiquity roughly 80 per cent of the population was engaged in agriculture, a statistic which he claims is a 'commonplace' in historical scholarship. Whatever the actual percentage may be, we can concede that agriculture functioned as the base of the ancient economy and the vast majority of the population lived off what they could cultivate (Aristotle, *Pol.* 1256a38–40).

[4] Jameson (1978: 138): 'The richer might be able to leave the farm to a manager, or to oversee the work without dirtying their hands. But the bulk of the landowners would have been *autourgoi* and if possible would have purchased *oiketai* in order to have men work with them, *synergous.*' For business affairs as a distraction and an annoyance to elite estate owners, see the numerous complaints of Pliny the Younger (*Ep.* 2.15; 4.6; 5.14; 7.30; 9.15; 9.20; 9.36).

[5] Rostovtzeff (1957: 18); Aubert (1994: 121). Finley (1980: 83–4) argues that Rome had become a slave society no later than the third century BCE and implies that *vilici* would have been appointed regularly by then.

Subordination

Absentee landownership generally took one of two forms, tenancy or agency, the difference generally being in who made the payments and who kept the proceeds. Tenancy required an estate to be leased to an occupant farmer, who could further sublet the estate or cultivate the land personally with his own staff. The benefit for tenants was that, after the base amount was paid to the landlord (in cash and/or kind), they were able to keep the remainder of the yields for themselves. Agency, on the other hand, required estates to be entrusted to the care of managers, who then might lease all or parts of a property to tenants, farm the land personally, or supervise a team of their own labourers. In the agency model, landowners (κύριοι/*domini*) were entitled to the proceeds, but were also responsible for all of the estate's operating expenses and for maintaining the manager's loyalty.[6]

Despite its popularity during the early to mid republic, by the principate tenancy became the expert's preferred method of estate management.[7] In the first century CE, for example, Columella insisted that 'it is better for every kind of land to be under free farmers [*liberis colonis*] than under slave overseers [*vilicis servis*]' (*Rust.* 1.7.6), especially for distant estates out of easy reach of the owner. This warning, however, did not deter every estate owner from appointing agents. The model was used enough throughout the early empire that even Columella composed a detailed profile and job description for *vilici* and advised those property owners employing agents to purchase estates within easy reach of the city, in order to sustain the loyalty of the manager through the ever-present possibility of a surprise inspection (*Rust.* 1.1.18–1.2.1).

Whereas the relationship between the landowner and tenant could have entailed a number of reciprocal obligations and involved different kinds of power dynamics,[8] the relationship between the principal and agent was decidedly asymmetrical. Administrators were always subordinate to the principal, being ranked directly beneath either the master or a *procurator* (e.g. Pliny, *Ep.* 3.19),[9] as is apparent in a host of

---

[6] Even though additional management options existed which adopted features from both models, the simple distinction between tenancy and agency will suffice for this study. For more on tenancy, see, e.g., Frier (1980); de Neeve (1984); Foxhall (1990).

[7] Garnsey and Saller (1987: 72). Still, Aubert (1994: 133) admits the difficulty of discerning whether absentee landowners preferred one system over the other, demonstrating that 'in many cases agency existed side-by-side with tenancy and independent smallholdings, and that the various systems of management supplemented each other'.

[8] Foxhall (1990: 100–4).

[9] The *procurator*/ἐπίτροπος as agent of the master and superior of an οἰκονόμος/*vilicus* appears increasingly after the first century CE; cf. Schäfer (2001). Corsten (2005: 11–13)

inscriptions.[10] Because these texts are often quite brief, normally being religious tributes or funerary epitaphs, they usually fail to mention much more than the administrator's name, title, and principal. The name appears often – although not exclusively – as a nominative absolute, and the title in apposition to the name. Both commonly stand in close proximity to – sometimes even bracketing – the name of the principal, which normally appears as a possessive genitive, creating a formula bearing close resemblance to the slave–master construction found in many other Greek and Latin inscriptions (e.g. Φίλων Κλαυδίας Γαλλίτης οἰκονόμος, *SEG* 28.1034/*INikaia* 196).

Legal status

It is impossible to be certain about the legal status of every private administrator, but it is generally safe to assume that most were slaves (δοῦλοι/*servi*; e.g. *RECAM* 2.34; *ILS* 4199) and freedmen (ἀπελεύθεροι/*liberti*; e.g. *TAM* 3.258; *ILS* 7372). Even eminent ancient historian Moses Finley in his celebrated volume on *The Ancient Economy* could generalise that 'management throughout the classical period, Greek as well as Roman, urban as well as rural, was the preserve of slaves and freedmen'.[11] There are exceptions to this rule,[12] yet there remain two significant reasons for regarding estate managers and other private business administrators from the Roman period as normally having servile standing.

First, the nomenclature of private administrative texts indicates that most managers had slave origins. Typically, Roman freedmen are demarcated in the documentary evidence by the adoption of the praenomen and/or nomen (gentilicium) of their former master.[13] This is the case for a number of private administrators, such as (i) the *vilicus* Gnaeus Vergilius Nyrius, freedman of Gnaeus (*Cn. Vergilio Cn. l. Nyrio ... vilico*,

---

observes how an ἐπίτροπος supervising the entire Ummidii estate delegated its three divisions to πραγματευταί and proposes that a similar hierarchy may have also been present on the nearby estate of M. Calpurnius Longus, which attests to an ἐπίτροπος and οἰκονόμοι (18); cf. S. Mitchell (1993: 164).

[10] Cf. Goodrich (2010b: 275–8).

[11] Finley (1973: 75–6). For the servile status of *oikonomoi* in the Roman period, see Landvogt (1908: 8, 13).

[12] Philodemus indicates that some estate managers were free-born: 'And how can he [Pseudo-Aristotle/Theophrastus] say that there are two kinds of slaves, the overseer and the worker, while both of them can also be free men?' (*Oec.* 9.16–20; cf. Xenophon, *Mem.* 2.8.1–4). See further Beare (1978); Scheidel (1990). But the suggestion of Tietler (1993: 213) is to be preferred, who recommends that historians 'consider those who occupied functions as *vilicus, oikonomos, actor* and the like as slaves unless the contrary is proved'. Cf. Maróti (1976: 115).

[13] Duff (1928: 52–3); Treggiari (1969: 250–1); Mouritsen (2011: 39).

CIL III 7147), and (ii) Claudius Thallos, *oikonomos* of Gaius Claudius Calpornianus (Κλαύδιος Θάλλος Γ. Κλαυδίου Καλπορνιανοῦ οἰκονόμος, *SEG* 29.1306/*INikaia* 205).[14] Slaves, on the other hand, were identified simply by a personal name, as were (i) Eutychos, slave agent of Julia Tabille (Εὔτυχος Ἰουλίας Ταβίλλης δοῦλος πραγματευτής, *TAM* 5.442), and (ii) Artemon, slave *oikonomos* of Marcus Calpurnius Longus (Ἀρτέμων Μ. Καλπουρνίου Λόγγου δοῦλος οἰκονόμος, *SEG* 48.1606/*IGRR* 4.895).[15] It is therefore quite significant that seven of the ten *oikonomoi* identified by Thomas Corsten in his study of the Bithynian population have only one name, while Jean-Jacques Aubert observes – mostly on the basis of nomenclature – that less than 10 per cent of the *vilici* in Italy and Sicily were freedmen and none were freeborn.[16] Thus, even though the majority of inscriptions mentioning private administrators fail to identify their legal status explicitly, it is generally safe based on convention to assume the servility of private administrators with a single name.

Secondly, the limitations of the Roman law of commercial agency made the employment of dependent intermediaries, such as slaves and freedmen, the safest and most convenient means for transacting business.[17] Aaron Kirschenbaum offers four reasons why slaves were those 'psychologically best suited' to occupy these roles: (i) 'self-respecting free men were unwilling to accept positions in which they had to obey the orders of an employer';[18] (ii) 'employers preferred to utilize the services of men whose character they knew and on whose obedience they could rely'; (iii) 'slaves could be chastised if they disobeyed instructions'; and (iv) 'slaves had formed the habit of executing their masters' orders'.[19]

[14] For *vilici* as freedmen, see Duff (1928: 93); Treggiari (1969: 106–10).

[15] Joshel (1992: 39), while conceding that 'a single name is not as secure an indication of servile status as a nomen is of free status', cautiously maintains that individuals with single personal names were normally slaves. For more on how to determine legal status, see Weaver (1972: 42–86); McLean (2002: 112–48, esp. 129–31).

[16] Corsten (2006: 89); Aubert (1994: 149–57).

[17] A. Watson (1987: 90–114); Andreau (1999: 64–70). This was the case in the western and eastern parts of the empire, even Roman Palestine (Hezser 2005: 275–84; cf. Udoh 2009: 315–24). Slave agency was more significant in Roman than in Greek law, largely because slaves were members of the Roman *familia*, and thus fell within the *potestas* of the *paterfamilias*. Slaves in the Greek *oikos*, on the other hand, were only considered property; cf. Pomeroy (1997: 21).

[18] There also existed a general disdain for commerce among the Roman elite; cf. D'Arms (1981); Pleket (1983); Wallace-Hadrill (1991); Andreau (1999: 9–29).

[19] Kirschenbaum (1987: 32). He also notes that 'the superior *savoir-faire* as well as the unscrupulous character of many hellenized Orientals that had been brought as slaves to Rome were the concomitant personal and psychological qualities that account for their generally uninhibited dynamic activity in the field of commerce and for their specific usefulness as agents' (149). It is additionally worth noting that slaves who were old enough to

But beyond these 'psychological' bases, Kirschenbaum explains that in Rome the employment of slave and freed agents was additionally beneficial on legal and pragmatic grounds.

To begin with, transacting business in the Roman world was complicated by the fact that there existed no law of direct agency. While free agents (e.g. clients, friends) could act as intermediaries in the negotiation of contracts and the transferral of property on behalf of a business owner (Gaius, *Inst.* 2.90–2),[20] third contracting parties were reluctant to make payments to free agents since there was no universal, extemporaneous legal device established to ensure the proceeds would be subsequently transferred to the intended party. Certain legal arrangements (*locationes conductio*; *mandata*; *negotiora gestio*) and legal remedies (*actiones*) were introduced to commercial law that made the principal responsible for specific liabilities incurred by an agent, but generally the principal himself remained unprotected if the agent was free.[21]

Roman law, however, possessed a built-in system of non-contractual obligations that permitted the heads of households (*paterfamiliae*) to make various kinds of commercial transactions (provisions and acquisitions) through certain household members. As the second-century CE jurist Gaius states, 'Acquisitions come to us not only by our own acts, but also through those whom we hold in *potestas*' (*Inst.* 2.86).[22] The *potestas*, or power of the head of the family, extended over not only one's wife and children, but also one's slaves. Because everything these dependants possessed practically (*de facto*) belonged legally (*de iure*) to the head of the household, whatever they acquired through their monetary grant (*peculium*) likewise became the property of the *paterfamilias/dominus* (Gaius, *Inst.* 2.87, 89).[23] This was also the case in Rabbinic Jewish practice. As the Tosefta states, 'The son who does business with what belongs to the father, and likewise the slave who does business with what belongs to his master, behold, they [the proceeds] belong to the father, they [the proceeds] belong to the master' (*t. B. Qam.* 11.2).[24] But despite the representative privileges slaves retained, in their commercial capacity they could not bring injury upon

---

serve in administration normally acquired significant education and experience growing up in the household and on the estates of their masters (Columella, *Rust.* 11.1.7); cf. Aubert (1994: 151).

[20] It was illegal for unqualified free men to act as intermediaries (Gaius, *Inst.* 2.95).

[21] Aubert (1994: 40–116).   [22] Trans. Zulueta.

[23] For more on the *peculium*, see Buckland (1908: 187–238); Zeber (1981); Kirschenbaum (1987: 31–88); Watson (1987: 90–101); Andreau (2004); Aubert (2009).

[24] For more on Rabbinic laws of commercial agency, see Hezser (2005: 276–82).

the master. As Kirschenbaum explains, '[A] person in *potestas* could not worsen the condition of the head of family economically or legally. Thus, a subordinate in power could neither create obligations for his master nor render him liable to suit. Moreover, since a slave could not be hailed into court ... it was useless to bring an action against [him].'[25] The liability of the slave was always limited to the extent of his *peculium*. Thus, while certain limitations remained, the use of slaves in commerce was often very advantageous.

Freedmen, on the other hand, whose ties of *potestas* were severed by manumission, also frequently functioned as agents for their former masters.[26] The freedman's competence in business administration was often derived from his prior education and experience as a commercial slave. But while many of the freedman's commercial dealings following manumission aimed to generate profit for himself, a significant portion of his efforts continued to be rendered on behalf of his patron, as was both customary and compulsory. As the jurist Ulpian states, 'A freedman and a son should always consider the person of a father and a patron honourable and inviolable' (*Dig.* 37.15.9; cf. *Lex Irnitana* 97).[27]

The filial reverence that the freedman owed to his former master was commonly described as deference (*obsequium*) and duty (*officium*), and was routinely exhibited in the freedman's fulfilment of certain services (*operae*) for his patron. These services, being semi-contractual by virtue of 'the oath of the freedman' (*iusiurandum liberti*, Gaius, *Inst.* 3.96), were legally binding and customarily rendered as payment for manumission.[28] But besides the formal, legal dimension of these obligations, the principle of loyalty (*fides*) served as an additional basis for the freedman's continued labour. Collectively, these factors contributed to the regular employment of freedmen as commercial agents. Thus, even without explicit mention of legal status in most of the documentary evidence, it can be deduced, with W. V. Harris, that '[a]mong the Romans it was largely freedmen and slaves ... who managed the commercial enterprises'.[29]

Once it is realised that private administrators were normally slaves and freedmen, their subordinate rank and compulsory obedience to their master or patron become more apparent. In antiquity it was simply accepted that 'the free rules [ἄρχει] the slave' (Aristotle, *Pol.*

---

[25] Kirschenbaum (1987: 38).
[26] Mouritsen (2011: 206–47, esp. 213–22).   [27] Trans. Watson.
[28] Duff (1928: 36–49); Treggiari (1969: 68–81); Mouritsen (2011: 51–65).
[29] W. V. Harris (2000: 732–3).

1260a10).[30] As Peter Garnsey explains, 'The slaveowner's rights over his slave-property were total, covering the person as well as the labour of the slave.'[31] K. R. Bradley clarifies the asymmetry and exploitative nature of slavery in Roman society:

> In the master–slave relationship ... there were no restricting factors: the slave was at the complete and permanent disposal of the master and except by an act of resistance could never find relief from the necessity of obeying because there were no countervailing rights or powers in the condition of slavery itself to which the slave had recourse. From the slave it was complete submission that the master expected.[32]

Bradley's portrayal is also the perception of slavery represented in much ancient popular literature. In Chariton's mid-first-century CE novel, the administrator (διοικητής) Leonas, speaking to his master Dionysius about the newly acquired slave Callirhoe, remarked, 'You are her master, with full power over her, so she must do your will whether she likes it or not [κύριος γὰρ εἶ καὶ τὴν ἐξουσίαν ἔχεις αὐτῆς, ὥστε καὶ ἑκοῦσα καὶ ἄκουσα ποιήσει τὸ σοὶ δοκοῦν]' (*Chaer.* 2.6.2). As slaves, then, administrators were considered forced labour, mere chattel, and basically powerless with respect to their masters.

The outlook of most freedmen was not markedly different from that of a slave, as noted above. Caught somewhere between the status of slavery (*servitus*) and that of the freeborn person (*ingenuitas*), freedmen often enjoyed the privileges of citizenship, even while maintaining the stigma of servility (*macula servitutis*), as they continued to labour under the subjugation of the propertied class.[33] More on the low social status of slave administrators will be addressed in Chapter 6. For now, however, we conclude that private administrators gazing up the chain of command, even in the physical absence of their masters or patrons, perceived themselves as delegates, and were fully aware of their vulnerability to the power of their superiors.

---

[30] The *Digest* defines the slave as one who is 'subjected to an alien dominion' (*Dig.* 1.5.4.1). For a survey of ancient ideologies of slavery, see Garnsey (1996). For a modern sociological analysis of the institution, see Patterson (1982: 13), who famously defines slavery as 'the permanent, violent domination of natally alienated and generally dishonored persons'.

[31] Garnsey (1996: 1); cf. Finley (1980: 77).   [32] Bradley (1994: 5).

[33] Andreau (1993: 179); Mouritsen (2005: 62); Mouritsen (2011: 10–35). For the assimilation of freedmen, see Petersen (2006: 228).

Authority

Though subordinate to a principal and often of marginal socio-legal status, estate managers and business administrators normally occupied an
elevated position within the household or managerial unit to which they
were assigned. Due to their aptitude for business, for instance, freedmen administrators during the Roman period were commonly appointed
as legal guardians (*tutores*) of free minors and their patrimonies (Dio
Chrysostom, *Or.* 73.3; Philo, *Prob.* 35). These assignments attributed
to the administrator authority (*auctoritas*) to make investment decisions with respect to the ward's property, especially while the heir was
an infant (*Dig.* 26.1.1.pr; 41.2.32.2). Paul himself drew on this custom,
comparing the provisional authority of the Mosaic Law (Gal 4.1–5) to
that of guardians and managers (ἐπιτρόπους ... καὶ οἰκονόμους).[34]

Beyond guardianship appointments, most private administrators also
supervised a team of subordinate labourers (*subiecti*; cf. Columella,
Rust. 1.8.10). This workforce, which consisted largely of fellow slaves,
provided the administrator with extensive structural leverage with which
to issue commands. Just as the master was known 'to rule [*imperare*]
his slaves' (Cicero, *Resp.* 3.37), so the administrator was placed over
a business 'to rule [ἄρχειν] the labourers' (Xenophon, *Oec.* 12.3). But
the administrator's authority to command (*auctoritatem ad imperium,*
Columella, *Rust.* 1.8.3) did not originate with him. As the owner's representative, the administrator 'had provisionally been entrusted with some
of the powers of the *pater familias*'.[35] K. D. White reiterates this point:
'Where the owner was normally non-resident, the steward (*vilicus*) was
given virtually complete authority over the entire staff, whether of free
or of servile status.'[36] As one first-century BCE literary fragment reads,
'To be a bailiff far from the city, where the master seldom comes, is, in
my opinion, not to be a bailiff, but to be the master [*non vilicari, sed
dominari*]' (*CRF* 45–6).[37]

The same derivative authority was also afforded to the *dispensator.*
As urbanised accounting clerks of exceptionally large *familiae*, *dispensatores* did not normally oversee large workforces like *vilici* and
actores, but still acquired numerous personal slaves (*vicarii*/οὐικάριοι;

---

[34] Garnsey (1997: 106); Goodrich (2010b).
[35] Carlsen (1995: 75).   [36] K. D. White (1970: 350).
[37] Cited by Carlsen (1995: 77); Maróti (1976: 117). Carlsen supposes that the power of
the manager increased in direct proportion to the owner's ability to control him. Thus, the
greater the distance from the master to the estate, the greater the opportunity for the manager to do what he wished (78).

cf. *P.Oxy.* 735 (lines 6–7)) attached to their *peculia* and handled considerable sums of money in their master's name.[38] This was especially the case for the *dispensatores* and other intermediate clerical aids belonging to the household of Caesar (cf. *ILS* 1514).[39] Such administrators in the *familia Caesaris* – though technically neither regal officials in the Hellenistic sense nor public servants in the municipal sense, and also somewhat distinct from other private administrators in terms of the scale of their operations – managed the accounts of various departments and enterprises attached to the imperial administration, and thus possessed unique opportunities to exploit their master's purse and power for their own socio-economic gain.

More on the administrator's supervisory responsibilities, especially those of the *vilicus*, will be discussed below. It will suffice now simply to underscore that his 'managerial functions', as Aubert notes, 'were the source of considerable power for the *vilicus*, and the basis of patronage in the countryside'.[40]

Responsibilities

Administrators were normally responsible for supervising a branch of a particular business, whether appointed to a rural estate (*villa rustica*), a factory (*officina*), or an urban shop (*taberna*). *Vilici* and *actores*, for instance, have been attested in a number of private contexts, including mines (*CIL* X 1913), aqueducts (*CIL* X 3967), baths (*CIL* VI 8676), libraries (*CIL* VI 8744), gardens (*CIL* VI 623/*ILS* 3521), apartments (*CIL* VI 9483), amphitheatres (*CIL* VI 10163/*ILS* 5155), and granaries (*CIL* VI 36786).[41] *Dispensatores* managed military funds (*CIL* VI 8516, 8517, 33737), schools (*CIL* VI 10166), crops (*CIL* VI 544, 634, 8472), and gardens (*CIL* VI 8667, 8675), among other things.[42] Naturally, the commercial context and social location determined the scope of the administrator's tasks. But aside from minute differences, the general responsibilities of most private administrators were very similar,[43] usually involving 'the

---

[38] Carlsen (1992); Carlsen (1995: 147–58, esp. 151).

[39] Weaver (1972: 200–6). For imperial *oikonomoi*, see Strabo, *Geogr.* 17.1.12; Swiderek (1970: 159–60); Brunt (1975: 140).

[40] Aubert (1994: 171). For managerial slaves and patronage, see D. B. Martin (1990: 22–49).

[41] Carlsen (1995: 31–43). For the administrative staff of imperial mines, see Hirt (2010: 251–8).

[42] Carlsen (1992: 97); Carlsen (1995: 151).

[43] According to the jurist Pomponius, 'The man in charge of a block of flats is not very different from a bailiff, but he lives among urban slaves' (*Dig.* 50.16.166pr). Even Aubert

supervision of real estate and possibly other slaves'.[44] Given these basic areas of oversight, it should be noted that the chief objective of estate and business administration in antiquity was to yield some measure of monetary gain (κέρδος/*fructus*).[45] For this reason, it is important to begin our survey of the responsibilities of private administrators with a brief overview of the financial goals of business owners themselves.

Financial productivity

It is commonly acknowledged that in Graeco-Roman antiquity the vast majority of people from the free population who were not tenants were small-landholding peasants who lived at or near subsistence level.[46] Because survival was routinely at stake, these peasant landowners neither took great risks in their land development strategies nor sought to produce much beyond that which was required to meet their immediate needs.[47] Moreover, because this large portion of the landowning population was actively involved in the cultivation of their own properties, they did not appoint managers to run their estates.[48]

(1994: 38), who observes with respect to *institores* few strict commonalities between them, suggests that they at least shared similar administrative skills and duties. There was, however, a great social divide between urban and rural life which extended even to slaves. As MacMullen (1974: 31) explains, '[A]way from the city each mile marked a further deviation from correctness.' The rural estate manager could therefore sense some inadequacy when in the territory of his urban counterpart (cf. Plautus, *Cas.* 97–103). The absence of urban luxuries on country estates also affected the appeal of being assigned to a rural post. Accordingly, Columella warned not to appoint a city slave as a rural *vilicus* for want of the city's entertainment (*Rust.* 1.8.1–2), while Trimalchio mentions that after being suspected of abusing his mistress, he was punished by being banished to a country stewardship (*vilicatio*, Petronius, *Satyr.* 69). Horace learned the hard way, having once relocated an urban slave longing for the countryside to his Sabine farm, only to have the new *vilicus* grumble over what he missed in the city (*Ep.* 1.14.14–15).

[44] Carlsen (1995: 31). Chrysippus (*c.* 280–207 BCE) defines administration (οἰκονομία) in similar terms: 'as an arrangement concerned with expenditures and tasks and has to do with the care of possessions and of those who work on the land' (Stobaeus, *Ecl.* 2.95.12–14).

[45] Garnsey (1982: 105) indicates that the service of business slaves involved in the first place 'the creation of profit … on behalf of masters', and was made possible through 'their possession of a *peculium*'.

[46] Finley (1973: 105); Garnsey and Saller (1987: 43).

[47] Erdkamp (2005) suggests that while enough of a surplus would have been sought to fulfil community obligations, for smaller-scale peasant farmers 'long-term subsistence was prized higher than short-term profit' (96). He observes further that small landholders generally adopted a 'constrained profit maximisation' approach, whereby 'peasants pursue profit only within the limits that are set by their primary goal of long-term security' (100).

[48] Maróti (1976: 109) notes that the employment of an estate manager is '[t]he fundamental difference between the small-peasant farming based on autarchy, and the organization of the Villa-farmstead aimed at production for the market'.

The financial security of absentee landowners, on the other hand, afforded them other investment options. Living well above subsistence, owners of large estates who could afford to appoint managers established a variety of economic goals and implemented a range of administrative strategies, normally utilising their estates as a means for long-term investment. According to some ancient theorists, estate owners as well as managers were to seek to *maximise* profits.[49] The Greek philosophers, for instance, generally maintained that the very objective of private administration (οἰκονομία/οἰκονομικός) is to generate income.[50] The fourth-century BCE philosopher Xenophon reported how Critobulus informed Socrates that 'the business of a good estate manager [οἰκονόμου ἀγαθοῦ] is to manage his own estate well [εὖ]' (*Oec.* 1.2). While the appropriateness of the adverb εὖ would be contested outright three centuries later by Philodemus, it is clear from elsewhere in Xenophon's discourses that the ἀγαθὸς οἰκονόμος – who for Xenophon is a *free* gentleman farmer – should seek to increase one's assets, since as an expert investor he knew the right times to make purchases and the best ways for generating profit (*Mem.* 2.10.4; 3.4.11). For Xenophon, then, οἰκονομία, as the discipline of the οἰκονόμος, is the knowledge 'by which men can increase [αὔξειν] estates' (*Oec.* 6.4), and making large profits is its chief objective.[51]

Aristotle later downplayed the profit-generating responsibility of the *oikonomos* by drawing a distinction between money-making (χρηματιστική) and administration (οἰκονομική). According to Aristotle, 'the function of the former [i.e. χρηματιστική] is to provide [πορίσασθαι] and that of the latter [i.e. οἰκονομική] to use [χρήσασθαι]' (*Pol.* 1256a11–13). Thus, for Aristotle, riches (πλοῦτος) were simply tools (ὄργανα) which administrators use to manage the household (*Pol.* 1256b37–8). Pseudo-Aristotle, however, returned to Xenophon's perspective by emphasising the need for administrators both to obtain and employ wealth. According to Pseudo-Aristotle, οἰκονομική 'tells us first how to acquire a household [κτήσασθαι οἶκον] and then how to conduct its affairs [χρήσασθαι αὐτῷ]' (Aristotle, *Oec.* 1343a9). His profile of the ideal *oikonomos* reflected both of these aspects:

> There are four qualities which the [*oikonomos*] must possess in dealing with his property. Firstly, he must have the faculty of

[49] Aubert (2000: 93–4) differentiates between the *strategic* (global, long-term) decisions made by entrepreneurs and the *tactical* (narrower, short-term) decisions made by business managers. Even if such a distinction existed, the quantitative aspect of their investment goals was probably closely aligned.
[50] Spahn (1984); Natali (1995).
[51] Pomeroy (1994: 52); Pomeroy (1997: 22).

acquiring, and secondly that of preserving what he has acquired; otherwise there is no more benefit in acquiring than in baling with a colander, or in the proverbial wine-jar with a hole in the bottom. Thirdly and fourthly, he must know how to improve his property, and how to make use of it; since these are the ends for which the powers of acquisition and of preservation are sought.

(*Oec.* 1344b22–8)

According to this later Aristotelian tradition, money-making (χρηματιστική) was an important component of the larger discipline of administration (οἰκονομική). The ἀγαθὸς οἰκονόμος, then, was required to *acquire, retain, multiply,* and *utilise* property for the benefit of the household.

The first-century BCE philosopher Philodemus later disputed these definitions due to their implicit promotion of material greed. As an Epicurean, Philodemus rejected both poverty and wealth, and combated any philosophy that led to either of those two conditions. As Reumann explains,

> The basic problem for an Epicurean discussing *oikonomia* in the first century B.C. – when his philosophy still stood for an absence of pain and a neutral state of feeling as the goal, not sensual self-indulgence, as in its later perversion – was the fact that household management was *popularly* interpreted to mean money-making; but to an Epicurean the goal of this science was only to provide a comfortable living according to a mean of expediency.[52]

Philodemus' major opponents with respect to household management were Xenophon and Pseudo-Aristotle (Theophrastus). Philodemus' primary critique was directed at Xenophon's use of εὖ in *Oec.* 1.2. For the Epicurean to live and manage 'well' implied that he should live and manage comfortably, but also simply rather than lavishly, as Philodemus interpreted Xenophon to mean. In his treatise, then, Philodemus sought to explain 'not how to live nobly in a household [οὐχ ὡς ἐν οἴκωι καλῶς ἔστιν], but how one must take a stand regarding the acquisition and pres-ervation of property [ἀλλ᾽ ὡς ἵστασθαι δεῖ περὶ χρημάτων κτήσεώς τε καὶ φυλακῆς], with which *oikonomia* and *oikonomikos*, it is agreed, are strictly concerned' (*Oec.* 12.6–12).[53] Philodemus therefore distinguished himself from his predecessors by his emphasis on the preservation

---

[52] Reumann (1957: 193).   [53] Trans. adapted from Balch (2004).

(φυλακή) rather than the use and increase of property. He also explained that a philosopher should have a 'moderate mean of wealth [πλούτου μέτρον]' (*Oec.* 12.17–19), insisting on neither extreme prosperity nor poverty, but happiness and expediency. Still, financial productivity remained part of the administrator's concern. As Philodemus explained, 'We would say that the good household manager [τὸν ἀγαθὸν οἰκονόμον] is the provider of possessions and goods [τὸν κτημάτων καὶ χρημάτων ποριστήν] ... which he sets in order [ἃ διοικονομεῖ], and his function is to manage a household happily [τὸ μακαρίως οἶκον οἰκεῖν]' (*Oec.* 3a.6–14).

While the Greek philosophers debated the relationship between financial productivity and administration, their emphasis on profit-making was perpetuated in the Latin tradition. Varro, for instance, advised the estate owner to seek from his investments both 'profit and pleasure' (*utilitatem et voluptatem*), that is, both material return (*fructum*) and enjoyment (*delectationem*). Significantly, Varro immediately clarified that '[t]he profitable [*utile*] plays a more important role than the pleasurable' (Varro, *Rust.* 1.4.1; cf. 1.2.8; 1.16.2–3; 3.2.15–17).[54] Echoing Varro's concerns, Cicero underscored the importance of deriving profit from estate management when he asked, 'Which of us may not survey his estate or go to see his rural concerns, whether in quest of profit or of amusement [*vel fructus causa, vel delectationis*]?' (*De or.* 1.58.249).

The emphasis in Columella's treatise is even stronger. For one, Columella describes his target audience as the 'attentive head of a household [*diligens pater familiae*], whose heart is set on pursuing a sure method of increasing his fortune [*rei familiaris augendae*] from the tillage of his land' (*Rust.* 1.1.3).[55] His detailed discussion on the operation of a vineyard (*Rust.* 3.3) has been considered '[p]ossibly the single most important piece of evidence ... suggestive of the existence of capitalism in Roman agriculture'.[56] Not only do Columella's remarks on viticulture present 'valuable insights as regards the general attitude towards business and money making in Roman times', but '[h]is work is most illuminating as to the precise extent estate owners oriented their activities towards the generation of monetary profits'.[57] Well aware of these observations about estate *ownership*, White applied the point to estate *management*: 'In the

---

[54] Love (1986: 123) considers it 'undeniable' that the estates about which Varro writes 'are implicated to varying degrees in profit making'.
[55] Steiner (1954: 88): 'The whole point of Columella's handbook of course is to provide the special knowhow to guarantee that the hardships and the toil of farming will not be in vain but result in profit for the owner and in useful products to benefit society in general.'
[56] Love (1986: 124).   [57] Love (1986: 127).

appointment of a *vilicus* ... the sole consideration is the economic one of obtaining a *maximum* return for the heavy expenditure by placing the responsibility on the shoulders of one whose tact and firmness in handling the staff were matched by dependability and integrity.'[58]

It is significant to note, however, that even as some ancient economic theorists emphasised the pursuit of large, indeed optimised profits, it is also apparent that in antiquity certain, perhaps many, wealthy landowners preferred to minimise risk by implementing sensible, long-term production strategies on their landed investments at the expense of a considerable and immediate return.[59] Columella, for example, despite having the profit-seeking agenda just mentioned, prescribed a rather conservative approach in his instructions on viticulture. He affirms – contrary to his contemporaries – that 'the return from vineyards is a very rich one [*uberrimum esse reditum vinearium*]' (*Rust.* 3.3.2), and that it is 'consistent with good business to plant them' (3.3.15).[60] Still, Columella himself favoured – again, relative to other farmers – a steady and enduring production strategy, assured that his methods would reap greater dividends over time than the strategies of those who were less risk-averse. Columella's conservatism is especially apparent in his criticisms of those maximalists who 'strive for the richest possible yield at the earliest moment; they make no provision for the time to come, but, as if living merely from day to day, they put such demands upon their vines and load them so heavily with young shoots as to show no regard for succeeding generations' (3.3.6).

Furthermore, Dennis Kehoe in his studies on the letters of Pliny the Younger (esp. *Ep.* 3.19; 9.37) and several large estates in early Roman Egypt observes that certain senators purchased and cultivated large tracts of land not as a means to generate great profits and social advancement, but to secure a comparatively modest yet dependable return.[61] While he

---

[58] K. D. White (1970: 350–1, emphasis added).

[59] This would seem to challenge the view of Erdkamp (2005: 103), who argues, 'In general, risk aversion declines as wealth rises.' Nevertheless, relative to their lower-class counterparts, wealthy landowners still received sizable returns from their estates, as is apparent through their lavish life-styles and expensive civic benefactions; cf. Finley (1973: 103).

[60] Columella insists that those who take care in their viticulture 'will easily outdo in the increase of their ancestral estates all those who hold fast to their hay and pot-herbs. And he is not mistaken in this; for, like a careful accountant, he sees, when his calculations are made, that this kind of husbandry is of the greatest advantage to his estate [*maxime rei familiari conducere*]' (*Rust.* 3.3.7).

[61] Kehoe (1992: 168): 'This income depended primarily on the landowner's ability to achieve a sufficient level of productivity from his property, while his security required him to keep as low as possible the investment necessary to achieve this level of productivity.' Cf. Kehoe (1988); Kehoe (1989); Kehoe (1993); de Neeve (1990).

acknowledges that some landowners profited enormously from risky land-based investments (e.g. Pliny the Elder, *Nat.* 14.49–51), Kehoe has shown that others – perhaps due to the unpredictability of droughts in the Mediterranean region, or the uncertainty of the Nile's flooding – implemented rather conservative approaches to agricultural production with the intention of obtaining steady and lasting revenue.[62] Admittedly, Kehoe has been criticised in some cases for forcing the documentary evidence from Egypt to fit the model he abstracts from the investment strategies of Pliny.[63] But, even still, the data he gathers which does fit his model require us to adjust our suppositions about the investment goals of absentee landowners.

If, then, the primary goal of estate and business administration was social and economic security through slow and steady profits – at least for those wealthy enough to appoint an administrator – then it is reasonable to surmise that the financial aims and production methods of estate and commercial managers were somewhat modest as well. This, in fact, is what is perceived from some popular Graeco-Roman literature, particularly biblical parables. Commercial agents in the Synoptic gospels are responsible, on the one hand, solely for increasing their employers' property. In the Parable of the Unjust Steward, for instance, the *oikonomos* initially is threatened with termination and abandonment for squandering his master's wealth (Luke 16.1). But by the end of the narrative, the *oikonomos* is praised (ἐπαινέω), not for demanding the debts owed to his master *in their entirety*, but for prudently (φρονίμως) reducing them enough probably to coax the debtors to make payment while satisfying his master's financial expectations (v. 8).[64] Since such a tactic elicits commendation, it seems reasonable to conclude that the administrator was responsible only for producing a moderate return.

This is also the caricature of the good (and faithful) slave in the Parable of the Talents and the Parable of the Ten Mina (Matt 25.14–30//Luke 19.11–27).[65] In both accounts commercial agents were responsible not

---

[62] Garnsey and Saller (1987: 74):

> Landowners had a strictly limited notion of profit and how to seek it, and a gravely defective method of calculating it... Attitudes to profit-seeking in agriculture differed, even among the aristocracy. Yet profit-seeking is not the same as profit maximization, and a value system that put a premium on wealth-consumption could not at the same time promote productive investment.

[63] Cf. Bagnall (1993).   [64] Cf. Goodrich (forthcoming).

[65] On the relationship between the two parables, see Snodgrass (2008: 523–5). Neither version employs strictly administrative titles, but Matthean parables often use δοῦλος to denote slave administrators (cf. Matt 24.45//Luke 12.42). Luke's use of πραγματεύομαι

simply for maintaining the master's investments, but for increasing his possessions.[66] The more each agent earned, the more they were entrusted at their master's return. The need to generate a profit is further under-scored in each narrative through the case of the wicked (and lazy) slave. The failure of the slave to invest his allowance resulted in his dismissal and violent death (Matt 25.26–30//Luke 19.24–7). The gruesome finale, even if somewhat hyperbolic, illustrates the urgency laid upon the slave to generate profit, while also showing the uselessness of the one who failed to do so. But it is perhaps equally surprising to notice that the mas-ter's expectation of the final slave was not, it would seem, beyond reason. While a profit was required, the master's investment goals seem rather modest, since the minimal bank interest such a small deposit could have generated would have been sufficient to meet the master's demands and spare the slave his life (Matt 25.27//Luke 19.23).

Finally, Jesus' remarks following the Parable of the Faithful and Wise Steward (Luke 12.42–8) likewise indicate that an agent who was appointed to an estate was expected to multiply what had been entrusted to him.[67] As Jesus is reported to have explained, 'From everyone to whom much [πολύ] has been given, much [πολύ] will be required; and from the one to whom much [πολύ] has been entrusted, *even more* [περισσότερον] will be demanded' (Luke 12.48).[68] But while Jesus' remark implies that a profit had to be earned, he does not suggest that a maximum return was expected. Generating especially large profits, in fact, could have been problematic for the estate manager. As Jesper Carlsen explains,

> The bailiff did not have any incentive to boost the farm's pro-duction or increase its profits year after year, as that could cre-ate expectations from the owner of a constantly rising yield; expectations which would be still more difficult to meet if the means of production remained unchanged; therefore the easiest and safest thing for the *vilicus* was to keep production ticking over at a level which could be reached without problems year after year.[69]

(19.13) suggests a managerial position similar to that of an οἰκονόμος. For managerial slav-ery in Matthew, see Glancy (2002: 112–22).

[66] Cf. κερδαίνω, Matt 25.16, 17, 20, 22; πραγματεύομαι, Luke 19.13; διαπραγματεύομαι, Luke 19.15. The force of πραγματεύομαι is 'make a profit'; cf. Mauer (1968: 641); Bock (1996: 1533); Snodgrass (2008: 532).

[67] Green (1997: 504).

[68] Even though the term οἰκονόμος is replaced with δοῦλος following verse 42, the administrator remains in view throughout the parable; cf. K.-J. Kim (1998: 137).

[69] Carlsen (1995: 74).

Since a satisfactory return from a landed investment was relative to the kind and size of the enterprise in view as well as the aims of the individual entrepreneur, it is impossible to be precise about how productive administrators were expected to be in each circumstance. We can generalise, however, that it was always advantageous for estate and business owners to find an ambitious administrator, one who, as Socrates described, was 'covetous of gain [φιλοκέρδεια] in a moderate degree' (Xenophon, *Oec.* 12.16).

Trade and transactions

Generating profit for one's master required that business administrators engage in a variety of monetary transactions. This is of course to be expected of those commercial agents entrusted with large sums of money for the purpose of making investments. But administrators of large enterprises also frequently had to engage in the exchange of various kinds of resource in order to generate revenue. Estate managers, for instance, were responsible for buying tools, slaves, animals, seed, fodder, and various other kinds of agricultural equipment (Columella, *Rust.* 11.1.23). They might hire labourers for special tasks (Cato, *Agr.* 2.6; 5.3; Petronius, *Satyr.* 53.10; Matt 20.8) and let contracts for leases, workers, and farm supplies. They also handled credits and deposits (Cato, *Agr.* 2.6), and registered all transactions involving cash, grain, wine, oil, and fodder in the estate's records (Cato, *Agr.* 2.5; Luke 16.2).[70] Finally, they were responsible for selling the surpluses of produce and other commodities, including everything that was considered superfluous and marketable, such as sick slaves, weak animals, and old tools (Cato, *Agr.* 2.1; Varro, *Rust.* 1.16.4; 1.22.1; 1.27.4).[71]

Managers whose business transactions involved writing contracts, however, were normally required to receive official authorisation from

---

[70] See P.Oxy. 3804 for the mid-sixth-century CE records of an estate manager.

[71] The agronomists, to be sure, were reluctant to allow managers to become overly involved in trade (Cato, *Agr.* 5.3–4; Varro, *Rust.* 1.16.5; 2.5–7; Columella, *Rust.* 1.8.13; 3.21.6). Columella particularly warns against spending too much time trading: 'He [the administrator] should not employ his master's money [*pecuniam domini*] in purchasing cattle or anything else which is bought or sold; for doing this diverts him from his duties as a bailiff and makes him a trader [*negotiatorem*] rather than a farmer [*agricolam*] and makes it impossible to balance accounts with his master' (*Rust.* 11.1.24). Although these remarks underscore the supplementary nature of trade in certain kinds of production (esp. agriculture), they are the exceptions which prove the rule (cf. Columella, *Rust.* 1.8.6). As Aubert (1994: 8 n. 30) maintains, 'There is no doubt that farm managers were often involved in moneylending, trading, and contracting'; cf. 170–1. See also Aubert (2004: 137); H. Forbes and Foxhall (1995: 78–81). *Contra* Erdkamp (2005: 109–10).

their principal to do so. This stipulation was not always mandatory by law, but was frequently observed by business owners due to the risks involved in using middlemen. Principals, for example, could not sue third contracting parties as a result of the contracts negotiated by their extraneous agents. Even more significant, third contracting parties could not sue principals directly as a result of those very same mediated contracts, as liability was restricted to the extent of the slave's *peculium*.[72] Over time, however, several legal remedies were introduced to Roman commercial law which aimed to enforce the contracts established by agents. The most significant remedy for our purposes is the second-century BCE *actio institoria* (*Dig.* 14.3). As Aubert explains,

> The *actio institoria* was based on the idea that principals who benefited from the transactions of their dependent business managers should also incur liabilities arising from them. According to the terms of the praetorian Edict, the principal who had appointed an agent (*institor*) to run his business expected him to negotiate contracts with customers, suppliers, and contractors, in a specifically designated place (estate, workshop, store, or any other facility) or elsewhere, and accepted full liability for the transactions performed by his agent on the basis, and within the scope, of his appointment (*praepositio*). Consequently, third contracting parties were given a legal remedy against either the agent or the principal.[73]

Institores were generally slaves.[74] By the principate free persons could also receive such authorisation, but this concession was probably introduced only to permit slave *institores* who had been freed to continue working for their former masters without interruption. In such cases, the principal no longer appears to have been able to sue a third contracting party, even if he himself could be sued.[75]

The use of *institores* had several immediate commercial benefits. One advantage for principals was the opportunity to offer legal assurance to third contracting parties through low-risk, mediated business transactions. Still, the third party had to be sure about the authorisation of the agent with whom they were entering into negotiations. As Aubert explains,

---

[72] Aubert (1994: 196–8).
[73] Aubert (1994: 52–3). Cf. Andreau (1999: 66).
[74] A. Watson (1987: 94).   [75] Lintott (2002: 558).

Circumspection was required on the part of a third contracting party entering into a business transaction with an agent, so that the transaction did not fall outside the scope of the [agent's] appointment. For instance, a moneylender had to make sure that the money borrowed by the *institor* would likely be used in fulfilment of the task entrusted to him.[76]

Such assurance could be supplied through the agent's authorising documentation. Thus, another benefit of the *institor* arrangement was the ability of the principal to restrict the kinds of transaction his manager could conduct by specifying the scope of the commission through a charter (*lex praepositionis*). The charter could then be disclosed to prospective clients to ensure the precise nature of the agent's authorisation. These advantages are apparent in the following mid-second-century CE contract:

> I have empowered you [συνέστησά σοι] by this document to administer [φροντιοῦντα] my estate in Arsinoe, and to collect the rents and, if need be, to arrange new leases or to cultivate some land yourself, and to give receipts in my name, and to transact any business connected with stewardship [πάντα τῇ ἐπιτροπῇ ἀνήκοντα ἐπιτελέσαντα], just as I can transact it when I am present [καθὰ κἀμοὶ παρόντι ἔξεστιν], and to distribute the plots in Karamis, restoring to me what remains over, as to which matter I rely on your good faith [πίστι], and I confirm whatever you decide about them [εὐδοκῶ οἷς ἐὰν πρὸς ταῦτα ἐπιτελέσῃ].   (BGU 1.300)[77]

This document shows with significant clarity the representative nature of an agency appointment. In this sort of arrangement, the administrator was able to manage the principal's many financial responsibilities just as if the owner were present (καθὰ κἀμοὶ παρόντι ἔξεστιν), since the principal's confirmation accompanied the decisions made by the administrator (εὐδοκῶ οἷς ἐὰν πρὸς ταῦτα ἐπιτελέσῃ). For this reason it was important when appointing an agent to specify the scope of the commission by listing each of their constituent tasks. By doing so, the principal not only made himself liable for those actions performed by the agent within the scope of the appointment, but the principal

---

[76] Aubert (1994: 14).
[77] Trans. Daube (1985: 2335). The document technically is not a *lex praepositionis*, but a temporary agreement (ὁμολογία) between a principal and his agent. It nonetheless contains many of the features expected in a *lex praepositionis*. Cf. Hamza (1977: 61–2); Aubert (1994: 11).

formalised and publicised his authorisation. The principal's liability would then be sufficiently disclosed to prospective third contracting parties.

In light of the first two benefits of the *institor* arrangement, an additional advantage was that principals could maximise their production by authorising and then stationing various business managers in strategic locations all across the empire. And just such use of multi-branch enterprises has been detected in various kinds of ancient commerce, such as the ceramics industry. For example, through the study of production signatures, W. V. Harris has proposed that certain entrepreneurs commissioned numerous agents to various locations to widen the base of their production and sale of terracotta lamps. Harris suggests that one manufacturer (Fortis) may have had between twenty and thirty workshops – although not necessarily all active at once – including branches in northern and central Italy, Gaul, Germany, Pannonia, Dalmatia, and Dacia. A second firm (C. Oppi Res.) had branches in Gaul, Sardinia, Spain, and Rome, and several in North Africa.[78] Thus, the authorisation of *institores* in Roman commerce became a significant means by which business owners were able to expand their commercial presence while simultaneously offering third contracting parties confidence and security when entering into trade negotiations.

Many kinds of commercial agent were able to take advantage of the *institor* arrangement, including extraneous agents and business managers, and those employed in urban contexts as well as those in rural ones.[79] But not all managerial slaves were required to receive such formal authorisation. A *dispensator*, whose service as an accountant required the grant of a sizable purse (*peculium*), was normally responsible for making and receiving payments without having to be formally commissioned as an *institor*.[80] But regardless of the legal arrangement, trade was an inevitable part of private administration. It was therefore generally important for administrators to have conceived, like Petronius' Trimalchio, 'a passion for business [*concupivi negotiari*]' (*Satyr.* 76).

[78] W. V. Harris (1980: 141–2).
[79] For the authorisation of rural estate managers, see *Dig.* 14.3.5.2; 14.3.16.
[80] Carlsen (1995: 149): '*Dispensatores* fundamentally differed from *vilici* and *actores* by not being *institores*: the legal foundation for their work was the consent of the master, *permissu domini*, which was considered as the precondition for the slaves' *peculium*.' Aubert (1994: 196) notes, 'The position of *dispensatores* was comparable in many ways to that of *vilici* or *actores*.' However, 'each time a *dispensator* entered a contract on behalf of his master, he did so upon request (*iussum*) from the master himself or from his *procurator*' (198).

Supervision

In order to generate profit, whether in agriculture or industry, private administrators were also responsible for overseeing a team of subordinates.[81] It would be misleading, in fact, to make any sharp distinction between revenue acquisition and labour supervision in the ancient economy, for the outcome of the former objective was heavily reliant on the success of the latter. Greek and Latin authors alike observed that the manner in which an administrator commanded his labourers greatly influenced the productivity of the enterprise. For instance, while many of his contemporaries blamed their small harvests on the severe climate and disposition of the elemental beings (*Natura* and *Tellura*), Columella maintained that most estate failures were caused by poor management (*Rust.* 1.*praef.*3). Since slaves were known to contribute to low production, it was critical for an administrator who wished to run a profitable business to be able to direct his team of subordinates efficiently.[82]

The group of slaves (*familia*) that an administrator supervised could be quite large. Although the size of a given workforce depended generally on the nature of the business, the depth of its managerial structure, and the entrepreneurial strategy of the owner, managers of large enterprises could be responsible for upward to several dozen slaves.[83] Seneca, in fact, intimates that some estates were so large that the administrator could be compared to a consul (*Ira* 1.21.2) or king (*Ep.* 89.20). Apuleius, in his second-century CE novel, may have alluded to such a manager, 'whose master had entrusted him with the stewardship of his entire household [*cunctam familiae tutelam*] and who acted as overseer of that extensive holding [*possessionem maximam … villicabat*]' (*Metam.* 8.22). Zenon, the mid-third-century BCE *oikonomos* of Apollonius – though clearly an exceptional case – also possessed considerable supervisory responsibilities as the manager of two very large estates in the Arsinoe and Memphis nomes.[84] While most managers of large estates and businesses

---

[81] Carlsen (1995: 54) maintains that managing his staff was in many ways the estate administrator's 'most important task'.

[82] The administrators themselves probably participated in manual labour in order to set an example for and win the respect of their subordinates, as the agronomists repeatedly advised (Cato, *Agr.* 5.5; Varro, *Rust.* 1.17.5; Columella, *Rust.* 11.1.4, 7–9, 14–18, 26–7; 11.3.65). But given their need to keep track of the agricultural yields and record the tasks performed on and off the estate by members of the staff (Cato, *Agr.* 2.1–2), the manager's time was probably in large part monopolised by his supervisory and administrative duties; cf. Aubert (1994: 172).

[83] Bradley (1994: 58–65).

[84] For Zenon as an *oikonomos*, see P.Lond. 7.2133. For Zenon's subordinates, see Rostovtzeff (1922: 87–9); Edgar (1931: 22–3).

were not able to rival the breadth and depth of Zenon's administrative staff, many were responsible for supervising numerous kinds of delegate (e.g. *vilica, subvilici, praefecti, monitores, magisteri*) and even more menial labourers.[85]

Not as much is known about the size and organisation of non-agricultural businesses, such as factories and workshops (*officinae*). Studies on the Roman brick and ceramics industries have shown that owners often delegated production responsibilities to business managers. Although the legal status of these overseers has been the subject of some debate (particularly the identity of the *officinatores*),[86] several studies have shown that not a few of these enterprises were managed by slave or freed *vilici* and *actores*.[87] As Aubert argues, the methods of administration commonly employed in these factories and workshops probably originated from the managerial model utilised on the *villa rustica*.[88] Thus, despite the shortage of data available on the size and structure of these non-agricultural businesses, it is reasonable to suppose that the administrators of factories and workshops shared many of the same responsibilities as those on rural estates. But how did these administrators motivate their subordinates and what kinds of skills were required to manage them?

In order to run a business well, it was preferred that managers possess a number of specific attributes. Beyond the desire and skill for money-making and trade, managers were expected to be diligent leaders (Xenophon, *Mem.* 3.4.7–9) with significant experience in their area of production. As such, the administrator was expected to motivate his subordinates to work productively. This could be accomplished in several ways. According to Ischomachus, the truly great leader is able to

---

[85] For the administrator's associates and subordinates, see K. D. White (1970: 355–6); Carlsen (1993; 2000); Aubert (1994: 175–99).

[86] In the brick industry, Helen (1975: 108–9) has argued that *officinatores* were normally (nearly 80 per cent) freeborn contractors, rather than slave or freedman agents, as previously thought (cf. Duff 1928: 92). Bodel (1983: 4) contests this point, suggesting that the title *officinator* could have been borne by a variety of persons, including 'anything from a slave foreman in his master's service to a powerful industrialist of equestrian rank'. Cf. Aubert (1994: 222–36); Weaver (1998).

[87] Aubert (1993: 174); Aubert (1994: 201–321). For other industries, see Carlsen (1995: 31–55).

[88] Aubert (1994: 319):

> The managerial system used in the clay industry seems to have been borrowed from agricultural concerns (*fundi*), and was adapted to both rural and urban contexts. The manufacture of containers for the export of staples produced in agricultural estates and the exploitation of clay districts located in the vicinity of farmsteads for the production of building material must have directly benefited from the existence of the *vilicus* system.

motivate his staff 'by his will [γνώμη] rather than his strength [ῥώμη]' (Xenophon, *Oec.* 21.8). As Ischomachus explained,

> [I]n private industries, the man in authority [ὁ ἐφεστηκὼς] – bailiff [ἐπίτροπος] or manager [ἐπιστάτης] – who can make the workers keen, industrious and persevering – he is the man who gives a lift to the business and swells the surplus [πολλὴν τὴν περιουσίαν ποιοῦντες]... [I]f at sight of him they bestir themselves, and a spirit of determination and rivalry and eagerness to excel falls on every workman, then I should say: this man has a touch of the kingly nature in him [τι ἤθους βασιλικοῦ]. And this, in my judgment, is the greatest thing in every operation that makes any demand on the labour of men, and therefore in agriculture. (Xenophon, *Oec.* 21.9–11)[89]

But managing a successful estate purely by will was hardly realistic. Eventually, administrators were expected to utilise force, as Cato explains: 'If anyone commits an offence he must punish him [*vindicet*] properly in proportion to the fault... If the overseer sets his face against wrongdoing, they will not do it; if he allows it, the master must not let him go unpunished' (*Agr.* 5.1–2). Administrators punished subordinates primarily through beatings and incarceration (Columella, *Rust.* 1.8.16).[90] The manager's brutality and readiness to penalise disobedience is well illustrated in Plautus' *Casina*, when the *vilicus* Olympio explained emphatically to his master Lysidamus how, given the opportunity, he would happily discipline the urban slave Chalinus: 'Only let him come to the farm! I'll send the fine fellow back to town to you, under a yoke like a charcoal peddler' (*Cas.* 2.8.437; cf. *Pseud.* 38–61).

Administrators who were overly reliant on the whip, however, also ran the risk of developing enmity with their labourers. As Columella cautioned, the *vilicus* who wished to manage a productive estate was required to strike a balance between ruling with laxness (*remisse imperet*) and leniency (*lenius*), on the one hand, and ruling with cruelty (*crudeliter imperet*) and severity (*dominorum*), on the other; for it was preferred that labourers 'fear his sternness than detest his cruelty' (Columella, *Rust.* 1.8.10; 11.1.6, 25; cf. Aristotle, *Oec.* 1344a29). Failure to avoid

---

[89] Although by line 10 of the discourse the δεσπότης is the kind of leader in view, it is clear from line 9 that the generic concept under consideration is 'the man in authority' (ὁ ἐφεστηκώς), of which the ἐπίτροπος, ἐπιστάτης, and δεσπότης each serve as examples.

[90] Alternatively, managers were urged by the philosophers and agronomists to encourage hard-working slaves with food, clothing, praise, and leisure (Aristotle, *Oec.* 1344a29–1344b12; Cato, *Agr.* 5.2).

extremes could be met with grave personal consequences, as illustrated in the Parable of the Faithful and Wise Steward. In both the Lucan and Matthean accounts, Jesus explains that the manager set over the master's slaves and entrusted with the responsibility of issuing to them allowances of food and drink would eventually be punished once his master discovered that the manager was hoarding the rations and beating the slaves without cause (Matt 24.45–51//Luke 12.42–6). Alternatively, Hippocrates, the real-life *vilicus* of a certain Plautus, exercised his command so judiciously that his subordinates paid tribute to him through a funerary inscription, signing it, 'the rural slaves, over whom he exercised authority with moderation [*quibus imperavit modeste*]' (*ILS* 7367).[91]

In addition to being strict with his subordinates, the manager of an estate was required also to be learned in farming and physically strong (*robustissimus*), so he could both 'teach those under his orders and himself adequately carry out the instructions which he gives' (Columella, *Rust.* 11.1.3). The manager was required to be neither too young nor too old, but of middle age, preferably around 35 years old, so as to be hardy and experienced enough to earn the respect of his subordinates while setting an example for them in work ethic (*Rust.* 1.8.3; 11.1.3–4).[92] As Pseudo-Aristotle summarises, 'Right administration of a household [οἰκονομεῖν] demands in the first place familiarity with the sphere of one's action; in the second place, good natural endowments; and in the third, an upright and industrious way of life. For the lack of any of these qualifications will involve many a failure in the task one takes in hand' (Aristotle, *Oec.* 1345b6–12).[93]

Accountability

The desired ethical make up of private administrators consisted chiefly of loyalty (πίστις/*fides*), which was visibly demonstrated through deference (*obsequium*) to the master.[94] Such compliance with the master's wishes

---

[91] Trans. *GRS* §152.
[92] As Plutarch remarks,

> Nowadays, the common practice of many persons is more than ridiculous; for some of their trustworthy [lit. diligent] slaves [δούλων τῶν σπουδαίων] they appoint to manage their farms [γεωργούς], others they make masters of their ships, others their factors, others they make house-stewards [οἰκονόμους], and some even money-lenders; but any slave whom they find to be a wine-bibber and a glutton, and useless for any kind of business [πραγματείαν], to him they bring their sons and put them in his charge (*Mor.* 4a–b).

[93] Cf. K. D. White (1970: 353–4).
[94] Bradley (1987: 21–45). Cf. Cicero, *Verr.* 29.1; Valerius Maximus, *Lib.* 6.8.*praef.*

could also be indicated through a range of others terms. Ischomachus, for instance, prescribed goodwill (εὔνοια) as the primary character trait to teach a new estate manager (Xenophon, *Oec.* 12.5).[95] Columella similarly warned that a new *vilicus* should always be tested early by his master in order to ensure the bailiff's competence in farming and his 'fidelity and attachment to his master [*domino fidem ac benevolentiam*]'; 'without these qualities, the most perfect knowledge possessed by a bailiff is of no use' (*Rust.* 11.1.7).

Numerous fictitious tales and real-life testimonials also affirm that loyalty was the principal trait of administrators. In his novel *Callirhoe*, Chariton used πίστος and πίστις several times to characterise private administrators. On one occasion, the master Dionysius commended his *oikonomos* Phocas, calling him his benefactor (εὐεργέτης), true guardian (κηδεμὼν ἀληθής), and most loyal supporter (πιστότατος) in confidential affairs (*Chaer.* 3.9.11–12; cf. 2.4.6; 5.1). The same *oikonomos* was elsewhere praised as a φιλοδέσποτος for his eagerness to ensure his master's security (*Chaer.* 3.7.2).[96] Loyalty also typified the administrators in the biblical tradition. In their repeated casting of trusted slaves in gospel parables, the evangelists portray faithfulness (πίστος) as the principal virtue of good managers (e.g. Matt 24.25//Luke 12.42; Matt 25.21–3// Luke 19.17). According to Jennifer Glancy, a faithful slave is 'one who occupies a managerial position and has moreover internalized the master's interests to the extent that he will work unsupervised when his master is away'.[97] Fabian Udoh similarly remarks, 'The faithful manager (ὁ πιστὸς οἰκονόμος [Luke 12.42]) is defined by the symbiosis between him and the master, such that he knows, anticipates, and does the master's will, that is, what promotes the master's best interest.'[98]

The testimony of funerary epitaphs – while probably containing a certain degree of embellishment – still further suggests that some real-life administrators aspired to, and perhaps even achieved, fidelity.[99] The first-century CE *oikonomos* Italos, for example, apparently exhibited such faithfulness (πιστός) and industrious service (δουλοσύνης φιλοεργοῦ)

---

[95] Aubert (1994: 159–62); Carlsen (1995: 57).

[96] Φιλοδέσποτος was also the name of a second-century CE *oikonomos* from Sparta (*CIG* 1276) and an *actor* (Philodespotus) in Apuleius' *Metamorphoses* (2.26), just as the name Pistus was given to one of Plautus' fictional *vilici* (*Mer.* 2.2.1).

[97] Glancy (2002: 114).   [98] Udoh (2009: 330).

[99] Despite the ubiquity of the rebellious slave, Vogt (1975: 130) maintains that there were many actual slaves, especially those serving in close proximity to the master, 'who reciprocated their master's good will and concern for them by industrious and dedicated work; there were always slaves who were dependable ... slaves to whom one could readily entrust one's property'.

that at his death his master wept and personally erected a memorial for him as a gift (*SEG* 28.1033/*NewDocs* 3.10). Another monument was raised for 'the most faithful [*fidelissimo*] Gallicanus', the *vilicus* of Afinianus (*ILS* 7371). Still another tribute was dedicated to a certain Sabinianus, who is described as 'a *vilicus* and a good and most faithful man [*vilico et homini bono et fidelissimo*]' (*ILS* 7370).[100] Similar honours were also paid to Cerdontus and Junius, who were both remembered as most faithful *actores* (*ILS* 7376/*CIL* XIV 469; *CIL* 6.9119/*CIL* XIV 2301). Collectively, these texts show that the quintessential administrator was characterised by loyalty. And so long as this virtue was apparent, the satisfaction of the master and the longevity of the administrator's tenure were secure.

The fidelity of managers was constantly reinforced through the structural hierarchy of the managerial unit. Over the course of his tenure, an administrator would be called to account by his master or immediate superior through sporadic and unannounced inspections (Xenophon, *Oec.* 12.19–20; Aristotle, *Oec.* 1345a). In Chariton's *Callirhoe*, for instance, Dionysius waited until just before the harvest to inspect the herds and crops at his seaside estate, presumably to ensure the profitability of the harvest (2.3.1). But beyond seasonal assessments, masters also made random and unannounced visits in order to observe the work ethic of their labourers.[101] In the gospel parables, it was the unknown date of the master's return which was to maintain the administrator's diligence while left unsupervised (Matt 24.51//Luke 12.46). Surprise inspections therefore served two functions: (i) they enabled the master to examine the various areas of production and the unveiled loyalty of the administrator and his staff; this then (ii) kept the administrator managing the enterprise well.

Reward

The outcome of the inspection normally resulted in either the reward or penalisation of the administrator. If the agent managed reliably, he could receive various kinds of reward.[102] To begin with, slave

---

[100] Trans. *GRS* §153.

[101] Inspections involved, among other things, the examination of the condition of the estate's produce, equipment, labourers, and accounts (Cato, *Agr.* 2.1–7; Columella, *Rust.* 1.8.20; Matt 25.19; Luke 16.2).

[102] Immediately following Ischomachus' prioritisation of fidelity in administrators, Socrates inquired of him, 'And how, in heaven's name, do you teach your man to be loyal to you and yours?' Ischomachus responded, 'By rewarding him [εὐεργετῶν], of course, whenever the gods bestow some good thing on us in abundance' (*Oec.* 12.6).

administrators – along with menial slaves – would receive certain basic necessities, such as food and clothing. As Pseudo-Aristotle cautioned, 'Unless we pay men, we cannot control them [ἀμίσθων γὰρ οὐχ οἷόν τε ἄρχειν]; and food is a slave's pay [δούλῳ δὲ μισθὸς τροφή]' (Aristotle, *Oec.* 1344b3). Ischomachus, in fact, instructs estate owners to provide their administrators with the best of the food and clothes, since the better servants deserve the superior provisions (Xenophon, *Oec.* 13.10).[103] Administrators might also receive verbal commendation. Ischomachus explains that slaves with 'an ambitious disposition [φιλότιμοι τῶν φύσεων] are also spurred on by praise [τῷ ἐπαίνῳ παροξύνονται], some natures being hungry for praise as others for meat and drink' (Xenophon, *Oec.* 13.9; cf. 13.12; Luke 16.8). Still other administrators might be awarded opportunities for leisure and mates to bear children (Varro, *Rust.* 1.17.5–7), or even promotions with increased responsibility (Matt 25.20–3//Luke 19.16–19), including additional financial and personnel oversight (Matt 24.46–7//Luke 12.43–4).[104] Finally, administrators might be afforded some kind of monetary compensation. If one was a freeman or freedman, the administrator would receive a wage (μισθός), in either cash or kind.[105] If one was a slave, however, the master might award the administrator with a salary (ὀψώνιον, σύνταξις; cf. P.Oxy. 3048; Rom 6.20–3).[106]

Administrators who did not receive a salary, however, may have benefited from an alternative financial arrangement, the grant of a

[103] Pomeroy (2010: 36–40).

[104] Some NT scholars doubt that real-life administrators would have been motivated by the rewards presented to Jesus' parabolic slaves, since they would have prized manumission over occupational promotion and material gain. But extra-biblical sources confirm that promotions up the slave hierarchy were desirable to slaves. Columella suggests that the *vilicus* himself should be promoted to his post from among the hardened, experienced, and hardworking slaves (*Rust.* 1.8.2). These managerial positions not only had the bonus of appearing to be freemen's work (Aristotle, *Oec.* 1344a), but also provided slaves with increased contact with the master, which in turn afforded them more privileges and better prospects for future manumission; cf. Beavis (1992: 43); Mouritsen (2011: 198).

[105] Eusebius, quoting a letter of Dionysios, bishop of Alexandria, for instance, recalls the martyrdom of Ischyrion, 'the hired steward of one of the rulers' (ἐπετρόπευέν τινι τῶν ἀρχόντων ἐπὶ μισθῷ, *Hist. eccl.* 6.42.1). It is not clear, however, if Ischyrion was a slave, freed, or free person. Xenophon (*Oec.* 1.3–4), reporting on a conversation between Socrates and Critobulus, explains how the gentleman farmer (οἰκονομικός) who is able to manage his own estate well would also be competent to manage the estate of another in exchange for a μισθός. Xenophon almost certainly does not have a slave administrator in view, although Pomeroy (1994: 218) suggests the possibility of a freedman. For the salary of free or freed agents in *mandatum*, see Bürge (1993).

[106] Rathbone (1991: 91–2); Rowlandson (1996: 205).

peculium.[107] The *peculium* of a slave could include money, provisions, and even other slaves. Although legally belonging to the master, it functioned as an allowance with which the slave could conduct business on his master's behalf (Matt 25.14–30//Luke 19.11–27). But before returning one's *peculium* to his master, the slave lived off what he earned, for the purse supplied his financial needs and thus motivated him to manage responsibly. In fact, Jean Andreau has argued that the entire *peculium* arrangement was intended to enable the slave to make a fortune and then return part or all of the sum to the master in exchange for manumission.[108] An anonymous freedman friend of Petronius' Trimalchio, for instance, admits to having purchased his freedom for 1,000 denarii (*Satyr.* 57),[109] while the real-life freedman Publius Decimius Eros Merula obtained his for 50,000 sesterces (*CIL* XI 5400/*ILS* 7812). Both sums could have only been supplied by just this sort of *peculium* arrangement. All of these kinds of award were quite commonplace and were thought – by the agronomists anyway – to benefit the farm. As Columella reasons, 'Such justice and consideration [*iustitia et cura*] on the part of the master contributes easily to the increase of his estate [*multum confert augendo patrimonio*]' (*Rust.* 1.8.19).

Punishment

Much has been written about the punishment of menial slaves in the ancient world that applies directly to administrators as well. Normally, if an administrator was found unfaithful and disobedient, he would be liable to professional and physical penalty. But in some instances of

---

[107] As Varro explains, 'The foremen [*praefectos*] are to be made more zealous by rewards, and care must be taken that they have a bit of property of their own [*peculium*]' (*Rust.* 1.17.5).

[108] Andreau (2004: 116–17): 'Au moment où l'esclave allait être affranchi, le maître pouvait lui redemander le pécule tout entier tel qu'il était au moment de l'affranchissement, ou bien lui en reprendre seulement une partie. Quelle partie? Assez souvent, semble-t-il, le maître demandait une somme équivalant au prix d'achat de l'esclave, afin qu'elle lui permît de racheter un esclave de valeur analogue.' Cf. Pliny the Elder, *Nat.* 7.39.128–9. Mouritsen (2011: 159–80) shows that many freed slaves were able to retain part of the sum after manumission.

[109] Although the LCL translation suggests that the freedman's purchase was for his own manumission, Petronius' Latin text is ambiguous and may indicate that the freedom of the freedman's wife (*contubernalis*) is in view. In either case, the story depicts the great monetary possessions of a slave. The boast of the fictitious bailiff Olympio, 'I can get freed for a farthing [*una libella liber possum fieri*]' (Plautus, *Cas.* 316), is of course hyperbole, but nevertheless demonstrates that slave stewards could possess adequate funds to purchase manumission.

administrative carelessness, it appears that they were punished rather lightly. After all, administrators were specially skilled and educated labourers who possessed great money-making potential for their master. Severely injuring or killing one's administrator was therefore not always in the best interests of the proprietor. Ischomachus, for instance, remarked that he punished his estate managers not vindictively, but for the purpose of training them, that is, to teach them how better to superintend the estate. As Ischomachus explained, 'Whenever I notice that they are careful [ἐπιμελομένους], I commend them and try to show them honour [ἐπαινῶ καὶ τιμᾶν πειρῶμαι αὐτούς]; but when they appear careless, I try to say and do the sort of things that will sting them [δήξεται αὐτούς]' (Xenophon, *Oec.* 12.16). These kinds of gentle punishment were suitable for generally obedient administrators, those who, even when deserving of punishment, were still of great value to their masters.

But some administrators were punished quite violently, especially when they had caused their masters great misfortune.[110] Rural estate managers and business agents were especially liable to the master's aggression, for as Ramsay MacMullen observes, 'It was easy for [the master] to hurt people he never saw.'[111] While some administrators were banished to a distant country estate (Petronius, *Satyr.* 69), others were heavily beaten and whipped (Chariton, *Chaer.* 3.9.5–7).[112] In his novel, Chariton shows how during an inspection a master's anger toward his administrator might be expressed in a subtle complaint (μέμψις) or in such fury (βαρύθυμος) as to require a lover's intercession and rescue from death (*Chaer.* 2.7.2–6; cf. Cicero, *Resp.* 1.59). The masters in the gospel parables are also quite famous for viciously penalising disobedient managers. In certain cases they desert or demote their managers to menial servitude (Luke 16.2–3),[113] and in others they have them cut into pieces (διχοτομέω, Matt 24.51//Luke 12.46).[114] These horrific images were not exceptional. As Richard Saller maintains, 'Romans regularly *and legitimately* inflicted on their fellow men corporal punishments that maimed and even killed.'[115]

---

[110] Cicero remarked, 'If a man, as a guardian, or as a partner, or as a person in a place of trust, or as any one's agent, has cheated any one, the greater his offence is, the slower is his punishment' (*Caecin.* 2.7).
[111] MacMullen (1974: 6). Alternatively, Seneca's *vilicus* appealed to the intimacy and longevity of their relationship in an attempt to appease his master's anger (*Ep.* 12.1–3).
[112] W. Fitzgerald (2000: 32–50).
[113] Beavis (1992: 49) argues that demotion and desertion were suitable forms of punishment for slaves, because the inflicted slaves would either be left to fend for themselves and probably die, or be demoted to digging as a drudge.
[114] Luz (2005: 224–5); cf. Beavis (1992: 43).
[115] Saller (1994: 134, original emphasis).

Summary

In the preceding analysis of private administrators we have sought through the use of the title οἰκονόμος and several Greek and Latin correlatives to identify their main occupational characteristics and personal attributes. Several features of the position were consistently observed. Although οἰκονόμος originally referred to a free proprietor of an estate, over time the title and responsibilities of estate and business management came to be identified almost exclusively with slaves and freedmen. Administrators therefore were typically the servile subordinates of wealthy masters/ patrons, although administrators themselves also possessed some structural authority. Granted the responsibility of running an enterprise, private administrators were charged with making steady – though not excessive – profits for the proprietor and with directing a staff of subordinate labourers to achieve that end.[116] Administrators were often authorised to enter into contract negotiations with potential third contracting parties. Both to their slave staff as well as to third parties, then, administrators acted as representatives of their principal and were entrusted with the authority to act for them on their behalf. Administrators, however, generally were not liable for their contracts. Rather, when formally authorised, the principal himself remained responsible for all commercial dealings, as long as the agent acted within the scope of his commission. But even though third parties could not charge the administrator with fault, business managers were always held accountable to their principal for the work they performed. Depending on their fidelity to the principal, they received either rewards (e.g. promotion, commendation, allowance) or punishment (e.g. demotion, chastisement, death).

---

[116] Thus, Ischomachus indicates that an administrator is valuable (ἄξιος) and ready to manage once

> you have implanted in him a desire for your prosperity and have made him also careful to see that you achieve it, and have obtained for him, besides, the knowledge needful to ensure that every piece of work done shall add to the profits [ὠφελιμώτερα], and, further, have made him capable of ruling [ἄρχειν], and when, besides all this, he takes as much delight in producing heavy crops for you in due season as you would take if you did the work yourself (Xenophon, *Oec.* 15.1).

PART II

Paul's administrator metaphor in 1 Corinthians

During the past few decades, many have explored the notions of apocalypticism, revelation, and mystery in the Pauline corpus. In these expeditions, however, one stone appears to be left unturned: Paul's enigmatic phrase 'stewards of the mysteries of God'.[1]

Interpreting the Apostle Paul's portrayal of himself as an administrator of God in 1 Corinthians 4 and 9 has long troubled NT interpreters. This difficulty is not due, however, to the infrequency with which the term οἰκονόμος was used in antiquity. As was made apparent in Part I, the title was used so commonly in the ancient Greek-speaking world that many modern scholars disagree about the precise source domain of Paul's metaphor. Just as troubling is that only a handful of studies on Paul's use of the term has been conducted in any detail, and even fewer have paid much attention to the differences between its regal, municipal, and private contexts. This is especially surprising given that the metaphor occupies an important place in the two passages where it appears in 1 Corinthians.[2]

However, when Paul's portrayal of his administration is analysed in light of the various models surveyed in Part I, it becomes clear that Paul adopted the term from just one of those contexts, and employed it strategically in an effort to elucidate the nature of his apostleship and to elicit a response from his readers. Part II of this investigation therefore seeks to apply the socio-historical insights gained in Part I to Paul's *oikonomos* metaphor in 1 Cor 4.1–5 and 9.16–23, in order to expose how those texts contribute to the scholarly study of Paul's apostolic authority. In Chapter 5 we shall implement a basic method for

[1] Gladd (2008: 165).

[2] Given that Paul's metaphor concludes one of the most instructive passages in the early part of Paul's letter (3.5–4.5) and is central to one of the most disputed sections in the middle portion of the epistle (9.16–23), the lack of attention Paul's *oikonomos* metaphor has received remains quite disproportionate to the rhetorical and theological significance it carries in 1 Corinthians.

identifying metaphors and thereby make a case for the source domain of Paul's analogy in our two passages. Then in Chapters 6 and 7 we shall turn to Paul's employment of the metaphor in 1 Corinthians 4 and 9 respectively, seeking to show how Paul deployed the image in two distinct epistolary contexts to meet his particular rhetorical and theological objectives.

5

IDENTIFYING PAUL'S METAPHOR
IN 1 CORINTHIANS

It is metaphor above all that gives perspicuity, pleasure, and a foreign air ... but we must make use of metaphors and epithets that are appropriate.   Aristotle, *Rhet.* 1405a8–9[1]

Having surveyed in Part I the three distinct administrative contexts in which *oikonomoi* are most attested in Graeco-Roman antiquity, in this chapter we shall seek to identify from which context Paul's metaphor originated. But in seeking to identify the image's source domain, we shall greatly increase the plausibility of our results if we examine Paul's letter, including its epistolary and social contexts, employing strict hermeneutical criteria that can direct and clarify our analysis. Our investigation of Paul's metaphor will benefit significantly from the principles recommended by Nijay Gupta.

In a 2009 article, Gupta has introduced a series of seven principles and related questions which aid in the identification and interpretation of Pauline metaphors. Three of those principles are of particular relevance here. The first, *cotextual coherence*, asks the question: 'Is the source domain made prominent elsewhere in the discourse?' The second principle, *analogy*, asks the question: 'Is the metaphorical term or phrase used in similar ways elsewhere?' Finally, the third principle, *exposure*, asks the question: 'To what extent were the author and reader exposed to, or in contact with, the source domain?'[2] Significantly, when these questions are posed of Paul's metaphor in 1 Corinthians, the metaphor resonates with only one source domain examined in Part I: private commercial administration. In what follows we shall demonstrate how these principles reveal that Paul borrowed from this particular source domain.

---

[1] Trans. Freese (1926).
[2] Gupta (2009: 174). The sequence of these principles has been reversed here.

Cotextual coherence

Evidence that commercial agency, or the private administrative sphere, is the appropriate source domain of Paul's *oikonomos* metaphor is, in the first place, supplied in 1 Cor 4.1–5 and the larger discourse in which this passage is located. The first indication is in the hierarchy Paul constructs involving apostles and God/Christ. In 4.1–5 Paul portrays apostles as serving in a subordinate role closely resembling those occupied by *oikonomoi* in private structures from Graeco-Roman antiquity. This is most apparent when Paul declares that apostles serve a κύριος, namely Christ (4.4–5). Paul indicates that it is Christ who will return to examine and acquit him. At that time the Lord will expose the secret things of darkness and the desires of the heart, and issue either rewards or penalty to his apostles (4.5; cf. 3.8, 14–15).

This hierarchy is reinforced in 4.1–3. First, the genitive constructions ὑπηρέται Χριστοῦ and οἰκονόμοι μυστηρίων θεοῦ (4.1) bear close resemblance to the administrator–master relationship exhibited in both Greek and Latin inscriptions. The use of the genitive in the phrase ὑπηρέτας Χριστοῦ is possessive. Since οἰκονόμος, on the other hand, is a cognate of the verb οἰκονομεῶ (LSJ I.1–2), the construction οἰκονόμοι μυστηρίων θεοῦ probably constitutes an objective genitive, so that apostles are those who manage, or dispense, God's mysteries.[3] Nevertheless, because the mysteries belong to God, the *oikonomoi* are by implication his subordinates.[4] Secondly, a hierarchical structure is apparent when Paul states that it is required of *oikonomoi* that they be found faithful (4.2). But who is it that will in fact examine Paul's faithfulness? Verses 3–4a reveal the wrong persons, namely other believers, human judiciaries, and even the apostle himself. While Paul considers it the mission of the apostolate to serve the church (3.21–2), their subordination and accountability are to none other than Christ (4.4b–5). Finally, the fact that apostles were entrusted with oversight of a particular commodity, the μυστήρια θεοῦ (4.1), implies the metaphor's commercial derivation, since *oikonomoi* who managed a specific product normally served in private commercial contexts, as did Genealis, the commercial slave of

---

[3] This goes slightly against Gladd (2008: 168 n. 9), who suggests a genitive of subordination ('stewards over the mysteries of God'), although, in light of *IKios* 46/*IGRR* 3.25, Gladd may be correct.

[4] Schrage (1991: 320): 'ὑπηρέται Χριστοῦ und οἰκονόμοι der Geheimnisse Gottes, nicht Besitzer eigener Mysterien'. For additional indicators in 4.1–5 of the subordination of apostles to God/Christ, see Chapter 6.

Caesar: Γενεάλ[ιος] Καίσαρος δούλου οἰκονόμου ἐπὶ τοῦ σείτου [*sic*, σίτου] (*IKios* 46/*IGRR* 3.25).⁵

Collectively, these textual features suggest that Paul served in an administrative configuration that was markedly different from the democratic and republican structures of both Greek and Roman cities. Furthermore, since by the time of Paul's ministry the regal *oikonomos* (in the Hellenistic sense) was a thing of the distant past, the source domain of Paul's metaphor must be the private administrative sphere. This is confirmed by Paul's frequent use of other private domestic metaphors in 1 Corinthians, especially in the letter's opening four chapters: ἀδελφοί (*passim*); διάκονοι (3.5); τέκνα (4.14, 17); παιδαγωγοί (4.15); πατήρ (4.15).⁶

Analogy

The commercial use of the *oikonomos* metaphor in 1 Cor 4.1–5 finds additional support in 9.17. In the earlier passage, Paul uses the noun οἰκονόμος in an effort to portray the role that apostles occupy in God's administration. It is significant, then, that Paul employs the abstract noun οἰκονομία in 9.17 for a similar purpose. In the latter instance, however, Paul uses the metaphor in order to explain how as God's slave he can be entitled to a μισθός (9.18), and why his primary ministerial objective is to 'gain' (κερδαίνω) converts. The intricacies of this difficult passage will be addressed at length in Chapter 7. Now it is sufficient to observe that Paul's concerns with slavery, remuneration, and making evangelistic 'profits' suggest that the source domain of his οἰκονομία metaphor in 9.17 is the realm of private commercial administration, especially since municipal *oikonomoi* were often wealthy freemen, normally did not receive a wage, and seem to have been more instrumental in making payments than profits. Therefore, because Paul figuratively utilises the οἰκονομ- lexical stem to refer to his apostleship in two passages in the same letter, we can with great certainty conclude that Paul drew both metaphors from the same private administrative context.

---

⁵ The original Greek text of this bilingual inscription probably presented Genealis' name in the genitive case (Γενεάλ[ιος]), although the Latin renders it in the nominative: *[Ge]nealis, Caesaris Aug(usti) [se]rvos [servus] verna, dispens(ator) [ad] frumentum.*

⁶ A. Robertson and Plummer (1911: 75): 'God is the master (iii. 23) of the Christian household (1 Tim. iii. 15), and the stores entrusted to His stewards are the "mysteries of God".' Cf. Fee (1987: 159); Joubert (1995: 216); Witherington (1995: 138); Hays (1997: 65); Thiselton (2000: 336).

Exposure

Paul was familiar with many features of the urban sector of the ancient world. As Wayne Meeks remarks, 'Paul was a city person. The city breathes through his language.'[7] For this reason, it is not surprising that on several occasions in 1 Corinthians Paul borrows images from Corinthian city life for the purpose of illustrating his theology (e.g. 1 Cor 3.10–17; 4.9–10; 9.24–7). The metaphor under investigation in our study functions similarly. Paul's portrayal of apostles as *oikonomoi* would have resonated deeply in the colony's flourishing commercial context. Even as early as the fifth century BCE, Thucydides could affirm that 'Corinth had from time out of mind been a commercial emporium [ἐμπόριον]' (*War* 1.13.5).[8] This was also true of the first-century city Paul knew.[9] But Corinth's success as a trade centre was not accidental: the city's wealth was due largely to geography.

Corinth's strategic location

Because of its location, Corinth served to unite the eastern and western parts of the Mediterranean, resting as it were 'at the cross-roads [ἐν τριόδῳ] of Greece' (Dio Chrysostom, *Or.* 8.5). Writing during the period of Corinth's desolation – Corinth remained in ruins from 146–44 BCE after being sacked by the Roman general Lucius Mummius – Cicero considered Corinth's location to be a navigational centrepiece: '[I]ts position was such on the straits and the entrance to Greece, that by land it held the keys of various places and almost united two seas, set over against each

---

[7] Meeks (1983: 9). Paul's acquaintance with the city began in his youth. Luke reports that Paul was born in Tarsus (Acts 22.3; cf. 9.11; 21.39), a philosophical and commercial centre as well as the capital of the Roman province of Cilicia. Paul then spent an unspecified number of years in Jerusalem, where he received his Pharisaic education (Acts 22.3; 26.4; cf. Gal 1.14, 22; Phil 3.5–6); cf. Hengel (1991: 18–39); van Unnik (1962); Dunn (2009: 330–3). Finally, he devoted over three decades to missionary activity, during which time he established numerous churches in some of the leading cities in the northeast Mediterranean basin (Rom 15.19). We can therefore without hesitancy affirm with Meeks that 'the mission of the Pauline circle was conceived from start to finish as an urban movement' (10).

[8] Trans. Crawley. Frayn (1993: 10): 'The Greek term ἐμπόριον denotes a market centre, mainly on the coast, importing and exporting goods to and from distant places, either in the same country or in foreign parts.' Thus, it may be, as Livy implies, that Corinth's harbours rather than the city proper formed the isthmus' famed emporium (*Libri* 32.17.3); cf. Pettegrew (in press). Regardless, trade occurring both at the harbours and in the city marketplace made Corinth a major commercial centre throughout its history. For the city up to the mid fourth century BCE, see J. B. Salmon (1984); for 228–44 BCE, see Wiseman (1979: 450–96).

[9] Cf. Meeks (1983: 47–9); Oakes (2009: 32–4).

other especially for purposes of navigation, separated by a very small intervening space' (*Agr.* 2.87). The narrow isthmus on which Corinth was built was an advantageous site on all accounts, even serving to join numerous people groups. As Aelius Aristides (117–81 CE) lauded,

> [Corinth] is, as it were, a kind of marketplace [ἀγορά], and at that common to all Greeks, and a national festival, not like this present one which the Greek race celebrates here every two years, but one which is celebrated every year and daily. If just as men enjoy the official status of being public friends with foreign cities, so too did cities enter into this relationship with one another, the city [Corinth] would have this title and honor everywhere. For it receives all cities and sends them off again and is a common refuge for all, like a kind of route [ὁδός] and passage [διέξοδος] for all mankind, no matter where one would travel, and it is a common city for all Greeks, indeed, as it were, a kind of metropolis and mother in this respect. For among other reasons, there is no place where one would rest as on a mother's lap with more pleasure or enjoyment. Such is the relaxation, refuge, and safety for all who come to it.
>
> (*Or.* 46.23–4)[10]

Corinth, then, was a city of repute throughout antiquity, and many of its accolades were owed to its auspicious location.

Corinth's location was also its primary reason for being refounded. Strabo credits Julius Caesar's decision to recolonise Corinth to its 'favourable position' (εὐφυΐαν, *Geogr.* 8.6.23),[11] the payoff being the city's potential to serve as a centre for all kinds of trade.[12] For this reason, in June 44 BCE, after the city had lain nearly uninhabited for over a century, Caesar's plan to resettle the site was implemented by Antony.[13] It is especially noteworthy that the city's colonists included a large contingent of freedmen, many of whom had become entrepreneurs or were

---

[10] Trans. Behr.

[11] M. E. Hoskins (1997: 99): 'The refounding of Corinth, a great commercial centre of the past, was in keeping with Julius Caesar's economic and colonial policies of relieving economic distress at home, particularly at Rome, and of developing the provinces.' Cf. E. T. Salmon (1969: 135).

[12] Cicero's appreciation of the ease of access to every city on the Peloponnese was especially true of Corinth: '[A]ll the products of the world can be brought by water to the city in which you live, and your people in turn can convey or send whatever their own fields produce to any country they like' (*Resp.* 2.9).

[13] Appian, *Hist. rom.* 8.136; Strabo, *Geogr.* 8.6.23; Plutarch, *Caes.* 57.8; Diodorus Siculus, *Libr.* 32.27.1. For the circumstances and date of Corinth's refounding, see M. E. Hoskins Walbank (1997: 97–9).

serving their patrons as business agents.[14] So strategic was Corinth's location that by the late first century CE the colony had already become a 'flourishing centre of commerce, administration, the imperial cult, and entertainment'.[15] As Strabo explained,

> Corinth is called 'wealthy' [ἀφνειός] because of its commerce [lit. emporium; τὸ ἐμπόριον], since it is situated on the Isthmus and is master of two harbors, of which the one leads straight to Asia, and the other to Italy; and it makes easy the exchange of merchandise from both countries that are so far distant from each other. And just as in early times the Strait of Sicily was not easy to navigate, so also the high seas, and particularly the sea beyond Maleae, were not, on account of the contrary winds; and hence the proverb, 'But when you double Maleae, forget your home.' At any rate, it was a welcome alternative, for the merchants both from Italy and from Asia, to avoid the voyage to Maleae and to land their cargoes here. And also the duties on what by land was exported from the Peloponnesus and what was imported to it fell to those who held the keys. And to later times this remained ever so.   (*Geogr.* 8.6.20)[16]

The Maleae was the infamous cape of the southeast Peloponnese which for centuries had posed a terrible risk for seafarers.[17] Crossing at the isthmus therefore provided a welcome relief for those who wished to avoid the dangerous trek around Greece's southern tip.

---

[14] M. E. Hoskins Walbank (1997: 107): 'These new Corinthians were entrepreneurs, eager to seize onto a good thing, and ready to exploit their resources and connections as far as possible; just the sort of people to make a commercial success of their city.' Cf. M. E. Hoskins Walbank (2002: 261). For the limited number of army veterans in Corinth, compared to freedmen and businessmen, see Spawforth (1996: 168–73). Millis (2010: 23–30) argues that many of Corinth's freedmen colonists originated from the eastern provinces. For an overview of the colony from its foundation in 44 BCE to 267 CE, see Wiseman (1979: 497–533).

[15] Spawforth (2003: 391). Based on the results of the Eastern Korinthia Archaeological Survey, Gregory (2010: 434–49) argues that by the early Roman period Corinth had already surpassed the economic prosperity that the city witnessed during the Greek period.

[16] Sanders (2005: 15):

> Well-watered, overlooked by an imposing acropolis, flanked by a large fertile plain to the north and northwest, and located between two seas, Corinth commanded the principal nodal point in the land and sea communications of southern Greece. Its strategic and commercial position was supplemented by valuable natural resources for export, including building materials, excellent clays for ceramic and mortars, wood, and agricultural produce. It was not so much Corinth's own riches that were being moved, however. The importance of Corinth was as an entrepôt through which the produce of other regions was shipped.

[17] Murphy-O'Connor (2002: 54).

The isthmus benefited transport primarily by way of the two major harbours at its opposing ends.[18] At these ports goods were imported, stored, traded, and exported. The Lechaion Harbour, located directly north of the colony on the Corinthian Gulf, was used for shipping to and from Italy, and was easily reached from the city's marketplace by the 3,150 metre-long Lechaion Road.[19] The Cenchreae Habour, on the other hand, being the lesser of the two, was located to the east of Corinth on the Saronic Gulf and served to facilitate trade with Asia.[20] Both Cenchreae and Lechaion grew quite famous in antiquity for their shipping and attest to the sheer volume of Corinth's commercial interests during the early empire.[21]

Corinth's prosperous marketplace

Many of the goods transported to the vicinity of Corinth, whether by land or sea, for the Pan-Hellenic festivities or everyday use, eventually made their way to be sold in the Corinthian marketplace (ἀγορά/*forum*).[22] And it was there where many local and international tradesmen exchanged their goods.[23] As Kathleen Warner Slane remarks, 'It is noteworthy ... that the ports of Corinth were located not at the *diolkos* but at the locations on their respective coasts closest to Corinth. This suggests that cargoes arriving from either direction were normally off-loaded and broken up, that Corinth acted as a middleman, and perhaps also as a market in the trade between east and west.'[24] Mary Hoskins Walbank similarly

[18] Corinth also had two simpler docking facilities at Schoenus and Poseidona which served either end of the *diolkos*, the 6 kilometre-long strip stretching across the narrowest part of the isthmus (Strabo, *Geogr.* 8.6.22; Pliny the Elder, *Nat.* 4.10). Some scholars have argued that the *diolkos* also functioned as a commercial thoroughfare, whereby smaller ships heading either east or west could be carried by trolleys from one end of the isthmus to the other. For a case against this position, see Pettegrew (2011).

[19] Strabo, *Geogr.* 8.6.22; Pausanias, *Descr.* 2.2.3. For the products and destinations of the Lechaion Harbour, see Engels (1990: 12).

[20] Dio Chrysostom, *Or.* 37.8; Apuleius, *Metam.* 10.35; Aristides, *Or.* 46.23; Livy, *Libri* 32.17.3. Cf. Murphy-O'Connor (2002: 16–19).

[21] Sanders (2005: 14–15).

[22] Corinth's bustling economy also owed much to the Isthmian Games, the second largest of the Pan-Hellenic festivals (Strabo, *Geogr.* 8.6.20).

[23] Pausanias provides a detailed description of the layout of the marketplace during the second century CE (*Descr.* 2.2.6–3.1). Unfortunately, in 77 CE an earthquake destroyed much of the city Paul knew. The marketplace then went under extensive reconstruction, so that much of what is discussed in ancient literature about the city's appearance post-dates the first century CE and is irrelevant for our study. Nevertheless, some archaeology and ancient sources are able to provide reliable evidence for the nature of Corinthian commerce in the mid first century CE.

[24] Slane (1989: 219). C. K. Williams (1993: 38–9): '[M]any of the market buildings at Corinth probably served as distribution centers for the various products that were to be

notes, 'Although Corinth's agricultural resources provided a valuable underpinning, the city's prosperity rested primarily on trade and on its function as an entrepôt between east and west, in addition to an invisible trade in usury and bottomry.'[25] Aristides vividly described the busyness of Corinth's marketplace and the profusion of its merchandise: 'Indeed, you would see it everywhere full of wealth [πλούτου] and an abundance of goods [πλήθους ἀγαθῶν], as much as is likely, since the earth on every side and the sea on every side flood it with these, as if it dwelled in the midst of its goods and was washed all around by them, like a merchant ship' (*Or.* 46.27).

Donald Engels' study on Roman Corinth has attempted to demonstrate that the city's economy was fuelled by something other than trade. While most cities in the Graeco-Roman period survived on agriculture and consumerism, Engels has controversially proposed that Corinth should be categorised as neither an agro- nor consumer-town. Rather, Engels contends that Corinth's economy was supported by services, that is, its numerous religious, educational, cultural, and judicial activities.[26] It is beyond the scope of this study to attempt either to confirm or deny Engels' thesis, but it is safe to affirm that Corinth had an unusually robust economy and relied to a large extent on trade. This owes much to the poor agricultural conditions of the *territorium* surrounding the city. Although some farming was possible, and in fact recent studies have shown that there was more arable land than some ancients supposed (cf. Strabo, *Geogr.* 8.6.23),[27] neither the size nor soil of the hinterland was suitable to sustain the Corinthian population and local economy.[28] The colony, then, was forced to take advantage of its easy access to trade routes and the services it could offer guests.

---

shipped abroad and for other products that were to be sold in the city and nearby, as well as for products destined for the eastern part of the Peloponnese and inland Arcadia.'

[25] M. E. Hoskins Walbank (2002: 259).

[26] For critiques of Engels' study, see Saller (1991); Spawforth (1991).

[27] Oakes (2009: 35): 'So much space seems to have been centuriated [in Corinth] that even if, as Strabo asserts, farming was difficult, it must have been a major component of the city's economic activity.' Cf. Romano (2003: 289–90); Romano (2005: 43).

[28] Engels (1990: 25): 'Corinth provided a huge market for agricultural surplus whose size had far outstripped the ability of its hinterland (*territorium*) to supply.' Williams (1993: 38): 'The Corinthia was not suited to raise a large crop of grain, at least not enough for export after the Augustan period. In fact, with the population that the Corinthia had after the initial colony took root – let us say in the Flavian-Hadrianic period – grain surely was imported on a regular basis to supply the needs of the area. Foodstuffs that were not able to be produced locally would have been much in demand in a provincial capital.' Cf. M. E. Hoskins Walbank (2002: 258–9).

Roman Corinth was well known for distributing a wide range of merchandise. C. K. Williams indicates that the items in especially high surplus there included wool, dyed woven goods, olive oil, honey, and wine.[29] Corinth also developed a reputation for its artisans. As Strabo reported, 'The city ... was always great and wealthy, and it was well equipped with men skilled both in the affairs of state and in the craftsman's arts; for both here and in Sicyon the arts of painting and modelling and all such arts of the craftsman flourished most' (*Geogr.* 8.6.23). Of its manufactured goods, Roman Corinth was best known for producing bronze, marble, and various kinds of pottery (e.g. terracotta lamps, terra sigillata, bowls, roof tiles).[30] Moreover, the large quantity of imports made Corinth an ideal location for those industries whose products required a combination of goods.[31] These locally manufactured items were probably produced in small factories outside the city, or even workshops in the marketplace.[32] In either case, business owners living in distant cities would have appointed various kinds of commercial administrator (*institores*) to supervise their local operations,[33] some of whom undoubtedly bore the title οἰκονόμος, ἐπίτροπος, *vilicus*, *actor*, or *dispensator*.[34]

Plutarch alludes to the prominence of these commercial middlemen when he uses πραγματευτής – another widely recognised synonym for οἰκονόμος – to describe the aggression of Achaean business agents and the threat they posed to habitual debtors: 'And so "one after another

[29] C. K. Williams (1993: 38); cf. Slane (1989: 220).

[30] Engels (1990: 33–9); cf. Broneer (1930); Spitzer (1942); Wright (1977: 453–73); Mattusch (2003); M. L. Zimmerman (2003). For the high volume of imported pottery during the first century CE, see Slane (1989: 221–3).

[31] Engels (1990: 33).

[32] For the excavations of workshops in the Corinthian marketplace, see C. K. Williams (1993: 37–8).

[33] Spawforth (1996: 171) argues that 'the new colony drew off eastern *negotiatores* from less well-located communities in Greece and the Aegean'. But a number of these wealthy entrepreneurs sent their freedmen commercial agents to the city to set up shop in their place. Spawforth suggests that the C. Heius family may serve as an example. Although these colonists were wealthy enough to hold public office shortly after the colony's founding (cf. *IKorinthKent* 151), it may be that this family of freedmen was commissioned to Corinth by the prominent Delian *negotiator* C. Heius Libo. If so, then 'we have here a case of a leading family of Roman businessmen which sent freedmen to represent its interests in the new colony' (172). But the stream of servile agents did not end at the city's inception. Spawforth surmises that 'colonial Corinth's reputation for being "freedman-friendly" continued to attract freedmen in the years after the foundation' (170).

[34] The only extant epigraphic occurrence of οἰκονόμος in Corinth attests to the purchase (ἀγοράζω) of a sepulchre in the later-Roman period by a certain Loukas from the οἰκονόμος Andreas (*SEG* 11.171b; *IKorinthKent* 558). Kent suggests that the two individuals were imperial employees.

takes over" the borrower,[35] first a usurer or broker of Corinth [τοκιστὴς ἢ πραγματευτὴς Κορίνθιος], then one of Patrae, then an Athenian, until, attacked on all sides by all of them, he is dissolved and chopped up into the small change of interest payments' (*Mor.* 831a).[36] The early colony had a large contingent of just these kinds of business agent. As Williams remarks,

> The freedmen-agents were an important part of the population sent to Corinth, serving the wealthy families who foresaw the colony as a potentially strong commercial center. These freedmen were sent out to ensure Roman control of the markets at this point on the east-west trade route and to secure positions for interested Roman families in this new distribution center in the eastern Peloponnesos.[37]

Corinth's commercial prosperity, then, clearly developed a reputation that was widely recognised both inside and outside the city, that is, among its residents as well as among itinerant philosophers and visiting apostles. The constant influx of potential converts was probably even a major reason why Paul devoted to this church so much time, energy, and letter-writing. For at Corinth Paul had an ideal base for his Gentile mission – to secure viable churches there would be to guarantee the proliferation of the gospel all across the Mediterranean world.[38] Most importantly for our purposes, however, Corinth's commercial fame provided Paul with a familiar metaphorical field from which to draw an illustrative portrait of his apostolic position. Paul's *oikonomos* metaphor would have resonated deeply in Corinth's commercial context, carrying with it not a few implications about who Paul was, what he was sent to do, and what kind of authority he possessed.

Paul and ancient commerce

The plausibility of Paul's use of a distinctly commercial metaphor finds additional support once it is recognised that the apostle spent considerable time in such commercial-related contexts. According to Luke, Paul

---

[35] Here Plutarch quotes the Greek philosopher Empedocles (*c.* 490–430 BCE).

[36] Based on this text, C. K. Williams (1993: 31 n. 3) reasons that 'Corinth especially was known for its business representatives'. Commenting on the wretchedness and desperation of Corinthian retailers, Dio Chrysostom remarks how one can observe in Corinth 'peddlers [καπήλων] not a few peddling [διακαπηλευόντων] whatever they happened to have' (*Or.* 8.9).

[37] C. K. Williams (1993: 33).   [38] Sanders (2005: 15).

preached in the marketplace daily while in Athens (Acts 17.17), and he probably did the same in other cities as well. Indeed, Paul was especially well acquainted with the Corinthian marketplace, for it was there he stood trial before Gallio (Acts 18.12–16) and it was the ἀγορά he had in view when urging the Corinthians not to dispute over the consumption of polluted foods purchased from the local meat market (1 Cor 10.25). In fact, Paul and his co-workers themselves would probably have been familiar faces in the marketplace of Corinth – as well as in Thessalonica, Ephesus, and elsewhere – where they are reported to have laboured as artisans from dawn to dusk for eighteen months (Acts 18.3, 11; 1 Cor 4.12; cf. 1 Thess 2.9).[39]

Paul's particular trade as a tentmaker (σκηνοποιός) also situated the apostle in various urban workshops (ἐργαστήρια/*officinae/tabernae*).[40] According to Ronald Hock, Paul would have laboured in such shops 'wherever and whenever he was doing missionary preaching and teaching'.[41] Although Hock explains that the size of these workshops depended on their location, he suggests that the average shop accommodated between about a half-dozen and a dozen artisans. Paul's workshop in Corinth was at least large enough to accommodate him, Aquila, and Priscilla, and functioned also as their residence (Acts 18.3).[42] Furthermore, although the NT does not indicate whether Paul himself laboured in an administrative hierarchy significant enough to require a manager, Aeschines explains that in the fourth century BCE a certain Athenian workshop which employed nine or ten slave leatherworkers was large enough to require a superintendent (ἡγεμών, *Tim.* 97). Thus, it is very plausible that the apostle was personally familiar with how local businesses and commercial enterprises were managed, making private administration the likely source domain of his *oikonomos* metaphor.[43]

---

[39] Hock (1979: 440): 'Paul's reference to Barnabas' working to support himself (1 Cor 9:6) would thus cover the so-called first missionary journey and the stays in Antioch (Acts 13:1–14:25 and 14:26–28; 15:30–35), the periods when Luke has Barnabas as Paul's travel and missionary companion.'

[40] For Paul's trade, see Hock (1980: 20–1), who also notes that 'most workshops would be located in or near the *agora*', and in close proximity to businesses specialising in the same trade (30).

[41] Hock (1979: 440).

[42] Hock (1980: 33); Murphy-O'Connor (2002: 194).

[43] Note also Paul's frequent use of commercial terminology: ἀγοράζω, κτλ. (1 Cor 6.20; 7.23; Gal 3.13; 4.5); ἀπέχω (Phil 4.18; Phlm 15); κερδαίνω, κτλ. (1 Cor 9.19–22; Phil 3.7, 8); μισθός/ὀψώνιον (Rom 4.4; 6.23; 1 Cor 3.8, 14; 9.17–18); ὀφείλω, κτλ. (Rom 1.14; 4.4; 8.12; 13.7, 8; 15.27; 1 Cor 7.3; Gal 5.3; Phlm 18, 19); πιπράσκω (Rom 7.14); ζημιόω, κτλ. (1 Cor 3.15; Phil 1.21; 3.7–8). Cf. Zenos (1891: 75–6); Arzt-Grabner (2011).

Summary

Through just a cursory analysis of Paul's metaphorical use of οἰκονόμος and οἰκονομία in 1 Corinthians 4 and 9, we noticed that the managerial structure in which Paul served as apostle far more closely resembles the systems implemented in ancient private administration than in Hellenistic kingdoms and Graeco-Roman cities. Moreover, this source domain would have resonated deeply with the church in Corinth, since the colony was renowned throughout antiquity as a centre for international trade and was during the Roman period the home to many servile business agents. Beyond this, Paul's gospel preaching and leatherworking profession situated him among all sorts of merchants and craftsmen for many hours at a time, exposing him to the social, legal, and administrative intricacies of the commercial world. With this first-hand experience in the realm of the ἀγορά and ἐργαστήριον, it seems to be well within the capability of Paul to draw on his understanding of the commercial world for the purpose of illustrating to a church all too familiar with trade and business his role and responsibilities as an administrator of God.

6

INTERPRETING PAUL'S METAPHOR
IN 1 CORINTHIANS 4.1–5

Think of us in this way, as servants of Christ and administrators
of God's mysteries.   1 Cor 4.1

Having established the private commercial world of Roman Corinth as
the most plausible context in which to read Paul's *oikonomos* metaphor,
over the next two chapters we shall investigate how Paul utilises the metaphor in 1 Corinthians to elucidate his apostolic authority. The concept of
authority in Paul is, however, quite complex, and admittedly a number
of avenues could have yielded results. But this particular metaphor has
been selected because of its relative neglect in Pauline scholarship and
its repeated use in key Pauline discourses. Even more importantly, this
image provides a unique insight into our larger theological concerns:
the *construction* and *assertion* of authority. Over the course of the next
two chapters we shall therefore seek to demonstrate how Paul employs
the *oikonomos* metaphor in both 1 Corinthians 4 and 9 to negotiate his
identity as a person of privilege and authority, on the one hand, and one
of relative insignificance and obligatory service, on the other. Moreover,
in both passages Paul applies the metaphor in an effort to respond to
perceived or anticipated critics. These texts therefore provide ample
opportunity to analyse Paul's description and exercise of authority in
contexts where apostolic rights are expressly in view and, indeed, a
matter of some dispute.[1]

In the present chapter, we shall seek (i) to identify *what* Paul's metaphor in 1 Cor 4.1–5 indicates about his understanding of apostolic ministry (especially concerning hierarchy, responsibility, and accountability),
and (ii) to trace *how* Paul employs the image there to bring about ecclesial

---

[1] Our two passages have significant commonalities. Aside from Paul's shared metaphorical use of οἰκονόμος/οἰκονομία (1 Cor 4.1–2; 9.17), in both texts Paul is on the defensive, as there were apparently some in the church who were scrutinising him (ἀνακρίνω,
4.3–4; 9.3; cf. 2.15–16). For additional thematic parallels, see Still III (2004); Phua (2005:
179–85).

and ethical change. To meet these two goals, it will also be important to identify the problems Paul faced in Corinth, including the kinds of resistance, or power play, the apostle perceived himself to be confronting. It will be argued that 1 Corinthians 1–4 reveals not only the existence of fractures in the church at Corinth, but that the divisions themselves materialised as a result of a fundamental misunderstanding about who, or what, apostles are, and a corresponding misapprehension about how the church should relate to them. Moreover, based on the content, style, and tone of Paul's discourse, it will be argued that Paul perceived his authority to be the subject of criticism in Corinth. Unfortunately, the validity of some of these socio-rhetorical assumptions has been challenged in recent scholarship. We must therefore begin our investigation by addressing the socio-rhetorical context of 1 Corinthians 1–4. Once a plausible case is made for reading the letter this way, we shall then turn our attention to Paul's discourse in 4.1–5.

Socio-rhetorical context

Our investigation must begin with an analysis of the socio-rhetorical context of the first four chapters of the letter so as to establish as best we can something of the relationship Paul perceived himself to have had with the Corinthians when he wrote. The central questions to ask at this stage are: What is Paul's primary rhetorical objective in 1 Corinthians? What are his subsidiary rhetorical objectives in 1.18–4.21? What does he perceive to be the current status of his relationship with the Corinthian church? What has Paul attempted to accomplish by the time he reaches 4.1–5?

The appearance of Margaret Mitchell's 1991 book-length treatment on the rhetoric of 1 Corinthians marked a significant watershed in the analysis of Paul's letter. In her seminal study, *Paul and the Rhetoric of Reconciliation*, Mitchell argued that 1 Corinthians is a unified composition with a single rhetorical objective, and as a case of deliberative rhetoric, the letter has ecclesial reconciliation as its primary goal.[2] Her argument rests on both the letter's form and its thematic congruencies, which closely resemble those modelled on ancient rhetorical handbooks and exhibited in both ancient speeches and letters.

---

[2] M. M. Mitchell (1991: 24): 'Deliberative rhetoric is argumentation which urges an audience, either public or private, to pursue a particular course of action in the future.' For 1 Corinthians as deliberative rhetoric, see also Kennedy (1984: 87); Welborn (1987a: 326); Welborn (1987b: 89); Pogoloff (1992: 25); Witherington (1995: 75). For critiques of Mitchell and Witherington, see Porter (1997: 551–4); Anderson (1999: 254–65).

Mitchell's conclusions are largely convincing since, when 1 Corinthians is taken as a compositional unit, Paul's reconciliatory objective is apparent from beginning to end.[3] Most telling of the letter's deliberative intentions are: (i) its prospective outlook, or future orientation, most evident in Paul's use of παρακαλῶ ὑμᾶς in 1.10, 4.16, and 16.15, the first and last instances forming an inclusio around most of the epistle; (ii) the repeated appeals to 'advantage', explicit in the use of συμφέρω/σύμφορος (6.12; 7.5, 35; 10.23, 33; 12.7); (iii) the use of a variety of examples, in this case from the Hebrew Scriptures, Hellenistic culture, and Paul's own life and ministry; and (iv) the presence of factions in the community (σχίσματα, 1.10; 11.28; αἱρέσεις, 11.19; ἔριδες, 1.11; 3.3), which Paul repeatedly sought to resolve.[4] Furthermore, if the inclusio formed by παρακαλῶ ὑμᾶς in 1.10 and 16.15 marks the compositional and rhetorical unity of the entire letter, then the inclusio formed by the phrase in 1.10 and 4.16 indicates that 1.18–4.21 forms a subsection within it.[5] The separateness of this unit is also indicated by the inclusio formed by Paul's descriptions of his evangelistic role in the community (1.17; 4.15).

In Mitchell's framework, 1.10 serves as the letter's thesis statement (πρόθεσις/*propositio*) and 1.11–17 functions as the statement of facts (διήγησις/*narratio*). The proof sections (πίστεις/*probationes*) are (a) 1.18–4.21, (b) 5.1–11.1, (c) 11.2–14.40, and (d) 15.1–57,[6] with 15.58 functioning as the conclusion (ἐπίλογος) and 16.1–24 as the epistolary closing.[7] But while many scholars now agree with Mitchell about the general deliberative character of 1 Corinthians, there remains some uncertainty concerning the rhetorical function of the first proof (1.18–4.21).[8] If the entire letter is deliberative, then how does this unit contribute to Paul's argument?

---

[3] Cf. R. F. Collins (1999: 20). Ciampa and Rosner (2006) argue that Paul's primary objective in 1 Corinthians is to establish the purity of the church.

[4] M. M. Mitchell (1991: 65–183). For the church as embroiled in bickering, yet undivided, see Munck (1959).

[5] M. M. Mitchell (1991: 207). Ciampa and Rosner (2006: 210–12) argue that the first major section ends at 4.17, while 4.18 begins a new section concerning sexual immorality and greed that extends to 7.40.

[6] M. M. Mitchell (1991: 207). For an alternative approach to framing the proofs, see Witherington (1995: vi–viii).

[7] Some of Mitchell's advocates consider 16.1–12 to be an additional proof, 16.13–18 the recapitulation (*peroratio*), and 16.18–24 the letter closing; cf. Witherington (1995: 313–24).

[8] M. M. Mitchell (1991: 207): 'While scholars are virtually unanimous in regarding 1:18 (or 1:10) – 4:21 as a discrete section of the letter, a section which treats the problem of Corinthian factions, there is debate about the function and purpose of this section within the whole composition.'

Prior to Mitchell's influential volume, many interpreters considered 1.18–4.21 to be a defence of Paul's apostolic authority, due to the seemingly apologetic function of many of his self-referential statements (esp. 2.1–5; 3.1–4; 4.1–5, 8–16).[9] More recently, however, Mitchell and others have contended that Paul had no opponents during the writing of the epistle, his apostleship was not being challenged by anybody in the church, and those passages which appear to be polemical only do so on the basis of illegitimate mirror-reading.[10] Furthermore, because these scholars insist that Paul's letter must conform to one rhetorical genre,[11] and 1 Corinthians is a case of deliberative rhetoric, all self-referential and seemingly apologetic elements are dismissed as *exempla*.[12] These interpreters even find textual support for their readings in Paul's use of μιμητής (4.16) and the verb μετασχηματίζω (4.6), the latter implying through 'covert allusion' that the disputes between the parties which attached themselves to Paul, Apollos, and Cephas (1.12; 3.4, 22) were purely figurative and represented by way of analogy altogether different quarrels centring on unnamed leaders in the church.[13] Paul's apostleship at the time was therefore unchallenged.

In spite of these arguments, there remain good reasons for regarding 1.18–4.21 as serving a defensive function. First, although some interpreters reject the possibility that a deliberative letter might simultaneously have an apologetic objective, the rhetorical flexibility of the epistolary genre permits certain passages in a deliberative piece to have

---

[9] A chief proponent of this position was Dahl (1967). The final footnote in the essay's re-publication, however, reveals some of Dahl's later reservations; Dahl (1977b: 61 n. 50): 'To call the section "apologetic" is to downplay the degree to which Paul is critical of his own adherents as well as of his opponents. Nevertheless, the section lays a foundation for the subsequent parts of the letter, it serves to reestablish Paul's true authority, and it does contain apologetic elements, see esp. 1 Cor. 4:2–5 and 18–21.' Cf. Baur (1873); J. Weiss (1910: 92); Barrett (1968: 101); Schütz (1975: 190); Theissen (1975); Chance (1982); Bünker (1984: 52–9); Marshall (1987: 217); Plank (1987: 11–24); Fee (1987: 48–9).

[10] M. M. Mitchell (1991: 54–5); Pogoloff (1992: 102); Witherington (1995: 74).

[11] Anderson (1999: 255).

[12] J. T. Fitzgerald (1988: 120–2); M. M. Mitchell (1991: 54–5, 209); Pickett (1997: 74–84); B. J. Dodd (1999: 45).

[13] The literary device was typically used to admonish an audience by way of analogy. Fiore (1985: 95), for instance, recognises that Paul uses covert allusion through the metaphors in 3.5–4.5, which seek to instruct the church how to regard their leaders. Hall (1994), on the other hand, claims that the apostolic parties mentioned in the letter represent entirely different quarrels, so that the parties and disputes Paul attaches to the apostles did not actually concern them. In a later essay, however, Hall (2003: 3–29) argues that the party leaders in 1 Corinthians were Christian sophists who did in fact criticise the apostle for his lack of rhetorical skill and were the false apostles whom Paul targeted in 2 Corinthians 10–13.

a defensive posture.[14] Several units within 1 Corinthians, in fact, feature characteristics of non-deliberative rhetoric. Mitchell herself concedes that 1.18–4.21 includes epideictic elements and 'has as its purpose the censuring of the Corinthians for their factionalism'.[15] George Kennedy also observes that, even though 1 Corinthians is 'largely deliberative', 'it contains some judicial [i.e. apologetic] passages, for example 1:13–17 claiming that [Paul] had not created faction in Corinth and chapter 9 defending his rights as an apostle'.[16] Such rhetorical licence even within a deliberative letter opens the door for the possibility of also attributing to 1.18–4.21 an apologetic function.

Secondly, there remain clues that the apostles mentioned by Paul in the party slogans (1.12; 3.4, 21–3) represent themselves, so that they were the very leaders who were the focus of inappropriate partisanship. Despite the objection of interpreters who, on account of Paul's use of 'covert allusion', fictionalise the disclosed *apostolic* parties (Paul, Apollos, Cephas) and assume the existence of parties attached to undisclosed *local* leaders, it seems quite excessive to allow Paul's use of μετασχηματίζω in 4.6 to mask *which* leaders are in view. In fact, there is no indication that unnamed leaders were ever the objects of boasting in 1 Corinthians. And if Paul was not included among the revered leaders, then why did he remove himself from the disputes by denying his participation in baptism (1.13–16) when local leaders almost certainly could not have denied the same? Rather, as Morna Hooker has argued, the ταῦτα in 4.6, as the direct object of μετασχηματίζω, refers only to the three metaphors employed in 3.5–4.5 (gardeners, builders, servants/administrators). These were 'figuratively applied' to Paul, Apollos, and perhaps Cephas not to hide the identities of the actual party leaders, but to demonstrate that apostles are merely intermediaries and should not be the objects of adulation.[17] Thus, a minimalist reading of this rhetorical device is preferred, as it simply highlights the use of analogy,

---

[14] R. F. Collins (1996: 60–1): '[T]he modes of rhetorical argumentation were sometimes so intermingled in a single sustained argument that one could speak of a mixed type of rhetoric.' Aune (1987: 23): 'Greco-Roman literary composition often departed from the prescriptions of ancient literary and rhetorical theory.' Cf. F. J. Long (2004: 24–8).

[15] M. M. Mitchell (1991: 209–10, cf. 213–25). Cf. Smit (2003). For the use of epideictic rhetoric in deliberative and forensic speeches, see the comment ascribed to Cicero: 'And if epideictic is only seldom employed by itself independently, still in judicial and deliberative causes extensive sections are often devoted to praise or censure' (*Rhet. her.* 3.8.15).

[16] Kennedy (1984: 87). Cf. Schüssler Fiorenza (1987: 393). For recent advocates of the apologetic function of 1 Corinthians 1–4, or parts of it, see Litfin (1994: 171); Vos (1996: 87, 90, 119); Ker (2000: 90–1); Smit (2002: 250); Wanamaker (2003: 136); F. J. Long (2004: 120).

[17] Hooker (1963: 131); cf. Ker (2000: 92).

not an undisclosed agenda. Accordingly, while the slogans which Paul recites to the Corinthians in 1.12 may not be '*actual* party-cries from the Corinthians themselves', we can reasonably conclude that 'underlying Paul's statements in 1:12 is an historical truth that people at Corinth are lining up behind the various missionaries', namely, Paul, Apollos, and Cephas.[18]

Thirdly, there is significant evidence to support the case that Paul at least *perceived* his authority to be in jeopardy. While at the time of this letter there was probably neither any intrusion of false teachers in Corinth nor the outright rejection of the apostle by the Corinthians, there remain indications that Paul considered his apostolic authority, or primacy, to be a matter of real dispute. Admittedly, Nils Dahl goes too far when he deduces that '[t]he other slogans are all to be understood as declarations of independence from Paul'.[19] Nevertheless, since Paul himself indicates that the parties in the church included a group *loyal* to him, it is reasonable to suppose that there were also persons in Corinth who were *critical* of him. This is also apparent in Paul's repeated efforts to clarify his apostolic role and manner of preaching (1.17; 2.1–5; 3.1–4; 4.1–5).

Not every exegete will agree with this assessment, since some mirror-reading is required. Mirror-reading as a hermeneutical method has, after all, been heavily criticised by a number of NT interpreters.[20] Mitchell, for instance, prudently challenges the assumption that whenever Paul speaks about himself, he seeks 'always to ward off charges'.[21] Nevertheless, one should be wary of any methodological protest that calls for a radical reversal of the hermeneutical pendulum. Mitchell's suspicions about mirror-reading, while valid, need not result in the absolute abandonment of the technique. After all, the decision to interpret every Pauline self-reference merely as an *exemplum* requires just as much presumption as the judgments made in mirror-reading. To obtain carefully formulated exegesis, one needs only to apply a cautious and consistent methodology.[22] Our

---

[18] M. M. Mitchell (1991: 83, original emphasis).

[19] Dahl (1967: 322).

[20] Lyons (1985) suggests that mirror-reading is 'an inappropriate, if not entirely fallacious, method for identifying either Paul's opponents or the function of his autobiographical remarks: (1) It does not give sufficient weight to the argumentative origins of Paul's denials and antithetical formulations, while (2) it gives too much weight to extra-textual assumptions' (96); '[s]ince we have only Paul's presumed defense and not the accusation, it is necessary to exercise restraint in asserting too confidently that a specific charge existed, and if so, what it may have been' (97). Cf. Baird (1990: 119).

[21] M. M. Mitchell (1991: 55 n. 156). She does consider 2 Corinthians 10–13 to be a defence.

[22] Ironically, it was Dahl (1967: 317–18) who first issued 'a strict method' in the study of 1 Corinthians 1–4; cf. Sumney (2005: 44).

study, then, will benefit further from the methodological principles proposed by John Barclay and Jerry Sumney.[23]

In his influential article on mirror-reading, Barclay offers seven criteria useful in the evaluation of a polemical letter. (1) The *type of utterance* requires that the reader consider the significance and limitations of certain kinds of statement (assertions, commands, etc.). Barclay explains, among other things, the implications of Pauline *denials*: 'If Paul makes a *denial*, we may assume that, *at least*, those whom he addresses may be prone to regard what he denies as true, and *at most*, someone has explicitly asserted it.'[24] (2) *Tone* demands due attention to be given to those statements made with emphasis and urgency. (3) *Frequency* suggests that statements made in repetition are probably central themes. (4) *Clarity* insists that the interpreter consider whether the text contains any significant ambiguities that might prevent the reader from giving it priority. (5) *Unfamiliarity* asks whether a theological motif is so uncommon that it stands out as something against which Paul might be reacting. (6) *Consistency* considers whether the previously mentioned criteria taken collectively point to a single opponent. (7) *Historical plausibility* allows what other evidence is available to be considered in order to demonstrate the likelihood of the hypothesis.

These criteria when applied collectively suggest that in 1 Corinthians Paul was reacting polemically to an urgent matter in the church. Since, according to Barclay's method, the very presence of a denial permits the reader to assume that the audience was at least inclined to believe the contrary, then Paul's *clear*, *emphatic*, and *repeated denials* about the role of eloquent speech in his preaching (1.17; 2.1–5; cf. 2 Cor 10.10) suggest that these issues – which are relatively *unfamiliar* outside the Corinthian correspondence (cf. 1 Thess 2.1–12) – were probably misunderstood by, and were of particular importance to, the church in Corinth. Moreover, Bruce Winter and others have convincingly demonstrated the *historical*

---

[23] Barclay (1987: 84) considers mirror-reading to be 'a good deal more difficult than is usually acknowledged, but not wholly impossible. What is needed is a carefully controlled method of working which uses logical criteria and proceeds with suitable caution.' In some ways, mirror-reading 1 Corinthians is on surer ground than many other Pauline letters, since certain difficulties present elsewhere do not apply here. In 1 Corinthians, for example, Paul directly addresses his so-called critics, rather than responding to one party about the remarks made by another, as in 2 Corinthians. Similarly, while Paul utilises some hyperbole and sarcasm in 1 Corinthians – the quarrels probably did not involve 'each' believer (1.12), Paul was not completely indifferent to personal scrutiny (4.3; cf. 4.14–16), and he did not actually consider the Corinthians to be wealthy, wise, strong, and honoured kings (4.8–10) – the distorting effects of polemic apparent perhaps in Galatians are less of a concern in 1 Corithians.

[24] Barclay (1987: 84, original emphasis).

plausibility of this reading in their reconstructions of the Corinthian disputes against the backdrop of Graeco-Roman oratory and the budding Second Sophistic (the second-century CE Hellenistic Renaissance).[25]

Sumney's basic methodology for identifying Pauline opponents also confirms our suspicions. In order to prioritise certain kinds of Pauline pericopae over others, Sumney differentiates between *explicit statements* ('those in which the author speaks directly about the opponents'), *allusions* ('statements which seem to address opponents, but are indirect, and so more or less oblique references to them'), and *affirmations* ('statements which neither explicitly refer to opponents nor obviously allude to them').[26] When seeking to identify which texts make reference to opponents, Sumney naturally grants more weight, or 'certainty', to explicit rather than allusive statements – even though he is suspicious of the 'reliability' of data arising from polemical and apologetic contexts, over against didactic, thanksgivings, and similar kinds of discourse.[27] But since the *reliability* of Paul's report need not prevent us from concluding that during this early period Paul at least *perceived* himself to have had critics in Corinth (even if not opponents/false teachers), it is notable that Sumney's methodology enabled him to identify no fewer than eleven verses in 1 Corinthians 1–4 explicitly referring to critics (1.10–12; 3.3–4, 21–2; 4.3, 6–7, 18–19) and another thirty alluding to them (1.13–17, 18–25; 2.1–5, 13–16; 3.5–9; 4.8–13). As Sumney remarks, 'Our search for opponents has yielded no evidence that the problems in Corinth are the result of intruders who are attempting to take Paul's place. Rather, the questions raised about Paul come from the Corinthians themselves. There are clearly challenges to his authority as he is compared to other leaders, specifically at least Cephas and Apollos.'[28] With Sumney, then, we can conclude that Paul's apostolic authority was being scrutinised by some in the church when he wrote 1 Corinthians.

This reconstruction becomes even more plausible once it is realised that Paul's preaching, presence, and apostleship came under heavier attack, provoking an even more comprehensive defence, in 2 Corinthians. Indeed, it seems quite unlikely that the themes included in Paul's self-referential statements in 1 Corinthians 1–4 (esp. 1.17; 2.1–5) would become the basis of the accusations addressed in subsequent correspondence (cf. 2 Cor 10.10) unless they were already in dispute – even

---

[25] Winter (2000: 31–43); Winter (2002: 180–202); cf. Clarke (1993: 36–9, 101–5); Litfin (1994: 137–209); Shi (2008: 112–86); Mihaila (2009).

[26] Sumney (1999: 23).   [27] Sumney (1999: 25–32).

[28] Sumney (1999: 79).

in embryonic form – during this earlier period. Such a scenario is highly improbable.

If 1.18–4.21 does have an apologetic function, however, then it must also be explained briefly how Paul's autobiographical remarks and reflections about his preaching serve the reconciliatory (deliberative) intentions of 1 Corinthians while also functioning as more than paradigms to be imitated (*exempla*).[29] After all, how can Paul instruct the Corinthians to imitate him if they are against him? But as we have already conceded, when Paul wrote the letter his apostolic authority was neither totally under attack nor even the primary problem in Corinth. And because the Corinthians had not been introduced to formal opponents during this period, there was no need for Paul to deliver a full apologetic just yet. After all, nobody in antiquity wanted to hear others praise themselves, for 'to speak to others of one's own importance or power is offensive' (Plutarch, *Mor.* 539a).[30] Rather, Paul sought only briefly to censure the Corinthian believers and justify his *modus operandi*, in order to eliminate the church's party mentality while also regaining their confidence so he could instruct them further about ecclesial unity and Christian maturity. As Duane Litfin explains, 'The fact is that in raising the subject of his preaching Paul has not left the Corinthian quarrels at all. On the contrary, he has moved to the heart of them.'[31]

Thus, we can with confidence agree with Peter Marshall when he asserts, 'It is clear through 1:10–4:21 Paul is defending himself in an endeavour to re-restablish his apostolic authority in Corinth and that the divisions in Corinth were related to criticisms that some had made against Paul's conduct as an apostle.'[32] Furthermore, while the reader need not conclude that Paul was facing formal opponents, Paul's censuring of the Corinthians for their apparent criticisms of his preaching (2.1–5; 3.1–4; 4.3–5) suggests that Paul was facing more hostility from the church than many recent interpreters have realised.

Literary context

Interpreters of 1 Corinthians have not infrequently attempted to subdivide 1.18–4.21 into smaller units. Among these approaches, Joop Smit's

---

[29] F. J. Long (2004: 55) observes that, although examples (παραδείγματα/*exempla*) were employed often in deliberative rhetoric, they were also commonly used in forensic rhetoric.

[30] See, e.g., Favorinus (Dio Chrysostom, *Or.* 37), who defended his former statue rather than himself in order to avoid self-praise; cf. Gleason (1995: 9); L. M. White (2005: 67–73).

[31] Litfin (1994: 188).   [32] Marshall (1987: 217).

analysis is to be preferred. Smit contends that 'this passage consists of four general reflections, each in a different, highly rhetorical style and followed by a practical conclusion formulated with much less rhetorical flourish'.[33] Smit argues that the stylised reflections and corresponding conclusions are divided as follows: (a) 1.18–31 followed by 2.1–5; (b) 2.6–16 followed by 3.1–4; (c) 3.5–23 followed by 4.1–5; and (d) 4.6–13 followed by 4.14–21.[34] As Smit argues,

> In 1 Cor 1,10–4,21 Paul builds up an argument to justify his rather unimpressive performance. To that end, from the four encomia [1.18–31; 2.6–16; 3.5–23; 4.6–13], evaluations of a more general character, he draws four specific conclusions regarding his former preaching at Corinth: this is in accordance with the highest, divine norms (2,1–5); this has been consciously adapted to the starting-position of the Corinthians (3,1–4); the Corinthians do not have the right to judge Paul, because he is in the service of God (4,1–5); as founder of the community Paul is entitled to the respect of the Corinthians (4,14–21).[35]

What is striking about Smit's proposed pattern is that the four conclusions clearly stand apart from their corresponding reflections, not simply in their lack of rhetorical flourish, but also in the directness with which Paul communicates with the Corinthians. In each conclusion Paul turns from a primarily third-person point of view to address the church in the first and second person.[36] Also, the transitions in 2.1 and 3.1 are marked

[33] Smit (2003: 185). It could be that in this discourse, despite his verbal dismissal of rhetoric, Paul was attempting to demonstrate his rhetorical skill; cf. Wire (1990: 47); Smit (2002: 247).

[34] For these divisions, consider the terminological associations observed by Smit (2002: 236–9): (a) the relationship between ὁ λόγος and δύναμις θεοῦ from 1.18 resurfaces in 2.1–5; Χριστὸς ἐσταυρωμένος from 1.23 reappears in 2.2; τὰ ἀσθενῆ from 1.25–7 becomes ἐν ἀσθενείᾳ in 2.3; the rejection of σοφία ἀνθρώπων at the end of the first unit (2.5) announces the theme of the second (2.6–3.4); (b) λαλέω (2.6, 7, 13) and πνευματικός (2.13(2x), 15) reappear in 3.1; λαλοῦμεν ἐν τοῖς τελείοις in 2.6 is in opposition to λαλῆσαι … ὡς νηπίοις in 3.1; the formula οὐ … ἀλλά from 2.6–7, 8–9, 12–13 is repeated twice in 3.1–2; Paul and Apollos, who are mentioned in the slogans at the end of the second unit (3.4), announce the theme of the third (3.5–4.5); (c) Paul's explicit use of metaphor in 3.5–17 resurfaces in 4.1–5, with the ὑπηρέται and οἰκονόμοι in 4.1 corresponding especially with the διάκονοι and συνεργοί from 3.5 and 9; the judgment theme in 3.12–17 is repeated in 4.3–5; the synecdochic use of ἡμέρα for judgment in 3.13 recurs at 4.3; the hierarchy exhibited in 3.18–23 is qualified in 4.1–5; (d) the verb φυσιόω stated at 4.6 is repeated as the main theme in 4.18–19.

[35] Smit (2003: 200).

[36] Paul occasionally addresses the church in the second person outside these conclusions, but the conclusions stand apart in tone; cf. Fiore (1985: 87–8); Smit (2002: 232); Smit (2003: 185, 200).

by the expression κἀγώ ἀδελφοί, demonstrating that 2.1–5 and 3.1–4 share the same function in their respective units.

Smit's analysis has significant implications for how one reads 1 Corinthians 1–4. Based on placement, directness, and tone, the conclusion passages should be given far more weight when interpreting Paul's rhetorical objectives than they have received in much recent scholarship. By concentrating on these smaller units, the reader will no doubt detect Paul's stern tone of blame and defence. In the following survey, then, we shall briefly summarise Paul's arguments in 1.18–2.5, 2.6–3.4, and 3.5–4.5 in order to prepare for a more comprehensive analysis of 4.1–5.

1 Cor 1.18–2.5

Paul's primary concern in 1.18–2.5 is to demonstrate the centrality of the power of God and alternatively the powerlessness of persuasion in gospel proclamation. This emphasis is apparent through the way 1.17 and 2.4–5 bracket the unit, as both texts (i) deny Paul's use of words of wisdom (οὐκ ἐν σοφίᾳ λόγου, 1.17; οὐκ ἐν πειθοῖς σοφίας λόγοις, 2.4), and (ii) convey the rationale for Paul's *modus operandi* (ἵνα μὴ κενωθῇ ὁ σταυρὸς τοῦ Χριστοῦ, 1.17; ἵνα ἡ πίστις ὑμῶν μὴ ᾖ ἐν σοφίᾳ ἀνθρώπων ἀλλ' ἐν δυνάμει θεοῦ, 2.5).[37] For the remainder of the unit (1.18–31), Paul responds to those in the church who desire that persuasion play a central role in his preaching by demonstrating how such an approach to ministry would obstruct the receipt of the wisdom and power intrinsic to the message itself (1.18, 24, 30). But while Paul surely seeks to illustrate the power of the word of the cross, he emphasises to an even greater extent the utter weakness of conventional wisdom by demonstrating the inability of the σάρξ to grasp such a foolish gospel (1.26, 29). Indeed, the rejection of the gospel by professional academics (σοφός, γραμματεύς, συζητητής, 1.20), the dismissal of the message by sign-demanding Jews and wisdom-seeking Greeks (1.22–3), and yet the salvation of the unimpressive Corinthian believers – most of whom lacked worldly wisdom, power, and nobility (1.26) – indicate that conventional wisdom and power are at odds with the wisdom and power of God.[38]

---

[37] Litfin (1994: 190): 'The close parallelism of these two statements is no accident. The first looks forward, the second looks back; the first states the theme to be developed in 1.18–2.5, the second restates the same theme, this time as a conclusion of what has just been developed.'

[38] M. M. Mitchell (1991: 212) maintains that Paul intended here to show how 'God's wisdom has the power to unite all those who are called, both Jew and Greek (1:24; cf. 12:13), thus ending ethnic separation in the common acceptance of the scandal of the cross

Instead, God saves those whose minds have been transformed to regard real wisdom and power as exhibited in the cross (1.30), so that no one can boast before God (1.29), but only in him (1.31).[39] As Litfin explains, '[I]n his wisdom God chooses to work through means which the world finds weak, foolish, and unimpressive so that there can be no question in the end as to who has accomplished the result.'[40]

Thus, in 1.18–2.5 Paul explains that he could not have utilised 'words of wisdom' (i.e. persuasive speech) in his articulation of the gospel because the gospel is utter foolishness from the perspective of conventional wisdom. Only divine wisdom transmitted through God's mystery (2.1) and divine power applied through God's spirit (2.4) are able to produce faith in the unbeliever (2.5). In this unit, then, Paul aims to re-establish the validity of his seemingly unimpressive mode of gospel proclamation and to censure the church for preferring an alternative approach. As Litfin aptly summarises, 'Paul's goal is nothing less than to defend his modus operandi as a preacher. To do so he must demonstrate that it is theologically inspired. Hence he argues that he could not have operated otherwise; he was locked into simple proclamation – in contrast to the impressive εὐγλωττία of the rhetor – by the demands of the Gospel itself.'[41]

1 Cor 2.6–3.4

After establishing in 1.18–2.5 the rationale for his unimpressive manner of preaching, Paul in 2.6–3.4 explains why it was that he brought the Corinthians an equally unimpressive message. Paul's primary concern in

---

(1:23–24).' This interpretation would support her emphasis on reconciliation in the letter. But Paul's reference to the crucifixion of Christ in 1.23 does not demonstrate God's unifying intentions for Jews and Greeks, but the paradoxical power and wisdom of his seemingly unimpressive gospel. As becomes clear in 1.24, Paul sought to demonstrate that Christ's humiliating death (1.23) was counter-intuitively δύναμις (rather than σκάνδαλον) for believing Jews and σοφία (rather than μωρία) for believing Greeks. As Hays (1997: 30) explains,

> The fundamental theological point is that if the cross itself is God's saving event, all human standards of evaluation are overturned. This outlandish message confounds Jews and Greeks alike, who quite understandably seek evidence of a more credible sort, either empirical demonstrations of power ('signs') or rationally persuasive argumentation ('wisdom'). But the apostle offers neither. Instead, 'we proclaim Christ crucified' (v. 23).

[39] Hays (1999: 113): 'Paul has taken the central event at the heart of the Christian story – the death of Jesus – and used it as the lens through which all human experience must be projected and thereby seen afresh. The cross becomes the starting point for an epistemological revolution, a *conversion of the imagination*.'

[40] Litfin (1994: 193–4).

[41] Litfin (1994: 201). Cf. Mihaila (2009: 17–24).

2.6–3.4 is to demonstrate why the Corinthians were not ready for deeper theological insight in the preaching they received during his earlier visit, and thus to defend the content of his preaching at that time.[42] Throughout this section Paul explains how divine wisdom is intended for mature believers, the τέλειοι and πνευματικοί, while being incomprehensible to immature believers and unbelievers, the νήπιοι, ψυχικοί, and σαρκίνοι. As Corin Mihaila summarises, '[T]he wisdom of God identified with the message of the cross is perceived only by the "mature" and "spiritual" as a result of the revelation of God's Spirit and not as a result of human wisdom, and much less of the teachers' eloquence.'[43] But in the conclusion of this section (3.1–4), Paul explains that while his preaching to the Corinthians contained the basic ingredients of wisdom, he did not share with them the depths of his divine insight as if they were mature enough to grasp it. Due to their immaturity, Paul was not even *able* (οὐκ ἠδυνήθην) to speak to the Corinthians this way (3.1). They were simply unprepared for the depths of God's wisdom and at that time could only consume milk, not solid food (3.3). And just in case the Corinthians take exception to Paul's accusation, he conveniently points to their factions – the topic of the next unit – as symptomatic of their very condition.

1 Cor 3.5–4.5

First Corinthians 3.5–4.5 has been labelled the 'centerpiece in the rhetorical structure of 1 Cor 1:10–4:21', since it is there where 'Paul deals explicitly and at length with the problem of social disunity in the Corinthian church'.[44] In order to eliminate inappropriate partisanship and criticism of individual apostles, it is in this pericope that Paul, through the employment of three elaborate metaphors (3.6–9a; 3.9b-17; 4.1–5), elucidates *what* (τί, 3.5)[45] apostles are and *how* (οὕτως, ὡς, 4.1) the early believers should regard them in relation to God and the church.[46]

---

[42] Bassler (1990: 180): 'It was the inept way he preached the gospel (2:3–4) and the way he seemed to hold back from the Corinthians the "meat" of the message (3:1–3) that the Corinthians objected to.'

[43] Mihaila (2009: 26).   [44] Kuck (1992: 220).

[45] Clarke (1999: 241): 'It may be argued that Paul's use of the neuter interrogative pronoun τί, as opposed to the masculine form τίς, implies a stress on the task which is performed, rather than on the importance of the relationship between the διάκονος and the Lord. Thus, he writes that the one who plants and the one who waters are comparatively "nothing".'

[46] Paul's temple metaphor in 3.16–17 has been considered a third analogy, but its close association with the preceding building metaphor suggests that they are actually the same image; cf. Bitner (2010). It is the servant/administrator metaphor (4.1–5) that functions as the third.

First, Paul explains that the church is a field in which apostles labour by sowing and watering seed – the gospel (3.7). It is God, however, who is the primary agent in salvation and maturation, enabling the harvest by causing its growth (ὁ αὐξάνων); he is therefore the only one who is 'anything' (τι), that is, deserving of adulation and undying allegiance. Secondly, the church is a building/temple which apostles construct.⁴⁷ Unlike the field analogy, the structural image focuses primarily on the labourers, rather than on God. And instead of concentrating on the nothingness of God's agents, this metaphor seeks to remind the church that the builder is responsible for how he builds (πῶς ἐποικοδομεῖ, 3.10).⁴⁸ In this metaphor, Christ is the edifice's foundation (θεμέλιος, 3.11) and apostles are the builders who must choose carefully which materials they will employ in their construction. Their labour will ultimately be tested (δοκιμάζω) by God, and at that time the quality of their work will become apparent (φανερός, δηλόω, ἀποκαλύπτω, 3.13).⁴⁹ Based on how the work of the individual labourers fare, they will receive just payment (μισθός, 3.14) or penalty (ζημιόω, 3.15).⁵⁰

Paul had three central aims with these metaphors. First, Paul sought to eliminate partisanship among believers (ὥστε μηδεὶς καυχάσθω ἐν ἀνθρώποις, 3.21) by showing God to be the one responsible for the conversion and maturation of believers, and apostles to be only complementary and subordinate agents of the gospel (συνεργοί, 3.9; cf. 3.5, 8, 22). By placing the primary focus on God, Paul aimed to make him alone the object of their boasting. Secondly, by portraying the church as God's temple (3.16–17) and as vulnerable to poor construction (3.13–14), Paul challenged believers to be discriminating about whom they permit to be teachers. While apostles are considered colleagues of one another, they are individually assigned, assessed, and compensated (ἕκαστος δὲ τὸν ἴδιον μισθὸν λήμψεται κατὰ τὸν ἴδιον κόπον, 3.9) and should therefore take care how they build, utilising the right materials in accordance

⁴⁷ For the political use of architectural metaphors, see Welborn (1987a: 337); M. M. Mitchell (1991: 99–111); Martin (1999: 39–41).

⁴⁸ Kuck (1992: 181–2); Konradt (2003: 258–84).

⁴⁹ Hollander (1994: 96): 'It is God who, at the Final Judgment, will disclose their work and will administer justice to each of them individually.' *Contra* Evans (1984), who suggests that the 'testing' in 1 Cor 3.10–15 refers to the earthly occasions when the faith and maturity of the church are assessed in persecution and difficult circumstances (cf. 2 Thess 1.6–10).

⁵⁰ Smit (2002: 242) is probably correct to conclude that Apollos, rather than Cephas, is the unnamed apostle building on Paul's work, and '[a]pparently his arrival has negatively influenced the valuation of certain believers at Corinth concerning Paul's former visit'. *Contra* Baur (1873: 269–81); Barrett (1963); Vielhauer (1975); Goulder (2001: 22–3); and possibly Fitzmyer (2008: 192).

with the building's Christological foundation (3.10–12). The church should at the same time be careful not to permit precarious building to take place, since what is poorly erected will eventually be tested and give way (3.13). Thirdly, in order to re-establish his standing among the Corinthians, Paul aimed to elicit their trust in him by emphasising how his work had been faithful to the pattern he prescribes. It is perhaps significant that in both the agricultural and architectural metaphors Paul presents himself in the founding position (3.6, 10). By doing so, Paul sought to re-establish his authority in the community, not in an effort to marginalise the other apostles, but to re-secure his right to address their ethical shortcomings and to offer them fatherly direction in their pursuit of Christian maturity.

Summary

Paul's discourse up to 3.23 has posed a considerable challenge to this infantile church. In fact, the groundwork for Paul's apologetic and reconciliatory objectives has been satisfactorily laid by the end of the letter's first three chapters. But one critical issue remains unaddressed: the impropriety of the Corinthians' criticisms of apostles. Therefore, in 4.1–5 Paul will introduce the *oikonomos* metaphor initially to reiterate several of the same apostolic attributes he has already stressed, namely, the apostles' relative insignificance as subordinates of God, their accountability to him, their shared responsibility, and thus their collegiality in gospel ministry. But this time Paul will portray these attributes with a particular view toward underscoring the apostle's authority and immunity from community judgment. It is only by emphasising these traits that Paul's apostolic ethos can be fully restored in the Corinthian church.

Paul as an administrator of God's mysteries

Once Paul reaches the conclusion of the unit at 4.1–5, he shifts back to describing the role of apostles in relation to God and the church. But this time the tone and urgency of Paul's discourse is significantly more emphatic, his *description* turning here into *prescription* as he employs the imperative mood for only the seventh time in the letter so far and the first time regarding the conceptualisation of leaders.[51] Since Paul's

---

[51] Peterson (1998: 146) considers 1 Cor 4.1–5 to be Paul's clearest response to the Corinthians' criticisms of him in chapters 1–4 and thus the centrepiece (*statis*) of the argument.

instructions concern the manner of the church's perception of apostles (οὕτως, ὡς),[52] he clearly assumes that the Corinthians had certain pre-conceived notions of church leadership.[53] It was, in fact, their promotion of patronage, boasting, wisdom, jealousy, strife, and other such leader-ship principles and practices foreign to his cruciform ideology which granted Paul the opportunity earlier to charge the church with thinking and behaving as mere humans (ἄνθρωποι, 3.3–4). For this reason, in 4.1 Paul must review how the *human* should consider apostles (οὕτως ἡμᾶς λογιζέσθω ἄνθρωπος ὡς).[54] Furthermore, the conceptual and collect-ive nature of this exhortation functions to support his earlier appeal for believers to agree with one another (1.10).[55] But what do the metaphors employed here indicate about Christian apostleship, and how were they supposed to bring an end to the Corinthian factions? It is our under-standing that in 4.1–5 Paul uses the *oikonomos* metaphor to negotiate the difficult task of portraying apostles as subordinate functionaries, on the one hand, and as God's authoritative representatives, on the other. Thus, Paul's concern here is simultaneously to eliminate the church's adula-tion of apostles while also reprimanding the Corinthians for their critical evaluations of them.

Hierarchy

As demonstrated in Chapter 4, the term οἰκονόμος implies the presence of an administrative hierarchy and the manager's possession of an inter-mediate position within that structure. In private administration, the rank of the *oikonomos* varied according to context. But regardless of the size and scope of the managerial unit to which the *oikonomos* was assigned, during the mid first century CE the administrator nearly always served directly beneath the proprietor as his immediate delegate. In 1 Cor 4.1–5, the *oikonomos* metaphor similarly carries certain social and structural implications which Paul exploits in order to elucidate his apostolic role, so that the Corinthian church will (i) understand precisely who, or what, apostles are, and (ii) allow this new outlook to shape both their ecclesi-ology and ethics.

---

[52] The οὕτως is cataphoric and signals the use of metaphor; cf. Fee (1987: 158 n. 3); Welborn (2005: 243); Fitzmyer (2008: 212). *Contra* Conzelmann (1975: 82); Fascher (1975: 142); Merklein (1992: 290); Zeller (2010: 173).

[53] For the influence of non-Christian leadership norms on the Corinthian church, see Clarke (1993: 89–107).

[54] All of Paul's fifteen uses of ἄνθρωπος/ἀνθρώπινος in 1 Corinthians 1–4 seem to be pejorative (esp. 3.21; 4.3, 9); cf. J. Weiss (1910: 92); R. F. Collins (1999: 171).

[55] Winter (2002: 181).

Subordination

By applying the *oikonomos* metaphor to himself, Apollos, and perhaps Cephas, Paul underscores the subordinate role they all share within God's administration. As discussed briefly in Chapter 5, this hierarchical relationship is indicated especially by the genitives in the construction ὑπηρέτας Χριστοῦ καὶ οἰκονόμους μυστηρίων θεοῦ (4.1) and the presence of a κύριος (4.5) within the structure. This apostolic hierarchy is affirmed elsewhere in 1 Corinthians. In the letter opening, for instance, Paul asserts that he was called to be an ἀπόστολος Χριστοῦ Ἰησοῦ διὰ θελήματος θεου (1.1), which points to the subordination of apostles to God/Christ. Moreover, as an apostle Paul could say that it was Christ who sent him (ἀπέστειλέν με Χριστὸς, 1.17). Paul's manner of speaking about his commission is exactly that used for dispatching commercial agents. According to one third-century CE letter, for example, Herakleidus, the *oikonomos* of the proprietor Alypios, was sent (ἀπέστειλα τὸν οἰκονόμον) to an estate to make arrangements for an approaching harvest (P.Flor. 2.134). Paul's repeated reference to his commission suggests that, like Herakleidus, he too occupies a subordinate rank.[56]

Legal and social status

Paul's *oikonomos* metaphor also carries socio-legal connotations which significantly shape his portrait of apostleship.[57] The social and legal aspects of Paul's description, however, are often overlooked in exegetical treatments of 1 Corinthians 4, and those scholars who treat the issues have opposing perspectives. Dale Martin, for instance, whose historical analysis of *oikonomoi* as private commercial administrators reached many of the same conclusions we reached in Chapter 4, applied the concept of managerial slavery to Paul's use of οἰκονομία in 1 Cor 9.17, arguing that Paul's metaphor would have elicited a plurality of responses from the socially stratified Corinthian congregations.[58] But Martin's assumptions about the social and legal implications of Paul's metaphor have been forcefully challenged by a number of interpreters.

---

[56] Schrage (1991: 320) notes that apostles are 'radikal von ihm abhängig und ihm untergeordnet'.

[57] *Contra* Michel (1967: 150).

[58] Cf. D. B. Martin (1990: 68–85), whose assumptions about the social make-up of, and relational dynamics within, the Corinthian church (119, 126–8) were largely influenced by Theissen (1982). Curiously, Martin never considered 1 Cor 4.1–2 in his investigation. For the slave status of Paul's metaphor in 4.1–2, see also Schrage (1991: 320–1).

John Byron, for example, has contended that the *oikonomos* image, far from having servile connotations, actually casts Paul and the apostles as free and voluntary servants.[59] Byron's detailed analysis, however, fails to account for several historical and exegetical insights which are critical for discerning the legal implications of Paul's metaphor. First, Byron criticises Martin for failing to notice that the phrase 'slave of Christ' does not appear in 1 Corinthians with reference to Paul. According to Byron, Martin 'overlooks that not only does Paul not describe himself as δοῦλος Χριστοῦ in 1 Corinthians, also Paul never describes himself as οἰκονόμος Χριστοῦ. In fact, this phrase does not appear anywhere in the NT.'[60] Presumably, this statement is intended to suggest that if Paul had referred to himself as either δοῦλος Χριστοῦ or οἰκονόμος Χριστοῦ in 1 Corinthians, then Martin's argument would find support; because they are not employed in 1 Corinthians, however, Martin's argument is somehow weakened. On the surface, Byron is correct: the precise phrases he identifies are not employed anywhere in the letter. But it is illegitimate for Byron to demand so much direct terminological congruency. Although Paul fails to use these exact phrases in 1 Corinthians, or anywhere else in the case of the latter, it simply does not follow that the expression οἰκονομίαν πεπίστευμαι in 9.17 cannot carry the meaning Martin attributes to it. Besides this, Paul does use, as Byron later observes, the phrase οἰκονόμους μυστηρίων θεοῦ in 4.1 with reference to himself, Apollos, and perhaps other apostles, and this metaphor is immediately preceded by Paul's portrayal of apostles as servants *of Christ* (ὑπηρέτας Χριστοῦ). In light of Christ's superordinate role in Paul's very similar and adjacent self-description, the phrase '*oikonomoi* of the mysteries of God' certainly implies the same kind of position as '*oikonomos* of Christ'.

Secondly, Byron charges Martin with assuming the synonymity of οἰκονόμος and δοῦλος in Pauline literature, since they both stand as terms for slaves in Martin's framework.[61] But this accusation is simply false; Martin nowhere suggests that the two terms were strictly synonymous. Instead, Martin argued that οἰκονόμοι were *mostly* slaves, specifically *managerial* slaves, and therefore a subset (hyponym) of δοῦλοι.[62] But even so, Martin conceded that not all οἰκονόμοι were slaves,[63] an

---

[59] Byron (2003: 241–57); cf. Galloway (2004: 184 n. 148).
[60] Byron (2003: 242). Cf. M. J. Harris (1999: 129).
[61] Byron (2003: 243).   [62] D. B. Martin (1990: 11–15).
[63] D. B. Martin (1990: 17): '[F]or the Roman Empire as a whole and for the Roman imperial period, the oikonomoi were of servile status (slave or freed). Furthermore, in private life they were almost always of servile status and were mostly slaves.'

admission which Byron himself eventually seeks to exploit.[64] Therefore, while Martin maintains that by the early empire οἰκονόμοι often shared the same referents as δοῦλοι, Byron incorrectly charges Martin with strictly identifying the two concepts.

Thirdly, Byron accuses Martin of misunderstanding Paul's argument in 1 Cor 9.17. Martin, along with most scholars, regards Paul's depiction of preaching involuntarily (ἄκων) in 9.17 as indicative of slavery and being unentitled to a wage (μισθός). Furthermore, since Paul links involuntary preaching with being entrusted with an administration (οἰκονομίαν πεπίστευμαι), Martin considers Paul's *oikonomos* (*oikonomia*) metaphor to be an admission to his servile status and descriptive of his actual condition. Byron, on the other hand, interprets Paul's preaching in 9.17 not as involuntary, but as voluntary (ἑκών) and deserving of a wage. The logic of Paul's argument in 9.16–18 will be treated extensively in Chapter 7. It is sufficient here simply to point out that despite his attempt to demonstrate that Paul's preaching was performed voluntarily, Byron never adequately explains how he is able to dissociate Paul's explicit correlation of involuntary preaching (i.e. slavery) with being entrusted with an οἰκονομία; regardless of Paul's actual condition, the apostle seems to link these two concepts.

Fourthly, in order to demonstrate the statistical uncertainty of the legal status of *oikonomoi*, Byron attempts to use Martin's catalogue of *oikonomoi* inscriptions against him. As Byron observes,

> Of the 81 inscriptions catalogued by Martin, only 8 can be identified as slaves, 3 as freed, 12 as free, and another 21 can only be listed as 'probably' slave or freed. A total of 41, roughly half, are of unknown status making identification impossible. Indeed a total of 62 of the inscriptions, roughly 75 percent, offer no evidence in support of a conclusion that οἰκονόμος usually indicated a slave status.[65]

Although Byron's statistics initially appear damning for Martin's thesis, it must be observed that Martin's catalogue includes both private *and* civic *oikonomoi*. Yet Byron repeatedly fails to discriminate between these very different kinds of administrator, a categorical distinction with significant socio-legal implications. Indeed, on two occasions Byron attempts to demonstrate the free status of the private *oikonomoi* under investigation in Martin's study by presenting as evidence *oikonomoi* who held some form of civic office: (i) Erastus, the first-century CE *oikonomos* of

---

[64] Byron (2003: 243).   [65] Byron (2003: 243–4).

Corinth (Rom 16.23); and (ii) Philokalos, the third-century CE citizen of Ephesus (*CIG* 2717/*IStratonikea* 1103).[66] But comparing as he does municipal *oikonomoi* of the likes of Erastus from Romans 16 with private *oikonomoi* of the likes of the Unjust Steward from Luke 16 is perhaps akin to comparing the rank and status of the *Secretary* of the State with the rank and status of the *secretary* of a small firm;[67] obviously, the two persons are not comparable simply because they share the same title. In fact, nearly all the *oikonomoi* falling within Martin's 'Free and Probably Free' and 'Unknown' categories were municipal administrators and served as treasury magistrates.[68] This classification is clearly indicated in most of those inscriptions; many even explicitly state the domain of their appointment (e.g. ἡ πόλις, *CIG* 2717; ἡ βουλή, *CIG* 2811; ἡ πατρίς, *CIG* 4132). Therefore, while the general usefulness of Martin's catalogue suffers considerably due to its integration of private and municipal administrators, the general reliability of his thesis should not be dismissed prematurely.

Despite the weaknesses of his criticisms of Martin, Byron concludes that οἰκονόμος is a legally ambiguous term and any attempt to retrieve Paul's meaning from 1 Corinthians 4 and 9 would require that ὑπηρέτης, the corresponding and supposedly more legally implicit term from 4.1, be examined for support. It was therefore Byron's next contention that ὑπηρέτης connotes voluntary service, a theory he defends by presenting several examples from ancient literature where the term carried this significance.[69] Two objections, however, must be raised against Byron's conclusions concerning the legal status of ὑπηρέται. First, it is quite significant that Byron in his brief overview of the word conceded that a ὑπηρέτης could be obliged to obey when the superordinate figure in the hierarchy is a deity.[70] Since the superordinate figure in the apostolic hierarchy is God/Christ, then at the very least the sense of obligatory rather than 'free-will' service associated with divinely appointed ὑπηρέται should be present in 1 Corinthians 4. Secondly, and more importantly,

---

[66] Byron (2003: 243–4).

[67] According to Byron (2003: 244), the Unjust Steward (Luke 16.1–8) is 'clearly not a slave but a "free treasurer" who expects to be able … to continue his work outside his master's household after being removed from his position as steward' (244). But what Byron assumes to be clear is in actuality still a matter of great dispute; cf. Beavis (1992: 43–53). For a more recent defence of the steward's servile (slave or freed) status, see Udoh (2009: 333).

[68] Most of these municipal *oikonomoi* are discussed by A. Weiss (2004: 51–5).

[69] Much of Byron's argumentation is indebted to Rengstorf (1972: 532–4, 537), who repeatedly describes ὑπηρέται as free and voluntary servants.

[70] Byron (2003: 245–6).

the strictly free status of ὑπηρέται assumed by Byron is dubious. In fact, there remain numerous ancient texts which demonstrate that ὑπηρέτης could connote slavery. These testimonies, however, either went undiscussed or were misrepresented in Byron's analysis.

Byron does not, for example, consider the early first-century BCE divinations of Artemidorus of Ephesus. Yet in his multi-volume treatise, *The Interpretation of Dreams*, Artemidorus seems to consider ὑπηρέται to be a category of domestic slave. Showing how a number of household articles, when dreamt about, correspond to various domestic servants, Artemidorus itemises these associations in what appears to be an ascending slave hierarchy (οἱ θεραπεύοντες, ὑπηρέται, οἰκονόμοι, ταμίαι) and even lists ὑπηρέται and οἰκονόμοι consecutively (*Onir.* 1.74).[71] Because ὑπηρέται fall between οἱ θεραπεύοντες and οἰκονόμοι (which for Artemidorus are servile positions; cf. 2.30), it is reasonably clear that ὑπηρέται were also considered slaves in Artemidorus' servile framework. This in no way indicates that ὑπηρέται, or for that matter οἰκονόμοι, were always slaves, but it demonstrates that ὑπηρέται could possess slave status, even in a piece of popular literature like Artemidorus' divinations.

The legal ambiguity of ὑπηρέται is also apparent in Aristotle's *Politics*, another treatise that went undiscussed by Byron. In a famous passage revealing the philosopher's impressions about the near personhood of slaves, Aristotle compares δοῦλοι to ὑπηρέται in order to explain their auxiliary function.[72] Aristotle explains that just as 'an assistant [ὁ ὑπηρέτης] in the arts belongs to the class of tools' and 'every assistant [πᾶς ὑπηρέτης] is as it were a tool that serves for several tools', so slaves (δοῦλοι) are living tools (τὰ ἔμψυχα) which utilise those tools that are lifeless (τὰ ἄψυχα, *Pol.* 1253b). Moreover, 'if every [lifeless] tool could perform its own work when ordered', then 'mastercraftsmen would have no need of assistants [ὑπηρετῶν] and masters no need of slaves [δούλων]' (1253b). Finally, and quite significantly, just as certain tools are instruments of production, while other tools are instruments of action, so an assistant (ὑπηρέτης) of a mastercraftsman is an instrument of production, while 'a slave is an assistant [ὁ δοῦλος ὑπηρέτης]' insofar as it is an instrument of action (1254a). This elaborate – and indeed tortured – analogy demonstrates the functional overlap between δοῦλοι and ὑπηρέται. Although it must be conceded that ὑπηρέτης is not depicted here as a strict synonym for δοῦλος, it is clear that Aristotle observed

[71] Cf. D. B. Martin (1990: 34).   [72] Cf. Garnsey (1996: 122).

and exploited certain similarities between them, which apparently were close enough for him to consider a δοῦλος to be a subset (hyponym) of ὑπηρέτης.

Furthermore, in his analysis of Plato's *Statesman*, Byron misrepresents the discourse when he implies that Plato delineated strictly between δοῦλοι and ὑπηρέται by classifying the former as 'tame animals' and the latter as 'free persons (ἐλεύθεροι) who serve willingly'.[73] While these descriptions do appear in the text, the legal classification that Plato attributes to the two groups is more complex than Byron acknowledges. First, Byron seems to miss that in this Socratic dialogue the Stranger (Ξένος) considers δοῦλοι and ὑπηρέται to comprise a single category of possessions, explaining at one point, 'There remains the class of slaves and servants in general [τὸ δὲ δὴ δούλων καὶ πάντων ὑπηρετῶν λοιπόν]' (*Pol.* 289c). Therein the Stranger couples δοῦλοι and ὑπηρέται together under one 'final' rubric (τὸ λοιπόν), that of living property (ζῴων κτῆσιν, 289b–c). Moreover, the phrase δούλων καὶ πάντων ὑπηρετῶν suggests that δοῦλοι belong to the larger category referred to as πάντων ὑπηρετῶν. Secondly, the interchangeability of δοῦλοι and ὑπηρέται is apparent in the Stranger's immediately preceding statement, when he refers to the class consisting of δοῦλοι and ὑπηρέται simply as δοῦλοι (289b). Finally, the close identification of δοῦλοι with ὑπηρέται is made abundantly clear when later in the passage the Stranger – contrary to his own intuition – asserts that the greatest servants (μεγίστους ὑπηρέτας) were indeed those 'bought servants, acquired by purchase, whom we can without question call slaves [τοὺς ὠνητούς τε καὶ τῷ τρόπῳ τούτῳ κτητούς: οὓς ἀναμφισβητήτως δούλους ἔχομεν εἰπεῖν]' (289d–e).[74]

These complex uses of ὑπηρέτης allow us to reach several conclusions about how the term was used in antiquity. On the one hand, since Plato used ὑπηρέτης with reference to free persons, the term should not be taken on its own to imply slavery. On the other hand, since authors such as Artemidorus, Aristotle, and Plato do on occasion refer to ὑπηρέται as slaves, it is incorrect for Byron to maintain that ὑπηρέται must have been by necessity free-will servants. One may be able to find additional texts to challenge Byron's conclusions. The preceding analysis, however, is sufficient to show that the term ὑπηρέτης was quite ambiguous

---

[73] Byron (2003: 246).

[74] But lest one assume that Plato *always* considered ὑπηρέται to be slaves, it should be observed how, after announcing that the greatest servants were slaves, the Stranger abruptly transitioned to speak of 'those free men who put themselves voluntarily in the position of servants [τῶν ἐλευθέρων ὅσοι τοῖς νυνδὴ ῥηθεῖσιν εἰς ὑπηρετικὴν ἑκόντες]' (*Pol.* 289e).

and probably intimated less about one's legal status than about one's rank and function in a given hierarchy. Perhaps a better description, then, is that ὑπηρέται were attendants, or subordinates (LSJ II.1), without any preconditioned legal status, even if in the majority of instances they happened to have been free.[75] As Rengstorf remarked, 'In all these instances ὑπηρέτης κτλ. serve to characterise someone, whether man, god, or divine being, in terms of the fact that he stands and acts in the service of a higher will and is fully at the disposal of this will.'[76] If this description is accurate, then Byron's approach to the titles in 1 Cor 4.1 must be reversed. Rather than interpreting οἰκονόμος in the light of ὑπηρέτης, it is better to understand ὑπηρέτης in the light of οἰκονόμος. The word order progresses therefore from abstract to concrete, just as the epexegetical καί implies.[77] Furthermore, it is best to consider private *oikonomoi* as *normally* slaves, as argued by Martin and shown further in this study in Chapter 4. The advice of H. C. Tietler on this matter is just as appropriate here as it was there: '[C]onsider those who occupied functions as *vilicus, oikonomos, actor* and the like as slaves unless the contrary is proved.'[78]

But while Martin's conclusions about the legal status of Paul's *oikonomos* metaphor remain secure, his theory about the social connotations of the image also needs to be revisited. Martin argued that slave *oikonomoi* could have possessed status inconsistency, so that their humble legal status contradicted the considerable social status they acquired through managerial privileges and their master's patronage. The status-inconsistent nature of Paul's metaphor would therefore have elicited a plurality of responses from his diverse readership. But the notion that Paul's metaphor would have evoked such a contrast of impressions in the Corinthian church has also been subject to much criticism. Few would object to the assumption that, as a servile position, an *oikonomos* connoted disrepute to free persons, especially those who possessed impressive socio-economic status.[79] But Martin also quite controversially claims that managerial slaves had opportunities for social mobility, and therefore Paul's metaphor would have elicited admiration from those lower on

---

[75] Thiselton (2000: 335).   [76] Rengstorf (1972: 531).

[77] Rengstorf (1972: 543); Léon-Dufour (1980: 146). Probably also Fee (1987: 159).

[78] Tietler (1993: 213).

[79] Horsley (1998b: 56): 'The wealth they acquired and influence they wielded did not give the "managerial" slave or freedperson any dignity or standing in the society. As literary sources, particularly satire, indicate quite clearly, the more wealthy and powerful the slave or freedperson, the more contemptuous he would be in the eyes of honourable people.'

the social pyramid.[80] While Martin's proposal about Paul's strategy to portray himself as a high-status-by-association administrator has been accepted by some interpreters,[81] a number of scholars have raised objections against Martin's theory that must be considered.

On the one hand, a number of weak criticisms have been presented which do not give Martin's thesis a fair reading. These require an initial response so that the stronger protests against Martin's theory can be heard. Some interpreters, for instance, have suggested that Paul's metaphor cannot carry the positive connotations Martin suggests it does in 1 Cor 9.17 simply because the context of the metaphor in 4.1–2, where Paul seeks to diminish the church's regard for apostles, will not allow for it. However, the fact that Paul describes apostleship in 1 Corinthians 3–4 in various ways with diverse social implications – that is, as a διάκονος in one instance and a σοφὸς ἀρχιτέκτων in another, as a μωρός on the one hand and as a πατήρ on the other – suggests that Paul's portrayal of himself as an *oikonomos* need not necessitate that the metaphor be understood negatively simply because, for example, it surfaces near the *peristasis* catalogue (4.9–13); the context simply does not demand this understanding as some have suggested.[82] Moreover, even though some interpreters acknowledge that slavery could be portrayed positively in certain contexts, others remain sceptical that Paul's Corinthian readers would have understood slavery so optimistically. As Murray Harris observes,

> '[M]iddle-level, managerial slaves' formed such a small minority that we may question whether that particular connotation of slavery would have ousted the dominant notion of slavery as humble subjection to a master in the minds of Paul's converts. Would not Paul's Corinthian readers or any typical Greco-Roman urbanites have interpreted the term *doulos* in light of their own experience or observation of slavery? And would that understanding of slavery not correspond precisely to the contextual indicators of 1 Corinthians 9, where the slave is someone who has no rights (vv. 12, 15, 18) and is under obligation to serve another (vv. 16–17)?[83]

[80] D. B. Martin (1990: 31) observes that managerial slaves were charged with 'tasks befitting the free' and considered more free (οἱ ἐλευθεριωτέροι) than menial slaves (Aristotle, *Oec.* 1344a28–30). Cf. Weaver (1972); Weaver (1974).
[81] See, e.g., R. H. Williams (2006: 82).
[82] *Contra* M. J. Harris (1999: 129).   [83] M. J. Harris (1999: 129–30).

But while Harris' initial observation demands consideration, his later comments neglect three important points. First, some slaves, such as *oikonomoi*, did in fact have certain 'rights'. How this applies to 1 Corinthians 9 will be explained in Chapter 7. It is sufficient now simply to note that obligation did not necessarily exclude servile privileges. Secondly, it is not a decisive matter in this instance how urbanites would have interpreted the term δοῦλος, since Paul's metaphor in 1 Corinthians 4 and 9 is that of an οἰκονόμος. It is, then, the early Christians' experiences and observations about this particular form of slavery that is crucial for interpreting Paul's metaphor. Finally, and very significantly, 'Paul's Corinthian readers', as identified by Harris, would have understood that business slaves, such as *oikonomoi*, were among the privileged slave class. We are not here suggesting that this provided *oikonomoi* elevated social status. But because business slaves and freedmen formed a significant portion of the population in commercially saturated Corinth (as noted in Chapter 5), it is plausible that the church in Corinth was well aware of some of the material (if not social) benefits these managerial slaves experienced.

At the same time, there remain grounds for doubting that many slave administrators were highly admired and honoured in antiquity as persons with significant social status, even by the menial slave population. Although slave administrators possessed representative authority and had access to certain material privileges, this hardly indicates that they acquired elevated social status. In fact, the material privileges enjoyed by administrators along with the right they possessed to abuse their subordinates could promote, not admiration and envy from other slaves, but apathy and indifference, or even hatred and resentment. As K. R. Bradley remarks, 'As the slaveowner's representative on the spot, the bailiff gave the slave orders for work, managed his daily routine, and disciplined him. In so doing he became the object of intense anger and defiance: he was after all only a slave himself.'[84] Moreover, the upward mobility of the servile class was so restricted that it is highly unlikely that the typical slave administrator was regarded as

---

[84] Bradley (1994: 72). In response to Martin, Combes (1998: 80) argues,
> We are hampered … by the lack of evidence shaped by the attitudes of the lower classes and Martin's use of funerary inscriptions to make up this deficiency is admirable. But such ritualized sentiments as those found in such a context cannot be regarded as complete evidence of an entirely different mindset from the enormous resentment that so often arose against the power of favoured slaves.

possessing significant social status in the ancient world.[85] As Richard Horsley explains,

> Roman imperial society generally consisted of a static pyramid of legally mandated orders and a relatively rigid hierarchy of statuses. For what minimal social mobility there was, slavery, even most 'managerial' roles, would not have provided a very promising launching pad, considering the social stigma that still attached to the minority of slaves who became freedmen/women – unless we are thinking of a social mobility that happened over three or four generations. The experience of the vast majority of slaves cannot be mitigated by focusing on the unusual influence or atypical mobility of a 'select few'.[86]

After comparing the Roman slave system with several other slave cultures, Orlando Patterson's sociological investigation reached similar conclusions. Patterson remarks,

> [I]f we consider not the content of what the elite slave did, but the structural significance of his role, we find immediately that it is identical with that of the most miserable of field slaves. He was always structurally marginal, whether economically or socially, politically or culturally. His marginality made it possible for him to be used in ways that were not possible with a person who truly belonged.[87]

These objections do not indicate that there existed in Roman society anything like slave homogeneity and a shared slave identity; there did exist,

---

[85] Even if some freedmen became upwardly mobile (and even this was quite difficult), it was nearly impossible for unmanumitted slaves to achieve social separation from their enslaved peers; cf. Quiroga (1995); Saller (2000: 834–8). Although Garnsey (1982: 105) concedes that business slaves were, 'as a whole, socially mobile', and that their 'most successful members founded families which ... advanced into the upper strata of Roman society', he notes that such advancement only took place 'in due course' – that is, following manumission and probably in subsequent generations. As Garnsey (1996: 186) later states in direct response to Martin, 'Slavery for most slaves was highly undesirable and anything but an avenue of upward mobility.'

[86] Horsley (1998b: 57; cf. 58).

[87] Patterson (1982: 332). Harrill (1992: 426) remarks, 'Martin's sharp separation of upper-class values and perceptions from those of the lower class looks at times artificial and exaggerated... It is questionable whether the humble freeborn population felt "class" or even "order" solidarity with the servile masses. Lower-status persons often share, if not exaggerate, the values and prejudices of their social betters'; Harrill provides as an example Petronius' Hermeros (*Satyr.* 38). Moreover, Joshel (1992: 91) shows that even when slave values departed from those of their social superiors, menial slaves do not appear to have been any more embarrassed about their labour than administrators.

after all, a variation of slave jobs, the desirability of which was affected largely by proximity to the master.[88] But regardless of variations in rank and privilege, the vast majority of slaves were considered dishonoured persons.[89] This is underscored by the fact that even administrators were subject to their master's wrath, being vulnerable to beatings and even murder, and such personal bodily violations were indicative of social disrepute.[90] Therefore, since Paul's metaphor implies legal restraint and the possibility of penalisation (1 Cor 4.5; 9.16), it is improbable that it would have also connoted social superiority even to low-status believers.

Thus, we conclude that through the *oikonomos* metaphor Paul sought to demonstrate the vast insignificance of apostles in comparison with their principal. Not only are apostles subordinate to God/Christ, but they are his slaves who serve him out of compulsion and humility. Understood in this way, apostles should not be regarded as in competition with one another.[91] As administrators of the same principal and of the same resources, the apostles were to be considered colleagues (συνεργοί, 3.9) who contributed to the growth of the church in complementary ways (3.6, 10).[92] As Paul maintains later in the epistle, 'Whether then it was I or they, so we preach and so you believed' (15.11). By disregarding which apostle mediated the gospel and emphasising instead their shared rank and objectives, Paul sought to eliminate boasting in leaders. In this sense, the *oikonomos* metaphor functions much like the διάκονος metaphor in 3.5–9, where Paul draws out the intermediary role which he and other apostles occupy between God and the church. Likewise, the apostles in 4.1–2 are mere *oikonomoi*, authorised slave agents commissioned by God to distribute his mysteries. And by illustrating the subordinate, servile, and functionary role of apostles, Paul seeks to convey their depressed status relative to Christ their κύριος, and thus to eliminate inappropriate adulation and partisanship in the Corinthian community.

Authority

While Paul's *oikonomos* metaphor is pregnant with shameful connotations, the image is not entirely void of notions of influence. Even as

[88] Bradley (1994: 72–3).

[89] Patterson (1982: 331–2); Brown (2001: 731–2). Harrill (1992: 427): '[F]rom a historical perspective, any "honor" conferred even on high-ranking servile persons was always fragile.'

[90] Saller (1994: 134–9).

[91] Mihaila (2009: 212). *Contra* Joubert (1995: 216), who curiously claims, 'Only Paul had access to the "mysteries of God" (1 Cor. 2:1, 7; 4:1), and only he could communicate its contents to others.'

[92] Furnish (1961).

Paul's metaphor implies subordination and servility, it simultaneously casts the apostolate as a position of unique power.[93] By virtue of having been appointed by the resurrected Christ and entrusted with the mysteries of God, Paul's metaphor portrays apostles as authorised representatives sent from God to speak and act on his behalf to the church and all humanity.[94]

Private administrators were appointed to supervise a managerial unit, which entitled them to a significant measure of representative authority in the handling of the principal's resources and the management of his personnel. But, generally speaking, administrators were not able to utilise the principal's resources in any way they wished; normally the manager's authorisation was limited to the scope of his commission (*praepositio*). Paul's *oikonomos* metaphor implies that apostles were entrusted with a similar kind of restricted authority. The apostle's authorisation to speak and act for God was limited to the domain of the resources with which he was entrusted, namely, the divine mysteries (4.1).[95] Apostles were also subordinate to these mysteries, so that their words and actions lost divine authorisation if and when they contradicted God's revelation (cf. Gal 1.8–9; 2.11–14). But within that realm, so long as their life and speech were consonant with the gospel they proclaimed, the words and actions of apostles were considered authoritative (1 Thess 2.13).[96]

---

[93] Michel (1967: 150).

[94] The authority which the apostle possessed was not, as some interpreters assume, entirely unique to Paul. Polaski (1999: 122–3), for instance, argues that through his use of grace language, 'Paul claims an unassailable position of power, an authority over his correspondents which is his alone precisely *because* he is the subject of the undeserved favor of a powerful God'; 'Paul emphasizes the universality of God's act in Christ and seeks to reserve to himself unique authority as interpreter of the divine gift.' But Paul's designation of apostles as administrators of God's mysteries implies that Paul's role and authority as a mediator and interpreter of the gospel was shared by all apostles. Of course, Paul elsewhere underscores his apostolic primacy in Corinth as the church's founder (4.14–16; 9.1–2). But his depiction of all apostles as *oikonomoi* of God indicates that each possessed the revelatory authority to announce and interpret God's grace. This is indeed one of the central points Paul seeks to establish through the metaphor, for only by demonstrating that all apostles who ministered in Corinth were entrusted with God's mysteries is Paul able to extinguish the partisanship which permeated the church.

[95] In the same way that administrators were not appointed until after they had first been tested by many trials (Columella, *Rust.* 11.1.7), so Paul asserts that he had to be approved by God to be entrusted with the gospel (1 Thess 2.4; cf. Gal 2.7).

[96] Campenhausen (1969: 36); Schütz (1975: 282). Even though Paul possessed authority in the gospel he received through the revelation of Jesus Christ (Gal 1.12), he himself also became an instantiation, or embodiment, of that very revelation by virtue of having witnessed the resurrection (1.16) and having been commissioned to proclaim it. As Schütz explains, Paul 'identifies gospel with apostle. He makes the apostle the paradigm of the gospel he proclaims. Both the message and the messenger proclaim grace and both embody grace, grace as event' (135).

As Paul's analogy situates him and other apostles equally beneath the Lord, the location of the Corinthians in Paul's metaphorical framework remains somewhat obscure. On the one hand, since God is the principal and Paul is the agent, those whom Paul seeks to 'gain' (κερδαίνω, 1 Cor 9.19–22) are at once the 'profits' he acquires and the third contracting parties with whom he conducts the 'kerygmatic transaction'. From this perspective, Paul positions himself alongside, rather than above, the church. At an initial glance, this would reinforce the non-hierarchical ecclesial structure which many scholars have suggested is implied in Paul's earliest letters.[97]

Paul's metaphor, however, also implies that he was appointed to manage God's personnel. This was the structural model established in commercial enterprises, and Paul's portrayal of apostles as *oikonomoi* suggests that they were afforded this kind of administrative rank and structural authority in the household of God.[98] This connotation finds support elsewhere in 1 Corinthians and Paul's other letters where he articulates structural superiority over immediate delegates, local church leaders, and other believers.[99] Timothy, for instance, while remaining Paul's ἀδελφός and συνεργός in the gospel (1 Thess 3.2; Rom 16.21), is also subordinate to him as the apostle's τέκνος ἀγαπητός (1 Cor 4.17) whom he sends to visit the Corinthians and other churches to lead and speak on his behalf (cf. 1 Cor 16.10; 1 Thess 3.2).[100] Paul also sent a number of other delegates to represent him, including Titus (2 Cor 8.16–17, 22–3; 12.18), Epaphroditus (Phil 2.25; 4.28), and Epaphras (Phlm 23; cf. Col 1.7; 4.12). Since Paul commissioned them, these delegates should be considered subordinate to the apostle.[101]

Beyond his immediate delegates, Paul also recognises the existence of certain local church leaders, including the ἐπισκόποι and διακόνοι in Philippi (Phil 1.1) and those leading (οἱ προϊστάμενοι) in Thessalonica and Rome (1 Thess 5.12–13; Rom 12.8).[102] There were also a number of

---

[97] Bartchy (1999: 77) argues that Paul sought to create a 'dynamic "horizontal" network of exchanges of spiritual power and material goods rather than affirming a fixed hierarchy of any kind'. Cf. Schüssler Fiorenza (1983: 205–41); Bartchy (2003).

[98] Admittedly, Paul does not expressly state that structural authority is bound up with the metaphor. But the usual practice of appointing administrators over estates and businesses, along with the normal use of the metaphor in Pauline and non-Pauline texts (e.g. Luke 12.42; Gal 4.2; Titus 1.7; Ign. *Pol.* 6.1; Epictetus, *Diatr.* 3.22.3), suggests that structural authority is implied by the image.

[99] Clarke (2008: 81); cf. Horrell (1997a).   [100] Aasgaard (2004: 289–90).

[101] Holmberg (1980: 60); Bash (1997: 121); Ehrensperger (2007: 53, 57); Clarke (2008: 93).

[102] The distinction between apostolic delegates and local leaders may seem tenuous. But since apostolic delegates normally represented Paul to local churches in his absence, it is

named and unnamed local leaders in Corinth. Paul identifies such persons as Stephanas, Fortunatus, and Achaicus as those whom the Corinthian believers must recognise (ἐπιγινώσκω) and submit to (ὑποτάσσω) on account of their work and toil (1 Cor 16.15–18). Giaus, Chloe, and Crispus may also have been leaders in Corinth, since the former two hosted house churches and the latter may have once been the leader of the local synagogue (Rom 16.23; 1 Cor 1.11, 14; cf. Acts 18.8). There were then those unnamed figures in the community who were gifted in administration (κυβέρνησις, 12.28), which may also indicate local leadership.[103] Paul's authority extended over all of these local leaders because he as the founder of the community was the ἀρχιτέκτων (3.10) while they were subordinate contractors.[104]

Finally, Paul considers his converts to be persons over whom he possesses structural authority. The Corinthian believers, as Paul's own work in the Lord and the seal of his apostleship (1 Cor 9.1–2), are nothing less than Paul's spiritual children (4.14–16). As such, Paul possesses the right to admonish and instruct them to imitate him as he imitates Christ (4.16; 11.1). It is significant that the believers in Corinth were regarded as slaves (δοῦλοι) and freedmen (ἀπελεύθεροι) of Christ (7.22–3; cf. 6.20). Given this metaphorical identification, Paul's rank as *oikonomos* provides him with a more senior position in the ecclesial household. One can then imagine up to five layers in the early ecclesiastical hierarchy: (i) God/Christ; (ii) Paul/apostles; (iii) apostolic delegates; (iv) local leaders; (v) believers.[105]

---

reasonable to conclude that they possessed structural authority over those churches and their local leaders (1 Cor 4.17; 16.2; 1 Thess 3.2).

[103] Clarke (2008: 84–5).

[104] Shanor (1988: 465–6): 'As ἀρχιτέκτων, Paul assumes responsibility for overseeing the coordination and general progress of the work, a fact to which his authoritative posture in the Corinthian Epistle itself bears cogent testimony.' See also Burford (1969: 139): 'There was no other distinction, technically speaking, between the architect and the craftsmen who worked with him on the temple than that the architect was more skilled and thus competent to command them.' Cf. Fitzmyer (2008: 192).

[105] Some interpreters have charged Paul with confusing his authority with that of Christ's. Castelli (1991: 112) remarks,

> However *imitatio Christi* is defined, Paul's act of imitation is an act of mediation. But it is also a presumptuous move on Paul's part, because he is setting himself in a structurally similar position to that of Christ... Paul does appear at times to confuse his own position with that of Christ or God. Here, the call to imitation is interwoven with this confusion of identity.

Paul's *oikonomos* metaphor, however, seeks to demonstrate his structural authority without confusing his identity with Christ's. Even if Paul's position in the apostolic hierarchy is situated between Christ and the church, Paul's deployment of the image clearly distinguishes himself from Christ his κύριος by establishing himself as Christ's servile intermediary. Thus, Paul's *oikonomos* metaphor significantly nuances Castelli's construal of the structural authority inherent in Paul's position.

Together these attest to the fact that the Pauline churches had at least a simple hierarchy, and that in some cases, like Corinth, an even more complex structure was present.[106]

Responsibilities

Paul's description of apostolic ministry in 4.1–5 does little more than imply what constituted his responsibilities as God's agent. His characterisation of apostles as ὑπηρέται Χριστοῦ suggests only their subordinate and auxiliary role as assistants in God's administration. The construction οἰκονόμοι μυστηρίων θεοῦ, on the other hand, indicates that the responsibilities of apostles primarily involved the dissemination of the heavenly goods entrusted to them. As stated earlier, the genitive in οἰκονόμοι μυστηρίων is objective, so that the apostles are administrators who dispense μυστήρια θεοῦ. But what is it that Paul refers to here as God's mysteries?

In both early Jewish and Christian literature, the general sense of μυστήριον, as Markus Bockmuehl explains, involves 'any reality of divine or heavenly origin specifically characterized as hidden, secret, or otherwise inaccessible to human knowledge'.[107] Bockmuehl further notes that God's mysteries generally involve two main areas: 'redemption (eschatology, cosmology) and sanctification (halakhah)'; '[b]oth are God's property and prerogative ... and can be described as stored up in heaven'.[108] In general agreement with Bockmuehl, Benjamin Gladd adds that God's mysteries have an inherently polemical role, functioning as an apocalyptic motif to subvert conventional knowledge of the present age.[109] The mysteries to which Paul refers in 1 Corinthians imply these very themes.

According to 1 Corinthians, the mysteries entrusted to apostles consist of divine and eternal wisdom (2.7) specially disclosed through God's spirit (2.10). More specifically, Paul equates the μυστήριον τοῦ θεοῦ with the message of the crucifixion of Jesus Christ (2.1–2) – the gospel (1.17–18; 15.1–8).[110] In the first, then, God's mysteries have

---

[106] Clarke (2008: 80–8).   [107] Bockmuehl (1990: 2).

[108] Bockmuehl (1990: 125). 'With few exceptions ... the writers' interest centres on secrets of the celestial world, where the privileged seer glimpses prepared storehouses of the eschatological *Heilsgüter* along with other furnishings of heaven which demonstrate God's universal saving sovereignty' (125–6).

[109] Gladd (2008: 105–7).

[110] For the original reading of 2.1 with μυστήριον rather than μαρτύριον, see Koperski (2002); Gladd (2008: 123–6).

a decidedly Christological focus and comprise Paul's theology of the cross.[111] Furthermore, God's mysteries include the 'wider *implications* of the work of God in Christ', namely righteousness, sanctification, and redemption (1.30), including the unimaginable future inheritance which remains unknown to the rulers of this age (2.8) yet awaits those who love God (2.9).[112] These insights have been disclosed to apostles, and it is they who are responsible for proclaiming God's mysteries, first to unbelievers for the purpose of salvation (1.18, 21, 24), and secondly to believers for maturation (3.2).[113]

Central to Paul's understanding of his apostolic task, however, is the manner in which the gospel message is to be communicated. Paul maintains that he was sent to proclaim the gospel (εὐαγγελίζομαι) not with rhetorical flair – that is, without eloquent speech (σοφία λόγου, 1.17; cf. 2.1, 4) and impressive bodily presence (2 Cor 10.10; cf. 1 Cor 2.3) – but by simply announcing the message of the crucified messiah (1.17–18; 2.2).[114] Paul's gospel consists of the message of the death, burial, resurrection, and appearances of Jesus Christ (15.1–8). When stripped of all rhetorical adornment, this gospel is no less than the power of God for salvation (1.18; cf. 1.24; Rom 1.16; 1 Thess 1.5) and the very means by which the Corinthians themselves are being saved (1 Cor 15.2).[115] Paul insists therefore that his proclamation must not aim to manipulate his audiences, but simply relay the revelation with which he has been entrusted. In his ministry Paul seeks to remove unnecessary ornamentation from God's message so that faith might rest on Christ's power, rather than on the apostle's own persuasiveness (1.17; 2.4–5).

Paul's understanding of the agency and power of the gospel, together with his disavowal of rhetorical invention, is underscored throughout 1 Corinthians 1–4 through the way he refers to his preaching. As Litfin explains,

> The verbs Paul uses to describe his public speaking, such as εὐαγγελίζω, κηρύσσω, καταγγέλλω, and μαρτυρέω, are decidedly non-rhetorical. No self-respecting orator could have

---

[111] Bockmuehl (1990: 165): 'Paul's message about Christ crucified is called the mystery of God.'

[112] Bockmuehl (1990: 162).

[113] Throughout 1 Corinthians 1–4 Paul associates apostleship almost entirely with the task of preaching (1.17, 23; 2.1, 4, 6–7, 13; 3.1–2, 6, 10; 4.15, 17), although this is occasionally veiled in metaphor.

[114] Litfin (1994: 181–209); Winter (2002: 141–64).

[115] Schütz (1975: 40–53). For the word of the cross as empowering epistemological and ethical transformation, see Brown (1995: 157–67).

used such verbs to describe his own *modus operandi*. Indeed, even though they deal with the subject of public speaking such verbs play no significant role in the rhetorical literature. This is understandable because these verbs describe a form of speaking which is at its core the antithesis of rhetorical behavior. The principles of rhetorical adaptation are irrelevant to the κῆρυξ... The herald's task is not to create a persuasive message at all, but to convey effectively the already articulated message of another... It is not surprising, then, that such verbs were largely unusable to the rhetoricians. Nor, in the light of Paul's understanding of his mission, is it surprising that he should embrace such verbs for his own. He perceived his public speaking in a profoundly different light from the orators who were so prominent in his day. He had been entrusted with a message and it was his task to announce it in simplicity to all who would listen.[116]

Given Paul's manner of describing his preaching ministry elsewhere, his portrayal of apostles as *oikonomoi* of God's mysteries becomes more understandable. As a commercial agent Paul is a messenger, a mere conduit of the word of the cross.[117] His chief responsibility is to take the currency entrusted to him – the foolish message of the crucified messiah (1.21, 23) – and to invest it in the market of the unbelieving world. But whereas commercial administrators generate profits, apostles produce converts (cf. κερδαίνω, 9.19–22). Paul's investments require neither flamboyance nor clever marketing, only the simple depositing of God's heavenly resources (1.21; 3.5; 15.2, 11). As agents commissioned to various parts of the Roman world, apostles are simply purveyors of God's salvific message. And all profits are ultimately for God's benefit.

Accountability

After expressing what role and corresponding responsibilities have been entrusted to apostles, Paul proceeds to explain what God expects of them and how he secures their obedience. Verse 2 begins with the particles ὧδε λοιπόν, a complex phrase which functions to connect Paul's preceding assertion with that which follows. The difficulty with the phrase lies with λοιπός. While ὧδε in this instance means 'in this case' (BDAG 2) and draws an inference from verse 1, λοιπός here can either strengthen the

---

[116] Litfin (1994: 195–6).
[117] Bockmuehl (1990: 166): '[T]his metaphor fits perfectly with the function of Paul's ministry as a source of revelation.'

inferential sense already present from ὧδε ('in this case, moreover'; cf. *BDF* §451 [6]; Epictetus, *Diatr.* 2.12.24) or introduce a new idea ('now'), so that 'λοιπόν becomes an inceptive particle, looking forward, rather than an inferential connective, looking back'.[118] Since the following gnomic statement transitions somewhat awkwardly from what precedes (see especially the verb's change in person and mood) and Paul introduces it entirely for the purpose of addressing the matter of apostolic judgment in 4.3–5, the latter inceptive sense is to be preferred. Together the phrase should be translated 'in this case, now', so that ὧδε looks backward and λοιπόν points forward.[119]

However one translates ὧδε λοιπόν, the phrase clearly makes way for Paul's forthcoming proverbial statement ('sprichwortartige Satz').[120] As he continues, Paul reminds his audience that 'it is required in administrators that a faithful one is found [ζητεῖται ἐν τοῖς οἰκονόμοις, ἵνα πιστός τις εὑρεθῇ]' (4.2). The proverb recalls the surprise inspections to which absentee business owners subjected their representative agents in ancient commerce. The primacy of loyalty in servile relationships, including private administration, was common knowledge in Graeco-Roman antiquity and was probably especially so in Roman Corinth where a large portion of the population had servile roots. The primary function of Paul's statement, however, is not to divulge original insight about what principals expected of their subordinates. Paul seeks simply to raise the issues of servile responsibility and accountability in anticipation of 4.3–5, which he does by introducing two complementary evaluative verbs commonly associated with servile acountability (ζητέω, εὑρίσκω; cf. Luke 12.43, 48).[121]

But Paul's articulation of the proverb is deliberately vague, for the apostle maintains the anonymity of the evaluating party by using the passive voice for both verbs. Of course Paul's point is not entirely concealed; clearly the administrator's principal is the only one competent to judge his manager. But Paul initially omits the identity of the evaluating

---

[118] Thrall (1962: 26–8, here at 27). Based on Epictetus' use of the phrase, Welborn (2005: 244) suggests that it is a 'verbal gesture of annoyance by one who is forced to concede that a general truth is applicable in the present case'.

[119] Schrage (1991: 321) translates it 'hierbei nun'.

[120] Fascher (1975: 143).

[121] Gladd (2008: 172) argues that Paul here alludes to Dan 6.4 (Theo). But his case is tenuous, since in the latter text εὑρίσκω has no syntactical relationship with πιστός and God is not the subject of the verb, as he is implied to be in 1 Cor 4.2. A better (though imperfect) Pauline parallel is Phil 3.9, where, following a clear commercial metaphor in 3.7–8, Paul expresses his need to be found (εὑρεθῶ) righteous διὰ πίστεως Χριστοῦ. Although the two metaphors are not the same, both 1 Cor 4.1–5 and Phil 3.7–9 employ commercial language and refer to Paul's calling to account.

party for rhetorical effect, that is, to prepare the way for his renunciation of phoney and inappropriate judges in the three forthcoming verses.[122] In other words, by not disclosing precisely who judges God's administrators, Paul is able to present and reject three unsuitable critics (the church, a court, oneself), ultimately for the sake of demonstrating the impropriety of just one of them – ὑμῶν.

Paul's censure of the Corinthians for their apostolic evaluations in 4.3–5 marks a major escalation in the tone of the discourse. Paul has resisted addressing their criticisms particularly of him for the initial three chapters of the letter. But here the apostle meets their judgments head-on, for Paul considers them to be a great affront, probably not because he is in anyway affected by them, but because judging teachers and public speakers implied the exercise of power over them. This association is easily overlooked outside the context of Graeco-Roman oratory. Therefore, before proceeding to Paul's censure, it is important to address the power of the audience in ancient oratory in order to show how criticisms might be perceived by orators.

Corinth's oratorical context

In addition to being renowned as a focal point in trans-provincial trade, Corinth was also a famous centre for education during the early empire. Especially during the Second Sophistic the city attracted many philosophers and rhetors, whose schools and oratorical skills became quite famous throughout Greece.[123] Auditing speeches therefore became one of Corinth's most popular and important spectator activities. As Tim Whitmarsh explains, 'Oratory was not just a gentle pastime of the rich: it was one of the primary means that Greek culture of the period, constrained as it was by Roman rule, had to explore issues of identity, society, family, and power.'[124] As some orators acquired great fame for their rhetorical

---

[122] This rhetorical strategy is apparent especially by the way the ἵνα + aorist-passive-subjunctive verb (εὑρεθῇ) construction in 4.2 is mirrored by the ἵνα + aorist-passive-subjunctive verb (ἀνακριθῶ) construction in 4.3.

[123] Bowersock (1969: 17–29) does not include Corinth among the most visited cities of the sophists, but recognises it as a client city of Herodes Atticus (Philostratus, *Vit. soph.* 551). Demetrius the Cynic, a late first-century intimate of Seneca, was an orator and resident of Corinth (Tacitus, *Hist.* 4.40; Lucian, *Ind.* 10; Seneca, *Ep.* 20, 62; *Vit. beat.* 18; *Prov.* 3.3, 5.5; Philostratus, *Vit. Apoll.* 4.25; *Ep.* 36, 37), while Aelius Aristides (*Or.* 46.23), Apollonius of Tyana (Philostratus, *Vit. Apoll.* 4.25, 7.10), Dio Chrysostom (*Or.* 31.121), and Plutarch (*Mor.* 723a) also frequented the city. The Corinthians even erected a bronze statue to Favorinus in front of the city library to stimulate the youth in scholastics (Dio Chrysostom, *Or.* 37.8). Cf. Engels (1990: 45); Dutch (2005: 95–138).

[124] Whitmarsh (2005: 1). Cf. Steel (2006: 54).

skill, others were handicapped by their failure to impress crowds. As a performance-oriented profession, oratory established a reciprocal relationship between the speaker and audience. Whether the orator delivered a speech in order to educate or amuse, the audience offered honour in return, providing them with a kind of power over the speaker.[125] This interplay, as will be shown, was something of a microcosm of the entire Roman honour system.

J. E. Lendon describes life in the Roman world as a 'ceaseless, restless quest for distinction in the eyes of one's peers and of posterity'.[126] And ceaseless it was. The pursuit of honour was a cultural addiction driven by a tenacious and competitive aspiration for public approval. Plutarch describes the competitive and irrepressible lust for honour and praise that saturated the early empire:

> [W]hen others are praised [ἐπαίνοις], our rivalry [τὸ φιλότιμον] erupts, as we said, into praise of self; it is seized with a certain barely controllable yearning and urge for glory [δόξαν] that stings and tickles like an itch, especially when the other is praised for something in which he is our equal or inferior. For just as in the hungry the sight of others eating makes the appetite sharper and keener, so the praise of others not far removed inflames with jealousy [τῇ ζηλοτυπίᾳ] those who are intemperate in seeking glory.   (*Mor.* 546c)

The love of honour (φιλοτιμία) about which Plutarch writes was not restricted to the privileged elite, but was endemic to all of Roman society. In Rome the pursuit of honour was, as Carlin Barton explains, 'the fire in the bones'.[127] Thus, Cicero's famous motto: 'To be equal to others in liberty, and first in honour' (*Phil.* 1.34).

Honour, however, was not an individualistic enterprise, but a public pursuit so that the honouree acquired his or her status only through community recognition. 'Renown [*claritas*]',[128] remarked Seneca, 'is the favourable opinion of good men; for just as reputation does not consist of one person's remarks, and as ill repute does not consist of one person's disapproval, so renown does not mean that we have merely pleased one good person. In order to constitute renown, the agreement of many distinguished and praiseworthy men is necessary' (*Ep.* 102.8).[129] As Lendon

---

[125] Bell (1997: 16–20).   [126] Lendon (1997: 35).   [127] C. A. Barton (2001).

[128] For a sampling of Greek and Latin terms belonging to honour discourse, see Lendon (1997: 272–9); deSilva (2000: 27–8).

[129] Pitt-Rivers (1965: 21): 'Honour is the value of a person in his own eyes, but also in the eyes of his society.' Cf. Malina (1993: 31–3).

explains, 'No quality was honourable in and of itself. Honour was mediated through the perceptions of others, and even a superfluity of worthy
qualities was of no use unless these qualities were publicly known, and
approved by other aristocrats.'[130] The pursuit of honour, then, kept the
typical Roman preoccupied with his or her public performance. Indeed,
life in Rome was, as V. Henry Nguyen suggests, a 'grand spectacle'.[131]

It is often recognised that during the empire the possession of honour implied the acquisition of power, since honour could be used to
influence one's peers.[132] But it is not as often realised that the ability
to confer honour also translated into power for the purveyor. Lendon
insightfully refers to the conferral of honour as 'power directed
upwards'. While recognising that honour in the context of Roman government 'contributed to the power of the rulers over the ruled', Lendon
notes that honour also 'contributed to the power of the ruled over the
rulers'.[133]

This inversion of the power dynamic is perhaps most apparent in the
practice of deference in the realm of politics. Desiring to gain public
approval as much as any commodity, it was not uncommon in legislation
for politicians to succumb to the wishes of the citizens when arriving
at a decision. Lendon explains, 'A governor treated his subjects with
deference not least because men … in whose hands his reputation lay
were watching. Appalling failures of deference on the part of governors
attracted unfavourable attention, perhaps even a blistering speech from
Libanius.'[134] And if conferring honour and shame was associated with
the possession of power in the assembly, so it was in the marketplace as
well. As Dio Chrysostom remarks,

> If one were acquainted with spells learned from Medea or the
> Thessalians which were so potent that by uttering them he
> could make any one he pleased weep and suffer pain though
> confronted by no misfortune, would not his power [δύναμις]
> be regarded as tyranny [τυραννίς]? While, in dealing with
> one who has become puffed up by reputation [τὸν ἐπὶ δόξῃ
> καχαυνωμένον] there is none who does not have this power
> [ἰσχύν]; for by speaking two or three words you have plunged
> him into misery and anguish.   (*Or.* 66.16–17)

---

[130] Lendon (1997: 37).   [131] Nguyen (2008: 33).
[132] For other ways that honour contributed to power, see Garnsey (1970); Saller (1982);
MacMullen (1986).
[133] Lendon (1997: 24).   [134] Lendon (1997: 204; cf. 230–4).

It was, then, the vulnerability of persons to the pleasure of honour and pain of shame that provoked them to seek, at whatever cost, the approval of their peers.

The power of bestowing reputation was also often couched in judicial terms. In the public arena the honouree was considered the defendant, and his or her peers functioned as the judge, jury, and witnesses. Bruce Malina appropriately remarks that 'honor is all about the tribunal or court of public opinion and the reputation that court bestows'.[135] Lendon similarly suggests, 'A man's honour was a public verdict on his qualities and standing.'[136] Dio Chrysostom's conceptualisation of the public exchange of honour and shame demonstrates this point clearly:

> Is not the trial concerning reputation [ὁ περὶ τῆς δόξης ἀγών] always in progress wherever there are men – that is, foolish men – not merely once a day but many times, and not before a definite panel of judges [δικασταῖς] but before all men without distinction, and, moreover, men not bound by oath, men without regard for either witnesses [μαρτύρων] or evidence [τεκμηρίων]? For they sit in judgement [δικάζουσι] without either having knowledge of the case or listening to testimony or having been chosen by lot, and it makes no difference to them if they cast their vote at a drinking bout or at the bath and, most outrageous of all, he who today is acquitted [ἀπολύσῃ] tomorrow is condemned [καταδικάζει].   (*Or.* 66.18)

Thus, in the Roman world the pursuit of honour and praise placed an individual in a position of social dependence where he or she remained vulnerable to the capricious estimations of one's community of on-lookers.

Given the significance of honour in the Roman world, it comes as no surprise that orators were among Rome's most notorious 'popularity-seekers' (φιλόδοξοι). Quintilian admits that declaimers consider the 'applause of a large audience [*laude plurium*]' to be 'that most coveted of all prizes [*ex illa quae maxime petitur*]' (*Inst.* 2.7.5). This preoccupation is frequently criticised by the moral philosophers. Epictetus is but one who repeatedly and colourfully indicated how common it was for orators during the early empire to covet the praises of their

[135] Malina (1993: 42).
[136] Lendon (1997: 36). Barton (2001: 212): 'Calling on spectators – or judges, for they were inseparable notions in the Roman mind – of an oath or an action was a Roman's way of saying, "Go ahead: put me in the spotlight. My words and my actions will stand the test of your scrutiny." The presence of witnesses made every act into an ordeal.'

audiences. In one monologue, after Epictetus asked his interlocutor about the benefits of being an orator, the interlocutor responded, 'But praise me [ἀλλ' ἐπαίνεσόν με]', prompting Epictetus to enquire, 'What do you mean by "praise"?' The orator then explained, 'Cry out to me, "Bravo!" or "Marvellous!"' (*Diatr.* 3.23.23). The same preoccupation with praise surfaces in Epictetus' instructions to orators before taking the stage. According to Epictetus, just before lecturing the orator should ask himself, 'Do you wish to do good or to be praised [ὠφελῆσαι θέλεις ἢ ἐπαινεθῆναι]?' (*Diatr.* 3.23.7). The question was of course rhetorical and supposed to remind the orator that his lecture ought to benefit his audience, not himself. But it also reveals for the modern reader how often ancient orators were enticed by their own ambition. Epictetus, in fact, considered 'sorry' (κακῶς) those orators who were found 'gaping for the praises of men [χάσκων περὶ τοὺς ἐπαινέσοντας]' and counting heads in their audiences (*Diatr.* 3.23.19). So pervasive was the preoccupation with honour among orators that Aristides considered himself to be one of only a few orators who lectured not for the sake of 'wealth, reputation, honor, marriage, power, or any acquisition', but because he genuinely loved speeches (*Or.* 33.19–20). Similar criticisms abound in the orations of Dio Chrysostom (e.g. *Or.* 32, 33, 35), who time and again distanced himself from the popular philosophers owing to their self-interest.

This lust for praise afforded spectators significant influence over orators before, during, and after a rhetorical performance. The fate of an orator, then, always rested in the hands of his audience, as they possessed the power to make or break the speaker's reputation and self-confidence.[137] Epictetus alludes to the susceptibility of the orator to the emotional impact of an audience's response:

> For why is it that the orator, although he knows that he has composed a good speech, has memorized what he has written

[137] The power of the spectator is apparent in many areas of Roman society, especially politics. Bell (1997: 19) notes about Cicero:

> *Virtus* was a key ideological quality and, because his career was short of military indications that he possessed it, Cicero had no recourse but to performance at a *contio* in order to record the popular approbation that warranted his claim. The Populus, therefore, had the power to make Cicero the sort of man he could never be on solely his own merits.

Aldrete (1999: 154) explains that 'acclamations do not just confer authority, power, and legitimacy upon a ruler; they also bestow power upon those who give them'. Of course orators also used persuasion as a form of power over their audiences. Aristides says that if he were to declaim frequently, 'everything would be mine and under my spell' (*Or.* 33.4). For more on the interplay between the political orator and audience, see Morstein-Marx (2004: 119–59).

and is bringing a pleasing voice to his task, is still anxious [ἔτι ἀγωνιᾷ] despite all that? Because he is not satisfied with the mere practice of oratory. What, then, does he want? He wants to be praised by his audience [ἐπαινεθῆναι ὑπὸ τῶν παρόντων]. Now he has trained himself with a view to being able to practise oratory, but he has not trained himself with reference to praise and blame [ἔπαινον δὲ καὶ ψόγον]... That is why, if he is praised [ἐπαινεθῇ], he goes off the stage all puffed up; but if he is laughed to scorn, that poor windbag of his conceit is pricked and flattens out.   (*Diatr.* 2.16.5–6, 10)

The ambitions of such orators made them quite vulnerable to praise and blame, honour and shame, and thus positioned them beneath, as it were, the power of their critics.

Many orators were successfully able to avoid public censure by giving the crowds what they wished. But as Dio Chrysostom explains (even if not specifically targeting orators), such manoeuvres themselves even imply a sense of subjection to one's on-lookers:

Clearly, therefore, if a person is going to be exceedingly anxious to win the praise of the crowd as well [τοῦ παρὰ τῶν πολλῶν ἐπαίνου], believing that its praise or censure has more weight [κυριώτερον] than his own judgement, his every act and wish will be aimed to show himself the sort of person that the crowd expects [lit. values; ἀξιοῦσιν οἱ πολλοί].   (*Or.* 77/78.24)

According to Dio, then, the individual – orator or otherwise – who adapts a performance due to anxiety of the crowd is beneath its power.

The audience's power over the orator is also implied when the enterprise is portrayed in forensic terms. According to the Athenians, it was through speech (λόγος) that the public was able to appraise (δοκιμάζω) the wise (Isocrates, *Nic.* 6–7). In fact, the entire goal of rhetoric was to establish a judgment (κρίσις), and therefore every auditor of speeches was a judge (κριτής) from whom the orator received a verdict (Aristotle, *Rhet.* 1377b2; cf. 1391b18). This was also the orator's perception under Roman rule and is perhaps no better exemplified than in Favorinus' Κορινθιακός. In the Corinthian Oration, Favorinus famously portrayed himself advocating for his missing statue as if it were on trial before the Corinthians. In an epideictic speech posing as an apology,[138] Favorinus blames the Corinthians for removing their statue of him:

---

[138] For Favorinus' rhetorical strategy, see Gleason (1995: 9); L. M. White (2005: 69–71).

Then supposing some such decree were to be passed in Corinth too, prescribing that statues should be subjected to an accounting [εὐθύνας] – or rather, if you please, supposing this to have been already decreed and a trial [ἀγῶνος] to have been instituted – permit me, pray permit me, to make my plea before you in my own behalf as if in court [ἐν δικαστηρίῳ]. Gentlemen of the jury [ἄνδρες δικασταί], it is said that anything may be expected in the course of time; but he who stands before you is in jeopardy of first being set up [τεθῆναι] as the noblest [ἄριστος] among the Greeks and then being cast out [ἐκπεσεῖν] as the worst [πονηρότατος], all in a brief span of time.

(Dio Chrysostom, *Or.* 37.22)

Courtroom language pervades much of the discourse (cf. 37.16). But even in this brief sampling, the repeated use of words from the δικ- root (δικαστήριον, δικαστής), the noun ἀγών for a generic trial, and the technical term εὔθυνα for a calling to account definitely signal a forensic perspective.[139] As L. Michael White has additionally demonstrated, τιθέναι and ἐκπίπτειν form a word-play, since both terms have architectural and legal connotations, further indicating that a trial scene is in view.[140] Moreover, it is significant for our purposes that Favorinus expressly acknowledges the power of the audience, as it possesses the authority to pronounce nobility (ἄριστος) and villainy (πονηρότατος).

The use of forensic language, then, was a familiar feature in ancient oratory and was used to convey the susceptibility of the speaker to the judgments of his audience. Furthermore, since oratory was caught up in the honour system of the early empire, the privilege to award praise or blame provided the audience with a position of power over the orator, which is occasionally acknowledged even in the speech. With this context in view, let us return to 1 Corinthians 4 to evaluate how Paul portrays and responds to the interrogation of his jury, the Corinthian church.

Paul's judgment

It is within the context of oratorical verdicts as 'power directed upwards' that Paul portrays and ultimately rejects the evaluations of his Corinthian

---

[139] Ἀγών can also denote an oratorical performance (e.g. Philostratus, *Vit. soph.* 526, 580, 601); cf. Whitmarsh (2005: 39). For εὔθυνα in magisterial trials, see Roberts (1982: 17–18); M. H. Hansen (1999: 222–4).

[140] L. M. White (2005: 69–70).

critics. In the following exposition we shall demonstrate that Paul repudiates these criticisms by playing the Corinthians, as it were, at their own game. By representing the Corinthian evaluations as a judicial proceeding, Paul casts the church as an audience scrutinising his rhetorical ability, an entirely normal procedure in the world of declamations. But Paul is not a rhetor and is therefore immune to these judgments. Instead, Paul is an *oikonomos* who is only accountable to and acquitted by his κύριος. It is the Lord alone who will announce Paul's verdict at his coming, and therefore the church must cease to judge him and other apostles. In this way Paul mixes oratorical and administrative metaphors in order to demonstrate the absurdity of the church's behaviour.

Paul's use of forensic language begins in 4.3–5, where the presence of courtroom terminology is quite explicit.[141] Paul's use of ἡμέρα in 4.3, for instance, is widely regarded as parallel to its use in 3.13 where Paul refers to the 'Day' of God's eschatological judgment. From there it is no large step to observe that Paul uses the phrase ἀνθρωπίνης ἡμέρας to refer to an earthly tribunal; the phrase even refers to a judicial proceeding on an early Christian amulet.[142] The use of δικαιόω for 'acquittal' (4.4) also clearly indicates that a courtroom motif is present in this pericope. Furthermore, the verb κρίνω (4.5) conveys the notion of reaching a legal verdict, as it does in 1 Corinthians 5–6 and elsewhere.

The verb ἀνακρίνω, which appears three times in this passage (4.3[2x], 4), is also a forensic term and alludes to a judicial proceeding. The verb ἀνακρίνειν can carry the meanings (i) 'to question or examine' generally (cf. Acts 17.11) and (ii) 'to discern' a matter of information, but it can also indicate (iii) 'to scrutinise' in a judicial hearing.[143] The term, in fact, was used the latter way in Greek literature to refer to the performance of a preliminary judicial interrogation, the ἀνάκρισις.[144] Ἀνακρίνω surfaces in numerous Lucan courtroom accounts referring to just such a

---

[141] Papathomas (2009: 55–9). Cf. Kuck (1992: 197 n. 246), who observes Paul's abundant use of evaluative terms in 4.2–5 (ζητεῖται, εὑρεθῇ, πιστός, σύνοιδα, φωτίσει, φανερώσει, ἔπαινος).

[142] Bonner (1950: 167). It is possible that ἀνθρωπίνης ἡμέρας (4.4) also contrasts with the καιρός of the Lord's judgment (4.5).

[143] LSJ implies the high frequency of this judicial sense when it provides for its most basic definition '*examine closely, interrogate*, esp. judicially'. Papathomas (2009: 47): 'Der papyrologischen Dokumentation ist eindeutig zu entnehmen, daß der Begriff zur juristischen Terminologie gehört und wurde Bevölkerung des Nahen Ostens als Rechtsterminus empfunden wurde.'

[144] See, e.g., Isaeus, *Dicaeog.* 5.32; Andocides, *Myst.* 1.101; Demosthenes, *Olymp.* 48.31; Aristotle, *Ath. pol.* 56.6; *SIG* 953.46; Josephus, *Ant.* 17.131; Sus 45–51. Cf. Harrison (1971: 94–105); MacDowell (1978: 240–3).

pre-trial hearing (Luke 23.14; Acts 4.9; 12.19; 24.8; 28.18),[145] and the noun ἀνακρίσις is used this way in Acts when Festus explains why he sent Paul before King Agrippa (Acts 25.26). In Paul, ἀνακρίνω is used only in 1 Corinthians, where it appears no fewer than ten times (2.14, 15[2x]; 4.3[2x], 4; 9.3; 10.25, 27; 14.24) and in a forensic sense in at least 9.3, 4.3–4, and probably in 2.14–15. Based therefore on the legal connotations of ἀνακρίνω along with the other forensic terms in 4.3–5, it is clear that Paul was portraying himself as if he were in a preliminary hearing (ἀνακρίσις) before the Corinthian church. Moreover, in light of the oratorical context sketched above, it is plausible that Paul's use of forensic language in the passage draws on the conventional perception of an oration as a miniature trial. In 4.3–5, then, the Corinthians are portrayed as spectators/jurors who were evaluating the ministry of Paul, the orator/defendant.[146]

Since Paul's primary ministerial responsibility was the faithful communication of the mysteries of God, the church's evaluations of Paul were probably targeting his oratorical ability. As one whose bodily presence was weak and whose speech was contemptible (cf. 2 Cor 10.10), this evaluation was probably more of a shameful critique. As Dahl explains,

> From the statement, 'With me it is a very small thing that I should be judged by you or by any human court' (4:3), we may safely infer that some kind of criticism of Paul has been voiced at Corinth. And it is not difficult to find out what the main content of this criticism must have been. That becomes evident in phrases like, 'Not with eloquent wisdom' (οὐκ ἐν σοφίᾳ λόγου, 1:17), 'Not in lofty words of wisdom' (οὐ καθ' ὑπεροχὴν λόγου ἢ σοφίας, 2:1), 'Not in persuasiveness of wisdom' (οὐκ ἐν πειθοῖ σοφίας, 2:4), 'Milk, not solid food' (γάλα...οὐ βρῶμα, 3:2).[147]

In this statement Dahl correctly observes that Paul's seemingly amateurish oratorical skill was the subject of the church's criticisms here as

---

[145] Trites (1974: 279) notes the sense of power ἀνακρίνω implies when she observes how in Acts the verb demonstrates that 'both Paul and the Jerusalem apostles work in an atmosphere of hostility and contention'.

[146] Welborn (1987b: 107) states that 'Paul's language in 4:1–5 leaves little doubt that his opponents sought to "examine" his credentials in quasi-judicial proceedings'. But Paul's language cannot be taken literally, as Welborn seems to suggest. The Corinthians neither had nor intended to examine Paul in an actual hearing. Paul's forensic metaphor is employed only in order to expose the power implied in the Corinthians' evaluations. Cf. A. Robertson and Plummer (1911: 75–6); Lietzmann and Kümmel (1969: 18).

[147] Dahl (1967: 321).

well as earlier in the letter.[148] As Litfin explains, 'These status-conscious
Corinthians apparently harbored few reservations about rendering a
negative judgment of Paul's abilities as a speaker. They perceived the
wandering Jewish Apostle in this respect in much the same light as they
perceived other itinerant speakers: as fair game for their evaluations.'[149]
As observed above from our survey on oratory and honour, an audience's praise or blame could dramatically affect an orator, especially
one's professional standing and self-confidence. Paul therefore portrays
the Corinthian interrogation as if the church attempted to appraise his
ministry and thereby wield power over him. Whether or not this power
was wielded intentionally, the gesture itself was, in the apostle's view,
quite out of place.

But Paul's response is telling. For Paul, the evaluations of the church,
a Roman court, even himself, were of no consequence (4.3).[150] When it
came to human opinions about his ministry, Paul cared very little (ἐμοὶ
δὲ εἰς ἐλάχιστόν ἐστιν).[151] Not only was Paul himself unaware of any
ministerial, motivational, or spiritual shortcomings which either he or
the Corinthians could hold against him (οὐδὲν γὰρ ἐμαυτῷ σύνοιδα),
but as an *oikonomos* of Christ no opinion even mattered other than that
of his κύριος (4.4–5).[152] As he states elsewhere, 'Who are you who judge
another's servant [σὺ τίς εἶ ὁ κρίνων ἀλλότριον οἰκέτην]? It is before
one's own lord [τῷ ἰδίῳ κυρίῳ] that one stands or falls' (Rom 14.4).[153]
It is based on this principle of exclusive servitude that the apostle objects
to the Corinthian interrogations. Paul was concerned to be found faithful
in the eyes of his Lord only (1 Cor 4.2), for it was God/Christ alone who

---

[148] This is additionally supported by Paul's use of ἀνακρίνω in 1 Cor 9.3, where his critics are also said to have been scrutinising the apostle's ministerial practice.

[149] Litfin (1994: 163). Cf. Finney (2010: 34).

[150] Paul is mainly concerned here with the criticisms of the church, rather than a secular
court or his conscience. But since oratory was often practised and evaluated in court, the
reference to a human tribunal confirms that Paul's oratorical ability is in view. For Paul's
examination of his own conscience in 4.3–4 as it relates to unrecognised sin, see Chester
(2003: 195–202). But the ministerial and harmartological interpretations are perhaps not
as far apart as some scholars assume, since there were probably some in the church who
regarded certain ministerial practices or negligences as matters of actual sin (cf. 2 Cor 11.7).

[151] Admittedly, Paul showed great concern in 2 Corinthians and elsewhere for how the
church perceived him. But Paul's elaborate apology in 2 Corinthians was motivated more
by his hope that the church would dismiss false teachers and continue to embrace his
gospel than by his desire that the church would accurately understand and genuinely appre-
ciate his ministry (cf. 2 Cor 11.1–15).

[152] Paul of course was well aware and even ashamed of his pre-conversion persecutions
(1 Cor 15.9), but here he insists that he cannot recall anything that would render him liable
to community judgment. Even so, Paul concedes that his own self-evaluations cannot be
trusted; cf. Chester (2003: 198). Therefore, justification must come through Christ.

[153] Hays (1997: 67).

was authorised to evaluate (ἀνακρίνω), judge (κρίνω), and justify him (δικαιόω).[154] Indeed, any alternative pursuit of approval would mean that Paul was serving another master (cf. Gal 1.10).

Paul makes a similar case in 1 Thess 2.3–6, where he likewise expresses his indifference to popular opinion and pledges his undivided allegiance to God.[155] There Paul insists,

> [O]ur appeal does not come from error, impurity, or deceit, but just as we have been approved by God to be entrusted with the gospel [δεδοκιμάσμεθα ὑπὸ τοῦ θεοῦ πιστευθῆναι τὸ εὐαγγέλιον], so we speak, not to please people, but God who tests our hearts [λαλοῦμεν οὐχ ὡς ἀνθρώποις ἀρέσκοντες ἀλλὰ θεῷ τῷ δοκιμάζοντι τὰς καρδίας ἡμῶν]. For we did not come then with flattering speech, as you know, or a pretext for greed, God is witness [μάρτυς], or seeking glory from people [ζητοῦντες ἐξ ἀνθρώπων δόξαν], whether from you or from others.

Although the congruencies in these texts are occasionally inverted – for instance, Paul dismisses ecclesial evaluations in 1 Cor 4.3–5, but submits to God's testing in 1 Thess 2.4 – they are many and often explicit.[156] Most significant for our purposes is that Paul identifies the sole objective of his preaching ministry to be the pleasure of God rather than the pleasure and glory of people. While he does not say so as strongly as he does in 1 Cor 4.3, in 1 Thess 2.3–6 Paul wholly discounts his audience's evaluation of

---

[154] The perfect tense δεδικαίωμαι corresponds with the perfect tense of σύνοιδα (4.4), both having a present force. As Edwards (1885: 99) explains, 'the case is still pending'; cf. Thiselton (2000: 341). Although Fitzmyer (2008: 213) and others insist that δικαιόω here cannot imply the 'justification of the sinner' since 'it is not a matter of *pistis*', the verb should retain the meaning 'justify' because this is the sense of the verb's only other occurrence in 1 Corinthians (6.11), as well as because πιστός (4.2) and the final judgment are in view (4.5; cf. 3.13–15; Rom 2.6–10, 13); cf. Fee (1987: 162); Garland (2003: 128). Still, the present tense of ὁ δὲ ἀνακρίνων με κύριός ἐστιν indicates that Paul's ministry was already undergoing divine evaluation, thus his justification also has a present orientation; cf. Chester (2003: 200).

[155] For 1 Thess 2.1–12 as a defence, see Weima (1997); Kim (2005); *contra* Malherbe (1970). Cf. Donfried and Beutler (2000: 3–131).

[156] See especially the following parallels: (i) stewardship of the gospel (οἰκονόμους μυστηρίων θεοῦ, 1 Cor 4.1; πιστευθῆναι τὸ εὐαγγέλιον, 1 Thess 2.4; cf. οἰκονομίαν πεπίστευμαι, 1 Cor 9.17); (ii) repetition of forensic language (ἀνακρίνω, ἡμέρα, δικαιόω, κρίνω, 1 Cor 4.3–5; δοκιμάζω, μάρτυς, 1 Thess 2.4–5); (iii) ζητέω (1 Cor 4.2; 1 Thess 2.6); (iv) ἄνθρωπος (1 Cor 4.1; 1 Thess 2.4, 6); (v) emphasis on καρδία and other internal qualifications (1 Cor 4.2, 5; 1 Thess 2.3–4); (vi) use of honour discourse as a ministerial incentive (ἔπαινος, 1 Cor 4.5; δόξα, 1 Thess 2.6).

his rhetorical skill,[157] seeking instead divine approval of his motivations (καρδία). And as in 1 Corinthians 4, this focus is based on the fact that God alone is the one who has commissioned Paul for apostolic ministry and will ultimately call him to account (2.4).[158]

Given the oratorical and administrative contexts of the discourse, Paul's stern rebuke in 1 Cor 4.1–5 should be interpreted as his response to what he perceived to be a power play on the part of the Corinthians. Their criticisms of Paul as Christ's slave agent amounted to nothing less than an implicit usurpation of the exclusive authority God possesses over his apostle. As Richard Hays explains, 'Paul's point is simply that [the Corinthians] have arrogated to themselves the right to pass judgment on his work in a way that is inappropriate to their position and impossible for any human being on this side of the *parousia*.'[159] In response to such presumption, Paul employs the *oikonomos* metaphor to construct his authority (i.e. his rank and immunity) and asserts that authority by deflecting the power play of the Corinthians and calling them to cease their judgments. Paul concedes that his life and ministry will undergo scrutiny, but only by his Lord and at his return. At that eschatological hearing, Christ will not consider the apostle's eloquence, physical presence, or any tangible marker of ministerial success, as were the Corinthians. Only the apostle's internal qualities will matter, for all of his secret motivations will be laid bare (φωτίσει τὰ κρυπτὰ τοῦ σκότους) as Christ alone searches the apostle's heart (φανερώσει τὰς

---

[157] It is significant that Paul uses the generic verb λαλέω (cf. 1 Cor 2.6–7, 13), for it portrays his preaching not as a rhetorical performance, but as the simple articulation of the gospel. Thus, just as in 1 Corinthians, Paul's concern is to distance his *modus operandi* from that of sophists and popular philosophers; cf. Winter (1993).

[158] Since God can already testify (μάρτυς) to Paul's lack of flattery and greed, he must have already begun testing (δοκιμάζω) Paul's heart. Therefore, just as in 1 Cor 4.4, in 1 Thess 2.4 Paul's justification has a present reality. Malherbe (2000: 141) suggests that Paul's use of δοκιμάζω stems from the LXX tradition of prophetic testing (e.g. Jer 11.20; 12.3; 17.10; 20.12; Psalm 17.3), but it could be that Paul has a Graeco-Roman forensic setting in view: the apostle, just like municipal magistrates, had to undergo an initial *and* final scrutiny (Aeschines, *Ctes.* 3.15); cf. Richard (1995: 96); Weima (1997: 84).

[159] Hays (1997: 67). Thiselton (2000: 341) and others suggest that Paul was criticising the church's *inability* to judge due to the inaccessibility of the heart to human assessment before the Lord's coming (πρὸ καιροῦ). But while human fallibility may be a factor, Paul believed that the Corinthians also lacked the *right/authority* to judge apostles. As Kuck (1992: 221) remarks,

> Paul's admonition not to judge is warranted by his appeal to the higher court of God's judgment. The contrast is not only, or even primarily, between present and future judgment. It is more a matter of who does the judgment: Christians are ultimately accountable to God, not to one another, for their work is assigned and empowered by God.   Cf. Roetzel (1972: 168).

βουλὰς τῶν καρδιῶν, 4.5).[160] This will ensure that Paul's chief ambition is faithful compliance with the commission entrusted to him (4.2), that is, to proclaim and in no way impede the message of the cross.[161] And only after being acquitted will Paul then receive his grand reception of praise (ἔπαινος; cf. Luke 16.8; Xenophon, *Oec.* 13.9, 12), not from an earthly audience, but from God.[162]

Summary

In this chapter we addressed a number of socio-rhetorical, exegetical, and theological issues pertinent to the interpretation of 1 Corinthians 1–4. It was initially argued that despite the resistance of many recent interpreters, Paul's rhetoric in the first four chapters of the letter betray various features of apologetic. Utilising basic mirror-reading principles, the case was made that Paul at least perceived his apostolic authority to be the subject of criticism in the Corinthian church. Furthermore, we showed that 1 Cor 4.1–5 is an integral unit to the rhetorical strategy of the early part of Paul's letter. In this brief passage, Paul aims to eliminate several ecclesial and ethical shortcomings plaguing the Corinthians. As Jouette Bassler astutely observes, 'Paul thus had two serious problems to address – a general *over*valuation of human leadership in the community and a criticism or *under*valuation (by some) of his own ministry and gospel. Furthermore, he had to address these problems in such a way that his solution to one did not exacerbate the other.'[163] It has been our contention here that Paul sought to resolve this dilemma by portraying himself and other apostles as God's *oikonomoi*, thereby attributing to them certain social and structural characteristics that enabled him to negotiate the risky terrain of simultaneously diminishing *and* defending his apostleship. By casting apostles as enslaved, status-depleted subordinates, as well as divinely authorised, critically immune administrators, Paul sought to censure the Corinthians for their inappropriate, power-implicit evaluations – and thus to reaffirm his own apostolic ethos – without also

---

[160] Léon-Dufour (1980: 144): 'Le verset 5 radicalise et justifie le devoir de ne pas juger.'

[161] Konradt (2003: 286): 'Die geforderte "Treue" impliziert also, die Botschaft nicht durch eine ihr nicht angemessene Präsentation zu entstellen (und so zu "entleeren" [1,17]), um beim "Publikum" besser anzukommen (vgl. Gal 1,10; 1 Thess 2,4).' For Paul's doctrine of judgment according to deeds, see Yinger (1999).

[162] Kuck (1992: 208) correctly argues that ἔπαινος 'is parallel to μισθός (3:8 and 14) in that it expresses the thought of individually appropriate rewards, not just corporate salvation'.

[163] Bassler (1990: 180, emphasis added).

providing them with additional grounds for adulating their leaders. Moreover, the metaphor's ability to construct Paul's authority is coupled here with the apostle's assertion of his right as God's administrator to avoid human evaluations. For Paul, then, the apostle as *oikonomos* is a rhetorically ingenious, yet culturally subversive image, having both the contextual relevance to resonate with the community and the connotative diversity to serve its multi-purpose deployment.

7

INTERPRETING PAUL'S METAPHOR IN 1 CORINTHIANS 9.16–23

> If I preach the gospel, it is not a boast for me, for compulsion is laid upon me... For if I do this willingly, I have a wage; but if unwillingly, I have been entrusted with an administration.
>
> 1 Cor 9.16–17

As we saw in Chapter 6, Paul utilised the image of a private slave administrator (*oikonomos*) in 1 Cor 4.1–5 to illuminate various misunderstood characteristics of his apostleship. Among those characteristics were Paul's location in the ecclesiastical hierarchy, his responsibility to preach the unadorned gospel, his indifference to popular opinion, and his hope to be found faithful and praiseworthy before Christ at his coming. What was striking about the metaphor was its ability to portray Paul as a person of authority while also portraying him as a person of relative insignificance in comparison to God/Christ. In 1 Corinthians 9 Paul offers a similar portrayal of his apostolic role, but this time for a different purpose. The need has arisen again to clarify certain misunderstood aspects of his apostleship, not least his apostolic authority,[1] but in this instance he does so in order to explain how it is that he has the right to receive financial support from the Corinthian church while simultaneously being compelled to minister as an apostle. The metaphor of administration is cast once more, but the characteristics of apostleship that the image conveys are more veiled this time around.

In this chapter we shall therefore apply what we know about first-century private commercial administration to Paul's discourse in 1 Corinthians 9 in order (i) to elucidate the apostle's logic and argumentation, as well as (ii) to further our understanding of Pauline apostleship. But before we do so, we shall briefly examine the socio-rhetorical context of 1 Cor 8.1–11.1 in order to situate 9.1–27 appropriately. Next, the

---

[1] Dunn (1998: 577) considers 1 Corinthians 9 to be 'Paul's most sustained exposition of how he conceived of his authority *(exousia)*'.

text will be analysed, certain exegetical difficulties treated, and a general profile of Paul's apostleship constructed.

Socio-rhetorical context

The rhetorical function of 1 Corinthians 9 has long been a matter of scholarly debate. Many have argued that the chapter is a digression through which Paul defends his apostolic right to receive and refuse material support from churches that benefit from his preaching in order to ward off criticisms directed toward him for having plied a trade.[2] According to advocates of this position, not every person in the church was critical of Paul's apostolic lifestyle, as there remained some in the community who were 'of Paul' (1.12; 3.4, 22). Nevertheless, certain believers who preferred to support Paul financially – as they did Apollos and other itinerant teachers – were accusing Paul of lacking what they considered to be an appropriate apostolic ethos, and his apostolic authority was in jeopardy as a result. In his response to the Corinthians, Paul therefore offered a defence of his apostleship (9.3), his rights as an apostle (9.6–8), and his decision to lay those rights aside for the benefit of certain persons in the community (9.12, 15, 19).

This approach to Paul's rhetorical strategy is to be commended for its ability to explain the use of such explicit forensic language as ἀπολογία and ἀνακρίνω (9.3). Moreover, this view adequately handles the vigour of the rhetoric in verses 1–14 as well as the sheer length of the interruption, which points to the existence of real tension between the apostle and the church.[3] Furthermore, the reappearance of certain themes reminiscent of 1 Corinthians 1–4 – which was argued earlier to have a defensive posture – suggests that in chapter 9 Paul re-enlists the apologetic strategy introduced earlier in the letter. On the other hand, this position fails to explain adequately the chapter's relationship with those which frame it, making for a harsh transition and an out-of-place digression in the middle of a rather confrontational discourse. Additionally, if 8.1–11.1 forms a unified section, as most scholars

---

[2] Supporters of this position often recognise a secondary deliberative function of this passage, but prioritise Paul's apologetic intention. See, e.g., Barrett (1968: 200); Conzelmann (1975: 151–3); Fee (1987: 393); Horsley (1998a: 124); Winter (2002: 166); Fitzmyer (2008: 353). Some advocates of this position have argued that all or part of the apologetic interruption is actually an interpolation; cf. J. Weiss (1910: 231–4); Héring (1962: 75); Schmithals (1971: 92–3). Wuellner (1987) and Robbins (1996: 88–9) regard the passage as featuring a mixture of forensic and epideictic rhetoric.

[3] Barrett (1968: 200): 'Paul would hardly have spent so long on the question of apostolic rights if his own apostolic status had not been questioned in Corinth.'

recognise, and Paul's concluding admonition instructs the church to imitate him as he imitates Christ (11.1), then Paul's appeal for imitation must refer to 9.1–27, since this is the most significant personal example Paul presents in chapters 8–10.[4] Finally, the themes in chapter 9 which correspond to those found in chapters 8 and 10 suggest that chapter 9 has a more organic relationship with its neighbours than this position would otherwise permit.[5]

Due to the shortcomings of the strictly apologetic interpretation of 1 Corinthians 9, a number of exegetes contend that Paul situated chapter 9 between chapters 8 and 10 for the sole, or primary, purpose of offering an *exemplum* of self-sacrifice.[6] From this perspective, Paul's hypothetical refusal to eat meat in 8.13 functions to transition the discourse to 9.1, where he authors a fictitious defence of his rights as an apostle in order to demonstrate how he has given them up for the benefit of the church and the progress of the gospel. The example is especially directed toward those 'strong' Corinthians whose theological astuteness enabled them to justify their participation in certain pagan meals.[7] But those practices, while theologically defensible, proved to be morally destructive, as certain 'weak' believers had emulated the behaviour of the strong by also participating in pagan meals, which consequently wounded their consciences.[8] In chapter 8, then, Paul exhorts the strong in the church to

---

[4] Paul's call to imitation may have in view his renunciation of eating meat in 8.13, although it cannot refer to this alone since it is hypothetical. It may refer to 10.33, although this is largely a recapitulation of 9.1–27 (esp. vv. 19–23). More probably, Paul's call to imitation refers to all of these personal examples; cf. Ellington (2011).

[5] It is noteworthy how in both sections Paul addresses rights, obstacles to salvation, and a group of individuals considered 'weak'.

[6] See, e.g., A. Robertson and Plummer (1911: 176, 179); Jeremias (1958: 156); Willis (1985a); M. M. Mitchell (1991: 246); Witherington (1995: 203); Smit (1997: 478); Thiselton (2000: 666–7); Garland (2003: 404–6); Galloway (2004: 152); Delgado (2010: 110–15).

[7] Despite the many scholarly theories that exist concerning the cause of the conflicts addressed in 8.1–11.1, Paul provides the non-Corinthian reader with too little information to be sure about what specific socio-religious occasion or influence gave rise to the quarrel. In fact, it seems reasonably clear that Paul was addressing an ethical dilemma which was expected to surface regularly. According to Paul, the Corinthians encountered food offered to idols in venues that were specifically pagan (ἐν εἰδωλείῳ, 8.10; τραπέζης δαιμονίων, 10.21), commercial (ἐν μακέλλῳ, 10.25), and domestic (εἴ τις καλεῖ ὑμᾶς τῶν ἀπίστων, 10.27). It is therefore unnecessary to isolate a single occasion that gave rise to these particular conflicts, since Paul may have been addressing a rather ubiquitous problem about which there are simply too many unknown factors. For a review of scholarly research on the socio-religious context of 8.1–11.1, see Fotopoulos (2003: 1–48). Cf. Willis (1985b); Newton (1998); Cheung (1999); Phua (2005: 29–125).

[8] According to Paul, when peer pressure causes an individual to transgress one's conscience, he or she becomes ruined (ἀπόλλυμι, 8.11). Such provocation is a sin against the weaker believer and against Christ (8.12). Due to the consequences of such actions, Paul

forgo their right to eat idol meat, and in chapter 9 provides a personal example of self-sacrifice which the strong should imitate.

This position gives appropriate attention to the thematic parallels shared by chapter 9 and chapters 8 and 10. It fails, however, to take seriously the defensive posture apparent both in earlier parts of the letter and in chapter 9. While it is plausible that most of Paul's original readers were in full agreement with the case he constructs in 9.1–14, it is also true that Paul's refusal of rights could, and probably did, elicit objections from those who disapproved of him plying a trade. Many supporters of this position deny that 1 Corinthians betrays any indication that disputes had already risen about Paul's authority or that objections had been made about his refusal of financial support when Paul wrote the letter.[9] However, the fact that the important topics in 1 Corinthians 9 were already a matter of heated polemic in 4.10–13 and eventually became a matter of even greater dispute in 2 Corinthians 10–13 suggests that at least some Corinthian believers had challenged Paul's policy at this early period in his relationship with the church.

Given the strengths of both positions, then, it seems most likely that 1 Corinthians 9 serves not one, but two equally important rhetorical purposes: in chapter 9 the apostle seeks to demonstrate through personal example how believers should love and edify one another at each person's own expense, and also to defend Paul's refusal of a wage by explaining, albeit quite inexplicitly, his policy of material support.[10]

Literary context

After declaring that he would never eat meat again if it offended another believer (8.13), Paul begins his discourse in 9.1–27 by affirming his apostolic rights. The affirmation comes in the form of no fewer than seventeen rhetorical questions spanning verses 1–13.[11] The opening question is perhaps the most perplexing. Paul asks simply, 'Am I not free?' (v. 1a). The kind of freedom Paul has in view remains disputed, since in his letters the apostle describes freedom in different ways.[12] Based, however, on the

---

declares that he would go so far as to abstain from eating meat altogether if by eating he might cause another believer to stumble (8.13).

[9] M. M. Mitchell (1991: 246).

[10] Grosheide (1953: 202); Dungan (1971: 5–6); Schmithals (1971: 92); Orr and Walther (1976: 240); Hock (1980: 60–1); Marshall (1987: 283–4); D. B. Martin (1990: 83); Gardner (1994: 67–8); Horrell (1996: 205); Hays (1997: 146); Lehmeier (2006: 241); Butarbutar (2007: 109).

[11] Fitzmyer (2008: 355).

[12] See, e.g., Hock (1980: 60); Galloway (2004: 155–80). Cf. Betz (1994); Coppins (2009).

series of questions presented in verses 4–13, together with the way Paul contrasts freedom and slavery in verses 16–17 and 19, he probably has in view the freedom simply to exercise certain rights as an apostle. Through his next question Paul therefore seeks to affirm his apostolic legitimacy: 'Am I not an apostle?' (v. 1b). Paul then grounds his apostleship on two propositions: he has seen the risen Christ (v. 1c), and he is responsible for the conversion of the Corinthian believers (vv. 1d–2).

Having established the legitimacy of his apostleship in verses 1–2, in verse 3 Paul enters into a lengthy defence of the apostolic rights he implicitly affirmed in verse 1a. Each question in verses 4–13 seeks to expose the claim to material privileges which accompanied various kinds of labour, and collectively they demonstrate that apostles too have the right, or authority (ἐξουσία), to be supported financially for their preaching.[13] For just as a soldier does not serve without being provided with his meals (v. 7a), or a vineyard worker labour without eating his own fruit (v. 7b), or a shepherd tend without access to the flock's milk (v. 7c), or an ox thresh without eating grain (vv. 9–10), or a priest minister without sharing in temple sacrifices (v. 13), so neither should an apostle preach the gospel without the opportunity to receive material support from his beneficiaries (vv. 11–12a).[14] In fact, the Lord commanded apostles to live off the gospel (v. 14).[15] But after making an extensive case for his possession of the right to be paid for preaching, Paul twice insists that he has no interest in exercising that right (vv. 12a, 15a).

In his first refusal, Paul explains that he has not made use of his right to receive material support (οὐκ ἐχρησάμεθα τῇ ἐξουσίᾳ ταύτῃ), because he would rather endure all things (πάντα στέγομεν) than in any way place an obstacle (ἐγκοπή) in the way of the gospel of Christ (v. 12b). Paul employs the verb χράομαι here, as he does elsewhere, to denote exploitation for personal advantage (cf. 1 Cor 7.21; 2 Cor 13.10). The refusal to exercise his right to material support, however, results not in personal gain, but in loss, for as a result of his refusal he must endure the physical hardships and meagrely wages of manual labour (cf. 1 Cor 4.11–12).

---

[13] The apostle's right to eat and drink (v. 4) is the logical precursor to his right to material support, while his right to take along a believing wife (v. 5) assumes that she too has the right to be supported by those who support the apostle; cf. Garland (2003: 406).

[14] For closer treatments of Paul's analogies, see, e.g., Caragounis (1974: 51–2); Instone-Brewer (1992); Richardson (1994).

[15] Paul may have been referring to the teachings recorded in Matt 10.10 or Luke 10.7. Dungan (1971: 79–80) and D. B. Martin (1990: 69) suggest the former. Horrell (1997b: 595), on the other hand, says, 'It is just as likely that Paul is alluding to (some form of) this whole block of instruction as that the proverb "the worker is worthy of his wage" alone is in view.'

Paul's refusal to accept support is ultimately for the purpose of ensuring that the gospel remains unobstructed. But how would accepting support in any way impede the gospel?

We can assume that some similarities existed between the example he offers in chapter 9 and the conflict he sought to extinguish in chapter 8. In the earlier scenario, certain believers with weak consciences were avoiding food offered to idols (8.7). Paul therefore exhorted those with strong consciences – those who did not avoid idol food – to forgo their right (ἐξουσία) to eat idol food so that their right would not become a hindrance (πρόσκομμα) for weaker believers (οἱ ἀσθενεῖς, 8.9). Assuming that the presentation of Paul's *exemplum* in chapter 9 was modelled after the conflict between the Corinthians themselves in chapter 8, it can be deduced that 'the more/many' (τοὺς πλείονας, v. 19) for whom Paul sought to eliminate an obstacle through his refusal of material support were those he similarly labelled 'the weak' (οἱ ἀσθενεῖς, 9.22). This conclusion is supported further by the fact that, although Paul used the comparative particle ὡς when referring to his accommodation to Jews, those under the law, and those outside the law, he conspicuously omits ὡς in his admission to having become weak in order to win the weak. The weak believers therefore were those to whom Paul wished to accommodate by refusing material support.

Many theories have been proposed concerning the identity of the weak in 9.22 and how the obstacle placed before them could hinder the gospel.[16] Views range from classifying the weak as those who were suspicious of greed,[17] to those belonging to a low socio-economic stratum,[18] to those who closely associated the acceptance of tuition fees with sophistry,[19] to those for whom the gospel would have been inaccessible should Paul have become the exclusive client teacher of wealthy patrons.[20] These positions are not mutually exclusive, and most interpreters adopt some combination of them in their historical reconstructions. But there remains the possibility that Paul labelled this group 'weak' (ἀσθενής) not with the

---

[16] Not everyone identifies the weak (v. 22) with those for whom Paul sought not to obstruct the gospel (v. 12), but the following arguments are in no way affected by assuming their identification here.

[17] J. Weiss (1910: 262); Hurd (1965: 204–5); Barrett (1968: 207); Dahl (1977a: 34).

[18] J. Weiss (1910: 238); Dungan (1971: 30–1); Theissen (1982: 124–40); Hafemann (1990: 133). This meaning of ἀσθενής is supported in 1.26–7 where Paul contrasts the haves with the have-nots. In 4.10 Paul even identifies himself with 'the weak', where he associates weakness with social, economic, physical, and occupational disrepute, mentioning his artisanship as contributing to his weakness. For criticisms of this view, see Meggitt (1998: 107–8).

[19] Winter (2002: 164–9).   [20] Walton (2011: 223–4).

intention of describing their social or theological condition, but simply to draw a terminological link between chapters 8 and 9. If this is so, then ἀσθενής refers to an actual group, but in no way provides a window into their particular social circumstances.

But while it is perhaps too unclear to identify precisely who the weak in verse 22 are, Paul elsewhere provides several clues that may suggest how the acceptance of material support could function as an obstacle in certain circumstances. First, Paul was clearly under the impression that the acceptance of material support could strain some of his churches (2 Cor 11.9; 12.13–16; 1 Thess 2.9). Although he occasionally received funds from some communities to aid in meeting his material needs while serving in distant regions (2 Cor 11.8–9; Phil 4.15–16), Paul for the most part was self-sufficient (αὐτάρκης, Phil 4.11).[21] In fact, he considered his refusal of aid to be a gesture of his love for and exaltation of the Corinthians (2 Cor 11.7–8, 11). Secondly, Paul apparently considered it detrimental to the success of his ministry for him to be confused with certain teachers who boasted of their ability to charge students exorbitant fees.[22] Paul therefore desired to distinguish himself from those teachers so that comparisons could not be made between him and them (2 Cor 11.12). Thirdly, Paul may have believed that by not conforming to the contexts of the very people he aimed to save, he would not have been able to apply the gospel to their particular social and theological situations. Several times in 1 Cor 9.19–22 Paul reiterates his desire to conform to his target audiences, summarising his unique ministry approach by stating, 'I have become all things to all people, so that by all means I might save some' (9.22). Given that objective, the meaning of the statement 'we endure all things rather than put an obstacle in the way of the gospel of Christ' (9.12) might indicate that Paul was willing to overcome the hardships of working with his hands in order to associate with the working class.[23] Finally, Paul may have thought that receiving financial aid from converts who, despite their generosity, did not intend to participate in the apostle's sufferings could prevent the church from growing in maturity (Phil 1.7; 4.14). He may have therefore desired that the Corinthians envisage their gifts as symbols of partnership in Christ and the gospel before he accepted their support.[24]

---

[21] Pratscher (1979); Walton (2011: 221–5).

[22] Winter (2002: 166–9).

[23] Hafemann (1990: 133); Horrell (1996: 215).

[24] Savage (1996: 98–9). The possibility of this as a factor at work in the Corinthian church is questionable in light of the fact that Paul promises never to accept pay from them (2 Cor 11.9, 11).

The difficulty with unravelling Paul's monetary policy, as well as with identifying the weak and how they would have been obstructed from the gospel should Paul have accepted support, remains a matter for further investigation in Pauline scholarship.[25] Whatever the reason(s), Paul's refusal was on account of these disadvantaged believers, whose accessibility to the gospel was as a result unimpeded. Paul's financial policy was therefore a matter of utmost importance in his ministry to the Corinthians, as the second grounds for his refusal indicates.

Paul's second declaration of refusal is similar to the first.[26] Initially, Paul simply reaffirms that he has not used any of his rights (ἐγὼ δὲ οὐ κέχρημαι οὐδενὶ τούτων, v. 15a).[27] But this time he goes well beyond declaring his preference for experiencing hardships to obstructing the gospel when he states that he would in fact rather die than have anyone nullify his boast (καλὸν γάρ μοι μᾶλλον ἀποθανεῖν ἤ- τὸ καύχημά μου οὐδεὶς κενώσει, v. 15b).[28] In verse 15, Paul does not explicitly state the object of his boast. Nevertheless, since Paul considers preaching the gospel to be an activity about which he cannot boast (οὐκ ἔστιν μοι καύχημα, v. 16) as a *compulsory* task under the terms of his commission (v. 17), it is clear that the object of Paul's boast consists of a *voluntary* act, namely, his refusal of support (cf. 2 Cor 11.10). Paul can boast in his refusal because, as he will explain later, through such disciplined self-sacrifice and suffering for the sake of the gospel he proves his qualifications for his eternal reward (1 Cor 9.24–7; cf. 3.8, 14; 4.5).[29]

---

[25] Cf. Briones (2011).

[26] In both constructions Paul (i) announces his refusal (ἀλλ' οὐκ ἐχρησάμεθα τῇ ἐξουσίᾳ ταύτῃ, v. 12b; ἐγὼ δὲ οὐ κέχρημαι οὐδενὶ τούτων, v. 15a), (ii) asserts his acceptance of or preference for a course of action leading to personal affliction (ἀλλὰ πάντα στέγομεν, v. 12c; καλὸν γάρ μοι μᾶλλον ἀποθανεῖν, v. 15c), and (iii) reveals the negative ministerial consequences he avoids by virtue of that course (ἵνα μή τινα ἐγκοπὴν δῶμεν τῷ εὐαγγελίῳ τοῦ Χριστοῦ, v. 12d; ἤ- τὸ καύχημά μου οὐδεὶς κενώσει, v. 15d).

[27] The use of the plural τούτων (v. 15a) surely parallels τῇ ἐξουσίᾳ ταύτῃ (v. 12b). Even if Paul in verse 15a has multiple rights in view (cf. vv. 4–6), the right to material aid is the central concern here; cf. Fee (1987: 416 n. 12). The ταῦτα in verse 15b, however, refers to the arguments Paul presented (ἔγραψα) in support of his rights (cf. vv. 1–14). Furthermore, the use of the first person pronoun ἐγώ in verse 15 suggests, as Thiselton (2000: 693) explains, a sense of 'individuality and emphasis', by which Paul sets himself apart from those who made no such refusal.

[28] Hafemann (1990: 139): 'The reason for the almost inconceivable weight which Paul thus attaches to his practice of self-support lies in his understanding of this practice as his "boast," which would be "nullified" or "invalidated" should someone pay him for his ministry.'

[29] Praising oneself (i.e. boasting) was typically regarded as repugnant, since it was tied up with advancing one's own social status. But, according to Plutarch, there were occasions when an orator might justifiably affirm himself without being distasteful (*Mor.* 539E). Self-praise was permissible in order to instil confidence and good repute in one's audience

In summary, Paul boasts of the fact that he goes above and beyond his apostolic mandate in order that the gospel might reach its intended end. For by refusing material support, Paul has voluntarily done everything within his power to save unbelievers, and at great personal cost to himself. Paul's refusal, then, is closely tied up with his ministry strategy and his entire apostolic self-understanding. But in order to stress this point further in verses 19–23, Paul must first embark on a brief digression where he explains why preaching on its own is insufficient for him to merit a boast.

Paul as entrusted with an administration

Explaining the relationship between verses 16–18 and the sections which frame them has proved difficult for many interpreters.[30] Ernst Käsemann even suggested that verses 16–18 introduce a complete change of topic, so that the entire section is superfluous ('überflüssig').[31] But upon closer examination, it is apparent that the digression plays an important supportive function in the larger rhetorical strategy of 1 Corinthians 9. Paul's argument – without necessarily exhibiting syllogistic logic – is a rebuttal to the anticipated criticisms of certain philosophically astute Corinthians.[32] The passage's explanatory nature is apparent in Paul's repeated use of γάρ, which surfaces a surprising four times in verses 16–17. Through the use of the conjunction, the argument escalates from one clarifying note to another until Paul eventually ends the digression with the paradoxical assertion that his apostolic wage (μισθός) is in fact his very refusal of the right to be paid. Verses 16–18 therefore provide a unique glimpse into Paul's apostolic profile, albeit in the form of a seemingly detached excursus. As Gordon Fee explains, 'Although one has the feeling that the argument got away from him a bit, nonetheless the

---

(539F), to discredit harmful people (544F), and to counter and refute their self-praise (545E–F). Although Paul repudiated boasting earlier in the letter, his practice of it here is justified, because he does so with the intent to defend himself. For boasting in the Graeco-Roman world and Paul's letters, see Judge (1968); C. Forbes (1986); D. F. Watson (2003); Glancy (2004); Wojciechowski (2006); Donahoe (2008).

[30] Harnisch (2007: 38) states that verses 15–18 contain 'almost insoluble problems' ('kaum lösbare Probleme').

[31] Käsemann (1969: 218). For the original essay in German, see Käsemann (1959).

[32] Käsemann (1969: 218) refers to the passage as 'passionate' ('leidenschaftliche'), but 'quite illogical' ('völlig unlogischen'). Although the logic is difficult to follow, Sibinga (1998: 162) has shown through detailed statistical analysis of the ratio of syllables and verbal forms in 1 Corinthians 9 – especially in verses 16 and 17 – that this chapter was 'the careful and patient work of a highly trained literary craftsman, who gave full attention to the final shape of the whole composition as well as to the perfect form of innumerable details'.

explanations of vv. 16–17 probably help us as much as anything in his let-ters to understand what made Paul tick.'[33] It is this transparency together with the fact that Paul here refers to his commission as an administration which makes the passage so important for our study. In what follows, then, we shall examine Paul's digression in order to discover how he used the *oikonomos* (*oikonomia*) metaphor to clarify for the Corinthians certain significant aspects of his apostleship.

The digression begins in verse 16 with Paul's admission to compulsory preaching, which he concedes in order to explain why he must refuse sup-port to maintain his boast (v. 16a). Compulsion, Paul states, has been laid upon him through his commission (v. 16b), so that judgment awaits him if he does not preach the gospel (v. 16c). But Paul immediately anticipates an objection to this concession: if he is under compulsion to preach, then according to moral philosophy he is a slave of God; and if he is a slave of God, then how can Paul be entitled to a wage? Recognising his vulnerabil-ity to this protest, Paul pre-emptively clarifies his particular status as God's slave by indicating the precise position he holds in God's household: he is God's slave administrator (οἰκονομίαν πεπίστευμαι, v. 17). But what Paul's argument demonstrates about his entitlement to a wage is not immediately clear to the modern reader. In order to make the point, he presents what are usually regarded as two contrasting conditional sentences addressing the voluntary nature of his preaching: 'For if I do this willingly, I have a wage; but if unwillingly, I have been entrusted with an administration [εἰ γὰρ ἑκὼν τοῦτο πράσσω, μισθὸν ἔχω· εἰ δὲ ἄκων, οἰκονομίαν πεπίστευμαι]' (v. 17).[34] But did Paul preach the gospel willingly or unwillingly, and how does his volition affect his right to be paid? Although this is the very mat-ter which Paul seeks to illuminate in verses 16–18, interpreters remain divided over Paul's actual condition. We shall therefore need to analyse Paul's argument closely, carefully scrutinising the main existing views, in order to elucidate Paul's approach to his preaching.

Paul's preaching as unpaid and involuntary

In verse 17 Paul presents two conditional sentences involving the vol-itional nature of his preaching: either he preaches voluntarily as a wage labourer, or involuntarily as a slave administrator – an *oikonomos*. (See the table below.)

---

[33] Fee (1987: 415).

[34] Reumann (1967: 158) and Winger (1997: 225) suggest that the second conditional sentence ends as a question in verse 18a: 'But if I am unwillingly entrusted with a commis-sion, then what is my reward?' However, the Pauline parallels discussed below show that the symmetry of the two conditional sentences in verse 17 should be maintained.

The Clausal Structure of 1 Cor 9.17

Protasis 1	εἰ γὰρ ἑκὼν τοῦτο πράσσω,	v. 17a
Apodosis 1	μισθὸν ἔχω·	v. 17b
Protasis 2	εἰ δὲ ἄκων,	v. 17c
Apodosis 2	οἰκονομίαν πεπίστευμαι·	v. 17d

Most scholars interpret the former sentence as hypothetical and the latter as Paul's actual condition, so that verses 16–18 indicate that Paul preached the gospel involuntarily.[35] Proponents normally reach this position in part because they regard Paul's admission to having had compulsion (ἀνάγκη, v. 16) laid upon him as equivalent to preaching involuntarily (ἄκων, v. 17c) as God's slave.[36] After all, it was by the will of God (διὰ θελήματος θεοῦ) – not by Paul's own willpower – that he was called to be an apostle (1.1; cf. 15.10). Moreover, because preaching voluntarily is coupled with having a wage in verse 17a–b, it is normally concluded that Paul's admission to preaching involuntarily in verse 17c indicates that he was not entitled to receive pay. This is also due to the assumption that verse 17a–b contrasts entirely with 17c–d: if verse 17a contrasts with 17c, it is normally presumed that verse 17b contrasts with 17d. After all, one expects the antithesis of voluntarily preaching for a wage to be involuntarily preaching free of charge.[37]

This interpretation also owes much to the supposition that all forms of slavery – managerial slavery (οἰκονομία) included – connote unpaid labour. This assumption surfaces, for instance, in an important essay by Käsemann, who remarks, '[W]hen Paul describes his preaching as

---

[35] See, esp., Käsemann (1969: 229–30); D. B. Martin (1990: 71–85). Cf. Hodge (1862: 162); Edwards (1885: 235); Ellicott (1887: 164); Moffatt (1938: 120–1); Thrall (1965: 69–70); Barrett (1968: 209–10); Dautzenberg (1969: 227); Lietzmann and Kümmel (1969: 43); Conzelmann (1975: 158); Morris (1985: 135); Hafemann (1990: 141–4); Schrage (1995: 324–6); Horrell (1996: 207); Hays (1997: 152–3); Horsley (1998a: 129–30); M. J. Harris (1999: 130); Thiselton (2000: 696); Garland (2003: 425); Phua (2005: 191–2); Richter (2005: 45); Lehmeier (2006: 230–1); R. H. Williams (2006: 81); Butarbutar (2007: 161); Ciampa and Rosner (2010: 418); Delgado (2010: 198); Zeller (2010: 310).

[36] Käsemann (1969: 230): '*Ananke* describes here the power of the divine will which radically and successfully challenges man and makes its servant its instrument.'

[37] Cf. Käsemann (1969: 231): '[I]n the text we have today protasis and apodosis taken together produce a tautology. The rationale of such a construction can only be to exclude the reward motif altogether and thus, as in the preceding sentence, to bring out the will of the Gospel as the sole motivation in the apostle's work.' Fee (1987: 420): '[T]his first sentence [v. 17a–b] is intended merely to set up the opposite alternative, which rules out any possibility of "reward" or "pay" in his case.' Ciampa and Rosner (2010: 418): 'The former [ἑκών] is entitled to a reward for what he does, while the latter [ἄκων] is not.'

something that is laid upon him and thus not to be looked upon as a service which brings with it a reward, he is, in his own way, picking up the saying of Jesus in Luke 17.10: "We are unworthy servants; we have only done what was our duty".'[38] Dale Martin similarly concludes,

> By stating that he is compelled to preach and that he therefore does not do it willingly, Paul explains why he does not receive a wage from the Corinthians. When Paul asks, in verse 18, 'What then is my pay?' he does so having already rejected the possibility that he is entitled (that is, as Christ's slave agent) to receive pay in the normal sense, thus opening up the possibility that he may receive pay in an abnormal sense... Paul here says he is not able to accept pay because he is Christ's slave agent.[39]

The interpretation of verse 17 presented by Käsemann and Martin is representative of most scholars who interpret Paul's preaching as involuntary and therefore without pay.[40] But aside from the fact that this interpretation rests on certain misguided assumptions about slave privileges (as will be discussed further below), it struggles to make Paul's argument coherent. If Paul wished to communicate that he should not receive pay, then why did he not simply say so, perhaps stating εἰ δὲ ἄκων, οὐ μισθὸν ἔχω? Or, why did he not portray himself as a menial slave (δοῦλος), rather than a privileged commercial agent (οἰκονόμος)? Moreover, this reading must ignore Paul's larger objective in the discourse – the demonstration of the refusal of his right to receive material support. As observed above, in verses 4–14 Paul repeatedly insists that he has the right to receive pay from the Corinthians.[41] Käsemann and Martin, however, conclude that in verses 16–17 Paul contradicts what he so adamantly maintained for the entire first half of the chapter.[42] This reading absolutely strips Paul

---

[38] Käsemann (1969: 220). Kreuzer (1985), Marshall (1987: 303), and Fitzmyer (2008: 368) also identify resonances between verses 16–17 and Lucan sayings of Jesus.

[39] D. B. Martin (1990: 71). In order to make verses 17 and 18 cohere, Martin must interpret Paul's μισθός in verse 18 in an 'abnormal sense'. He rightly explains that 'the reward Paul receives for preaching as a slave of Christ is the opportunity to give up his authority, his power' (85). Cf. Fitzmyer (2008: 368). In so doing, Martin, with most interpreters, recognises the paradoxical nature of verse 18. But the fact that he must consider Paul's wage to be 'abnormal' (i.e. distinct from the μισθός defended in vv. 4–17) exposes the strain Martin's interpretation places on Paul's argument.

[40] Cf. Conzelmann (1975: 158): '[O]nly voluntary labor deserves and gains a reward'; Thiselton (2000: 696): 'Paul makes a *logical* point that only acts carried out from self-motivation or self-initiative belong to the logical order of "reward".'

[41] Malherbe (1994: 249 n. 35).

[42] Although Horsley (1978: 588) seeks to demonstrate that 'Paul surely knows what he is doing' in the juxtaposition of slavery and freedom throughout verses 16–19, he must

of his ἐξουσία, so that he has neither the right to *use* nor the right to *refuse* a wage for his preaching. Beyond that, the ensuing question, 'What therefore is my wage?' (v. 18a), suggests that Paul actually believed he was entitled to a μισθός. If Paul, after conceding in verse 17 that he is not entitled to a wage, reverses his position again and suggests that he is entitled to pay after all, then one must conclude that Paul's discourse is completely incoherent.

This interpretation, then, has the advantage of interpreting ἄκων in verse 17 as echoing ἀνάγκη in verse 16, and thus correctly regards verse 17c–d as Paul's real situation. But by understanding verse 17d as contrasting with 17b, Käsemann, Martin, and many others leave Paul without any entitlement to pay, which undercuts the apostle's entire argument in verses 4–14 and makes his claim to having a μισθός in verse 18 appear out of nowhere, a leap in logic that even an 'abnormal' reading like Martin's is unable to satisfy.

Paul's preaching as paid and voluntary

Due to the weaknesses of the conventional reading, Abraham Malherbe has defended an alternative position which places Paul's discourse in the context of Cynic-Stoic debates on predestination.[43] By reading Paul's application of the terms ἐλεύθερος, δουλόω, ἐξουσία, ἀνάγκη, ἑκών, and ἄκων in the light of their moral-philosophical significance, Malherbe seeks to make the apostle's volition compatible with divine necessity.[44] Malherbe argues that Paul's preaching, while on the one hand a compulsion (ἀνάγκη), was nevertheless conducted willingly (ἑκών), rather than unwillingly (ἄκων) as Käsemann and Martin understand him.[45]

According to Stoicism, the wise person alone can be free, but only by ridding oneself of all passions and desires which conflict with the predetermination of Fate.[46] As Seneca states, 'I have set freedom before my

admit that Paul's approach is 'seemingly contradictory'. See also Donahoe (2008: 194–5), whose conclusion that 'Paul avoids abusing his authority by making full use of his right' contradicts her earlier assertion that Paul 'is not entitled to material compensation', 'since he does not preach out of his own volition'.

[43] Malherbe (1994: 231–41).

[44] For Paul's freedom as financial independence from the Corinthians, see Hock (1980: 61). But the philosophical rather than socio-economic sense of freedom is to be preferred, since Paul speaks of being free interchangeably with possessing apostolic rights; cf. R. F. Collins (1999: 329); Galloway (2004: 164).

[45] Malherbe (1994: 249–50). Cf. Reumann (1967: 159); Bruce (1980: 85–6); Hock (1980: 100 n. 113); Robbins (1996: 85); Winger (1997: 226); R. F. Collins (1999: 348); Byron (2003: 249–53); Harnisch (2007: 41).

[46] For the influence of Stoicism on the Corinthian church, see Brookins (2011).

eyes; and I am striving for that reward. And what is freedom, you ask? It means not being a slave to any circumstance, to any constraint [*necessitati*], to any chance; it means compelling Fortune to enter the lists on equal terms' (*Ep.* 51.9). Epictetus agrees with Seneca's Stoic conception of freedom when he says, 'He is free who lives as he wills [ὡς βούλεται], who is subject neither to compulsion [ἀναγκάσαι], nor hindrance, nor force, whose choices are unhampered, whose desires attain their end, whose aversions do not fall into what they would avoid' (*Diatr.* 4.1.1; cf. 2.1.23).[47] But while compulsions impose themselves on all people, according to Stoicism they can be overcome through reason and philosophy by desiring those very things that are necessary. As Seneca insists, '[T]he wise man does nothing unwillingly [*invitus*]. He escapes necessity [*necessitatem*], because he wills to do [*vult*] what necessity is about to force upon him [*coactura*]' (*Ep.* 54.7; cf. 37.3); 'See to it that you never do anything unwillingly [*invitus*]. That which is bound to be a necessity if you rebel, is not a necessity if you desire it [*volenti necessitas non est*]. This is what I mean: he who takes his orders gladly, escapes the bitterest part of slavery, – doing what one does not want to do' (*Ep.* 61.3).[48] Epictetus also gives instructions about how to escape compulsions:

> Come, can anyone force [ἀναγκάσαι] you to choose something that you do not want? – He can; for when he threatens me with death or bonds, he compels [ἀναγκάζει] me to choose. – If, however, you despise death and bonds, do you pay any further heed to him? – No. – Is it, then, an act of your own to despise death, or is it not your own act? It is mine.
>
> (*Diatr.* 4.1.70–1; cf. 4.1.74)

Together, Seneca and Epictetus promoted philosophy as the great liberator of the soul, prescribing reason in the battle against the enslaving power of compulsions and those outward circumstances beyond one's control, for through reason the wise can redirect their desires toward that which is necessary. Apparently, even death, if one could resist fearing it, would cease serving as a person's master, since the one who went along with his or her outer compulsions became, as it were, inwardly free.

It is within this moral-philosophical context that Malherbe reads Paul's argument in 1 Cor 9.15–18. Malherbe initially acknowledges the dissimilarity between Paul and the Stoics (and the Cynics) since Paul, to the

---

[47] For Epictetus' concept of free will, see Bobzein (1998: 330–57); A. A. Long (2002: 221).
[48] The Vulgate at 1 Cor 9.16–17 translates ἀνάγκη as *necessitas*, ἑκών as *volens*, and ἄκων as *invitus*.

abhorrence of moral philosophy, grants that he has had compulsion laid upon him (v. 16).[49] But Malherbe proceeds to explain that Paul closes the gap between himself and the Stoics through his voluntary acceptance of divine necessity:

> As we have seen ... Stoics exercized [*sic*] their free will in the manner in which they conducted themselves within the providential scheme of things. So does Paul. He willingly does what necessity has laid upon him, thus exercizing [*sic*] his freedom, the topic that has engaged him throughout this long argument. That it is freedom of action that predominates in his thinking and not compulsion, is evident from vv. 18–19. There he provides the grounds for forgoing his exousia – his freedom did not compel him to insist on his exousia, but allowed him to forgo it.[50]

According to Malherbe, Paul conducts his preaching functionally as a Stoic: like the Stoics, Paul, though outwardly compelled, co-operates with divine necessity by inwardly desiring his apostolic mandate to preach the gospel. Malherbe concedes that Paul has been entrusted with an administration (notice the perfect tense of πιστεύω, v. 17d), which he possesses presumably by virtue of his compulsion, so that '[i]f Paul were to preach unwillingly (εἰ δὲ ἄκων is hypothetical)', he would have to preach anyway, for 'he nevertheless has been entrusted with an οἰκονομία'.[51] But even so, Paul's preaching is performed willingly, thus freely and deserving of pay.

In his examination, Malherbe insightfully applies to Paul's discourse the concepts of freedom and constraint found in the Stoics. Moreover, he carefully notices that in verses 18–19 Paul possesses the right and thus the freedom to receive and refuse material support. But Malherbe's contention for the actuality of verse 17a–b and the hypothetical nature of verse 17c fails to account for three exegetical details. First, from Malherbe's perspective, it remains unclear why Paul included verse 17c–d in the discourse at all. If verse 17a–b represents Paul's actual condition and becomes the topic of more focused discussion in verses 18–19, then Paul's inclusion of verse 17c–d – particularly the disclosure of his administration in verse 17d – merely reinforces the already revealed fact that Paul is externally compelled to preach (v. 16) and his underlying condition is

---

[49] Malherbe (1994: 249). D. B. Martin (1990: 76) regards Paul's admission to being compelled as a 'philosophical faux pas'.
[50] Malherbe (1994: 250).   [51] Malherbe (1994: 249; cf. 251).

that of a slave of God.[52] From Malherbe's perspective, then, verse 17c–d unnecessarily detracts from Paul's argument. Secondly, Malherbe fails to account for the ongoing presence of Paul's compulsion. In addition to the texts cited above, there are a number of passages from Paul's Stoic contemporaries which demonstrate that having any compulsion was equivalent to performing involuntary actions and being a slave (Philo, *Prob.*, 29–30, 59–61; Seneca, *Prov.* 5.6).[53] As Epictetus explains, 'The unhampered man, who finds things ready to hand as he wants them, is free. But the man who can be hampered, or subjected to compulsion [ἀναγκάσαι], or hindered, or thrown into something against his will [ἄκοντα], is a slave' (*Diatr.* 4.1.128; cf. 4.1.11; 4.1.56). Because moral philosophers consistently identify the person under compulsion with one who acts involuntarily, Paul's admission to having a compulsion laid upon him (notice the present tense of ἐπίκειμαι in v. 16) is equivalent to stating that his preaching is performed unwillingly.[54]

Furthermore, the perpetuation of Paul's constraint to preach the gospel is apparent from his fear of the consequences of not preaching: 'For woe is me if I do not preach the gospel [οὐαὶ γάρ μοί ἐστιν ἐὰν μὴ εὐαγγελίσωμαι]' (v. 16b). What would Paul have had to fear if indeed he wilfully preached? In Stoicism the very fear of pain and punishment was indicative of slavery, as Epictetus explained: '[A]nd if you hear him say, "Alas! What I must suffer [τάλας ἐγώ, οἷα πάσχω]!" call him a slave; and in short, if you see him wailing, complaining, in misery, call him a slave in a *toga praetexta*' (*Diatr.* 4.1.57).[55] Epictetus himself apparently overcame the fear of illness, torture, and death, and was therefore considered free, by desiring those very ends (4.1.89–90); as he says, quoting Diogenes, 'The one sure way to secure freedom is to die cheerfully' (4.1.30). In Paul's discourse, however, the apostle makes no such claims

---

[52] *Contra* Byron (2003: 243–53), who argues that Paul conceived of his administration as befitting free persons. For the use of οἰκονομία and πιστεύω as denoting a slave οἰκονόμος, see Luke 16.2–3, 11; Artemidorus, *Onir.* 1.35; 2.30; cf. D. B. Martin (1990: 75, 200 n. 44).

[53] Galloway (2004: 140). For ἐξουσία, ἑκών, and ἄκων in physical slavery, see Chariton, *Chaer.* 2.6.2.

[54] Harnisch (2007: 41) argues that ἀνάγκη corresponds with ἑκών. But in her study of volitional language in early Greek literature (esp. ἑκών, ἄκων, ἀνάγκη), Rickert (1989: 36) explains that ἀνάγκη always corresponds with ἄκων: 'The presence or absence or circumstances of ἀνάγκη exhaust, in effect, the significance of the personal descriptions ἑκών and ἄκων. Someone described as ἑκών is not acting in any particular way but rather is acting in any way at all when no circumstances of ἀνάγκη pertain; someone described as ἄκων is subject to circumstances of ἀνάγκη.'

[55] For τάλας used somewhat interchangeably with ὤ/οὐαί in the prophetic woes, see LXX Isa 6.5.

to compliance and desire, but only acknowledges through a prophetic woe the sentence he would face should he not fulfil his divine commission. Indeed, Paul insists that he cannot cheer or boast (καύχημα) for preaching the gospel (v. 16). Such is the condition of one who is *compelled* to preach. As Käsemann remarks, 'This power of God drives [Paul] without rest or respite like a slave through the Mediterranean.'[56]

In summary, while Malherbe's interpretation has the advantage of explaining that Paul is entitled to a μισθός (v. 18), there is no indication in verses 16–18 that Paul regards himself as having overcome his compulsion, and thus as inwardly free. Paul's argument suggests rather that he truly is compelled like a slave administrator of God, and his admission to being so would have been abhorrent to a Stoic. Therefore, since neither Martin nor Malherbe has articulated views which make coherent all the details in the passage, we shall offer a new reading of verse 17 that accounts for its literary, philosophical, and commercial contexts, that is, by arguing that Paul's preaching was both involuntary and deserving of pay.

Paul's preaching as paid and involuntary

It is our contention that not only did Paul preach involuntarily as a slave administrator, but his position as administrator, far from dismissing his right to receive compensation for preaching, actually supported such a right. Whether therefore he preached willingly or unwillingly – that is, as a free labourer or a slave steward – Paul was entitled to a μισθός.

The paying of private administrators and other privileged slaves for their labour is certainly not a new proposal. Martin himself conceded that business slaves, and especially commercial administrators, would normally have received compensation for their work. Yet Martin resisted the conclusion that Paul was issued a *paid* administration because of how the apostle referred to the arrangement.[57] Moreover, Martin assumes, along with the majority of scholars, that the conditional sentences in verse 17 completely contrast with one another. In other words, he considers the protasis in verse 17a (εἰ γὰρ ἑκὼν τοῦτο πράσσω) to be antithetical to the protasis in verse 17c (εἰ δὲ ἄκων), and the apodosis in verse 17b

---

[56] Käsemann (1969: 231).

[57] D. B. Martin (1990: 75): 'It is true that slaves were usually paid by their masters for their work. This was probably even more often true for managerial slaves than for common laborers, but *misthon echein* is not a normal way of referring to this financial arrangement.' Martin also discusses how slaves were able to circumvent the legal barriers which prevented them from obtaining possessions (7–11); cf. Winger (1997: 226).

(μισθὸν ἔχω) to be antithetical to the apodosis in verse 17d (οἰκονομίαν πεπίστευμαι).[58] When analysed closely, however, it becomes apparent that the two apodoses are not explicitly antithetical; while the protases in verse 17a and 17c are in direct contrast, the apodoses in verse 17b and 17d are not. Paul never actually states that he is without the right to receive a wage, but simply insists that he is a slave of God, and quite significantly, he is not a menial slave (δοῦλος), but a slave administrator by virtue of having been entrusted with an *oikonomia*.[59] And as an administrator, that is, a privileged commercial slave, Paul implies that he possesses the right to receive payment.

The compensation of slave administrators during the Roman period is apparent in both literary and non-literary texts.[60] The privileges of slave stewards in the Latin agronomists and other real-life bailiffs from Roman Egypt often included some form of monetary compensation. Jane Rowlandson, for instance, describes how the landowners of Oxyrhynchus paid their administrators in cash and/or kind. 'Like tenancy', she writes, 'agricultural wage labour took a variety of forms, from long-term employees (ranging in status from bailiffs to humble servants) to independent workers or craftsmen being paid for performing a single service. In both cases, but particularly the former, payment in kind was often supplemented by or substituted for cash wages.'[61] Dominic Rathbone makes a similar distinction between the forms of compensation, explaining that all permanent employees of the Appianus and related estates in the Arsinoite nome received either a salary (ὀψώνιον), in the form of 'a fixed monthly allowance of cash and wheat and sometimes vegetable oil', or a wage (μισθός).[62] A mid-third-century CE document from Oxyrhynchus even mentions a certain Calpurnia Heraclia, who in her corn registration reported that 'monthly allowances [from her corn holdings] are given to the agents and stewards and farmers and boys and monthly workers [δίδονται μηνιαῖαι συντάξεις πραγματευταῖς τε

---

[58] D. B. Martin (1990: 75): 'One last linguistic indication that Paul is here describing himself as Christ's slave agent lies in his opposition of "being entrusted with an oikonomia" to "having a wage" (*misthos*).'

[59] Even if Paul had stated that he was simply a δοῦλος, he would still be entitled to basic provisions, since, as Pseudo-Aristotle insists, 'food is a slave's pay [δούλῳ δὲ μισθὸς τροφή]' (*Oec.* 1344b3).

[60] Some slaves were paid during the Greek period also. According to Rihll (2011: 65), in Classical Athens '[t]he skilled slave could earn a living much as a free worker did'.

[61] Rowlandson (1996: 205).

[62] Rathbone (1991: 91–2). This policy, however, may not have been applied to Appianus' administrators, because they were probably free or freedmen already in possession of some wealth (70–1). Cf. Caragounis (1974: 44–5).

καὶ φροντισταῖς καὶ γεωργοῖς καὶ παιδαρίοις καὶ καταμηνείοις]' (P.Oxy. 3048, lines 19–20).[63] The labourers, of course, could have easily bartered these items in the marketplace to supply their cash needs.[64]

A more common form of compensation among slave administrators was the grant of a *peculium*.[65] As discussed in Chapter 4, the *peculium* of a slave, while legally belonging to the master, served as a purse or allowance of money, provisions, and other slaves on which the slave could live from day to day and even increase in order to purchase various luxuries. As the gospel parables demonstrate, a slave's administration commenced once he received his allotted sum (Matt 25.14–15//Luke 19.13).[66] Two kinds of purchase verify that administrators and other privileged slaves earned great sums of money which were then treated (*de facto*) as their own. First, the great monetary gain of some administrators is apparent in the epitaphs they are responsible for erecting. Although some of these inscriptions are modest, others are quite lavish and make a point of mentioning that the monuments were paid for by the administrator himself, presumably with his *peculium*.[67] But undoubtedly the most important purchase a slave could make was his manumission, and this would not have been possible without a sizable *peculium*. As Peter Garnsey remarks, 'Unless we grant that profits could be made in [trading ventures and manufactures], it is difficult or impossible to understand how it was that slaves were able to buy their freedom.'[68] Therefore, even though payments and allowances came in a variety of forms, it is clear that administrators and other privileged slaves could expect to be compensated for their labour.

---

[63] Rowlandson (1996: 207) states that the labourers listed in the letter were 'certainly estate employees'.

[64] Rathbone (1991: 111–12).

[65] Andreau (1999: 66):

> According to several texts in the *Digest*, the slave *institor* would often get a salary, a *merces*, in return for his work (*operae*). But, in some cases, he did not receive any direct reward. In such a case, his *operae* were free, *gratuitae*, but he probably had other benefits (for instance, some better opportunity to run his *peculium*). The money sunk in the business was not part of the *peculium* of the slave-agent. But that does not mean that the slave did not also possess a *peculium*, so that in practice a certain confusion could sometimes arise over which sums were entrusted to the slave as part of his *peculium* and which were those that he managed in his capacity as agent.
>
> Cf. A. Watson (1987: 90–101).

[66] For these sums as *peculia*, see Aubert (1994: 4 n. 18).

[67] Carlsen (1995: 95). Bradley (1987: 110): 'From epigraphic evidence it appears that at times [slaves] spent what must have been substantial sums on commemorative epitaphs and even public monuments.'

[68] Garnsey (1981: 370). Cf. Mouritsen (2011: 159–80).

The realisation that administrators normally received compensation for their labour has significant implications for our reading of 1 Cor 9.16–18. Far from implying that he is an unworthy slave who simply fulfils his duty (à la Käsemann), by asserting that he has been entrusted with an administration Paul insists that he is a privileged slave of God who, though compelled to preach, is entitled to some kind of pay or *peculium*.[69] The conditional sentences which make up verse 17 should therefore no longer be considered completely antithetical, as the scholarly consensus maintains.[70] Instead, the two apodoses correspond: if Paul preaches willingly, then naturally he is entitled to a wage; but (δέ) if he preaches unwillingly, as in fact he does, then he has been entrusted with an administration, which still entitles him to compensation.[71]

The plausibility of Paul utilising two corresponding rather than antithetical apodoses in adjacent conditional sentences in 1 Cor 9.17 is supported in several places in Paul's letters, even elsewhere in the Corinthian correspondence. In 1 Cor 12.26, for example, Paul states, 'If one member [ἓν μέλος] suffers, all members [πάντα τὰ μέλη] suffer together; if one member [(ἓν) μέλος] is honoured, all members [πάντα τὰ μέλη] rejoice together.' Although Paul describes quite dissimilar conditions in the two protases (individual suffering and honour), their respective apodoses are remarkably similar: mutual and collective empathy should characterise the body of Christ. Paul introduces both scenarios in order to illustrate the immediately preceding principle – that there may be no division in the body, but that all members may have the same concern for one

[69] Paul's belief that slaves could receive remuneration is implied in Rom 6.20–3, where death is identified as the proft (καρπός), dues (τέλος), and even wages (ὀψώνια) of slavery to sin; cf. Cranfield (1979: 329); D. B. Martin (1990: 62); Yinger (1999: 187–92); Jewett (2007: 425–6). Significantly, Paul uses μισθός and ὀψώνιον interchangeably when referring to his material support (cf. 1 Cor 9.17–18; 2 Cor 11.8). Therefore, even if, as D. B. Martin (1990: 75) maintains, μισθός was not the normal term used to designate a slave's pay, its meaning is close enough to ὀψώνιον and other payment terms for Paul to use here as a reference to his right to receive material support.

[70] Harnisch (2007: 41) argues that the apodoses in verse 17 correspond, but proposes that οἰκονομίαν πεπίστευμαι refers to Paul's dependence on the Corinthian elites. But God is normally the implied subject when Paul refers to being entrusted with something through πιστεύω (Rom 3.2; Gal 2.7; 1 Thess 2.4; cf. 1 Tim 1.11; Titus 1.3). Hall (2003: 190–8) also contends that the conditional sentences in verse 17 agree, though only insofar as they support Paul's denial in verse 16 that he has a right to boast for preaching the gospel: 'If I preach willingly, that is nothing to boast about because I am doing it for payment. If I preach unwillingly, that is also nothing to boast about, because I am performing a duty that has been laid upon me' (197). But Paul's primary objective in verse 17 is not to disqualify his boast for preaching – this possibility has already been eliminated in verse 16 – but to demonstrate his right to receive a wage, as verse 18 confirms.

[71] The δέ in verse 17 is adversative, but the terms being contrasted are ἑκών and ἄκων, not μισθὸν ἔχω and οἰκονομίαν πεπίστευμαι.

another (1 Cor 12.25). As Michelle Lee explains, 'Oneness for Paul has this multi-dimensional quality: rather than independence there is inter-dependence, and even more, an intimate unity leading to mutual care and a sharing of suffering and rejoicing.'[72]

Similar constructions surface in 2 Corinthians. After having explained that both the sufferings and comfort of Christ pour out onto him, Paul in 2 Cor 1.6 defends his apostolic ethos by insisting that he is afforded both sufferings and comfort for the benefit of the church, so long as they patiently share in his sufferings: 'If we suffer, it is for your comfort [ὑπὲρ τῆς ὑμῶν παρακλήσεως] and salvation; if we are comforted, it is for your comfort [ὑπὲρ τῆς ὑμῶν παρακλήσεως], which is effective in the endurance of the same afflictions which we also suffered.' The conditions in the two protases (suffering and comfort) are clearly anti-thetical. However, since both Paul's sufferings and eventual comfort produce comfort for the church, the apodoses are not antithetical, but in agreement. As Murray Harris remarks, 'The combination εἴτε … εἴτε does not introduce mutually exclusive alternatives but rather successive experiences.'[73] Thus, Paul Barnett explains, 'Paul is the receiver of suffering but also of comfort, which, as he stated in v. 4, is for their benefit. Therefore, "whether" distressed or, in consequence, "whether" comforted, it is for their comfort.'[74]

Again, in 2 Cor 5.13 Paul states, 'For if we are irrational, it is for God [θεῷ]; if we are rational, it is for you [ὑμῖν].' Having had experiences which have brought into question Paul's rationality, here the apostle defends himself and his actions by contrasting two alternative protases in order to legitimate a single proposition about his ministry – its selfless nature.[75] Paul's selflessness is expressed through two seemingly competing apodoses: his actions are performed either for the benefit of God (θεῷ) or for the benefit of the church (ὑμῖν). In either case, however, whether Paul is found to be out of his mind or with sound mind, a single proposition is upheld: he ministers for the benefit of others. As Moyer Hubbard maintains, '[H]owever vexing the parts may be, the whole is reasonably clear: Paul is stating that his actions are entirely free of self-ish ambition and wholly "other" directed.'[76] Ralph Martin concurs: 'On the surface, it comes into view that no matter the state of Paul's mind

---

[72] Lee (2006: 148).   [73] Harris (2005: 147).

[74] Barnett (1997: 76). Cf. R. P. Martin (1986: 10).

[75] The correspondence between 1 Cor 9.17 and 2 Cor 5.13 is further supported by their shared apologetic function and use of the explanatory γάρ. For the defence as targeting Paul's rhetorical lucidity, rather than sanity, see Hubbard (1998: 61).

[76] Hubbard (1998: 39).

or disposition, he does nothing for himself; all is done for God and the Corinthians... [W]hether Paul speaks of his exceptional behavior or his ordinary, all of his actions are directed towards someone else.'[77]

Finally, in Rom 14.8 Paul announces, 'For if we live, we live to the Lord [τῷ κυρίῳ ζῶμεν], and if we die, we die to the Lord [τῷ κυρίῳ ἀποθνῄσκομεν].'[78] Addressing a dispute in which believers are illegitimately judging one another based on personal dietary and calendrical preferences, Paul insists that both parties are equally acceptable to the Lord and that the more important concern in this circumstance is the disposition of the individual. All that matters is whether a believer observes or abstains, lives or dies, while honouring and giving thanks to the Lord of both life and death (Rom 14.6, 9). Thus, although the two protases are antithetical (living and dying), the two assertions in the apodoses are in agreement (τῷ κυρίῳ). As Paul remarks in the ensuing explanation, 'Therefore, whether we live or whether we die, we belong to the Lord [τοῦ κυρίου ἐσμέν]' (Rom 14.8).[79]

In summary, we have found four additional examples from Paul's letters (three from the Corinthian correspondence) where the apostle, in response to specific ecclesial disputes, employs two conditional sentences which contain antithetical protases yet corresponding apodoses in order to make a single affirmation. In light of these texts, the rhetorical approach we have argued for in 1 Cor 9.17 finds strong support. How then should verse 17 read, and how does this new reading correlate with the exegetical insights identified in the earlier critiques of the views represented by Martin and Malherbe?

The digression begun in verse 16 is introduced in order to ward off the anticipated criticisms of certain philosophically astute members in the church. While in verses 12 and 15 Paul boasts in the fact that he has refused his right to receive material support and thus has endured hardship for the sake of the gospel, in verse 16 he explains why preaching the gospel by itself is insufficient to merit a boast. He must preach because God has compelled him to preach. In fact, neglect of his commission, as with the other Hebrew prophets, will be met

[77] R. P. Martin (1986: 126–7).

[78] In Rom 14.8 (as in 1 Cor 9.17 and 2 Cor 5.13) Paul uses the explanatory γάρ. The correspondence between 1 Cor 9.17 and Rom 14.8 is further supported by the fact that much of Paul's ethical argumentation in Romans 12–15 was recast from 1 Corinthians; cf. Karris (1973); Toney (2008: 164–90).

[79] Cranfield (1979: 707): '[A]ll Christians live "to the Lord", that is, they live with the object of pleasing Christ, they seek to use their lives in His service, and, when it comes to dying, they glorify Him by committing themselves to His keeping.' Cf. Jewett (2007: 848).

with God's judgment.[80] But Paul anticipates that this concession will bring into question his freedom and right to receive remuneration. If Paul is compelled to preach the gospel, then his critics will assume that he is simply a slave of God and labours without the right and privilege of material support. In order to circumvent this charge, Paul in verse 17 explains that, despite his compulsion, his particular role in God's household allows him to retain certain apostolic rights. After all, if Paul preaches willingly, then naturally he would be entitled to receive a wage. But since he preaches unwillingly,[81] he is also entitled to compensation because his particular form of privileged slavery is that of a paid administrator. By the end of verse 17, Paul therefore still possesses the right to material support, which he argued for incessantly in verses 4–14 and is required to have in order to refuse that right in verses 12, 15, 18, and 19. He then in verse 18 without any insincerity or rhetorical abnormality can ask, 'What therefore is my wage?' And in typical Pauline fashion he explains that his payment is, quite paradoxically, the opportunity to deliver (τίθημι) the gospel free of charge, and thus not to make use of his right to receive pay.[82]

---

[80] Käsemann (1969: 230): '*Ananke* and Woe are personified here to convey the sense that in them the epiphany of divine power is taking place.' Crook (2004: 160) argues that Paul's ἀνάγκη and fear of divine retribution (οὐαί) indicate that he understood himself to be the client of his patron God. But Crook fails to notice how Paul's compulsion rhetoric more closely belongs to the realm of moral philosophy, and how both the notions of divine compulsion and curse are rooted in the Hebrew prophetic tradition (cf. LXX Jer 15.10; 51.33; Isa 6.5; Nasuti 1988: 257–8; Sandnes 1991: 125–30).

[81] Some interpreters reject the possibility that Paul preached unwillingly and under compulsion because they correlate motives with the acceptability of the service rendered; cf. Calvin (1960: 193); Grosheide (1953: 210). It cannot be denied that Paul elsewhere expresses great compassion for those to whom he preached (Rom 9.1–3) and insists that he ministers out of emulation of Christ's love (2 Cor 5.14). But Paul's ministry brought on him so many hardships, and future resurrection was such a consuming reality for him, that he consistently preferred (μᾶλλον) to be away from the body and at home with the Lord (2 Cor 5.8). In fact, when pressed to choose between persisting in ministry and departing to be with Christ, the apostle considered death to be more advantageous (κέρδος, Phil 1.21), admitting that being with Christ was his desire (ἐπιθυμία) and indeed far better (πολλῷ μᾶλλον κρεῖσσον, 1.23), even if ministering to the church was at the moment a greater necessity (ἀναγκαιότερον, 1.24). Moreover, it can be affirmed with Käsemann (1969: 230) that Paul fulfilled his commission not by his own will, but through the power of God's gospel and grace which took possession of him (1 Cor 15.10; Gal 2.20).

[82] Hafemann (1990: 143–4) and Gardner (1994: 94) avoid a paradoxical sense of μισθός by regarding Paul's wage in verse 18 as eschatological (cf. 1 Cor 3.8, 14). But while an eschatological reward awaits Paul at the faithful completion of his ministry, his μισθός in verse 18 (unless interpreted as metonymy) cannot refer directly to it since he expressly states that his μισθός is in fact his free preaching. Harnisch (2007: 41) comes closer to Paul's meaning by identifying the apostle's wage as his boast (v. 15). More probably, Paul's μισθός is his refusal of monetary support, an act of self-sacrifice for the sake of the gospel

Paul's responsibility: 'depositing' the gospel (9.18)

There remains some ambiguity concerning the kind of action τίθημι denotes in verse 18. Translations usually suggest 'make' (KJV; ASV; RSV; NRSV), 'offer' (NET; NASB; NIV), or 'present' (ESV) the gospel. Admittedly, the verb has a broad lexical range. But given the presence of Paul's *oikonomos* metaphor and the monetary theme in the passage, it is better to regard τίθημι as also having a commercial sense, as the term was occasionally used to mean in antiquity.[83] For instance, in the Parable of the Ten Mina the verb denotes the depositing of resources (Luke 19.21, 23; cf. NRSV).[84] Moreover, in Paul's remarks about the Jerusalem collection in 1 Corinthians, he instructs believers to 'put aside and save [παρ' ἑαυτῷ τιθέτω θησαυρίζων]' on the first day of each week (1 Cor 16.2), which undoubtedly denotes a monetary deposit (BDAG 2).[85]

Given the monetary sense of τίθημι apparent elsewhere in 1 Corinthians and in other ancient literature, the verb in 1 Cor 9.18 should be interpreted metaphorically, so that it portrays Paul's gospel preaching as if it were a commercial transaction. This sense of the verb is supported in 2 Cor 5.19, where Paul shows apostles to be the recipients of a similar kind of deposit, as those to whom God was '*entrusting* [θέμενος] the message of reconciliation' (NRSV; ESV). Therefore, 1 Cor 9.18 should read: '[As God's administrator], what then is my reward? Just this: that in my preaching I may *deposit/entrust* the gospel free of charge, so as not to make full use of my right in the gospel.'[86] As with Paul's *oikonomos*

which not only demonstrates his faithfulness to his commission (4.2; 9.23), but affords him a 'boast' and ensures his receipt of an eschatological μισθός (3.8, 14; cf. 4.5; 9.24–7).

[83] LSJ II.7–8; BDAG 2; MM 5087 (2); cf. Demosthenes, *Tim.* 49.5; Plutarch, *Mor.* 829b.

[84] Johnson (1991: 291).

[85] Certain related terms can also carry a monetary sense, such as παραθήκη (1 Tim 6.20; 2 Tim 1.12–14) and παρατίθημι (1 Tim 1.18; 2 Tim 2.2); cf. Quinn and Wacker (2000: 554–7); Tomlinson (2010). The cognate noun θέμα is widely attested in the papyri for grain deposits (P.Oxy. 2588–90, 4856–90; P.Ryl. 199 (line 12); P.Tebt. 120 (line 125), which were often handled by *oikonomoi* and other administrators (P.Oxy. 621; 2588; 4859; 4862; 4863; 4870; 4871; 4879; 4881); cf. Litinas (2007).

[86] Far from serving like 'the many who peddle the word of God' as a commodity for profit (2 Cor 2.17), Paul distinguishes himself as an apostle through his refusal of pay and by issuing the gospel as a benefaction (ἀδάπανος, 1 Cor 9.18; cf. δωρεάν, 2 Cor 11.7; Danker 1982: 333–4). The apostle as peddler differs from Paul as administrator in that the peddlar preaches selfishly and without accountability, whereas Paul as God's administrator preaches 'as from sincerity', 'in the sight of God' (2 Cor 2.17), seeking not money, but converts (1 Cor 9.19–23). In fact, in Paul's approach to apostolic support, he will not accept pay from those to whom he currently ministers, and never from certain churches (2 Cor 11.9, 12). Instead, he offers his own life and body as the expense for his services (1 Cor 9.27; cf. 9.18–19). As he states in 2 Cor 12.15, 'I will most gladly spend [δαπανήσω] and be spent [ἐκδαπανηθήσομαι] for you.'

metaphor in 4.1, such a metaphorical reading implies that the apostle is simply a dispenser and mediator of the gospel, rather than an orator sent to adorn the good news.

Paul's reward: 'gaining' converts (9.19–23)

To this point we have utilised what we know of commercial administrators to address the exegetical difficulties in 1 Cor 9.16–18. Earlier we observed how Paul employs the *oikonomos* metaphor to explicate how he can serve as a slave of God while also being entitled to material support, and thereby to reinforce the defence of his right to receive a wage in order to demonstrate emphatically that he has refused to exercise that right. But far from leaving the theme of administration behind, it is our contention that the apostle as *oikonomos* also serves as the controlling metaphor for verses 19–23. As the γάρ at the beginning of verse 19 indicates, Paul closely relates what he says earlier about his refusal of rights with his discourse on accommodation. And rather than introduce a new theme in order to showcase his ministry strategy, here Paul conspicuously enlists terms and concepts originating from the familiar metaphorical sphere of commercial administration, extending the analogy as far as verse 23.

Paul has already admitted in verse 17 that he is a slave administrator of God. Even so, he indicates in verse 19 that he is 'free from all [people]' (ἐλεύθερος γὰρ ὢν ἐκ πάντων, v. 19a), since he retains the right as an apostle not to ply a trade (vv. 1, 6) and instead to receive financial support from his churches (vv. 4, 12, 14).[87] But in verse 19 Paul indicates that he also has the right to refuse those rights and in that way to enslave himself to others (πᾶσιν ἐμαυτὸν ἐδούλωσα, v. 19b).[88]

---

[87] Because of Paul's compulsion and slavery to God, the scope of his freedom is limited to his independence 'from all *people*', namely, Jews, Gentiles, and the weak, who are clearly the target of his self-enslavement in verses 19–22.

[88] Cf. Garland (2003: 425): 'As God's slave, Paul ultimately sets himself free from others (7:22–23). Some are compelled to speak because of their need for money, which in turn means that they are compelled to preach only to those who can pay. By refusing fees, Paul was able to exercise freedom to preach to one and all.' Hall (1990), Galloway (2004: 183), and Walton (2011: 224) erroneously argue that Paul's ἀνάγκη extends even to his refusal of pay, so that his self-enslavement is not voluntary, but mandated by his call. In order to do so, they must redefine 'slavery', 'right', and 'freedom' and confuse those concepts to an utterly unrecognisable state, presumably because they misunderstand Paul's logic in verses 16–18. Although his own exegetical conclusions are quite ambiguous, see also the critical engagement of Coppins (2009: 62–77) with existing scholarly (esp. German) configurations of Paul's freedom and self-enslavement.

Several views have been proposed regarding the sense and implications of Paul's self-slavery in verse 19.[89] Perhaps most famously, Ronald Hock has contended that Paul's metaphor refers to the social degradation that accompanied his work as an artisan, a profession typically occupied by slaves.[90] But in addition to the fact that such a characterisation would have been offensive to at least a good number – almost certainly the vast majority – of Corinthian Christians, who in all probability shared his status as wage labourers,[91] Paul's explanation in verses 20–2 indicates that the metaphor is descriptive of his strategy of accommodation generally – that is, to Jews, Gentiles, *and* the weak, indeed 'to all people' (πᾶσιν, v. 19b) – and not simply his assumption of the status and lifestyle befitting a wage labourer. The slave metaphor, however, does have social connotations, implying the apostle's humiliation of self and exaltation of others (cf. 2 Cor 11.7).[92] Moreover, Paul's repeated use of Stoic themes throughout 1 Corinthians 8–9 (as seen above) suggests that his declaration of freedom (9.1, 19), together with his self-enslavement (v. 19), is to be interpreted (at least in part) within the context of moral philosophy.[93] By stating that he is free from all yet has enslaved himself to all, Paul explains in social *and* philosophical terms his relinquishing of apostolic rights for the benefit of those to whom he ministers.

Paul then explains how his strategy of accommodation plays out. To the Jews, Paul explains, he became as a Jew; to those under the law, he became as one under the law; to those outside the law, he became as one outside the law; finally, to the weak, he became weak. Driving his ministry strategy was Paul's chief objective of making converts. He thus summarises his approach by asserting that his adaptative lifestyle has a definite evangelistic purpose – 'I become all things to all people *that by all means I might save some* [ἵνα πάντως τινὰς σώσω]' (9.22).

---

[89] D. B. Martin (1990: 86–135) argues that Paul's approach resembles the Graeco-Roman demagogue leader topos.

[90] Hock (1978: 558–60); Hock (1980: 59–62).

[91] Cf. Still (2006: 787–9) and the response by Hock (2008). For the socio-economic status of early Pauline believers, see Longenecker (2010: 36–59).

[92] Gorman (2001: 181–92) shows that Paul's self-lowering in 1 Cor 9.19 closely – and probably intentionally – resembles the humiliation of Christ (cf. Phil 2.6–8), stating, 'Perhaps Paul's most sustained systematic reflection on his own experience of cruciform ministry appears in 1 Corinthians 9' (181). Cf. Horrell (1997c); S. Kim (2003). Since Hellerman (2005: 135–42) has convincingly shown how Paul's depiction of Christ as a δοῦλος (Phil 2.7) has humble social connotations without implying that Jesus actually lived like a slave, Paul's self-enslavement likewise implies social humiliation and self-sacrifice (δουλόω, 1 Cor 9.19) without necessarily referring to his living and work conditions.

[93] Malherbe (1994: 251–2).

But σῴζω is not Paul's preferred term for conversion in this passage. Instead, it is striking that Paul repeatedly refers to his missionary objective with the verb κερδαίνω ('gain', 'profit'). While many interpreters have noticed the oddity of Paul's reference to his evangelistic work with κερδαίνω, few have sought to explain Paul's application of it, and those who have offer competing explanations. Abraham Malherbe and Clarence Glad, on the one hand, suggest that Paul here is indebted to Cynic tradition. Both cite speeches by the Cynic philosopher Antisthenes, where κερδαίνω and σῴζω are used together to express Odysseus' preference to undergo ill-treatment if thereby he might gain something or save people.[94] Margaret Mitchell and Raymond Collins, on the other hand, have both advocated that κερδαίνω here carries the rhetorical sense of 'advantage'. Because Paul's letter has significant deliberative intentions, Mitchell and Collins suggest that Paul's use of the verb in 1 Corinthians is another occurrence of this rhetorical topos.[95] But while Paul has been interacting with moral philosophy, and his use of the verb certainly serves a rhetorical function (one objective of the chapter, after all, is to serve as an *exemplum*), these explanations do not give sufficient attention to the monetary theme that runs throughout the chapter.[96]

David Daube additionally noticed that the application of κερδαίνω in the sense 'to win over an unbeliever to one's faith' is 'quite un-Greek'; indeed, '[t]here is nothing remotely analogous in Liddell-Scott or the papyri'.[97] Nevertheless, Daube observed that the consistent way the NT authors use the verb as a 'missionary term' – that is, as either implying conversion (1 Pet 3.1) or turning from sin (Matt 18.15) – requires an explanation beyond mere coincidence. Since κερδαίνω appears nowhere in the LXX, Daube looked to Rabbinic Judaism, where he found a precedent for utilising commercial terms for 'the gaining by God of men whom he had cast away'.[98] But Daube was unable to demonstrate that

---

[94] Malherbe (1994: 253); Glad (1995: 251).

[95] M. M. Mitchell (1991: 248); R. F. Collins (1999: 353).

[96] For other scholarly views on the influence of Paul's thought in verses 19–23, see Mitchell (2001: 198) and Sandnes (2011: 130–1), who perhaps rightly question whether any single Hellenistic tradition is responsible for Paul's accommodation motif. Still, the plausibility of the commercial use of κερδαίνω is strengthened by the fact that it is not dependent on Paul's education or familiarity with popular philosophy and follows closely on the heels of other commercial terminology.

[97] Daube (1947: 109). Cf. Schlier (1965: 673).

[98] As Daube (1947: 109) remarks, 'No Rabbinic parallels have so far been adduced; but surely, they ought to exist, for if there had been no Rabbinic influence, it is difficult to see how the New Testament writers should have come to employ the verb in a way neither classical nor vernacular.' Daube's conclusions are followed by, e.g., Barrett (1968: 211);

there was ever in Judiasm an association between this commercial sense and God's gaining or winning of Gentiles.[99] Conceding this point, Daube proposed that both 1 Pet 3.1 and 1 Cor 9.19–22 are intertextually indebted to Rabbinic instruction. However, the associations Daube mapped out remain very weak, which provides room for exploring the possibility that Paul's use of κερδαίνω in 1 Cor 9.19–22 originated from the monetary theme already established earlier in the discourse.

It is not our objective here to show how non-Pauline Christian literature came to use κερδαίνω as a missionary idiom. Nevertheless, it is significant that in nearly all of its sixteen occurrences in the NT (whether literal or figurative) the verb retains a strong commercial or accounting sense. This meaning of κερδαίνω becomes explicit when on a number of occasions the verb is contrasted with its antonym ζημιόω ('lose', 'forfeit'). Each of the Synoptics, for instance, report Jesus cautioning his followers about 'gaining' the world and yet 'forfeiting' their souls/lives (Matt 16.26//Mark 8.36//Luke 9.25).[100] The verb is also used in Acts 27.21 during Paul's voyage to Rome, where it is ironically juxtaposed with ζημία to indicate the ship's 'accruing' of both damage and 'loss'. In Phil 3.7–8, Paul's only use of κερδαίνω outside 1 Cor 9.19–22, he used it quite famously along with κέρδος, ζημία, and ζημιόω to underscore the enormous 'gain' he considers to have obtained by knowing Christ, in contrast to the 'loss' which was his life before Christ.[101] Also quite significant is the occurrence of κερδαίνω in the Parable of the Talents, where the verb is used four times to indicate how commercial slaves made significant profits for their master (Matt 25.16, 17, 20, 22). Even in the verb's apparent 'missionary' sense regarding community discipline in Matt 18.15, it is perhaps significant that Jesus' discourse progresses shortly thereafter to the Parable of the Unforgiving Slave, which also involves a cast of commercial slaves (Matt 18.23–35). Finally, a commercial sense of the verb is also clear in Jas 3.1, where it is coupled with the explicit commercial term ἐμπορεύομαι.[102]

Lietzmann and Kümmel (1969: 180); Conzelmann (1975: 159–60 n. 17); D. B. Martin (1990: 209 n. 1); Schrage (1995: 339); Thiselton (2000: 701); Fitzmyer (2008: 369).

[99] Daube (1947: 117).

[100] It is striking that each of the Synoptics also uses ὠφελέω in the statement, further confirming that a monetary metaphor is in view, and employs σῴζω in a parallel expression in the immediately preceding verse.

[101] For Paul's use of these terms in a commercial or accounting sense, see O'Brien (1991: 382–91); Bockmuehl (1997: 204–8); Reumann (2008: 488–92). Fee (1995: 316) even observes that here Paul uses 'the language of the marketplace'.

[102] Thus, the only NT passage outside 1 Cor 9.19–22 where κερδαίνω surfaces without a context involving commerce or accounting is 1 Pet 3.1.

In light of the consistent monetary use of κερδαίνω by a host of NT authors and Paul's obvious application of the verb this way in Phil 3.8, it is probable that Paul also intended this sense in 1 Cor 9.19–22.[103] By using this verb, Paul indicates that as God's commercial administrator the chief objective of his apostolic administration is to generate a 'profit' for his divine principal.[104] As Thomas Edwards observed long ago, 'The word [κερδαίνω] both explains μισθός and carries on the metaphor of the steward. [Paul] refuses payment in money that he may make the greater gain in souls. But the gain is that which a faithful steward makes, not for himself, but for his master.'[105] In the same way that the commercial slaves in the Parable of the Talents were required to make more (ἄλλος) revenue for their master (Matt 25.20–2), so Paul seeks to generate sizable profits to deliver unto his.

In contrast to many real-life administrators, however, Paul was unsatisfied with producing only a modest return for his master. Surely, just as his apostolic colleagues, Paul could have preached the gospel while receiving financial support from his churches and still made a significant evangelistic return. But Paul went beyond the expectations of his master, God's other agents, and the church by forgoing his right to a wage in order to procure an even *greater* profit than he would have been able to obtain otherwise (ἵνα τοὺς πλείονας κερδήσω, v. 19).

Paul's refusal to be paid was only one example of his ministry strategy of accommodation. Adaptation was the hallmark of his apostleship and the means by which he was able to save a host of unbelievers in several socio-religious contexts.[106] The 'profit-seeking' objective of his ministerial strategy is apparent throughout the grammatically, syntactically, and verbally repetitive construction spanning verses 19–22, where Paul

---

[103] Cf. Hock (1980: 100 n. 114); Fee (1987: 426–7 n. 24); Marshall (1987: 314–15); Gorman (2001: 184); Garland (2003: 429); Delgado (2010: 245).

[104] Lehmeier (2006: 231): 'Das Handeln eines tüchtigen οἰκονόμος strebt nach Gewinn (κέρδος).' Cf. A. Robertson and Plummer (1911: 190).

[105] Edwards (1885: 237–8). Hock (1980: 100 n. 114) notices a similar association between Paul's use of κερδαίνω and the passage's monetary theme, arguing that Paul applied the verb in an anti-sophistic manner reminiscent of the philosophers. For while the sophists pursued financial profit (κέρδος) and fame (δόξα) by entertaining wealthy patrons (Philostratus, *Vit. Apoll.* 8.7.3), the philosophers opted for poverty in order to reap (κερδαίνω) learning and friendship (Epictetus, *Diatr.* 4.1.177; Xenophon, *Mem.* 1.2). According to Hock, Paul, in a similar anti-sophistic demonstration, impoverishes himself in order to acquire converts rather than a wage (62). Hock, however, fails to acknowledge the significant disparity between Paul and the philosophers, arguing that 'Paul's apologies of his tentmaking, and the criticisms implied therein, show the influence of the philosophers' debates over the appropriate means of support' (65). But, whereas the philosophers sought entirely to benefit themselves, the main beneficiary of Paul's pursuit is God.

[106] Chadwick (1955); Hall (1990); Glad (1995: 249–77); S. C. Barton (1996).

uses κερδαίνω five times. There it becomes clear that, by assuming the lifestyle of Jews, Gentiles, and perhaps other socio-ethnic groups, Paul sought to save more unbelievers than would have been possible had he not adopted such an accommodating approach. Thus, while he had rights as an apostle and was therefore free (ἐλεύθερος) to exercise them, Paul gave up his rights and so voluntarily enslaved himself to his churches (v. 19a) in order that he might make even more profits/converts for his master (v. 19).[107]

Finally, in verse 23 Paul offers an important explanatory note where he clarifies the purpose of his *modus operandi*. Paul explains that he refuses his rights and accommodates to his audiences 'for the sake of the gospel' (διὰ τὸ εὐαγγέλιον), that is, in order to facilitate its advancement in Corinth and elsewhere as its 'co-partner' (συγκοινωνός).[108] In this text, Paul's use of συγκοινωνός denotes business partnership (*societas*) in keeping with the commercial theme.[109] The term clearly carried this meaning in antiquity and would probably have been heard this way by the Corinthians in a discourse replete with commercial terminology (cf. BDAG; MM 609).[110] But precisely how does this partnership function?

The pairing in verse 23 of συγκοινωνός/συγκοινωνέω with εὐαγγέλιον (or the gospel in any implied sense) is unique for Paul and the rest of the NT authors. Elsewhere, for instance, Paul only uses those terms

---

[107] For Paul's chief apostolic mandate as the salvation of people, see Barram (2011: 238–40).

[108] The enigmatic phrase συγκοινωνὸς αὐτοῦ γένωμαι is troublesome for a number of reasons. Chief among them is how to understand the sense in which Paul actually is a συγκοινωνός. A number of translations and interpreters regard Paul as a sharer 'in the blessings of the gospel' (RSV, NRSV, NIV, ESV); cf. Bornkamm (1966: 197–8); Conzelmann (1975: 161); Fee (1987: 432); Witherington (1995: 213). But while the pronoun αὐτοῦ certainly refers back to τὸ εὐαγγέλιον, συγκοινωνός must be understood in an active, rather than a passive sense.

[109] For the Roman *societas*, see A. Watson (1965: 125–46); R. Zimmermann (1990: 451–76). Sampley (1980) argues that Paul conceptualises Christian communities (esp. the Philippian and Roman churches) as *societates*, but he does not apply the concept to 1 Cor 9.23. Sampley's proposal has been challenged by Peterman (1997: 123–7). But Paul's use of συγκοινωνός/συγκοινωνέω elsewhere with reference to other persons does not negate its use here as figuratively denoting a business partnership.

[110] P.CairMasp. 2.67158, a mid-sixth-century contract from Antinoopolis in Egypt, specifies how Aurelius Psois and Aurelius Josephus, brothers-in-law and business partners (συνκοινωνοί, συνπραγματεύται) in carpentry, divide their business shares (μέρα) and responsibilities, including their gains (κέρδοι, ὠφέλιμοι) and losses (ζημίαι). Cf. P.Bilabel 19 (line 2). Dio Chrysostom demonstrates the commercial sense of κοινωνέω when he states, '[T]he law protects the private individual from being easily wronged by men with whom he enters into business relations, either by entrusting them with money, or by making them agents of an estate, or by entering into partnership with them in some enterprise [ἔργου τινὸς κοινωνήσαντες]' (*Or.* 3.88). Cf. LSJ 2b; BGU 969.13. See also Thiselton (2000: 707).

for the relationship which believing Jews and Gentiles share in God's promises (Rom 11.17) and the active participation of the Philippians in various aspects of Paul's ministry (Phil 1.7; 4.14). The two examples from Philippians, however, serve as significant thematic and conceptual parallels for our text. Whereas Paul accepts financial support from the Philippians, and thus they become his 'co-partners' in grace and in the advancement of the gospel (Phil 4.14–18; cf. 1.7), he rejects support from the church in Corinth in order that he might become the gospel's 'co-partner' in its pursuit of the Corinthians. For in Paul's view, the gospel is an autonomous agent, a power or force with transformative potential (Rom 1.16; 1 Cor 1.18, 23–4). Realising the power that the gospel possesses independent of the apostle, Paul aims to co-operate with it as its co-partner, rather than to obstruct it as its competitor.[111] To this end, becoming the gospel's συγκοινωνός implies that Paul seeks to do, or in this case not to do, whatever is necessary in order for the gospel to reach its intended goal – the effecting of faith and salvation (Rom 1.17; 10.14; 1 Cor 15.1–2).[112] And since Paul understands his apostolic role as primarily involving the proclamation of the gospel (1 Cor 1.17; 4.1), he must advance that gospel without impeding its progress (9.12), which might occur if he were to utilise sophistic rhetoric (clearly Paul's concern earlier in the letter (1.17; 2.1–5)) or to exploit his apostolic rights (the focus of his attention here).

Verses 19–23 therefore recapitulate and further develop verses 12 and 15, forming an inclusio around the digression at verses 16–18. Taken together, it becomes apparent that Paul refuses to accept a wage from the Corinthians because such an act of self-sacrifice enables the gospel to advance further in Corinth, a noteworthy accomplishment which Paul can confidently identify, or boast in (9.15; cf. 2 Cor 1.14; Phil 2.16), as a demonstration of faithfulness to his commission (4.2). Thus, Paul forgoes his right to an immediate financial payoff in order to ensure that he will receive his incorruptible prize (9.24–5), an eschatological wage (3.8, 14) to be issued along with his master's praise (ἔπαινος, 4.5) at his return.

---

[111] Cf. R. Zimmermann (1990: 451): 'Societas is thus not based, primarily, on an antagonism of interests; its essence is the pooling of resources (money, property, expertise or labour, or a combination of them) for a *common purpose*' (original emphasis).

[112] Schütz (1975: 52): 'If vv. 19–23 repeat the same theme of renunciation as is found in the preceding portion of ch. 9, then Paul must mean that he has done all this to become a participant in the dynamic character of the gospel – to share in the gospel's *own* work. He is commissioned to preach the gospel (v. 17), but his *reward* comes in sharing in the effectiveness of the gospel, not hindering this force. That is accomplished by disregarding "apostolic" rights and claims' (original emphasis). Cf. Hooker (1996); R. F. Collins (1999: 356); Fitzmyer (2008: 372); Ellington (2011).

Summary

In this chapter we have attempted again to address a number of social-rhetorical, exegetical, and theological issues in Paul's first epistle to the Corinthians, this time targeting Paul's important and notoriously complex discourse in 1 Corinthians 9. Through this investigation we have seen for a second time the way Paul utilised the image of the apostle as an *oikonomos* to articulate at once several fundamental characteristics of his apostolic position which were misunderstood by those in the Corinthian church. First, we observed that Paul, who initially defended at great length his right to receive material support from the Corinthians (vv. 1–14), insisted that he would not exploit that right (in this particular church anyway) because it would prevent the gospel from accomplishing its intended goal (vv. 12, 15). In fact, we saw that Paul's right to receive payment was very different from his commission to preach the gospel, which was not a right at all. Paul's preaching was not a matter of choice; he was compelled to preach on account of his divine commission, and he did so, albeit 'unwillingly' (vv. 16–17), so as to avoid any negative divine recompense. He was therefore considered to be a slave not of men, but of God.

Much to the surprise of his critics, however, Paul's slavery to God did not nullify his right to receive pay, because Paul's particular form of slavery was a private administration through which he maintained his right to receive material support despite being forced to preach. Nevertheless, although he was free to exploit this right, Paul enslaved himself to the Corinthians by refusing to accept a wage from them, insisting instead as God's administrator that his 'kergymatic transactions', or 'deposits', would be made without cost to their recipients (v. 18). Moreover, Paul freely chose to assume the life of an artisan, because by forgoing his right to receive his own material benefits he was able to secure even greater evangelistic gains for God his principal than he would otherwise have been able to (v. 19). This accommodating approach to apostolic ministry became characteristic of many of Paul's missionary efforts (vv. 19–22), for he realised that in order to maximise his evangelistic profits he had to co-operate, rather than compete, with the gospel as if it were his business partner (v. 23). Moreover, these evangelistic gains, though strictly speaking belonging to God, nevertheless secure Paul's eschatological payoff, his incorruptible wage which awaits him at Christ's return.

Through the *oikonomos* metaphor, then, Paul is able to elucidate a number of otherwise confusing, and even conflicting, characteristics of his apostolic ministry. Not only does the image portray the apostle as a slave of God who is compelled to fulfil his commission, but it affords him the right, indeed the apostolic authority, to demand financial support from his churches. It is also significant that Paul casts the image in order to evade anticipated criticisms of his apostleship. Right when it seems that Paul has been rhetorically cornered into admitting that he as God's slave in fact does not possess the right to a wage as he had contended for the first half of the chapter, Paul then quickly turns the table on the argument by announcing his status as God's slave administrator. The metaphor not only exonerates him of the anticipated charge of financial disentitlement, but also paves the way for employing the other commercial terms which surface in the latter part of the passage (vv. 18–23). Finally, it is of utmost importance to this study that Paul, an apostle with dominical authorisation to be supported by his churches (v. 14), forfeits his freedom and authority in order that God, the gospel, and his churches might be further enriched through his poverty (cf. 2 Cor 8.9). Paul's exercise of authority, then, was not a precondition for his apostleship. For in this scenario, rather than assert authority over his churches, Paul subordinated his authority to his greater apostolic mandate – gaining converts for Christ. Thus, Paul embodies the very person of Christ (1 Cor 11.1; cf. Phil 2.6–11) by humiliating himself for the benefit of God (1 Cor 10.31) and those he seeks to save (10.33).

8

CONCLUSION

> Our authority ... the Lord gave for building you up and not for
> tearing you down.   2 Cor 10.8

In this final chapter we shall summarise the argument of the foregoing
investigation and briefly discuss its theological implications. The summary will trace the book's argument chapter by chapter and compare its
socio-historical and exegetical conclusions to those of Dale Martin. We
shall then consider what contributions this investigation has made to the
scholarly study of Paul's apostolic authority, paying special attention to
the way it addresses how Paul's authority is *constructed*, *asserted*, and
contested.

Summary

This study has sought to elucidate the nature of Paul's apostleship and
apostolic authority in 1 Corinthians. Although a number of important
passages and themes could have been examined as a possible means for
exploring these issues, this investigation has concentrated on Paul's portrayal of apostles as administrators (*oikonomoi*) of God in 1 Cor 4.1–5
and 9.16–23 because of the unique way Paul utilises the image in those
passages to construct and assert his authority in the face of opposition.
Unfortunately, this task was immediately recognised to be complicated
by the fact that Paul's description is a metaphor, and as such requires the
interpreter to identify as accurately as possible the origin of the image
and its source domain. In Chapter 1, several source domains previously proposed by NT scholars were ruled out as unlikely or unhelpful.
Moreover, while Dale Martin and others have suggested that managerial
slavery provides an adequate window into Paul's metaphor, it was shown
that the criticisms and counter-evidence marshalled against Martin's
historical assumptions and exegetical conclusions by other interpreters
were considerable enough to raise some doubts about the reliability of

Martin's thesis in its entirety. It was therefore concluded that a full-scale reassessment of the ancient evidence was necessary in order to interpret Paul's *oikonomos* metaphor appropriately.

In Part I, we surveyed the three kinds of *oikonomoi* most frequently attested in Graeco-Roman antiquity: those who served as regal, munici-pal, and private administrators. In this section we took special note of the rank and status that these administrators possessed within their respect-ive hierarchies, as well as their responsibilities and accountability to a superior person or body. In Chapter 2 we saw that the *oikonomoi* serv-ing as regal administrators were appointed exclusively in the Hellenistic kingdoms. There we observed that, despite variations in chronology, geography, and political hierarchy, the social and structural attributes of those administrators were surprisingly consistent. In each of the main four political powers of the Hellenistic period, *oikonomoi* served as regional financial managers and supervised significant resources in the divisions of those kingdoms. Being representatives of the king in matters of finance, these officials possessed the structural authority to make deci-sions in their area of supervision and in their respective regions. They served, however, beneath higher-ranking officials and were therefore held accountable for their administration by superiors, in most instances by the king or one of his delegates. Moreover, in return for their per-formance, they normally received either a promotion or dismissal, but no immediate monetary compensation.

In Chapter 3 we observed that the *oikonomoi* serving as municipal administrators in Graeco-Roman cities were characterised by a greater degree of social and structural diversification than their regal coun-terparts. The municipal *oikonomoi* serving in Greek cities during the Hellenistic period, for instance, were free persons and served as treasury magistrates. In fact, due to the poor economic conditions of Hellenistic cities, the persons occupying this office normally possessed significant socio-economic standing. This was the case as well for some *oikonomoi* serving in Greek cities during the Roman period, although there were also public slaves bearing this title who were from humbler conditions. Evidence for the rank and status of *oikonomoi* serving in Roman cities, particularly Roman colonies, is more difficult to uncover. The question of the position and corresponding socio-economic status of Erastus of Corinth (Rom 16.23) continues to be disputed. However, an inscription from the neighbouring city of Patras has demonstrated that the title in an Augustan colony in Achaea can refer to a local dignitary serving as *quaestor*, the civic treasury magistrate. Regardless of the socio-economic status of the persons who bore the title in a municipal context, these *oikonomoi* were not entrusted with great authority, or situated in a deep administrative hierarchy, or always subject to an accounting. And when these magistrates were held to account, they were normally answerable to a local governing body (ἐκκλησία/δικαστήριον; *ordo decurionum*), rather than an individual sovereign (κύριος).

In Chapter 4 we examined the *oikonomoi* serving as private commercial administrators. There we observed that the persons bearing this title (or any number of Greek and Latin equivalents), while being free farmers during the Classical Greek period, were almost always slaves during the Roman period, normally serving a κύριος/*dominus* as business managers. In this capacity they were given the responsibility of making profits for their owner through the production, trade, and investment of various goods and resources. Thus, they were also entrusted with a considerable measure of authority to speak and act on behalf of their principal, commanding whatever staff served beneath them and representing the master to third contracting parties. Because of their legal condition, they typically belonged to a humble social stratum, although they possessed certain servile privileges, including opportunities to circumvent the legal restraints preventing them from acquiring money and possessions. But as slaves, they were susceptible to various forms of punishment, including violent abuse and even death, should they prove unfaithful.

Having outlined in Part I the major social and structural differences between the *oikonomoi* serving in regal, municipal, and private administration, in Part II we sought to compare the portraits assembled in Part I to Paul's *oikonomos* metaphor in 1 Corinthians in order to identify its source domain and to interpret how Paul used the metaphor to meet his rhetorical, theological, and ethical objectives. In Chapter 5 we briefly analysed 1 Corinthians 4 and 9, arguing that Paul's metaphor should be interpreted in the context of private commercial administration. Our argument was based on the fact that in 1 Corinthians 4 Paul's apostolic framework consisted of a hierarchy with a κύριος in the superior position, and in 1 Corinthians 9 Paul's metaphor signified compulsory labour and his entitlement to a wage. Our argument was strengthened by an analysis of the commercial context of Roman Corinth. There we showed that Corinth was a thriving emporium during the early empire and home to a large population of private servile agents and administrators. Lastly, it was shown from his experience as an artisan and his use of commercial terminology that Paul was himself probably familiar with the commercial world of the Roman Empire.

With the private administrator in view, we then turned to Paul's metaphor in 1 Corinthians 4 and 9 in order to investigate how Paul utilised the *oikonomos* metaphor in his rhetorical strategy. In Chapter 6 we examined 1 Corinthians 1–4 initially to demonstrate that the church in Corinth was facing two major ecclesial and ethical shortcomings: the inappropriate adulation of apostles and the undue criticism of Paul's ministry. This led us to suggest that Paul utilised his *oikonomos* metaphor in 1 Cor 4.1–5 both to underscore the social and structural insignificance of apostles in relation to God/Christ, and to emphasise the authority of apostles and their immunity to the criticisms of the church. In addition to restoring his apostolic ethos to its proper place in Corinth, Paul sought to censure the Corinthians for passing judgment on him and his colleagues, since the church does not possess the authority either to convict or acquit apostles.

Finally, in Chapter 7 we examined Paul's metaphor in 1 Corinthians 9 where, in a discourse with both apologetic and deliberative functions, he portrayed himself as God's administrator in order to defend his apostolic right to receive and refuse a wage. We began by tracing Paul's argument from the beginning of 1 Corinthians 9 and critically assessed the two prevailing interpretive approaches to Paul's complex logic in verses 16–18. Rather than conclude that Paul preached voluntarily *with* the right to receive pay or involuntarily *without* such a right, we revisited what we observed in Chapter 4 about the monetary privileges of private administrators and concluded that Paul's metaphor was skilfully employed in order to demonstrate that he was a slave of Christ who preached involuntarily and yet was entitled to material support. Our impressions about the pattern of Paul's logic in 1 Cor 9.17 was even shown to find strong support from similar constructions used elsewhere in Paul's letters (Rom 14.8; 1 Cor 12.26; 2 Cor 1.6; 5.13). We argued further that Paul's commercial metaphor continues into 1 Cor 9.18, where Paul's preaching activity was portrayed as a financial 'deposit', and even into 9.19–23, where he described his ministry objective as 'gaining' converts and 'partnering' with the gospel. Quite significantly, however, we saw that the apostolic right which Paul incessantly defended for the first half of 1 Corinthians 9 was sacrificially forfeited for the benefit of the gospel, his converts, and his divine principal. We argued that, through plying a trade, Paul subjected his apostolic right and authority to his divine mandate of advancing the gospel in order that he might more definitively prove his faithfulness to the Lord and thereby secure more assuredly his eschatological reward.

By interpreting Paul's *oikonomos* metaphor in both 1 Corinthians 4 and 9 in this double-sided sense (social, legal, and structural degradation + authority, immunity, and privilege), this study has shown that

Paul's deployment of the image is far more versatile than NT scholars have previously shown it to be. Another case for the multi-faceted nature of this metaphor was proposed two decades ago by Dale Martin in his examination of 1 Corinthians 9. It was Martin's contention that Paul's metaphor connoted different things to different people. Martin argued that because *oikonomoi* were slaves, they were despised by the elite. But since they were empowered through patronal ties to their masters, they were esteemed and envied by those from a low socio-economic condition. In light of the alleged status inconsistency of *oikonomoi*, Martin argued that Paul's status-laden metaphor would have elicited disrepute from privileged believers, but honour from his lowly converts.

In this study, however, we are arguing for a significant revision of Martin's thesis. Having considered Paul's employment of the metaphor in both 1 Corinthians 4 *and* 9, it is our contention that Paul's metaphor is double-sided, but was employed to impart the same theological insights to, and elicit the same response from, the entire Corinthian church: Paul sought simultaneously to emphasise the servility *and* authority of apostles in order to eliminate partisanship and to defend himself against critics. For only if Paul in this situation were stressing the same concerns to, and seeking the same response from, all believers could they share the same mind and thoughts, and thus achieve complete unity (1.10).

Theological implications

This investigation has a number of implications for Paul's theology of apostolic authority. Because the metaphor analysed and the passages examined cannot address every aspect of Paul's authority, we shall, of course, not be able to exhaust the topic. Nevertheless, Paul's *oikonomos* metaphor has allowed us to analyse Paul's authority from a number of approaches, including how it is *constructed*, *asserted*, and *contested* in a single epistle. Moreover, because Paul's power relations are quite complex, it was important in this study not to over-simplify the concept, but instead to take into consideration several often-ignored hermeneutical factors. In this investigation we therefore sought to follow the recommendation of Andrew Clarke by exploring Paul's power rhetoric and power dealings 'within their wider context, including the ways in which Paul defined the limits of his power, the ways in which he undermined the power that was inherent in his own position, [and] how he responded to the power plays of others'.[1] Paul's use of the *oikonomos* metaphor in 1

[1] Clarke (2008: 106).

Corinthians has afforded us a fascinating insight into each of these areas and offers some helpful correctives to other recent construals.

It was important, in the first place, to show from 1 Corinthians 4 and 9 that Paul utilised the *oikonomos* metaphor to *construct* his apostolic authority. Paul's authority was shown in 1 Cor 4.1–5 to be structural and inherent in his position within the ecclesiastical hierarchy. It is quite telling, in fact, that in one of his longest sustained expositions of the nature of apostolic ministry (1 Corinthians 1–4), Paul indicates that he possesses a rank superior to that of his apostolic delegates, local church leaders, and the remaining believers in his faith communities. Additionally, Paul's authority was both derived from God and present in the gospel (divine mysteries), so that he believed he could legitimately speak and act on God's behalf. Moreover, Paul's commission afforded him certain apostolic rights, including the opportunity to be financially supported by those to whom he preached. His authority was therefore an ever-present and undeniable reality in his ministry.[2]

The imposition of Paul's authority, however, is tempered in 1 Corinthians by the context and manner in which it is exercised. As this study has shown, it is important to interpret Paul's power relations in Corinth while being cognisant of the power struggles present in the church and the numerous parties competing for prominence. By placing Paul's discourses in their socio-rhetorical context, we have demonstrated that Paul's power assertions in 1 Corinthians 4 and 9 were neither unprovoked nor unilateral. Rather, at the time the letter was written, Paul's authority (from his perspective anyway) was being strongly *contested* by status-conscious believers who objected to the style of his preaching, the content of his gospel, his manual labour, and his monetary policy. In fact, Paul portrayed himself as an administrator of God in both 1 Corinthians 4 and 9 precisely for the purpose of defending against and deflecting away such unwarranted scrutiny (ἀνακρίνω, 4.3; 9.3).

Paul's *oikonomos* metaphor also has significant implications for how we regard the limits and purpose of Paul's *assertion* of authority. As mentioned in Chapter 1, previous studies have identified in Paul's letters generally and in 1 Corinthians in particular various assertions of power in Paul's interaction with his churches. While this investigation has no intention of denying that Paul exercised power and authority in Corinth and elsewhere, it has sought to balance the scholarly portrayal of Paul

---

[2] *Contra* the non-hierarchical ecclesiastical structure proposed by Schüssler Fiorenza (1983: 205–41); Bartchy (1999); Bartchy (2003). For the diversity of Paul's hierarchically implicit metaphors, see Horrell (2001: 303).

as one who exercised authority manipulatively, selfishly, and unrelentingly. Indeed, this study has demonstrated that Paul portrayed himself as an authorised agent of God who, in certain circumstances, *refused* to exercise the authority inherent in his position. Although Paul possessed the right to receive financial aid from the Corinthians, to their surprise he chose not to assert that right, fearing that such an exercise of freedom might endanger the spiritual condition of the weak in Corinth. For when his authority became an obstacle to the spiritual good of others, Paul, well aware that he would answer to God according to the outcome of his administration (4.4–5; 9.16), considered it entirely appropriate for him to forgo exercising his authority so that the gospel, God, and the church might obtain greater gains.

Paul's exercise of authority, therefore, was not a precondition for his apostleship. Apostolic authority was afforded for the express purpose of obtaining converts and enabling them to reach maturity. As Paul programmatically states in later correspondence, the authority Christ entrusted to him was intended for building up rather than tearing down (εἰς οἰκοδομὴν καὶ οὐκ εἰς καθαίρεσιν, 2 Cor 10.8; 13.10). For that reason, when Paul's rights and authority in some way obstruct the power of the gospel and thus prohibit the expansion and maturation of the church, he subjects that authority to his greater apostolic mandate. As Schütz explains, '[T]he goal of this authority is not to subject others to the apostle, but to subject all, including the apostle, to the power which manifests itself in the gospel and will be manifest in the eschaton.'[3]

Given this purpose, the authority entrusted to Paul begins to resemble what Kathy Ehrensperger describes as 'transformative power'. As explained in Chapter 1, it was Ehrensperger's contention that Paul's apostolic authority was afforded him to empower the church toward maturation. While Paul provides no indication, as Ehrensperger supposes, that the apostolic hierarchy sought to render itself obsolete, Paul's apostolic authority had a distinctly constructive and empowering objective.[4]

---

[3] Schütz (1975: 286).

[4] This 'transformative', or even 'kyriadoularchic', approach to Christian leadership also goes some way toward explaining the hierarchy Paul constructs in the reversal of the Corinthian slogans in 3.21–3. If apostles are directly subordinate to Christ (4.1) and accountable to him alone (4.3–5), then how can they simultaneously 'belong' to the church (3.21–2)? It must have been Paul's policy that he and other apostles, in their effort to serve God faithfully, should labour to achieve both the salvation and maturation of the Corinthians to the extent that – practically speaking – they were at the service of the community. The inverted pyramid of 3.21–3 must therefore be regarded as an instance where Paul sought, as Clarke (2008: 101) remarks, 'to limit the perception of his status, whilst not removing it'.

When Paul's authority is recognised as having this transformative intention, his policy for asserting power seems quite benevolent. Of course many authority figures in ecclesiastical history have failed to understand the purpose for their power in just this way. For this reason modern interpreters of Paul are to some extent justified in their suspicions of the apostle's claims to and exercise of authority over others. But it is our hope that the insights gained through this study contribute to exonerating Paul of some of the charges raised against him by modern critics, while also providing a model of sensible church leadership for 21st-century practitioners.

BIBLIOGRAPHY

Aasgaard, Reidar (2004), *'My Beloved Brothers and Sisters!': Christian Siblingship in Paul* (JSNTSup 265; ECC; London: T&T Clark).

Abbott, F. F., and A. C. Johnson (1926), *Municipal Administration in the Roman Empire* (Princeton University Press).

Adams, Edward (2000), *Constructing the World: A Study in Paul's Cosmological Language* (SNTW; Edinburgh: T&T Clark).

Adeleye, Gabriel (1983), 'The Purpose of the *"Dokimasia"*', *GRBS* 24: 295–306.

Agnew, F. H. (1986), 'The Origin of the NT Apostle-Concept: A Review of Research', *JBL* 105: 75–96.

Aldrete, Gregory S. (1999), *Gestures and Acclamations in Ancient Rome* (Ancient Society and History; Baltimore: The Johns Hopkins University Press).

Allen, R. E. (1983), *The Attalid Kingdom: A Constitutional History* (Oxford: Clarendon Press).

Anderson, R. Dean (1999), *Ancient Rhetorical Theory and Paul* (rev. edn; CBET 18; Leuven: Peeters).

Andreau, Jean (1993), 'The Freedman' in *The Romans*, ed. Andrea Giardina (University of Chicago Press): 175–98.

(1999), *Banking and Business in the Roman World* (Key Themes in Ancient History; Cambridge University Press).

(2004), 'Les Esclaves "hommes d'affaires" et la gestion des ateliers et commerces' in *Mentalités et choix économiques des romains*, ed. Jean Andreau, Jérôme France, and Sylvie Pittia (Scripta Antiqua 7; Bordeaux: Ausonius): 111–26.

Aperghis, G. G. (2004), *The Seleukid Royal Economy: The Finances and Financial Administration of the Seleukid Empire* (Cambridge University Press).

Arzt-Grabner, Peter, Amfilochios Papathomas, Ruth Elisabeth Kritzer, and Franz Winter (2006), *1. Korinther* (Papyrologische Kommentare zum Neuen Testament; Göttingen: Vandenhoeck & Ruprecht).

(2011), 'Gott als verlässlicher Käufer: Einige papyrologische Anmerkungen und bibeltheologische Schlussfolgerungen zum Gottesbild der Paulusbriefe', *NTS* 57: 392–414.

Asboeck, Anton (1913), 'Das Staatswesen von Priene in hellenistischer Zeit' (Ph.D. Diss., University of Munich).

Aubert, Jean-Jacques (1993), 'Workshop Managers' in *The Inscribed Economy: Production and Distribution in the Roman Empire in the Light of instrumentum domesticum*, ed. W. V. Harris (JRASup 6; Ann Arbor: University of Michigan Press), 171–81.

(1994), *Business Managers in Ancient Rome: A Social and Economic Study of Institores, 200 BC – AD 250* (Columbia Studies in the Classical Tradition 21; Leiden: Brill).

(2000), 'The Fourth Factor: Managing Non-Agricultural Production in the Roman World' in *Economies Beyond Agriculture in the Classical World*, ed. D. J. Mattingly and John Salmon (Leicester-Nottingham Studies in Ancient Society 9; London: Routledge): 90–111.

(2004), 'De l'usage de l'écriture dans la gestion d'entreprise a l'époque romaine' in *Mentalités et choix économiques des romains*, ed. Jean Andreau, Jérôme France, and Sylvie Pittia (Scripta Antiqua 7; Bordeaux: Ausonius): 127–47.

(2009), 'Productive Investments in Agriculture: *instrumentum fundi* and *peculium* in the Later Roman Republic' in *Agricoltura e scambi nell'Italia tardo repubblicana*, ed. Jesper Carlsen and Elio Lo Cascio (Rome: Bari): 167–85.

Aune, David E. (1987), *The New Testament in its Literary Environment* (Library of Early Christianity; Louisville: WJK).

Bagnall, Roger S. (1976), *The Administration of the Ptolemaic Possessions Outside Egypt* (Columbia Studies in the Classical Tradition 4; Leiden: Brill).

(1993), 'Managing Estates in Roman Egypt: A Review Article', *BASP* 30: 127–35.

Baird, William (1990), '"One Against the Other": Intra-Church Conflict in 1 Corinthians' in *The Conversation Continues: Studies in Paul and John in Honor of J. Louis Martyn*, ed. Beverly R. Gaventa and Robert T. Fortna (Nashville: Abingdon Press): 116–36.

Balch, David L. (2004), 'Philodemus, "On Wealth" and "On Household Management": Naturally Wealthy Epicureans against Poor Cynics' in *Philodemus and the New Testament World*, ed. John T. Fitzgerald, Dirk Obbink, and Glen Holland (Leiden: Brill): 177–96.

Baldwin Bowsky, Martha W. (1989), 'Epigrams to an Elder Statesman and a Young Noble from Lato Pros Kamara (Crete)', *Hesperia* 58: 115–29.

Barclay, John M. G. (1987), 'Mirror-Reading a Polemical Letter: Galatians as a Test Case', *JSNT* 31: 73–93.

(1992), 'Thessalonica and Corinth: Social Contrasts in Pauline Christianity', *JSNT* 47: 49–74.

Barnett, Paul (1997), *The Second Epistle to the Corinthians* (NICNT; Grand Rapids: Eerdmans).

Barram, Michael (2011), 'Pauline Mission as Salvific Intentionality: Fostering a Missional Consciousness in 1 Corinthians 9.19–23 and 10.31–11.1' in *Paul as Missionary: Identity, Activity, Theology, and Practice*, ed. Trevor J. Burke and Brian S. Rosner (LNTS 420; London: T&T Clark): 234–46.

Barrett, C. K. (1963), 'Cephas and Corinth' in *Abraham unser Vater: Juden und Christen im Gespräch über die Bibel*, ed. Otto Betz (AGSU 5; Leiden: Brill): 1–12.

(1968), *A Commentary on the First Epistle to the Corinthians* (BNTC; London: A&C Black).

Bartchy, S. Scott (1999), 'Undermining Ancient Patriarchy: The Apostle Paul's Vision of a Society of Siblings', *BTB* 29: 68–78.

(2003), 'Who Should Be Called Father? Paul of Tarsus between the Jesus Tradition and Patria Potestas', *BTB* 33: 135–47.

Barton, Carlin A. (2001), *Roman Honor: The Fire in the Bones* (Berkeley: University of California Press).

Barton, Stephen C. (1996), '"All Things to All People": Paul and the Law in the Light of 1 Corinthians 9.19–23' in *Paul and the Mosaic Law: The Third Durham–Tübingen Research Symposium on Earliest Christianity and Judaism*, ed. James D. G. Dunn (WUNT 1/89; Tübingen: J.C.B. Mohr (Paul Siebeck)): 271–85.

Bash, Anthony (1997), *Ambassadors for Christ* (WUNT 2/92; Tübingen: J.C.B. Mohr (Paul Siebeck)).

Bassler, Jouette M. (1990), '1 Corinthians 4:1–5', *Interpretation* 44: 179–83.

Baur, F. C. (1873), 'The Two Epistles to the Corinthians' in *Paul: The Apostle of Jesus Christ, His Life and Work, His Epistles and His Doctrine*, vol. I (2nd edn; London: Williams and Norgate): 267–320.

Beare, Rhona (1978), 'Were Bailiffs Ever Free Born?', *CQ* 28: 398–401.

Beavis, Mary Ann (1992), 'Ancient Slavery as an Interpretive Context for the New Testament Servant Parables with Special Reference to the Unjust Steward (Luke 16:1–8)', *JBL* 111: 37–54.

Bell, Andrew J. E. (1997), 'Cicero and the Spectacle of Power', *JRS* 87: 1–22.

Best, Ernest (1986), 'Paul's Apostolic Authority?', *JSNT* 27: 3–25.

Betz, Hans Dieter (1994), 'Paul's Concept of Freedom in the Context of Hellenistic Discussions about the Possibilities of Human Freedom' in *Paulinische Studien* (Tübingen: J.C.B. Mohr (Paul Siebeck)): 110–25.

Billows, Richard A. (1990), *Antigonos the One-Eyed and the Creation of the Hellenistic State* (Hellenistic Culture and Society 4; Berkeley: University of California Press).

Bispham, Edward (2008), *From Asculum to Actium: The Municipalization of Italy from the Social War to Augustus* (Oxford Classical Monographs; Oxford University Press).

Bitner, Bradley J. (2010), 'Colonial and Ecclesial Construction in Roman Corinth: 1 Cor. 3:5–4:5 and Inscriptional Evidence' (paper presented at the Annual Meeting of the Society of Biblical Literature, Atlanta, GA, 22 November 2010).

Bobzein, Susanne (1998), *Determinism and Freedom in Stoic Philosophy* (Oxford: Clarendon Press).

Bock, Darrell L. (1996), *Luke 9:51–24:53* (BECNT; Grand Rapids: Baker).

Bockmuehl, Markus N. A. (1990), *Revelation and Mystery in Ancient Judaism and Pauline Christianity* (WUNT 2/36; Tübingen: J.C.B. Mohr (Paul Siebeck)).

(1997), *A Commentary on the Epistle to the Philippians* (BNTC; London: A&C Black).

Bodel, John P. (1983), *Roman Brick Stamps in the Kelsey Museum* (Kelsey Museum of Archaeology, Studies 6; Ann Arbor: University of Michigan Press).

Bonner, Campbell (1950), 'A Reminiscence of Paul on a Coin Amulet', *HTR* 43: 165–8.

Bornkamm, Günther (1966), 'The Missionary Stance of Paul in 1 Corinthians 9 and in Acts' in *Studies in Luke-Acts: Essays Presented in Honor of Paul Schubert*, ed. Leander E. Keck and J. Louis Martyn (Nashville: Abingdon Press): 194–207.

Bowersock, G. W. (1969), *Greek Sophists in the Roman Empire* (Oxford: Clarendon Press).

Bowman, Alan K. (1996), 'Provincial Administration and Taxation' in *The Cambridge Ancient History: The Augustan Empire, 43 BC–AD 69*, vol. X, ed. Alan K. Bowman, Edward Champlin, and Andrew Lintott (2nd edn; Cambridge University Press): 344–70.

Bradley, K. R. (1987), *Slaves and Masters in the Roman Empire: A Study in Social Control* (Oxford University Press).

(1994), *Slavery and Society at Rome* (Key Themes in Ancient History; Cambridge University Press).

Briones, David (2011), 'Paul's Financial Policy: A Socio-Theological Approach' (Ph.D. Diss., University of Durham).

Broneer, Oscar (1930), *Terracotta Lamps* (Corinth 4.2; Cambridge, MA: Harvard University Press).

Brookins, Tim (2011), 'The Wise Corinthians: Their Stoic Education and Outlook', *JTS* 62: 51–76.

Brown, Alexandra R. (1995), *The Cross and Human Transformation: Paul's Apocalyptic Word in 1 Corinthians* (Minneapolis: Fortress Press).

Brown, Michael Joseph (2001), 'Paul's Use of δοῦλος Χριστοῦ Ἰησοῦ in Romans 1:1', *JBL* 120: 723–37.

Brown, Raymond E. (1968), *The Semitic Background of the Term 'Mystery' in the New Testament* (Facet Books/Biblical Series 21; Philadelphia: Fortress Press).

Bruce, F. F. (1980), *1 and 2 Corinthians* (New Century Bible; London: Oliphants).

Brunt, P. A. (1975), 'The Administrators of Roman Egypt', *JRS* 65: 124–47.

Buckland, W. W. (1908), *The Roman Law of Slavery: The Condition of the Slave in Private Law from Augustus to Justinian* (Cambridge University Press).

Bünker, Michael (1984), *Briefformular und rhetorische Disposition im 1. Korintherbrief* (Göttinger theologische Arbeiten 28; Göttingen: Vandenhoeck & Ruprecht).

Burford, Alison (1969), *The Greek Temple Builders at Epidauros: A Social and Economic Study of Building in the Asklepian Sanctuary, during the Fourth and Early Third Centuries BC* (Liverpool University Press).

Bürge, Alfons (1993), 'Salarium und ähnliche Leistungsentgelte beim mandatum' in *Mandatum und Verwandtes: Beiträge zum römischen und modernen Recht*, ed. Dieter Nörr and Shigeo Nishimura (Berlin: Broschiert): 319–38.

Burke, Trevor J. (2003), 'Paul's Role as "Father" to His Corinthian "Children" in Socio-Historical Context (1 Corinthians 4:14–21)' in *Paul and the Corinthians: Studies on a Community in Conflict. Essays in Honour of Margaret Thrall*, ed. Trevor J. Burke and J. K. Elliott (NovTSup 109; Leiden: Brill): 95–113.

Butarbutar, Robinson (2007), *Paul and Conflict Resolution: An Exegetical Study of Paul's Apostolic Paradigm in 1 Corinthians 9* (Paternoster Biblical Monographs; Milton Keynes: Paternoster).

Byron, John (2003), *Slavery Metaphors in Early Judaism and Pauline Christianity: A Traditio-Historical and Exegetical Examination* (WUNT 2/162; Tübingen: J.C.B. Mohr (Paul Siebeck)).

Cadbury, Henry J. (1931), 'Erastus of Corinth', *JBL* 50: 42–58.

Calvin, John (1960), *The First Epistle of Paul the Apostle to the Corinthians* (Edinburgh: Oliver and Boyd).

Campenhausen, Hans von (1969), *Ecclesiastical Authority and Spiritual Power in the Church of the First Three Centuries* (Stanford University Press).

Caragounis, Chrys C. (1974), 'ΟΨΩΝΙΟΝ: A Reconsideration of Its Meaning', *NovT* 16: 35–57.

Carlsen, Jesper (1992), '*Dispensatores* in Roman North Africa' in *L'Africa romana: Atti del IX convegno di studio*, ed. Attilio Mastino (Pubblicazioni del Dipartimento di Storia dell'Università di Sassari 20; Nuoro: Gallizzi): 97–104.

(1993), 'The *Vilica* and Roman Estate Management' in *De Agricultura: In Memoriam Pieter Willem de Neeve (1945–1990)*, ed. H. Sancisi-Weerdenburg, R. J. Van Der Spek, and H. C. Teitler (Dutch Monographs on Ancient History and Archaeology 10; Amsterdam: Gieben): 197–205.

(1995), *Vilici and Roman Estate Managers until AD 284* (ARIDSup 24; Rome: L'Erma di Bretschneider).

(2000), 'Subvilicus: Subagent or Assistant Bailiff?', *ZPE* 132: 312–16.

(2002), 'Estate Managers in Ancient Greek Agriculture' in *Ancient History Matters: Studies Presented to Jens Erik Skydsgaard on His Seventieth Birthday*, ed. Karen Ascani, Vincent Gabrielsen, Kristen Krist, and Anders Holm Rasmnssen (ARIDSup 30; Rome: L'Erma di Bretschneider): 117–26.

Castelli, Elizabeth A. (1991), *Imitating Paul: A Discourse of Power* (Louisville: WJK).

Chadwick, H. (1955), '"All Things to All Men"', *NTS* 1: 261–75.

Chance, J. Bradley (1982), 'Paul's Apology to the Corinthians', *PRSt* 9: 144–55.

Chester, Stephen J. (2003), *Conversion at Corinth: Perspectives on Conversion in Paul's Theology and the Corinthian Church* (SNTW; Edinburgh: T&T Clark).

Cheung, Alex T. (1999), *Idol Food in Corinth: Jewish Background and Pauline Legacy* (JSNTSup 176; Sheffield Academic Press).

Chow, John K. (1992), *Patronage and Power: A Study of Social Networks in Corinth* (JSNTSup 75; Sheffield Academic Press).

Ciampa, Roy E., and Brian S. Rosner (2006), 'The Structure and Argument of 1 Corinthians: A Biblical/Jewish Approach', *NTS* 52: 205–18.

(2010), *The First Letter to the Corinthians* (PNTC; Grand Rapids: Eerdmans).

Clarke, Andrew D. (1993), *Secular and Christian Leadership in Corinth: A Socio-Historical and Exegetical Study of 1 Corinthians 1–6* (AGJU 18; Leiden: Brill).

(1998), '"Be Imitators of Me": Paul's Model of Leadership', *TynBul* 49: 329–60.

(1999), *Serve the Community of the Church: Christians as Leaders and Ministers* (First-Century Christians in the Graeco-Roman World; Grand Rapids: Eerdmans).

(2008), *A Pauline Theology of Church Leadership* (LNTS 362; London: T&T Clark).

Clarysse, W. (1976), 'Harmachis, Agent of the Oikonomos: An Archive from the Time of Philopator', *Ancient Society* 7: 185–207.

Collins, John N. (1990), *Diakonia: Re-Interpreting the Ancient Sources* (Oxford University Press).

Collins, Raymond F. (1996), '1 Corinthians as a Hellenistic Letter' in *The Corinthian Correspondence*, ed. Riemund Bieringer (BETL; Leuven: Peeters): 39–61.

(1999), *First Corinthians* (Sacra Pagina 7; Collegeville: Liturgical Press).

Combes, I. A. H. (1998), *The Metaphor of Slavery in the Writings of the Early Church from the New Testament to the Beginning of the Fifth Century* (JSNTSup 156; Sheffield Academic Press).

Conzelmann, Hans (1975), *1 Corinthians: A Commentary on the First Epistle to the Corinthians* (Hermeneia; Minneapolis: Fortress Press).

Copan, Victor (2007), *Saint Paul as Spiritual Director: An Analysis of the Imitation of Paul with Implications and Applications to the Practice of Spiritual Direction* (Milton Keynes: Paternoster).

Coppins, Wayne (2009), *The Interpretation of Freedom in the Letters of Paul: With Special Reference to the 'German' Tradition* (WUNT 2/261; Tübingen: J.C.B. Mohr (Paul Siebeck)).

Corsten, Thomas (2005), 'Estates in Roman Asia Minor: The Case of Kibyratis' in *Patterns in the Economy of Roman Asia Minor*, ed. Stephen Mitchell and Constantina Katsari (Swansea: Classical Press of Wales): 1–51.

(2006), 'The Role and Status of the Indigenous Population in Bithynia' in *Rome and the Black Sea Region: Domination, Romanisation, Resistance*, ed. Tønnes Bekker-Nielsen (Black Sea Studies 5; Aarhus University Press): 85–92.

Cranfield, C. E. B. (1979), *A Critical and Exegetical Commentary on the Epistle to the Romans, Volume II (IX–XVI)* (ICC; Edinburgh: T&T Clark).

Crawford, Dorothy J. (1976), 'Imperial Estates' in *Studies in Roman Property*, ed. M. I. Finley (Cambridge University Press): 35–70.

(1978), 'The Good Official of Ptolemaic Egypt' in *Das Ptolemäische Ägypten*, ed. Herwig Maehler and Volker Michael Strocka (Mainz am Rhein: Philipp von Zabern): 195–202.

Crook, Zeba (2004), *Reconceptualising Conversion: Patronage, Loyalty, and Conversion in the Religions of the Ancient Mediterranean* (BZNW 130; Berlin: Walter de Gruyter).

Cullmann, Oscar (1951), *Christ and Time: The Primitive Christian Conception of Time and History* (London: SCM Press).

Curchin, Leonard A. (1990), *The Local Magistrates of Roman Spain* (Phoenix Supplementary Series 28; University of Toronto Press).

D'Arms, John H. (1981), *Commerce and Social Standing in Ancient Rome* (Cambridge, MA: Harvard University Press).

Dahl, Nils A. (1967), 'Paul and the Church at Corinth According to 1 Corinthians 1:10–4:21' in *Christian History and Interpretation: Studies Presented to John Knox*, ed. William R. Farmer, C. F. D. Moule, and R. R. Niebuhr (Cambridge University Press): 313–35.

(1977a), 'Paul and Possessions' in *Studies in Paul: Theology for the Early Christian Mission* (Minneapolis: Augsburg Press): 22–39.

(1977b), 'Paul and the Church at Corinth' in *Studies in Paul: Theology for the Early Christian Mission* (Minneapolis: Augsburg Press): 40–61.

Danker, Frederick W. (1982), *Benefactor: Epigraphic Study of a Graeco-Roman and New Testament Semantic Field* (St Louis: Clayton).

Daube, David (1947), 'κερδαίνω as a Missionary Term', *HTR* 40: 109–20.

(1985), 'Neglected Nuances of Exposition in Luke–Acts', *ANRW* II 25.3: 2329–56.

Dautzenberg, Gerhard (1969), 'Der Verzicht auf das apostolische Unterhaltsrecht: Eine exegetische Untersuchung zu 1 Kor 9', *Biblica* 50: 212–32.

Davies, John Kenyon (2003), 'Economy: Hellenistic' in *OCD* (3rd rev. edn).

de Neeve, P. W. (1984), *Colonus: Private Farm-Tenancy in Roman Italy during the Republic and the Early Principate* (Amsterdam: Gieben).

——— (1990), 'A Roman Landowner and His Estates: Pliny the Younger', *Athenaeum* 68: 363–403.

de Ste Croix, G. E. M. (1975), 'Political Pay Outside Athens', *CQ* 25: 48–52.

——— (1981), *The Class Struggle in the Ancient Greek World: From the Archaic Age to the Arab Conquests* (London: Duckworth).

de Vos, Craig Steven (1999), *Church and Community Conflicts: The Relationships of the Thessalonian, Corinthian, and Philippian Churches with Their Wider Civic Communities* (SBLDS 168; Atlanta: Scholars Press).

Delgado, Álvaro Pereira (2010), *De apóstol a esclavo: El exemplum de Pablo en 1 Corintios 9* (Analecta Biblica 182; Rome: Gregorian & Biblical Press).

deSilva, David A. (2000), *Honor, Patronage, Kinship and Purity: Unlocking New Testament Culture* (Downers Grove: InterVarsity Press).

Dignas, Beate (2002), *Economy of the Sacred in Hellenistic and Roman Asia Minor* (Oxford Classical Monographs; Oxford University Press).

Dmitriev, Sviatoslav (2005), *City Government in Hellenistic and Roman Asia Minor* (Oxford University Press).

Dodd, Brian J. (1999), *Paul's Paradigmatic 'I': Personal Example as Literary Strategy* (JSNTSup 177; Sheffield Academic Press).

Dodd, C. H. (1935), *The Parables of the Kingdom* (London: Nisbet & Co. Ltd).

Donahoe, Kate C. (2008), 'From Self-Praise to Self-Boasting: Paul's Unmasking of the Conflicting Rhetorico-Linguistic Phenomena in 1 Corinthians' (Ph.D. Diss., University of St Andrews).

Donfried, Karl P., and Johannes Beutler, eds. (2000), *The Thessalonians Debate: Methodological Discord or Methodological Synthesis?* (Grand Rapids: Eerdmans).

Duff, A. M. (1928), *Freedmen in the Early Roman Empire* (Oxford University Press).

Dungan, David L. (1971), *The Sayings of Jesus in the Churches of Paul: The Use of the Synoptic Tradition in the Regulation of Early Church Life* (Oxford: Blackwell).

Dunn, James D. G. (1998), *The Theology of Paul the Apostle* (Grand Rapids: Eerdmans).

——— (2004), 'Reconstructions of Corinthian Christianity and the Interpretation of 1 Corinthians' in *Christianity at Corinth: The Quest for the Pauline Church*, ed. Edward Adams and David G. Horrell (Louisville: WJK): 295–310.

——— (2009), *Beginning from Jerusalem* (Christianity in the Making 2; Grand Rapids: Eerdmans).

Dutch, Robert S. (2005), *The Educated Elite in 1 Corinthians: Education and Community Conflict in Graeco-Roman Context* (JSNTSup 271; London: T&T Clark).

Edgar, C. C., ed. (1931), *Zenon Papyri in the University of Michigan Collection* (University of Michigan Studies, Humanistic Series; Ann Arbor: University of Michigan Press).

Edwards, Thomas C. (1885), *A Commentary on the First Epistle to the Corinthians* (London: Hodder and Stoughton).

Ehrensperger, Kathy (2007), *Paul and the Dynamics of Power: Communication and Interaction in the Early Christ-Movement* (LNTS 325; London: T&T Clark).

Ehrhardt, Arnold (1953), *The Apostolic Succession in the First Two Centuries of the Church* (London: Lutterworth Press).

Ellicott, Charles J. (1887), *St Paul's First Epistle to the Corinthians: With a Critical and Grammatical Commentary* (London: Longmans).

Ellington, Dustin W. (2011), 'Imitating Paul's Relationship to the Gospel: 1 Corinthians 8.1–11.1', *JSNT* 33: 303–15.

Engels, Donald (1990), *Roman Corinth: An Alternative Model for the Classical City* (University of Chicago Press).

Erdkamp, Paul (2005), *The Grain Market in the Roman Empire: A Social, Political and Economic Study* (Cambridge University Press).

Errington, R. M. (1990), *A History of Macedonia* (Hellenistic Culture and Society 5; Berkeley: University of California Press).

Esler, Philip F. (2000), 'Models in New Testament Interpretation: A Reply to David Horrell', *JSNT* 78: 107–13.

Evans, Craig A. (1984), 'How are the Apostles Judged? A Note on 1 Corinthians 3:10–15', *JETS* 27: 149–50.

Falivene, Maria Rosaria (1991), 'Government, Management, Literacy: Aspects of Ptolemaic Administration in the Early Hellenistic Period', *Ancient Society* 22: 203–27.

(2009), 'Geography and Administration in Egypt (332 BCE–642 CE)' in *The Oxford Handbook of Papyrology*, ed. Roger S. Bagnall (Oxford University Press): 521–40.

Fascher, Erich (1975), *Der erste Brief des Paulus an die Korinther* (THKNT 7/1; Berlin: Evangelische Verlagsanstalt).

Fee, Gordon D. (1987), *The First Epistle to the Corinthians* (NICNT; Grand Rapids: Eerdmans).

(1995), *Paul's Letter to the Philippians* (NICNT; Grand Rapids: Eerdmans).

Finley, M. I. (1973), *The Ancient Economy* (Berkeley: University of California Press).

(1980), *Ancient Slavery and Modern Ideology* (London: Chatto and Windus).

(1983), *Politics in the Ancient World* (The Wiles Lectures; Cambridge University Press).

Finney, Mark T. (2010), 'Honor, Rhetoric, and Factionalism in the Ancient World: 1 Corinthians 1–4 in its Social Context', *BTB* 40: 27–36.

Fiore, Benjamin (1985), '"Covert Allusion" in 1 Corinthians 1–4', *CBQ* 47: 85–102.

Fitzgerald, J. T. (1988), *Cracks in an Earthen Vessel: An Examination of the Catalogues of Hardships in the Corinthian Correspondence* (SBLDS 99; Atlanta: Scholars Press).

Fitzgerald, W. (2000), *Slavery and the Roman Literary Imagination* (Roman Literature and Its Contexts; Cambridge University Press).

Fitzmyer, Joseph A. (2008), *First Corinthians: A New Translation with Introduction and Commentary* (AYB 32; New Haven: Yale University Press).

Forbes, C. (1986), 'Comparison, Self-Praise and Irony: Paul's Boasting and the Conventions of Hellenistic Rhetoric', *NTS* 32: 1–30.

Forbes, H., and Lin Foxhall (1995), 'Ethnoarchaeology and Storage in the Ancient Mediterranean: Beyond Risk and Survival' in *Food in Antiquity*, ed. John Wilkins, David Harvey, and Mike Dobson (University of Exeter Press): 69–86.

Fotopoulos, John (2003), *Food Offered to Idols in Roman Corinth: A Social-Rhetorical Reconsideration of 1 Corinthians 8:1–11:1* (WUNT 2/151; Tübingen: J.C.B. Mohr (Paul Siebeck)).

Foxhall, Lin (1990), 'The Dependent Tenant: Land Leasing and Labour in Italy and Greece', *JRS* 80: 97–114.

Fraser, P. M. (1972), 'Notes on Two Rhodian Institutions', *Annals of the British School at Athens* 67: 113–24.

Frayn, Joan M. (1993), *Markets and Fairs in Roman Italy: Their Social and Economic Importance from the Second Century BC to the Third Century AD* (Oxford: Clarendon Press).

Freese, J. H. (1926), *Aristotle: The Art of Rhetoric* (LCL 193; London: Heinemann).

Frey, Jörg (2004), 'Apostelbegriff, Apostelamt und Apostolizität: Neutestamentliche Perspektiven zur Frage nach der "Apostolizität der Kirche"' in *Das kirchliche Amt in apostolischer Nachfolge. I, Grundlagen und Grundfragen*, ed. Theodor Schneider and Gunther Wenz (Dialog der Kirchen 12/1; Freiburg im Breisgau; Göttingen: Herder; Vandenhoeck & Ruprecht): 91–188.

Frier, Bruce W. (1980), *Landlords and Tenants in Imperial Rome* (Princeton University Press).

Friesen, Steven J. (2010), 'The Wrong Erastus' in *Corinth in Context: Comparative Studies on Religion and Society*, ed. Steven J. Friesen, Daniel N. Schowalter, and James C. Walters (NovTSup 134; Leiden: Brill): 231–56.

Fröhlich, Pierre (2004), *Les Cités grecques et le contrôle des magistrats (IVe–Ier siècle avant J.-C.)* (Hautes études du monde gréco-romain 33; Geneva: Droz).

Furnish, Victor P. (1961), '"Fellow Workers in God's Service"', *JBL* 80: 364–70.

    (1999), *The Theology of the First Letter to the Corinthians* (New Testament Theology; Cambridge University Press).

Galloway, Lincoln E. (2004), *Freedom in the Gospel: Paul's Exemplum in 1 Cor 9 in Conversation with the Discourses of Epictetus and Philo* (CBET 38; Leuven: Peeters).

Gardner, Paul Douglas (1994), *The Gifts of God and the Authentication of a Christian: An Exegetical Study of 1 Corinthians 8–11:1* (Lanham: University Press of America).

Garland, David E. (2003), *1 Corinthians* (BECNT; Grand Rapids: Baker).

Garnsey, Peter (1970), *Social Status and Legal Privilege in the Roman Empire* (Oxford: Clarendon Press).

    (1981), 'Independent Freedmen and the Economy of Roman Italy under the Principate', *Klio* 63: 359–71.

    (1982), 'Slaves in "Business"', *Opus* 1: 105–7.

    (1996), *Ideas of Slavery from Aristotle to Augustine* (Cambridge University Press).

    (1997), 'Sons, Slaves – and Christians' in *The Roman Family in Italy: Status, Sentiment, Space*, ed. Beryl Rawson and Paul Weaver (Oxford: Clarendon Press): 101–21.

Garnsey, Peter, and Richard P. Saller (1987), *The Roman Empire: Economy, Society and Culture* (Berkeley: University of California Press).

Gauthier, Philippe (1989), *Nouvelles Inscriptions de Sardes II* (Hautes études du monde gréco-romain 15; Geneva: Droz).

Gaventa, Beverly R. (2007), *Our Mother Saint Paul* (Louisville: WJK).

Gerber, Christine (2005), *Paulus und seine 'Kinder': Studien zur Beziehungsmetaphorik der paulinischen Briefe* (BZNW 136; Berlin: Walter de Gruyter).

Gill, David W. J. (1989), 'Erastus the Aedile', *TynBul* 40: 293–301.

Glad, Clarence E. (1995), *Paul and Philodemus: Adaptability in Epicurean and Early Christian Psychagogy* (NovTSup 81; Leiden: Brill).

Gladd, Benjamin L. (2008), *Revealing the Mysterion: The Use of Mystery in Daniel and Second Temple Judaism with Its Bearings on First Corinthians* (BZNW 160; Berlin: Walter de Gruyter).

Glancy, Jennifer A. (2002), *Slavery in Early Christianity* (Oxford University Press).

(2004), 'Boasting of Beatings (2 Corinthians 11:23–25)', *JBL* 123: 99–135.

Gleason, Maud W. (1995), *Making Men: Sophists and Self-Presentation in Ancient Rome* (Princeton University Press).

Gonzalez, Julian, and Michael H. Crawford (1986), 'The Lex Irnitana: A New Copy of the Flavian Municipal Law', *JRS* 76: 147–243.

Goodrich, John K. (2010a), 'Erastus, *Quaestor* of Corinth: The Administrative Rank of ὁ οἰκονόμος τῆς πόλεως (Rom 16.23) in an Achaean Colony', *NTS* 56: 90–115.

(2010b), 'Guardians, not Taskmasters: The Cultural Resonances of Paul's Metaphor in Galatians 4.1–2', *JSNT* 32: 251–84.

(2011), 'Erastus of Corinth (Rom 16.23): Responding to Recent Proposals on His Rank, Status, and Faith', *NTS* 57: 583–93.

(forthcoming), 'Debt Remission and the Parable of the Unjust Steward (Luke 16:1–13)', *JBL*.

Gorman, Michael J. (2001), *Cruciformity: Paul's Narrative Spirituality of the Cross* (Grand Rapids: Eerdmans).

Goulder, Michael D. (2001), *Paul and the Competing Mission in Corinth* (Peabody, MA: Hendrickson).

Green, Joel B. (1997), *The Gospel of Luke* (NICNT; Grand Rapids: Eerdmans).

Gregory, Timothy E. (2010), 'Religion and Society in the Roman Eastern Corinthia' in *Corinth in Context: Comparative Studies on Religion and Society*, ed. Steven J. Friesen, Daniel N. Schowalter, and James C. Walters (NovTSup 134; Leiden: Brill): 433–76.

Grosheide, F. W. (1953), *The First Epistle to the Corinthians* (NICNT; Grand Rapids: Eerdmans).

Gupta, Nijay K. (2009), 'Towards a Set of Principles for Identifying and Interpreting Metaphors in Paul: Romans 5:2 (Προσαγωγή) as a Test Case', *ResQ* 51: 169–81.

Hafemann, Scott J. (1990), *Suffering and Ministry in the Spirit: Paul's Defence of His Ministry in 2 Corinthians 2:14–3:3* (Paternoster Biblical and Theological Monographs; Carlisle: Paternoster).

Hall, Barbara (1990), '"All Things to All People": A Study of 1 Corinthians 9.19–23' in *The Conversation Continues: Studies in Paul and John in Honor of J. Louis Martyn*, ed. Beverly R. Gaventa and Robert T. Fortna (Nashville: Abingdon Press): 137–57.

Hall, David R. (1994), 'A Disguise for the Wise: μετασχηματισμός in 1 Corinthians 4.6', *NTS* 40: 143–9.

——— (2003), *The Unity of the Corinthian Correspondence* (JSNTSup 251; London: T&T Clark).

Hamza, Gábor (1977), 'Einige Fragen der Zulässigkeit der direkten Stellvertretung in den Papyri (Das Verhältnis zwischen Vollmacht und Auftrag im Recht der Papyri Ägyptens als romischer Provinz)', *Annales Universitatis Scientiarum Budapestinensis de Rolando Eötvös Nominatae, Sectio Iuridica* 19: 57–68.

Hansen, Esther V. (1947), *The Attalids of Pergamon* (Ithaca: Cornell University Press).

Hansen, Mogens Herman (1974), *The Sovereignty of the People's Court in Athens in the Fourth Century BC and the Public Action against Unconstitutional Proposals* (Odense University Classical Studies 4; Odense University Press).

——— (1975), *Eisangelia: The Sovereignty of the People's Court in Athens in the Fourth Century BC and the Impeachment of Generals and Politicians* (Odense University Classical Studies 6; Odense University Press).

——— (1979), 'Misthos for Magistrates in Classical Athens', *Symbolae Osloenses* 54: 5–22.

——— (1990), 'The Political Powers of the People's Court in Fourth-Century Athens' in *The Greek City: From Homer to Alexander*, ed. Oswyn Murray and Simon Price (Oxford: Clarendon Press): 215–43.

——— (1995), 'The "Autonomous City-State", Ancient Fact or Modern Fiction?' in *Studies in the Ancient Greek Polis*, ed. Mogens Herman Hansen and Kurt A. Raaflaub (Historia Einzelschriften 95; Stuttgart: Franz Steiner): 21–43.

——— (1999), *The Athenian Democracy in the Age of Demosthenes: Structure, Principles, and Ideology* (Norman: University of Oklahoma Press).

Harnisch, Wolfgang (2007), 'Der paulinische Lohn (I Kor 9,1–23)', *ZTK* 104: 25–43.

Harrill, J. Albert (1992), 'Review: Dale B. Martin, *Slavery as Salvation*', *Journal of Religion* 72: 426–7.

——— (1995), *The Manumission of Slaves in Early Christianity* (HUT 32; Tübingen: J.C.B. Mohr (Paul Siebeck)).

——— (2006), 'Subordinate to Another: Elite Slaves in the Agricultural Handbooks and the Household Codes' in *Slaves in the New Testament: Literary, Social, and Moral Dimensions* (Minneapolis: Fortress Press): 85–117.

Harris, Murray J. (1999), *Slave of Christ: A New Testament Metaphor for Total Devotion to Christ* (NSBT 8; Downers Grove: InterVarsity Press).

——— (2005), *The Second Epistle to the Corinthians: A Commentary on the Greek Text* (NIGTC; Grand Rapids: Eerdmans).

Harris, W. V. (1980), 'Roman Terracotta Lamps: The Organization of an Industry', *JRS* 70: 126–45.

——— (2000), 'Trade' in *The Cambridge Ancient History: The High Empire, AD 70–192*, vol. XI, ed. Alan K. Bowman, Peter Garnsey, and Dominic Rathbone (2nd edn; Cambridge University Press): 710–40.

Harrison, A. R. W. (1971), *The Law of Athens*, vol. II (Oxford: Clarendon Press).

Harvey, A. E. (1980), 'The Use of Mystery Language in the Bible', *JTS* 31: 320–36.

Hatzopoulos, M. B. (1996a), *Macedonian Institutions under the Kings: A Historical and Epigraphic Study* (Meletemata 22.1; Athens: Research Centre for Greek and Roman Antiquity/National Hellenic Research Foundation).

(1996b), *Macedonian Institutions under the Kings: Epigraphic Appendix* (Meletemata 22.2; Athens: Research Centre for Greek and Roman Antiquity/National Hellenic Research Foundation).

Hays, Richard B. (1997), *First Corinthians* (Interpretation; Louisville: John Knox Press).

(1999), 'Wisdom According to Paul' in *Where Shall Wisdom Be Found?: Wisdom in the Bible, the Church and the Contemporary World*, ed. Stephen C. Barton (Edinburgh: T&T Clark): 111–23.

Helen, Tapio (1975), *Organization of Roman Brick Production in the First and Second Centuries AD: An Interpretation of Roman Brick Stamps* (Annales Academiae Scientiarum Fennicae, Dissertationes Humanarum Litterarum 5; Helsinki: Suomalainen Tiedeakatemia).

Hellerman, Joseph H. (2005), *Reconstructing Honor in Roman Philippi: Carmen Christi as Cursus Pudorum* (SNTSMS 132; Cambridge University Press).

Hengel, Martin (1991), *The Pre-Christian Paul* (London: SCM Press).

Henry, Alan S. (1982), 'Polis/Acropolis, Paymasters and the Ten Talent Fund', *Chiron* 12: 91–118.

(1984), 'Athenian Financial Officials after 303 BC', *Chiron* 14: 49–91.

(1989), 'Provisions for the Payment of Athenian Decrees: A Study in Formulaic Language', *ZPE* 78: 247–93.

Hentschel, Anni (2007), *Diakonia im Neuen Testament: Studien zur Semantik unter besonderer Berücksichtigung der Rolle von Grauen* (WUNT 2/226; Tübingen: J.C.B. Mohr (Paul Siebeck)).

Héring, Jean (1962), *The First Epistle of Saint Paul to the Corinthians* (London: Epworth).

Hezser, Catherine (2005), *Jewish Slavery in Antiquity* (Oxford University Press).

Hirt, Alfred Michael (2010), *Imperial Mines and Quarries in the Roman World: Organizational Aspects 27 BC–AD 235* (Oxford Classical Monographs; Oxford University Press).

Hock, Ronald F. (1978), 'Paul's Tentmaking and the Problem of His Social Class', *JBL* 97: 555–64.

(1979), 'The Workshop as a Social Setting for Paul's Missionary Preaching', *CBQ* 41: 438–50.

(1980), *The Social Context of Paul's Ministry: Tentmaking and Apostleship* (Philadelphia: Fortress Press).

(2008), 'The Problem of Paul's Social Class: Further Reflections' in *Paul's World*, ed. Stanley E. Porter (Pauline Studies 4; Leiden: Brill): 7–18.

Hodge, Charles (1862), *An Exposition of the First Epistle to the Corinthians* (New York: Robert Carter & Brothers).

Hollander, Harm W. (1994), 'The Testing by Fire of the Builders' Works: 1 Corinthians 3.10–15', *NTS* 40: 89–104.

Holmberg, Bengt (1980), *Paul and Power: The Structure of Authority in the Primitive Church as Reflected in the Pauline Epistles* (Philadelphia: Fortress Press).

(1990), *Sociology and the New Testament: An Appraisal* (Minneapolis: Fortress Press).

(2004), 'The Methods of Historical Reconstruction in the Scholarly "Recovery" of Corinthian Christianity' in *Christianity at Corinth: The Quest for the Pauline Church*, ed. Edward Adams and David G. Horrell (Louisville: WJK): 255–71.

Hooker, Morna D. (1963), '"Beyond the Things which are Written": An Examination of 1 Cor. IV.6', *NTS* 10: 127–32.

(1996), 'A Partner in the Gospel: Paul's Understanding of His Ministry' in *Theology and Ethics in Paul and His Interpreters: Essays in Honor of Victor Paul Furnish*, ed. Eugene H. Lovering and Jerry L. Sumney (Nashville: Abingdon Press): 83–100.

Horrell, David G. (1996), *The Social Ethos of the Corinthian Correspondence: Interests and Ideology from 1 Corinthians to 1 Clement* (SNTW; Edinburgh: T&T Clark).

(1997a), 'Leadership Patterns and the Development of Ideology in Early Christianity', *Sociology of Religion* 58: 323–41.

(1997b), '"The Lord commanded... but I have not used...": Exegetical and Hermeneutical Reflections on 1 Cor 9.14–15', *NTS* 43: 587–603.

(1997c), 'Theological Principle or Christological Praxis? Pauline Ethics in 1 Corinthians 8.1–11.1', *JSNT* 67: 83–114.

(2000), 'Models and Methods in Social-Scientific Interpretation: A Response to Philip Esler', *JSNT* 78: 83–105.

(2001), 'From ἀδελφοί to οἶκος θεοῦ: Social Transformation in Pauline Christianity', *JBL* 120: 293–311.

(2009), 'Whither Social-Scientific Approaches to New Testament Interpretation: Reflections on Contested Methodologies and the Future' in *After the First Urban Christians: The Socio-Historical Study of Pauline Christianity Twenty-Five Years Later*, ed. Todd Still and David G. Horrell (London: T&T Clark): 6–20.

Horsley, Richard A. (1978), 'Consciousness and Freedom among the Corinthians: 1 Corinthians 8–10', *CBQ* 40: 574–89.

(1998a), *1 Corinthians* (ANTC; Nashville: Abingdon Press).

(1998b), 'The Slave Systems of Classical Antiquity and Their Reluctant Recognition by Modern Scholars' in *Slavery in Text and Interpretation*, ed. Allen Dwight Callahan, Richard A. Horsley, Abraham Smith, and David Jobling (Semeia 83/84; Atlanta: Society of Biblical Literature): 19–66.

(2005), 'Paul's Assembly in Corinth: An Alternative Society' in *Urban Religion in Roman Corinth: Interdisciplinary Approaches*, ed. Daniel N. Schowalter and Steven J. Friesen (HTS 53; Cambridge, MA: Harvard University Press): 371–95.

Hubbard, Moyer (1998), 'Was Paul out of His Mind? Re-Reading 2 Corinthians 5.13', *JSNT* 70: 39–64.

Hurd, John C. (1965), *The Origin of 1 Corinthians* (London: SPCK).

Ierodiakonou, Katerina (2007), 'The Philosopher as God's Messenger' in *The Philosophy of Epictetus*, ed. Theodore Scaltsas and Andrew S. Mason (Oxford University Press): 56–70.

Instone-Brewer, David (1992), '1 Corinthians 9.9–11: A Literal Interpretation of "Do Not Muzzle the Ox"', *NTS* 38: 554–65.

Jacques, François (1984), *Le Privilège de liberté: politique impériale et autonomie municipale dans les cités de l'Occident romain (161–244)* (Collection de l'École Française de Rome; École française de Rome).

Jameson, Michael H. (1978), 'Agriculture and Slavery in Classical Athens', *CJ* 73: 122–45.

Jeremias, Joachim (1958), 'Chiasmus in den Paulusbriefen', *ZNW* 49: 145–56.

Jewett, Robert (2007), *Romans: A Commentary* (Hermeneia; Minneapolis: Fortress Press).

Johnson, Luke Timothy (1991), *The Gospel of Luke* (Sacra Pagina 3; Collegeville: Liturgical Press).

Jones, A. H. M. (1940), *The Greek City: From Alexander to Justinian* (Oxford: Clarendon Press).

Jones, C. P. (1978), *The Roman World of Dio Chrysostom* (Loeb Classical Monographs; Cambridge, MA: Harvard University Press).

Joshel, Sandra R. (1992), *Work, Identity, and Legal Status at Rome: A Study of the Occupational Inscriptions* (Norman: University of Oklahoma Press).

Joubert, Stephan J. (1995), 'Managing the Household: Paul as *Paterfamilias* of the Christian Household Group in Corinth' in *Modelling Early Christianity: Social-Scientific Studies of the New Testament in Its Context*, ed. Philip F. Esler (London: Routledge): 213–23.

Judge, E. A. (1968), 'Paul's Boasting in Relation to Contemporary Professional Practice', *AusBR* 18: 37–50.

  (1980), 'The Social Identity of the First Christians: A Question of Method in Religious History', *Journal of Religious History* 11: 201–17.

Karris, Robert J. (1973), 'Rom 14:1–15:13 and the Occasion of Romans', *CBQ* 35: 155–78.

Käsemann, Ernst (1959), 'Eine paulinische Variation des "amor fati"', *ZTK*: 138–54.

  (1969), 'A Pauline Version of "Amor Fati"' in *New Testament Questions of Today* (Philadelphia: Fortress Press): 217–35.

Kehoe, Dennis P. (1988), 'Allocation of Risk and Investment on the Estates of Pliny the Younger', *Chiron* 18: 15–42.

  (1989), 'Approaches to Economic Problems in the "Letters" of Pliny the Younger: The Question of Risk in Agriculture', *ANRW* II 33.1: 555–90.

  (1992), *Management and Investment on Estates in Roman Egypt during the Early Empire* (Papyrologische Texte und Abhandlungen 40; Bonn: R. Habelt).

  (1993), 'Investment in Estates by Upper-Class Landowners in Early Imperial Italy: The Case of Pliny the Younger', in *De Agricultura: In Memoriam Pieter Willem de Neeve (1945–1990)*, ed. H. Sancisi–Weerdenbery, R. J. Van der Spek, and H. C. Teitler (Amsterdam: Gieben): 214–37.

Kennedy, George A. (1984), *New Testament Interpretation through Rhetorical Criticism* (Studies in Religion; Chapel Hill: University of North Carolina Press).

Ker, Donald P. (2000), 'Paul and Apollos – Colleagues or Rivals?', *JSNT* 77: 75–97.

Kim, Kyoung-Jin (1998), *Stewardship and Almsgiving in Luke's Theology* (JSNTSup 155; Sheffield Academic Press).

Kim, Seyoon (2003), '*Imitatio Christi* (1 Corinthians 11:1): How Paul Imitates Jesus Christ in Dealing with Idol Food (1 Corinthians 8–10)', *BBR* 13: 193–226.

  (2005), 'Paul's Entry (εἴσοδος) and the Thessalonians' Faith (1 Thessalonians 1–3)', *NTS* 51: 519–42.

Kirschenbaum, Aaron (1987), *Sons, Slaves and Freedmen in Roman Commerce* (Jerusalem: Magnes Press).

Kokkotake, Nikolitsa (1992), 'Στ' Εφορεία Προϊστορικών και Κλασικών Αρχαιοτήτων: Οδός Ηφαίστου 13 και Ηλία Μηνιάτη', *Archaiologikon Deltion* 47: 129–57.

Konradt, Matthias (2003), *Gericht und Gemeinde: Eine Studie zur Bedeutung und Funktion von Gerichtsaussagen im Rahmen der paulinischen Ekklesiologie und Ethik im 1 Thess und 1 Kor* (BZNW 117; Berlin: Walter de Gruyter).

Koperski, Veronica (2002), '"Mystery of God" or Testimony of God in 1 Cor 2,1: Textual and Exegetical Considerations' in *New Testament Textual Criticism and Exegesis: Festschrift J. Delobel*, ed. A. Denaux (BETL 161; Leuven: Peeters): 305–15.

Kövecses, Zoltán (2002), *Metaphor: A Practical Introduction* (Oxford University Press).

Kreuzer, Siegfried (1985), 'Der Zwang des Boten: Beobachtungen zu Lk 14 23 und 1 Kor 9 16', *ZNW* 76: 123–8.

Kruse, Thomas (2002), *Der königliche Schreiber und die Gauverwaltung: Untersuchungen zur Verwaltungsgeschichte Ägyptens in der Zeit von Augustus bis Philippus Arabs (30 v. Chr.–245 n. Chr.)* (2 vol.; Archiv für Papyrusforschung und verwandte Gebiete 11; Munich: K.G. Saur).

Kuck, David W. (1992), *Judgment and Community Conflict: Paul's Use of Apocalyptic Judgment Language in 1 Corinthians 3:5–4:5* (NovTSup 66; Leiden: Brill).

Landvogt, Peter (1908), 'Epigraphische Untersuchungen über den Οἰκονόμος: Ein Beitrag zum hellenistischen Beamtenwesen' (Ph.D. Diss., University of Strasburg).

Lebek, W. D. (1994), 'Domitians *Lex Lati* und die Duumvirn, Aedilen und Quaestoren in Tab. Irn. Paragraph 18–20', *ZPE* 103: 253–92.

Lee, Michelle V. (2006), *Paul, the Stoics, and the Body of Christ* (SNTSMS 137; Cambridge University Press).

Lehmeier, Karin (2006), *Oikos und Oikonomia: Antike Konzepte der Haushaltsführung und der Bau der Gemeinde bei Paulus* (Marburger theologische Studien 92; Marburg: Elwert).

Lendon, J. E. (1997), *Empire of Honour: The Art of Government in the Roman World* (Oxford: Clarendon Press).

Léon-Dufour, Xavier (1980), 'Jugement de l'homme et jugement de Dieu. 1 Co 4,1–5 dans le cadre de 3,18–4,5' in *Paolo a una chiesa divisa (1 Cor 1–4)*, ed. L. de Lorenzi (Rome: Benedictina): 137–53.

Levick, Barbara (1967), *Roman Colonies in Southern Asia Minor* (Oxford: Clarendon Press).

Lietzmann, Hans, and Werner George Kümmel (1969), *An die Korinther I/II* (3rd edn; HNT 9; Tübingen: J.C.B. Mohr (Paul Siebeck)).

Lightfoot, J. B. (1865), *The Epistle of St Paul to the Galatians* (London: Macmillan).

Lintott, Andrew W. (1993), *Imperium Romanum: Politics and Administration* (London: Routledge).

—— (2002), 'Freedmen and Slaves in the Light of Legal Documents from First-Century AD Campania', *CQ* 52: 555–65.

Litfin, Duane (1994), *St Paul's Theology of Proclamation: 1 Corinthians 1–4 and Greco-Roman Rhetoric* (SNTSMS 79; Cambridge University Press).

Litinas, Nikos (2007), 'Sitologi Documents Concerning Private Transactions in the Oxyrhynchite Nome', *ZPE* 160: 183–202.

Long, A. A. (2002), *Epictetus: A Stoic and Socratic Guide to Life* (Oxford: Clarendon Press).

Long, Adrian (2009), *Paul and Human Rights: A Dialogue with the Father of the Corinthian Community* (The Bible in the Modern World 26; Sheffield Phoenix Press).

Long, F. J. (2004), *Ancient Rhetoric and Paul's Apology: The Compositional Unity of 2 Corinthians* (SNTSMS 131; Cambridge University Press).

Longenecker, Bruce W. (2010), *Remember the Poor: Paul, Poverty, and the Greco-Roman World* (Grand Rapids: Eerdmans).

Love, J. (1986), 'The Character of Roman Agricultural Estates in the Light of Max Weber's Economic Sociology', *Chiron* 16: 99–146.

Luz, Ulrich (2005), *Matthew 21–28: A Commentary* (Hermeneia; Minneapolis: Fortress Press).

Lyons, George (1985), *Pauline Autobiography: Toward a New Understanding* (SBLDS 73; Atlanta: Scholars Press).

Ma, John (1999), *Antiochos III and the Cities of Western Asia Minor* (Oxford University Press).

MacDowell, Douglas M. (1978), *The Law in Classical Athens* (Aspects of Greek and Roman Life; London: Thames and Hudson).

MacMullen, Ramsay (1974), *Roman Social Relations: 50 BC to AD 284* (New Haven: Yale University Press).

——— (1981), *Paganism in the Roman Empire* (New Haven: Yale University Press).

——— (1986), 'Personal Power in the Roman Empire', *American Journal of Philology* 107: 512–24.

Macridy, T. (1905), 'Altertümer von Notion', *JÖAI* 8: 155–73.

Magie, David (1950), *Roman Rule in Asia Minor: To the End of the Third Century after Christ* (Princeton University Press).

Makarov, I. (2007), 'Les Données épigraphiques sur l'histoire de Chersonèse Taurique du Ier s.a.C. au Ier s.p.C.' in *XII Congressus Internationalis Epigraphiae Graecae et Latinae: Provinciae Imperii Romani inscriptionibus descriptae. Barcelona, 3–8 Septembris 2002*, vol. II, ed. Marc Mayer, Olivé G. Baratta, and A. Guzmán Almargo (Monografies de la Secció Histórico Arqueológica 10; Universitat de Barcelona): 877–83.

Malay, H. (1996), 'New Evidence Concerning the Administrative System of the Attalids', *Arkeoloji Dergisi* 4: 83–6.

Malay, H., and C. Nalbantoğlu (1996), 'The Cult of Apollon Pleurenos in Lydia', *Arkeoloji Dergisi* 4: 75–81.

Malherbe, Abraham J. (1970), '"Gentle as a Nurse": The Cynic Background to I Thess ii', *NovT* 12: 203–17.

——— (1994), 'Determinism and Free Will in Paul: The Argument of 1 Corinthians 8 and 9' in *Paul in His Hellenistic Context*, ed. Troels Engberg-Pedersen (SNTW; Edinburgh: T&T Clark): 231–55.

——— (2000), *The Letters to the Thessalonians: A New Translation with Introduction and Commentary* (AB 32b; New York: Doubleday).

Malina, Bruce J. (1993), *The New Testament World: Insights from Cultural Anthropology* (rev. edn; Louisville: WJK).

Manning, Joseph Gilbert (2003), *Land and Power in Ptolemaic Egypt: The Structure of Land Tenure* (Cambridge University Press).

Maróti, Egon (1976), 'The Vilicus and the Villa System in Ancient Italy', *Oikumene* 1: 109–24.

Marshall, Peter (1987), *Enmity in Corinth: Social Conventions in Paul's Relations with the Corinthians* (WUNT 2/23; Tübingen: J.C.B. Mohr (Paul Siebeck)).

Martin, Dale B. (1990), *Slavery as Salvation: The Metaphor of Slavery in Pauline Christianity* (New Haven: Yale University Press).

——— (1999), *The Corinthian Body* (New Haven: Yale University Press).

Martin, Ralph P. (1986), *2 Corinthians* (WBC 40; Waco: Word).

Mason, Hugh J. (1974), *Greek Terms for Roman Institutions: A Lexicon and Analysis* (American Studies in Papyrology 13; Toronto: Hakkert).

Mattusch, Carol C. (2003), 'Corinthian Bronze: Famous, but Elusive' in *Corinth, the Centenary, 1896–1996*, ed. Charles K. Williams II and Nancy Bookidis (Corinth 20; Princeton: American School of Classical Studies at Athens): 219–32.

Mauer, Christian (1968), 'πραγματεύομαι' in *TDNT*: 6: 641–2.

McCarthy, Kathleen (2000), *Slaves, Masters, and the Art of Authority in Plautine Comedy* (Princeton University Press).

McLean, B. H. (2002), *An Introduction to Greek Epigraphy of the Hellenistic and Roman Periods from Alexander the Great Down to the Reign of Constantine (323 BC–AD 337)* (Ann Arbor: University of Michigan Press).

Meeks, Wayne A. (1983), *The First Urban Christians: The Social World of the Apostle Paul* (New Haven: Yale University Press).

Meggitt, Justin J. (1996), 'The Social Status of Erastus (Rom. 16:23)', *NovT* 38: 218–23.

——— (1998), *Paul, Poverty and Survival* (SNTW; Edinburgh: T&T Clark).

——— (2004), 'Sources: Use, Abuse, Neglect. The Importance of Ancient Popular Culture' in *Christianity at Corinth: The Quest for the Pauline Church*, ed. Edward Adams and David G. Horrell (Louisville: WJK): 241–53.

Merklein, Helmut (1992), *Der erste Brief an die Korinther. Kapitel 1–4* (ÖTK 7.1; Gütersloh: Echter).

Michel, Otto (1967), 'οἰκονόμος' in *TDNT* 5: 149–51.

Migeotte, Léopold (2006a), 'La Haute Administration des finances publiques et sacrées dans les cités hellénistiques', *Chiron* 36: 379–94.

——— (2006b), 'La Planification des dépenses publiques dans les cités hellénistiques' in *Studi Ellenistici* 19, ed. Biagio Virgilio (Pisa: Giardini Editori e Stampatori): 77–97.

Mihaila, Corin (2009), *The Paul–Apollos Relationship and Paul's Stance toward Greco-Roman Rhetoric: An Exegetical and Socio-Historical Study of 1 Corinthians 1–4* (LNTS 399; London: T&T Clark).

Millar, Fergus (1981), 'The World of the *Golden Ass*', *JRS* 71: 63–75.

Millis, Benjamin W. (2010), 'The Social and Ethnic Origins of the Colonists in Early Roman Corinth' in *Corinth in Context: Comparative Studies on Religion and Society*, ed. Steven J. Friesen, Daniel N. Schowalter, and James C. Walters (NovTSup 134; Leiden: Brill): 13–35.

Mitchell, Margaret M. (1991), *Paul and the Rhetoric of Reconciliation: An Exegetical Investigation of the Language and Composition of 1 Corinthians* (Louisville: WJK).

(1992), 'Review: Elizabeth A. Castelli, *Imitating Paul*', *Journal of Religion* 72: 581–2.

(2001), 'Pauline Accommodation and "Condescension" (συγκατάβασις): 1 Cor 9:19–23 and the History of Influence' in *Paul Beyond the Judaism/Hellenism Divide*, ed. Troels Engberg-Pedersen (Louisville: WJK): 197–214.

Mitchell, S. (1993), *Anatolia: Land, Men, and Gods in Asia Minor* (Oxford: Clarendon Press).

Moffatt, James (1938), *The First Epistle of Paul to the Corinthians* (London: Hodder and Stoughton).

Morris, Leon (1985), *The First Epistle of Paul to the Corinthians: An Introduction and Commentary* (2nd edn; TNTC 7; Grand Rapids: Eerdmans).

Morstein-Marx, Robert (2004), *Mass Oratory and Political Power in the Late Roman Republic* (Cambridge University Press).

Mouritsen, Henrik (2005), 'Freedmen and Decurions: Epitaphs and Social History in Imperial Italy', *JRS* 95: 38–63.

(2011), *The Freedman in the Roman World* (Cambridge University Press).

Munck, Johannes (1950), 'Paul, the Apostles, and the Twelve', *Studia Theologica* 3: 96–110.

(1959), 'The Church without Factions: Studies in 1 Corinthians 1–4' in *Paul and the Salvation of Mankind* (London: SCM Press): 135–67.

Murphy-O'Connor, Jerome (2002), *St Paul's Corinth: Texts and Archaeology* (3rd edn; Collegeville: Liturgical Press).

Nasuti, Harry P. (1988), 'The Woes of the Prophets and the Rights of the Apostle: The Internal Dynamics of 1 Corinthians 9', *CBQ* 50: 246–64.

Natali, Carlo (1995), '*Oikonomia* in Hellenistic Political Thought', *Justice and Generosity: Studies in Hellenistic Social and Political Philosophy – Proceedings of the Sixth Symposium Hellenisticum*, ed. Andre Laks and Malcolm Schofield (Cambridge University Press): 95–128.

Newton, Derek (1998), *Deity and Diet: The Dilemma of Sacrificial Food at Corinth* (JSNTSup 169; Sheffield University Press).

Nguyen, V. Henry T. (2008), *Christian Identity in Corinth: A Comparative Study of 2 Corinthians, Epictetus and Valerius Maximus* (WUNT 2/243; Tübingen: J.C.B. Mohr (Paul Siebeck)).

O'Brien, Peter T. (1991), *The Epistle to the Philippians: A Commentary on the Greek Text* (NIGTC; Grand Rapids: Eerdmans).

Oakes, Peter (2009), 'Contours of the Urban Environment' in *After the First Urban Christians: The Socio-Historical Study of Pauline Christianity Twenty-Five Years Later*, ed. Todd Still and David G. Horrell (London: T&T Clark): 21–35.

Oliver, G. J. (2007), *War, Food, and Politics in Early Hellenistic Athens* (Oxford University Press).

Orr, William F., and James Arthur Walther (1976), *1 Corinthians: A New Translation with Introduction and Commentary* (AB 32; Garden City, NY: Doubleday).

Papathomas, Amphilochios (2009), *Juristische Begriffe im ersten Korintherbrief des Paulus: Eine semantisch-lexikalische Untersuchung auf der Basis der zeitgenössischen griechischen Papyri* (Tyche Supplementband 7; Vienna: Holzhausen).

Patterson, Orlando (1982), *Slavery and Social Death: A Comparative Study* (Cambridge, MA: Harvard University Press).

Peterman, G. W. (1997), *Paul's Gift from Philippi: Conventions of Gift-Exchange and Christian Giving* (SNTSMS 92; Cambridge University Press).

Petersen, Lauren Hackworth (2006), *The Freedman in Roman Art and Art History* (Cambridge University Press).

Peterson, Brian K. (1998), *Eloquence and the Proclamation of the Gospel in Corinth* (SBLDS 163; Atlanta: Scholars Press).

Pettegrew, David K. (2011), 'The *Diolkos* of Corinth', *AJA* 115: (2011): 549–74.
    'The *Diolkos* and the *Emporium*: How a Land Bridge Framed the Commercial Economy of Roman Corinth' in *Corinth in Contrast: Studies in Inequality*, ed. Steven J. Friesen, Sarah James, and Daniel N. Schowalter, *AJA* (in press).

Phua, Richard Liong-Seng (2005), *Idolatry and Authority: A Study of 1 Corinthians 8.1–11.1 in the Light of the Jewish Diaspora* (LNTS 299; London: T&T Clark).

Pickett, Raymond (1997), *The Cross in Corinth: The Social Significance of the Death of Jesus* (JSNTSup 143; Sheffield Academic Press).

Pitt-Rivers, J. A. (1965), 'Honor and Social Status' in *Honour and Shame: The Values of Mediterranean Society*, ed. J. G. Peristiany (London: Weidenfeld and Nicolson): 21–77.

Plank, Karl A. (1987), *Paul and the Irony of Affliction* (Semeia Studies; Atlanta: Scholars Press).

Pleket, H. W. (1983), 'Urban Elites and Business in the Greek Part of the Roman Empire' in *Trade in the Ancient Economy*, ed. Peter Garnsey, Keith Hopkins, and C. R. Whittaker (Berkeley: University of California Press): 131–44.

Plescia, Joseph (2001), 'Judicial Accountability and Immunity in Roman Law', *American Journal of Legal History* 45: 51–70.

Pogoloff, Stephen M. (1992), *Logos and Sophia: The Rhetorical Situation of 1 Corinthians* (SBLDS 134; Atlanta: Scholars Press).

Polaski, Sandra Hack (1999), *Paul and the Discourse of Power* (The Biblical Seminar 62; Gender, Culture, Theory 8; Sheffield Academic Press).

Pomeroy, Sarah B. (1994), *Xenophon Oeconomicus: A Social and Historical Commentary* (Oxford: Clarendon Press).
    (1997), *Families in Classical and Hellenistic Greece: Representations and Realities* (Oxford: Clarendon Press).
    (2010), 'Slavery in the Greek Domestic Economy in the Light of Xenophon's *Oeconomicus*' in *Xenophon*, ed. Vivienne J. Gray (Oxford Readings in Classical Studies; Oxford University Press): 31–40.

Porter, Stanley E. (1997), 'Paul of Tarsus and His Letters' in *Handbook of Classical Rhetoric in the Hellenistic Period, 330 BC–AD 400*, ed. Stanley E. Porter (Leiden: Brill): 533–85.

Pratscher, Wilhelm (1979), 'Der Verzicht des Paulus auf finanziellen Unterhalt durch seine Gemeinden: Ein Aspekt seiner Missionsweise', *NTS* 25: 284–98.

Price, S. R. F. (1999), *Religions of the Ancient Greeks* (Key Themes in Ancient History; Cambridge University Press).

Quinn, Jerome D., and William C. Wacker (2000), *The First and Second Letters to Timothy: A New Translation with Notes and Commentary* (Grand Rapids: Eerdmans).

Quiroga, Pedro López Barja de (1995), 'Freedmen Social Mobility in Roman Italy', *Historia: Zeitschrift für Alte Geschichte* 44: 326–48.

Rathbone, Dominic (1991), *Economic Rationalism and Rural Society in Third-Century AD Egypt: The Heroninos Archive and the Appianus Estate* (Cambridge Classical Studies; Cambridge University Press).

Rengstorf, Karl Heinrich (1964), 'ἀπόστολος' in *TDNT* 1: 407–45.

(1972), 'ὑπηρέτης' in *TDNT* 8: 530–44.

Reumann, John (1957), 'The Use of "Oikonomia" and Related Terms in Greek Sources to about AD 100, as a Background for Patristic Applications' (Ph.D. Diss., University of Pennsylvania).

(1958), '"Stewards of God": Pre-Christian Religious Application of *Oikonomos* in Greek', *JBL* 77: 339–49.

(1967), 'Οἰκονομία-Terms in Paul in Comparison with Lucan *Heilsgeschichte*', *NTS* 13: 147–67.

(1992), *Stewardship and the Economy of God* (Library of Christian Stewardship; Grand Rapids: Eerdmans).

(2008), *Philippians: A New Translation with Introduction and Commentary* (AYB; New Haven: Yale University Press).

Reynolds, Joyce (1988), 'Cities' in *The Administration of the Roman Empire, 241 BC–AD 193*, ed. David Braund (Exeter Studies in History; University of Exeter): 15–51.

Rhodes, P. J. (1972), *The Athenian Boule* (Oxford: Clarendon Press).

(1979), 'Εἰσαγγελία in Athens', *JHS* 99: 103–14.

(1980), 'Athenian Democracy after 403 BC', *CJ* 75: 305–23.

(2007), 'διοίκησις', *Chiron* 37: 349–62.

(2009), 'State and Religion in Athenian Inscriptions', *Greece & Rome* 56: 1–13.

Rhodes, P. J., and David M. Lewis (1997), *The Decrees of the Greek States* (Oxford: Clarendon Press).

Richard, Earl J. (1995), *First and Second Thessalonians* (Sacra Pagina 11; Collegeville: Liturgical Press).

Richardson, Peter (1994), 'Temples, Altars and Living from the Gospel (1 Cor. 9.12b–18)' in *Gospel in Paul: Studies on Corinthians, Galatians and Romans for Richard N. Longenecker*, ed. L. Ann Jervis and Peter Richardson (JSNTSup 108; Sheffield Academic Press): 89–110.

Richter, Gerhard (2005), *Oikonomia: Der Gebrauch des Wortes Oikonomia im Neuen Testament, bei den Kirchenvätern und in der theologischen Literatur bis ins 20. Jahrhundert* (Arbeiten zur Kirchengeschichte 90; Berlin: Walter de Gruyter).

Rickert, GailAnn (1989), *EKΩN and AKΩN in Early Greek Thought* (American Classical Studies 20; Atlanta: Scholars Press).

Rihll, R. E. (2011), 'Classical Athens' in *The Cambridge World History of Slavery: The Ancient Mediterranean*, vol. I, ed. Keith Bradley and Paul Cartledge (Cambridge University Press): 48–73.

Rizakis, A. D. (1989), 'La Colonie romaine de Petras en Achaie: le temoignage épigraphique' in *The Greek Renaissance in the Roman Empire: Papers from the Tenth British Museum Classical Colloquium*, ed. Susan Walker and Averil Cameron (BICS 55; University of London Institute of Classical Studies): 180–6.

(1998), *Achaïe II. La Cité de Patras: épigraphie et histoire* (Meletemata 25; Athens: Research Centre for Greek and Roman Antiquity/National Hellenic Research Foundation).

Robbins, Vernon K. (1996), *The Tapestry of Early Christian Discourse: Rhetoric, Society, and Ideology* (London: Routledge).

Roberts, Jennifer Tolbert (1982), *Accountability in Athenian Government* (Wisconsin Studies in Classics; Madison: University of Wisconsin Press).

Robertson, Archibald, and Alfred Plummer (1911), *A Critical and Exegetical Commentary on the First Epistle of St Paul to the Corinthians* (ICC; Edinburgh: T&T Clark).

Robertson, C. K. (2001), *Conflict in Corinth: Redefining the System* (SBL 42; Berne: Peter Lang).

Roetzel, Calvin J. (1972), *Judgement in the Community: A Study of the Relationship between Eschatology and Ecclesiology in Paul* (Leiden: Brill).

Romano, David Gilman (2003), 'City Planning, Centuriation, and Land Division in Roman Corinth: *Colonia Laus Iulia Corinthiensis* & *Colonia Iulia Flavia Augusta Corinthiensis*' in *Corinth, the Centenary, 1896–1996*, ed. Charles K. Williams II and Nancy Bookidis (Corinth 20; Princeton: American School of Classical Studies at Athens): 279–301.

(2005), 'Urban and Rural Planning in Roman Corinth' in *Urban Religion in Roman Corinth: Interdisciplinary Approaches*, ed. Daniel N. Schowalter and Steven J. Friesen (HTS 53; Cambridge, MA: Harvard University Press): 25–59.

Rostovtzeff, Michael I. (1922), *A Large Estate in Egypt in the Third Century BC: A Study in Economic History* (University of Wisconsin Studies in the Social Sciences and History 6; Madison: University of Wisconsin Press).

(1933), '703' in *The Tebtunis Papyri*, ed. Arthur S. Hunt and J. Gilburt Smyly (3/1; London: Humphrey Milford): 66–102.

(1941), *The Social and Economic History of the Hellenistic World* (Oxford: Clarendon Press).

(1957), *The Social and Economic History of the Roman Empire* (2nd edn; Oxford University Press).

Rowlandson, Jane (1996), *Landowners and Tenants in Roman Egypt: The Social Relations of Agriculture in the Oxyrhynchite Nome* (Oxford: Clarendon Press).

Saller, Richard P. (1982), *Personal Patronage under the Early Empire* (Cambridge University Press).

(1991), 'Review: Donald Engels, *Roman Corinth*', *Classical Philology* 86: 351–7.

(1994), *Patriarchy, Property and Death in the Roman Family* (Cambridge Studies in Population, Economy and Society in Past Time; Cambridge University Press).

(2000), 'Status and Patronage' in *The Cambridge Ancient History: The High Empire, AD 70–192*, vol. XI, ed. Alan K. Bowman, Peter Garnsey, and Dominic Rathbone (2nd edn; Cambridge University Press): 817–54.

Salmon, Edward T. (1969), *Roman Colonization under the Republic* (Aspects of Greek and Roman Life; London: Thames and Hudson).

Salmon, J. B. (1984), *Wealthy Corinth: A History of the City to 338 BC* (Oxford: Clarendon Press).

Sampley, J. Paul (1980), *Pauline Partnership in Christ: Christian Community and Commitment in Light of Roman Law* (Philadelphia: Fortress Press).

Samuel, Alan E. (1966), 'The Judicial Competence of the Oikonomos in the Third Century BC' in *Atti dell'XI Congresso Internazionale di Papirologia. Milano, 2–8 settembre 1965* (Milan: Istituto Lombardo di Scienze e Lettere): 444–50.

(1971), 'P. Tebt 703' in *Studi in onore di Edoardo Volterra*, ed. Edoardo Volterra (Pubblicazioni della Facoltà di Giurisprudenza dell'Università di Roma 40–5; Milan: Giuffrè): 451–60.

Sanders, G. D. R (2005), 'Urban Corinth: An Introduction' in *Urban Religion in Roman Corinth: Interdisciplinary Approaches*, ed. Daniel N. Schowalter and Steven J. Friesen (HTS 53; Cambridge, MA: Harvard University Press): 11–24.

Sandmel, Samuel (1962), 'Parallelomania', *JBL* 81: 1–13.

Sandnes, Karl Olav (1991), *Paul – One of the Prophets? A Contribution to the Apostle's Self-Understanding* (WUNT 2/43; Tübingen: J.C.B. Mohr (Paul Siebeck)).

(2011), 'A Missionary Strategy in 1 Corinthians 9.19–23?' in *Paul as Missionary: Identity, Activity, Theology, and Practice*, ed. Trevor J. Burke and Brian S. Rosner (LNTS 420; London: T&T Clark): 128–41.

Savage, Timothy B. (1996), *Power through Weakness: Paul's Understanding of the Christian Ministry in 2 Corinthians* (SNTSMS 86; Cambridge University Press).

Schäfer, Christoph (2001), 'Procuratores, actores und vilici: Zur Leitung landwirtschaftlicher Betriebe im Imperium Romanum' in *Landwirtschaft im Imperium Romanum*, ed. Peter Herz and Gerhard Waldherr (Pharos 14; St Katharinen: Scripta Mercaturae): 273–84.

Scheidel, Walter (1990), 'Free-Born and Manumitted Bailiffs in the Graeco-Roman World', *CQ* 40: 591–3.

Schlier, Heinrich (1965), 'κερδαίνω' in *TDNT* 3: 672–3.

Schmithals, Walter (1969), *The Office of Apostle in the Early Church* (Nashville: Abingdon Press).

(1971), *Gnosticism in Corinth: An Investigation of the Letters to the Corinthians* (Nashville: Abingdon Press).

Schrage, Wolfgang (1991), *Der erste Brief an die Korinther: 1 Kor 1,1–6,11* (EKK 7/1; Zurich: Benziger).

(1995), *Der erste Brief an die Korinther: 1 Kor 6,12–11,16* (EKK 7/2; Zurich: Benziger).

Schuler, Christof (2005), 'Die διοίκησις τῆς πόλεως im öffentlichen Finanzwesen der hellenistischen Poleis', *Chiron* 35: 385–403.

Schüssler Fiorenza, Elisabeth (1983), *In Memory of Her: A Feminist Theological Reconstruction of Christian Origins* (New York: Crossroad).

(1987), 'Rhetorical Situation and Historical Reconstruction in 1 Corinthians', *NTS* 33: 386–403.

Schütz, John H. (1975), *Paul and the Anatomy of Apostolic Authority* (SNTSMS 26; Cambridge University Press).

Scott, John (2001), *Power* (Cambridge: Polity).

Shanor, Jay (1988), 'Paul as Master Builder: Construction Terms in First Corinthians', *NTS* 34: 461–71.

Shaw, Graham (1983), *The Cost of Authority: Manipulation and Freedom in the New Testament* (Philadelphia: Fortress Press).

Sherwin-White, Susan (1978), *Ancient Cos: An Historical Study from the Dorian Settlement to the Imperial Period* (Göttingen: Vandenhoeck & Ruprecht).

Sherwin-White, Susan, and Amélie Kuhrt (1993), *From Samarkhand to Sardis: A New Approach to the Seleucid Empire* (Hellenistic Culture and Society 13; London: Duckworth).

Shi, Wenhua (2008), *Paul's Message of the Cross as Body Language* (WUNT 2/254; Tübingen: J.C.B.Mohr (Paul Siebeck)).

Sibinga, Joost Smit (1998), 'The Composition of 1 Cor. 9 and Its Context', *NovT* 40: 136–63.

Silva, Moisés (1994), *Biblical Words and Their Meaning: An Introduction to Lexical Semantics* (rev. edn; Grand Rapids: Zondervan).

Slane, Kathleen Warner (1989), 'Corinthian Ceramic Imports: The Changing Pattern of Provincial Trade in the First and Second Centuries AD' in *The Greek Renaissance in the Roman Empire: Papers from the Tenth British Museum Classical Colloquium*, ed. Susan Walker and Averil Cameron (BICS 55; University of London; Institute of Classical Studies): 219–25.

Slater, William J., and Daniela Summa (2006), 'Crowns at Magnesia', *GRBS* 46: 275–99.

Smit, Joop F. M. (1997), 'The Rhetorical Disposition of First Corinthians 8:7–9:27', *CBQ* 59: 476–91.

—— (2002), '"What is Apollos? What is Paul?": In Search for the Coherence of First Corinthians 1:10–4:21', *NovT* 44: 231–51.

—— (2003), 'Epideictic Rhetoric in Paul's First Letter to the Corinthians 1–4', *Biblica* 84: 184–201.

Snodgrass, Klyne (2008), *Stories with Intent: A Comprehensive Guide to the Parables of Jesus* (Grand Rapids: Eerdmans).

Spahn, Peter (1984), 'Die Anfänge der antiken Ökonomik', *Chiron* 14: 301–23.

Spawforth, A. J. S. (1991), 'Roman Corinth and Ancient Roman Economy', *The Classical Review* 42: 119–20.

—— (1996), 'Roman Corinth: The Formation of a Colonial Elite' in *Roman Onomastics in the Greek East: Social and Political Aspects*, ed. A. D. Rizakis (Meletemata 21; Athens: Research Centre for Greek and Roman Antiquity/ National Hellenic Research Foundation): 167–82.

—— (2003), 'Corinth: Roman' in *OCD* (3rd rev. edn).

Spitzer, Doreen Canaday (1942), 'Roman Relief Bowls from Corinth', *Hesperia* 11: 162–92.

Steel, C. E. W. (2006), *Roman Oratory* (Greece & Rome, New Surveys in the Classics 36; Cambridge University Press).

Steiner, Grundy (1954), 'Columella and Martial on Living in the Country', *CJ* 50: 85–90.

Still III, E. Coye (2004), 'Divisions over Leaders and Food Offered to Idols: The Parallel Thematic Structures of 1 Corinthians 4:6–21 and 8:1–11:1', *TynBul* 55: 17–41.

Still, Todd D. (2006), 'Did Paul Loathe Manual Labor? Revisiting the Work of Ronald F. Hock on the Apostle's Tentmaking and Social Class', *JBL* 125: 781–95.

Sumney, Jerry L. (1999), *'Servants of Satan', 'False Brothers' and Other Opponents of Paul* (JSNTSup 188; Sheffield Academic Press).

(2005), 'Studying Paul's Opponents: Advances and Challenges' in *Paul and His Opponents*, ed. Stanley E. Porter (Pauline Studies 2; Leiden: Brill): 7–58.

Swiderek, Anna (1970), 'Les Καίσαρος οἰκονόμοι de l'Égypte romaine', *Chronique d'Égypte* 89: 157–60.

Talbott, Rick F. (2010), *Jesus, Paul, and Power: Rhetoric, Ritual, and Metaphor in Ancient Mediterranean Christianity* (Eugene: Cascade).

Theissen, Gerd (1974), 'Soziale Schichtung in der korinthischen Gemeinde: Ein Beitrag zur Soziologie des hellenistischen Urchristentums', *ZNW* 65: 232–72.

(1975), 'Legitimation und Lebensunterhalt: Ein Beitrag zur Soziologie Urchristlicher Missionare', *NTS* 21: 192–221.

(1982), 'The Strong and the Weak in Corinth: A Sociological Analysis of a Theological Quarrel' in *The Social Setting of Pauline Christianity: Essays on Corinth* (Philadelphia: Fortress Press): 121–43.

Thiselton, Anthony C. (2000), *The First Epistle to the Corinthians: A Commentary on the Greek Text* (NIGTC; Grand Rapids: Eerdmans).

Thomas, J. David (1978), 'Aspects of the Ptolemaic Civil Service: The Dioiketes and the Nomarch' in *Das Ptolemäische Ägypten*, ed. Herwig Maehler and Volker Michael Strocka (Aspects of the Ptolemaic Civil Service; Mainz: Philipp von Zabern): 187–94.

Thrall, Margaret E. (1962), *Greek Particles in the New Testament: Linguistic and Exegetical Studies* (New Testament Tools and Studies 3; Leiden: Brill).

(1965), *First and Second Letters of Paul to the Corinthians* (Cambridge Bible Commentary; Cambridge University Press).

Tietler, H. C. (1993), 'Free-Born Estate Managers in the Graeco-Roman World' in *De Agricultura: In Memoriam Pieter Willem de Neeve (1945–1990)*, ed. H. Sancisi-Weerdenburg, R. J. Van Der Spek, and H. C. Teitler (Dutch Monographs on Ancient History and Archaeology 10; Amsterdam: Gieben): 206–13.

Tomlinson, F. Alan (2010), 'The Purpose and Stewardship Theme within the Pastoral Epistles', in *Entrusted with the Gospel: Paul's Theology in the Pastoral Epistles*, ed. Andreas Köstenberger and Terry L. Wilder (Nashville: B&H Publishing Group), 52–83.

Toney, Carl N. (2008), *Paul's Inclusive Ethic: Resolving Community Conflicts and Promoting Mission in Romans 14–15* (WUNT 2/252; Tübingen: J.C.B. Mohr (Paul Siebeck)).

Tooley, Wilfred (1966), 'Stewards of God: An Examination of the Terms οἰκονόμος and οἰκονομία in the New Testament', *SJT* 19: 74–86.

Treggiari, Susan (1969), *Roman Freedmen during the Late Republic* (Oxford: Clarendon Press).

Trites, Allison A. (1974), 'The Importance of Legal Scenes and Language in the Book of Acts', *NovT* 16: 278–84.

Tsetskhladze, Gocha R. (2004), 'Greek Penetration of the Black Sea' in *The Archaeology of Greek Colonisation: Essays Dedicated to Sir John Boardman*, ed. Gocha R. Tsetskhladze and Franco De Angelis (Oxford University School of Archaeology Monographs; Oxford University School of Archaeology): 111–35.

Tucker, J. Brian (2010), *You Belong to Christ: Paul and the Formation of Social Identity in 1 Corinthians 1–4* (Eugene, Pickwick).

Turner, E. G. (1984), 'Ptolemaic Egypt' in *The Cambridge Ancient History: The Hellenistic World*, vol. VII.1, ed. F. W. Walbank, A. E. Austin, M. W. Frederiksen, and R. M. Ogilvie (2nd edn; Cambridge University Press): 118–74.

Udoh, Fabian E. (2009), 'The Tale of an Unrighteous Slave (Luke 16: 1–8 [13])', *JBL* 128: 311–35.

van Unnik, Willem Cornelis (1962), *Tarsus or Jerusalem: The City of Paul's Youth* (London: Epworth Press).

Vielhauer, Philipp (1975), 'Paulus und die Kephaspartei in Korinth', *NTS* 21: 341–52.

Vogt, Joseph (1975), *Ancient Slavery and the Ideal of Man* (Cambridge, MA: Harvard University Press).

Vos, J. S. (1996), 'Die Argumentation des Paulus in 1 Kor 1,10–3,4' in *The Corinthian Correspondence*, ed. R. Bieringer (BETL 125; Leuven: Peeters): 87–119.

Walbank, F. W. (1940), *Philip V of Macedon* (Cambridge University Press).
   (1984a), 'Macedonia and Greece' in *The Cambridge Ancient History: The Hellenistic World*, vol. VII.1, ed. F. W. Walbank, A. E. Austin, M. W. Frederiksen, and R. M. Ogilvie (2nd edn; Cambridge University Press): 221–56.
   (1984b), 'Sources for the Period' in *The Cambridge Ancient History: The Hellenistic World*, vol. VII.1, ed. F. W. Walbank, A. E. Austin, M. W. Frederiksen, and R. M. Ogilvie (2nd edn; Cambridge University Press): 1–22.

Walbank, Mary E. Hoskins (1997), 'The Foundation and Planning of Early Roman Corinth', *JRA* 10: 95–130.
   (2002), 'What's in a Name? Corinth under the Flavians', *ZPE* 139: 251–64.

Wallace-Hadrill, Andrew (1991), 'Elites and Trade in the Roman Town' in *City and Country in the Ancient World*, ed. John Rich and Andrew Wallace-Hadrill (Leicester-Nottingham Studies in Ancient Society 2; London: Routledge): 241–72.

Walton, Steve (2011), 'Paul, Patronage and Pay: What Do We Know about the Apostle's Financial Support?' in *Paul as Missionary: Identity, Activity, Theology, and Practice*, ed. Trevor J. Burke and Brian S. Rosner (LNTS 420; London: T&T Clark): 221–33.

Wanamaker, Charles A. (2003), 'A Rhetoric of Power: Ideology and 1 Corinthians 1–4' in *Paul and the Corinthians: Studies on a Community in Conflict. Essays in Honour of Margaret Thrall*, ed. Trevor J. Burke and J. K. Elliott (NovTSup 109; Leiden: Brill): 115–37.

Watson, Alan (1965), *The Law of Obligations in the Later Roman Republic* (Oxford: Clarendon Press).
   (1987), *Roman Slave Law* (Baltimore: The Johns Hopkins University Press).

Watson, Duane F. (2003), 'Paul and Boasting' in *Paul in the Greco-Roman World: A Handbook*, ed. J. Paul Sampley (Harrisburg: Trinity Press International): 77–100.

Weaver, P. R. C. (1972), *Familia Caesaris: A Social Study of the Emperor's Freedman and Slaves* (Cambridge University Press).
   (1974), 'Social Mobility in the Early Roman Empire: The Evidence of the Imperial Freedmen and Slaves' in *Studies in Ancient Society*, ed. M. I. Finley (London: Routledge and Kegan Paul): 121–40.

(1998), 'Imperial Slaves and Freedmen in the Brick Industry', *ZPE* 122: 238–46.

Weima, Jeffrey A. D. (1997), 'An Apology for the Apologetic Function of 1 Thessalonians 2.1–12', *JSNT* 68: 73–99.

Weinrib, E. J. (1968), 'The Prosecution of Roman Magistrates', *Phoenix* 2: 32–56.

Weiss, Alexander (2004), *Sklave der Stadt: Untersuchungen zur öffentlichen Sklaverei in den Städten des römischen Reiches* (Historia Einzelschriften 173; Stuttgart: Franz Steiner).

(2010), 'Keine Quästoren in Korinth: Zu Goodrichs (und Theißens) These über das Amt des Erastos (Röm 16.23)', *NTS* 56: 576–81.

Weiss, Johannes (1910), *Der erste Korintherbrief* (KEK 5; Göttingen: Vandenhoeck & Ruprecht).

Welborn, L. L. (1987a), 'A Conciliatory Principle in 1 Cor. 4:6', *NovT* 29: 320–46.

(1987b), 'On the Discord in Corinth: 1 Corinthians 1–4 and Ancient Politics', *JBL* 106: 85–111.

(2005), *Paul, the Fool of Christ: A Study of 1 Corinthians 1–4 in the Comic-Philosophic Tradition* (JSNTSup 293; ECC; Edinburgh: T&T Clark).

Welles, C. Bradford (1934), *Royal Correspondence in the Hellenistic Period* (New Haven: Yale University Press).

(1938), 'New Texts from the Chancery of Philip V of Macedonia and the Problem of the "Diagramma"', *AJA* 42: 245–60.

White, K. D. (1970), *Roman Farming* (Aspects of Greek and Roman Life; London: Thames and Hudson).

White, L. Michael (2005), 'Favorinus's "Corinthian Oration": A Piqued Panorama of the Hadrianic Forum' in *Urban Religion in Roman Corinth: Interdisciplinary Approaches*, ed. Daniel N. Schowalter and Steven J. Friesen (HTS 53; Cambridge, MA: Harvard University Press): 61–110.

White, L. M., and J. T. Fitzgerald (2003), 'Quod est comparandum: The Problem of Parallels' in *Early Christianity and Classical Culture: Comparative Studies in Honor of Abraham J. Malherbe*, ed. J. T. Fitzgerald, Thomas H. Olbricht, and L. Michael White (NovTSup 110; Leiden: Brill): 13–39.

Whitmarsh, Tim (2005), *The Second Sophistic* (Greece & Rome, New Surveys in the Classics 35; Oxford University Press).

Williams, C. K. (1993), 'Roman Corinth as a Commercial Center' in *The Corinthia in the Roman Period*, ed. Timothy E. Gregory (JRASup 8; Ann Arbor: JRA): 31–46.

Williams, Ritva H. (2006), *Stewards, Prophets, Keepers of the Word: Leadership in the Early Church* (Peabody, MA: Hendrickson).

Willis, Wendell L. (1985a), 'An Apostolic Apologia? The Form and Function of 1 Corinthians 9', *JSNT* 24: 33–48.

(1985b), *Idol Meat in Corinth: The Pauline Argument in 1 Corinthians 8 and 10* (SBLDS 68; Chico, CA: Scholars Press).

Windisch, Hans (1934), *Paulus und Christus: Ein biblisch-religionsgeschichtlicher Vergleich* (Untersuchungen zum Neuen Testament 24; Leipzig: Hindrichs).

Winger, Michael (1997), 'Freedom and the Apostle: Paul and the Paradoxes of Necessity and Choice' in *Putting Body and Soul Together: Essays in Honor of Robin Scroggs*, ed. Virginia Wiles, Graydon F. Snyder, and Alexandra Brown (Valley Forge, PA: Trinity Press International): 217–29.

Winter, Bruce W. (1993), 'The Entries and Ethics of Orators and Paul (1 Thessalonians 2:1–12)', *TynBul* 44: 55–74.

  (1994), *Seek the Welfare of the City: Christians as Benefactors and Citizens* (First-Century Christians in the Graeco-Roman World; Grand Rapids: Eerdmans).

  (2000), *After Paul Left Corinth: The Influence of Secular Ethics and Social Change* (Grand Rapids: Eerdmans).

  (2002), *Philo and Paul among the Sophists: Alexandrian and Corinthian Responses to a Julio-Claudian Movement* (2nd edn; Grand Rapids: Eerdmans).

Wire, Antoinette Clark (1990), *The Corinthian Women Prophets: A Reconstruction through Paul's Rhetoric* (Minneapolis: Fortress Press).

Wiseman, James (1979), 'Corinth and Rome I: 228 BC–AD 267', *ANRW* II 7.1: 438–548.

Witherington, Ben (1995), *Conflict and Community in Corinth: A Socio-Rhetorical Commentary on 1 and 2 Corinthians* (Grand Rapids: Eerdmans).

Wojciechowski, Michael (2006), 'Paul and Plutarch on Boasting', *JGRChJ* 3: 99–109.

Wörrle, Michael (1975), 'Antiochos I., Achaios der Ältere und die Galater: Eine neue Inschrift in Denizli', *Chiron* 5: 59–78.

  (1977), 'Epigraphische Forschungen zur Geschichte Lykiens I', *Chiron* 7: 43–66.

Wright, K. S. (1977), 'Early Roman Sigillata and Its Local Imitations from the Post-War Excavations at Corinth' (Ph.D. Diss., Bryn Mawr College).

Wuellner, Wilhelm (1987), 'Where is Rhetorical Criticism Taking Us?', *CBQ* 49: 448–63.

Yinger, Kent L. (1999), *Paul, Judaism, and Judgment According to Deeds* (SNTSMS 105; Cambridge University Press).

Zeber, Ireneusz (1981), *A Study of the Peculium of a Slave in Pre-Classical and Classical Roman Law* (Acta Universitatis Wratislaviensis 491; Wroclaw: Wydawn).

Zeller, Dieter (2010), *Der erste Brief an die Korinther* (KEK; Göttingen: Vandenhoeck & Ruprecht).

Zenos, A. C. (1891), 'St Paul as a Business-Man', *Old and New Testament Student* 12: 71–8.

Zimmerman, Mary Lou (2003), 'Corinthian Trade with the Punic West in the Classical Period' in *Corinth, the Centenary, 1896–1996*, ed. Charles K. Williams II and Nancy Bookidis (Corinth 20; Princeton: American School of Classical Studies at Athens): 195–217.

Zimmermann, Reinhard (1990), *The Law of Obligations: Roman Foundations of the Civilian Tradition* (Capetown: Juta).

Zuiderhoek, Arjan (2009), *The Politics of Munificence in the Roman Empire: Citizens, Elites and Benefactors in Asia Minor* (Greek Culture in the Roman World; Cambridge University Press).

INDEX OF PASSAGES

Ancient authors

Ancient literature

INDEX OF MODERN AUTHORS